MYSTIC MEG'S

ASTROSEX

NEW LOVERS' GUIDE TO THE STARS

Published by
Big Books
London
in association with
Peter Grose Ltd
Monmouth

First edition, February 1995
Copyright © Mystic Meg Ltd 1995

ISBN 1-898-885125

A CIP catalogue record for this book is available from the
British Library. Printed and bound in Great Britain by The
Bath Press. *AstroSex* is printed on re-cycled paper.

ACKNOWLEDGMENTS

For their input, help with the survey and follow-up interviews, and gifts of friendship and encouragement, I would like to thank Maggie Innes, Kate Andrew, Angela Wilkes, Patricia Stead and Millicent Taylor.

Cover Photographs
By Mark Lawrence

ACKNOWLEDGMENTS

MYSTIC MEG'S

ASTROSEX

NEW LOVERS' GUIDE TO THE STARS

Published by
Big Books
London

in association with
Peter Grose Ltd
Monmouth

CONTENTS

sex better in second marriages *Which starsigns are virgin brides and bridegrooms *Does marriage have a good or bad effect on sex lives.
THE 12 STARSIGNS' MARRIAGE PROFILES

Infidelity: 178

*Who have the most—and least—affairs *Understanding, revenge or goodbye—what happens when a partner is unfaithful *Real reasons for affairs.
THE 12 STARSIGNS' INFIDELITY PROFILES

Sexuality Profiles: 234

*Which starsigns make love most, and least, often *Who want more sex * Starsigns who get too much sex *Who have most sexual partners *Couples with different sex drives *Who do all they want to in bed *Which starsigns love the same sex *Raising the satisfaction levels.
THE 12 STARSIGNS' SEXUALITY PROFILES

Part Two - LoveMatches
The 288 zodiac partnerships: 300

ZODIAC SIGNS

ARIES
March 21 to April 20
Element: Fire
Planet: Mars

TAURUS
April 21 to May 21
Element: Earth
Planet: Venus

GEMINI
May 22 to June 21
Element: Air
Planet: Mercury

CANCER
June 22 to July 22
Element: Water
Ruler: Moon

LEO
July 23 to August 23
Element: Fire
Ruler: Sun

VIRGO
August 24 to September 22
Element: Earth
Planet: Mercury

LIBRA
September 23 to October 23
Element: Air
Planet: Venus

SCORPIO
October 24 to November 22
Element: Water
Planets: Pluto/Mars

SAGITTARIUS
Nov 23 to Dec 21
Element: Fire
Planet: Jupiter

CAPRICORN
December 22 to January 20
Element: Earth
Planet: Saturn

AQUARIUS
January 21 to February 18
Element: Air
Planets: Uranus/Saturn

PISCES
February 19 to March 20
Element: Water
Planets: Neptune/Jupiter

The sun changes from one zodiac sign to the next at a slightly different time each year and can be in one sign in the morning, another by the afternoon. If you were born near the beginning or end of your sign, look up your year in the sun sign tables on page 518 to find your true zodiac sign.

Introduction

In the autumn of 1993, I decided to put everything I believed in to the test. Astrology is based on the belief that the time of year you are born influences your character, emotions, actions and reactions, affects the way you behave in relationships and measures compatibility. And that each starsign is very different from the others.

But what would happen if astrology was scientifically tested by a large-scale survey? Would the beliefs and observations of astrologers over the last 6,000 years be proved, or shattered?

I devised a survey with very direct questions about sexual behaviour, love experiences and relationships. I asked all the people surveyed to give their own starsign, as well as the starsign of their partner, if they had one.

This questionnaire was printed in the News of The World's *Sunday* magazine, which sells five million copies each week, and has a readership of 12 million. Then 30,000 responses, covering all the age groups and social groups, the 12 starsigns, and both sexes were used to get the first scientific picture.

Computer analysis showed, at once, that there was a significant statistical difference between the starsigns' responses to each question. So, yes, the time of year you are born makes you different from people born at other times of the year. Astrology does work.

But the answers challenge and change many of astrology's traditional beliefs about each starsign's personality and sexuality. And this scientific survey revolutionises the view of which starsigns are right for each other. There is also a marked difference between the way starsigns influence men, and the way they influence women.

This survey reveals REAL STARSIGNS that in many important ways are different from TRADITIONAL STARSIGNS, as this taster shows.

TRADITIONALLY, ARIES WOMAN is believed to be a strong, selfish sexpot. Yet the answers to the AstroSex survey show REAL ARIES WOMAN rates kindness three times higher than sexual attraction, prefers the missionary position and is more turned on by the words "I love you" than any other woman.

TRADITIONALLY, TAURUS MAN is often described as a straitlaced stay-at-home. But the survey shows that REAL TAURUS MAN has made love in more positions and more places than any other male. Yet REAL TAURUS WOMAN is revealed as one of the zodiac's least sexually adventurous females. Showing how the same sign does affect the male and female very differently.

TRADITIONALLY, GEMINI MAN is often characterised as a curious, fickle, flirt, greedy to sample everything life and love can offer. But the survey shows REAL GEMINI MAN is the one most likely to be a virgin when he marries (21% of Gemini men are wedding night virgins, compared with 3% of Aquarius men).

TRADITIONALLY, CANCER MAN is characterised as protective, caring, and a top choice for lifelong commitment. Yet REAL CANCER MAN is the king of multiple marriages—almost half marry more than once, and 5% of them marry five times, and more!

TRADITIONALLY, LEO WOMAN bathes in the spotlight of flattery and needs constant high levels of luxury and excitement—not the recipe for life-matches. But the statistics from the AstroSex survey show that REAL LEO WOMAN works harder at staying together than any other woman, is most likely to marry once only and have only one lover.

TRADITIONALLY, VIRGO MAN has a deep and intense sexuality that remains hidden until a secure relationship sets it free. But

2

REAL VIRGO MAN says marriage makes his sexlife worse and he, more than any other man, wants to be caressed very gently.

TRADITIONALLY, LIBRA MAN is the charmer of the zodiac and REAL LIBRA MAN lives up to this. This survey shows he has the greatest number of lovers, and is the starsign mostly likely to have had five or more affairs while he is still married. Yet, unlike the traditional view of Libra woman, REAL LIBRA WOMAN tops the list for relationships that last more than 10 years.

TRADITIONALLY, SCORPIO WOMAN is the zodiac's sexiest woman, and the AstroSex survey shows that, yes, she makes love more often than any other woman in the zodiac—and wants to make love even more. But though REAL SCORPIO MAN is the number one in the sexual popularity list with women, as traditional astrology believes, he is also the man who is least likely to remarry.

TRADITIONALLY, SAGITTARIUS MAN loves freedom and adventure. But REAL SAGITTARIUS MAN, as the AstroSex survey shows, is by far the most faithful starsign, and the most likely to be celibate.

TRADITIONALLY, CAPRICORN WOMAN has a practical and conventional approach to sex. But REAL CAPRICORN WOMAN reveals in the survey that she has taken part in more threesomes, watched more sexy videos, and worn more rubber than any other woman.

TRADITIONALLY, AQUARIUS MAN is Mr Unconventional, yet has extra helpings of cool charisma that attract a love queue. But REAL AQUARIUS MAN, reveals he is the man most likely to rate his sex drive lower than his partner, and wrecks the traditional zodiac pairing system by choosing Taurus women to marry, but rating Aquarius women as the sexiest.

TRADITIONALLY PISCES WOMAN is seen as a victim of her emotions, who chases impossible dreams of love. REAL PISCES WOMAN is the most likely to have six or more affairs, after marriage. And she is the woman most likely to take a "revenge"

3

lover if her partner strays. Unlike REAL PISCES MAN who is the least likely to take a lover and the sign who most often answers that having children together makes his partner seem more sexy.

The computer analysis of the answers to the questionnaire, plus further more detailed studies of the survey, follow-up interviews and case-histories form the basis of this book. I would like to thank everyone who filled in the survey and shared their most personal feelings about love, sex and the starsigns.

Part One:

The AstroSex Survey

1
PARTNERS

* WHICH STARSIGNS END UP TOGETHER * WHO
IS SEXUALLY ATTRACTED TO WHO —AND WHO
ISN'T * WHAT FIRST DRAWS PARTNERS TO EACH
OTHER AND WHAT KEEPS THEM TOGETHER
* HOW SEX DEVELOPS WITHIN A PARTNERSHIP
* DOES HAVING CHILDREN MAKE OR SHAKE, A
LOVE BOND * THE 12 STARSIGNS' PARTNERSHIP
PROFILES FOR MEN AND FOR WOMEN

The survey's first shock is that when it comes to making permanent partnerships, almost no-one ends up with the starsign partner traditional astrology would predict. And very few people settle with the starsign that he, or she, rates as the most sexy. Men and women from the same starsign also make very different choices. But there is an intuitive logic underlying partnership choices that rewrites the rules of astrology.

WHO ENDS UP WITH WHO?
The new view of what couples need, and want, from each other starts here. For although the system of partner selection is broadly similar for both sexes, there are distinct differences between men and women.

6

MEN LOOKING FOR THEIR OPPOSITE

The ideal partnership, astrology has always believed, should be found within the same element. So fire signs (Aries, Leo, Sagittarius) should pair off with other fire signs, earth signs (Taurus, Virgo and Capricorn) with other earth signs. Air signs (Gemini, Libra and Aquarius) with other air signs. Water signs (Cancer, Scorpio and Pisces) with other water signs. But the single most striking discovery in this section of the survey is that this just doesn't happen, at least not among the men.

The vast majority of males do not list even one starsign from the same element in their top three choices of partners, let alone as their number one mate. So what's going on here? Could every man in the zodiac be stuck in an unsatisfactory and unfulfilling relationship?

Thankfully, no. What the results do show is that men instinctively choose a partner who will complement rather than compete with them. And this should give a partnership a greater chance of success long-term. In two out of three cases, men whose starsigns are classified positive (or masculine) with a dominant, forceful streak, end up with women from more submissive, supportive signs classified negative (or female). While more intuitive, emotional men from the "negative" starsigns choose long-term partners from assertive, "positive" women's signs. The positive signs are Aries, Gemini, Leo, Libra, Sagittarius and Aquarius. The negative signs are Taurus, Cancer, Virgo, Scorpio, Capricorn and Pisces.

This means hard-to-get-close-to Aries man, for instance, is most likely to pair off with tenderly loving Cancer (15%), Virgo (12%) or Pisces (12%) women. While intense Scorpio man finds his perfect match in easy-going Libra (14%) women.

There are a couple of notable exceptions to this pattern, however. First, with Sagittarius and Libra starsigns, which are both classified positive—and both most likely to end up with each other. Libra men choose Sagittarius women 14% of the time. And 12% of Sagittarius men opt for Libra partners. Two carefree, lively spirits with more than a touch of vanity...perhaps they understand each other better than we might expect.

The other exception is dreamy, sensitive Pisces man who over-whelmingly prefers a partner who is also Pisces (16%). He is the only man in the zodiac who does. In the vast majority of cases same sign partners don't even make the top three. It seems Pisces' offbeat, highly individual view on life, and love, may be best appreciated by someone who matches it.

STARWATCH
Men choose partners who fill in the gaps in their life and personality—and not mirror images of themselves. That's the opposite of what traditional astrology has always suggested.

CASE HISTORY OF A VIRGO MAN
Virgo Alex, 29, has lived with 30-year-old Robyn, who's Gemini, for three years

"Before I met Robyn, I always seemed to go out with girls who were very like me—quiet and a bit serious. And who tended to get in a state over nothing, just like I do. I remember one time I locked myself and a girlfriend out of my house, we both got so worked up we just couldn't think what to do next. Luckily a policeman friend of mine was passing and was able to take charge for us.

"I can safely say it was dislike, if not sheer hate, at first sight when I met Robyn. I'm a nurse and she started on my shift—she seemed so incredibly scatty and almost hyperactive. But I soon saw how good she was at her job, and her bubbly, cheerful personality started to grow on me.

"Needless to say, Robyn had to ask me out—it if was left up to me I'd still be thinking about it. And it was her idea to move in together, too. We suit each other pretty well, although if there was one thing

I'd change about her it's her chatty, flirtatious nature. I love her, but she drives me mad when she talks to absolutely everyone we meet.

"Would she change anything about me? Probably the way I won't buy anything for the house, however small, without thinking about it, discussing it, and looking at every option for weeks. Then after we've bought it, worrying if I've made the right decision!"

When it comes to the partners men choose least often, an obvious pattern is less easy to see. But in general the same starsign, or immediate neighbours on either side, are not popular choices. Looks like a case of just too close for comfort. Partners from the same element usually rate quite low results too.

Capricorn man illustrates all these points very well. For he is least likely to choose as his partner neighbouring sign Sagittarius (5%), his own sign Capricorn (5%) or fellow earth sign Taurus (just 3%). While Libra man turns down fellow air signs Aquarius (4%) and Gemini (6%), and neighbour Virgo (4%).

WOMEN LOOKING FOR THEMSELVES
In partner choice for women, another surprising finding emerges. For while men look for a permanent partner who is very different to themselves, women tend to prefer someone very similar.

Yet, in general the majority of women will, like men, end up with a "negative" partner if their own starsign is classified "positive."

But leaving averages aside and looking, starsign by starsign, at women's number one choice of partner in a stunning five out of every six cases, women from positive signs opt most often for other positive signs. And negatives choose fellow negatives.

Among women, there is also a higher likelihood of partners being selected from the same sign, or from the same element. For example, Taurus woman's most popular partner is Taurus man (12%), while 10% of Sagittarius also choose men from the same sign. Aquarius women opt for Aquarius (11%). Gemini (11%) and Libra (10%), a full complement of air signs.

So what influences women, in their choice of partner? It seems, compared to men, they are looking for different things from a long-term relationship, and prefer a partner who thinks and feels the same way they do. "I want a combination of equals, not a lifetime spent massaging a man's ego," says Aquarius-born Louise, 33.

"I'm with Mark now, who's a Libra, and I know a lot of my friends —not to mention my family—think our relationship is really strange. Just because we go out separately and go on holidays alone.

"We've worked out a way of life that suits us, and that's what matters. I don't believe in bonds, however loving—and I wouldn't want a man who tried to tie me down, no way."

STARWATCH
Women follow more closely traditional astrology's idea of which starsigns settle down together. But perhaps not for the reasons we might expect...

So who are female starsigns least likely to choose? Reflecting the men's results, signs that are immediate neighbours are not particularly popular partners, but looking directly at each female starsign's least popular choice, shows women's preference for men who share various vital characteristics. For in three out of four cases, negative starsigns are least likely to settle with positive, and vice versa.

One man does deserve a special mention here, however—and that's Sagittarius. For alone among men, he features in the bottom three of over half the female starsigns, as the man they're least likely to settle down with. Is this because Sagittarius is so notoriously hard to pin down, or because wary women believe he is a bad bet long-term, even though he's not, really?

CASE HISTORY OF A CAPRICORN WOMAN

Capricorn Diana, 40, is currently dating Sagittarius man Simon, 45

"Simon wants to move in with me and I've had to put my foot down and say absolutely no way. He's a lovely man and we have wonderful times together, but I don't need another child in my life —I have enough trouble coping with the three I already have.

"And I certainly don't see Simon as stepfather material for my kids. I'd want someone a lot steadier and more reliable. Simon's full of great ideas but he hardly ever sees them through. He doesn't seem to realise how hurt the kids get when he breaks a promise or changes an arrangement at the last minute.

"But having said all that, it's been great having Simon in my life for the last few months. I'd just come through a bad divorce and felt unlovable and unattractive. Simon's made me feel sexy and young again and I can never thank him enough for that. But I'm realistic enough to know he won't stick around, whatever he thinks. I'm just enjoying our fling while it lasts and forgetting about the future."

WHICH SIGNS ARE MOST—AND LEAST—SEXY?

If ever proof was needed that sexual attraction alone is not something to base a relationship on, the AstroSex Survey provides it. For it shows that the majority of people do not settle down with the starsigns they find most sexy—they seem to save them for flings.

But again, there is a split between the sexes—almost twice as many women as men say they have found a permanent partner from the starsign they rate most sexy.

Perhaps this simply means that women are more loyal to their partner, but less honest, in their answers.

The survey also highlights how much variation can be found within one starsign. For surprisingly often the same starsign is voted both most, and least sexy. Showing that they do stir strong reactions.

WHO DO MEN FIND MOST SEXY?

This is the section where traditional astrology comes into its own. For almost without exception each man who replied to the survey selected a partner from the same starsign, or the same element, as himself as the sexiest sign.

Perhaps when it comes to sex, shared energy levels, or adventurousness and sheer sex drive gain in importance. But these become secondary in a long-term relationship, for again almost without exception the starsign men name as most sexy is not the one they have chosen to pair off with permanently.

So although 23% of Aries men rate Aries women as the most sexy, when they choose a life partner, Aries doesn't even make the top three—which are Cancer, Virgo and Taurus. And a stunning 24% of Scorpio men may go wild over Scorpio women—but the ones they end up with most are Libra and Virgo.

CASE HISTORY OF A SCORPIO MAN

Scorpio-born Don, 34, had an intense affair with a Scorpio woman
"I'll never forget our lovemaking till the day I die—we were almost physically drunk with the pleasure of each other and even now, thinking about Lorraine, I find myself getting aroused.

"But we had to get out of bed some time, and when we did the problems started. We were both so intense, possessive and jealous, yet somehow also driven to test our attractiveness to others by almost—but not quite— having affairs.

"I remember once I'd taken a new girl from work for a quiet drink when Lorraine burst in and started making a scene. Then she took my beer and poured it in my crotch. That night when we got home we started wrestling and slapping on the bed. We almost killed each other—and ended up making love. The sex was fantastic, but next day I packed my bag and left. We were basically no good for each other anywhere except between the sheets.

"I'm with another girlfriend now and things are better. Yes, if I'm honest I have to say sex is less exciting—but it's less traumatic too.

And now it's just one part of a good relationship, not the only good part of a bad one"

While most men across the zodiac do not settle down with the partners they find most sexy, there are three lucky male starsigns who do.

First, Gemini men rate Virgo women among the most sexy (14%), and they're also most likely to pair off with Gemini (13%). And the reverse is also true for Virgo men and Gemini partners. So these must be two very contented starsigns.

And Pisces men, who so overwhelmingly prefer to pick permanent partners from their own sign (see above) are also far more likely to rate other Pisces people as most sexy (20%).

Adding all the results together, every starsign is rated one of the sexiest by someone. But the starsigns men find most sexy overall are energetic Aries (11%), charming Gemini (10%), sensuous Taurus, tender Cancer and attentive Virgo (all 9%).

League Table
The lover's league of sexy women (chosen by men):

1. **Aries**
2. **Gemini**
3. **Virgo**
4. **Taurus**
5. **Cancer**
6. **Scorpio**
7. **Leo**
8. **Libra**
9. **Pisces**
10. **Sagittarius**
11. **Capricorn**
12. **Aquarius**

The survey does show a link between men actively not finding a sign sexy and not pairing off with someone from that sign.

13

For example, Taurus men fancy Pisces least and only end up with Pisces partners 6% of the time. And Capricorn men rate Taurus partners least sexy, so just 3% choose them. Scorpio men don't take to assertive Aries women—a staggering 27%, over a quarter, vote them least sexy of all. And Leos have the same reaction to Cancer partners. But these are the signs everyone else seems to like.

STARWATCH
Patterns of sexual attraction between starsigns stick far more closely to what traditional astrology would expect—that like attracts like. But for all but a few men this is not the main factor in choosing a life partner. We now need a new way of looking at zodiac love.

WHO DO WOMEN FIND MOST SEXY?
Like men, women from all starsigns find partners from the same sign or same element sexiest in the vast majority of cases. So Sagittarius women rate Aries the sexiest starsign (13%), Capricorn goes for Taurus (13%) and so on. But again, the signs that turn different women on most are not necessarily the ones they will settle down with. Although in fact this does happen to women almost twice as often as to the zodiac's men.

Once again, the starsign with by far the greatest opinion of themselves is Scorpio. One in four (25%) Scorpio women rate their own sign as the sexiest—and for men the figure is almost identical (24%). This much certainly backs up traditional astrology's profile of Scorpio as the sex bomb of the zodiac.

But neither men nor women seem to manage to make a go of a Scorpio-Scorpio partnership. Twin Taurus couples fare better, according to the survey results. Taurus women rate partners from the same sign most sexy 13% of the time—and they're also most likely to end up with another Taurus (12%).

Taking all the women's starsigns together, the partners they rate as most sexy overall are Scorpio (12%), Aries (10%) and Leo (9%).

League Table
The lover's league of sexy men (chosen by women):
1. **Scorpio**
2. **Aries**
3. **Leo**
4. **Taurus**
5. **Gemini**
6. **Cancer**
7. **Libra**
8. **Virgo**
9. **Pisces**
10. **Sagittarius**
11. **Capricorn**
12. **Aquarius**

Least sexy, according to the women, are Aries (12%), Taurus (10%), Gemini, Cancer and Virgo (all 9%).

Once again, just as with the men, Aries arouses very strong feelings, one way or another! And this can happen even within individual signs—Gemini and Sagittarius women both vote Aries man the most sexy AND the least sexy starsign of all!

CASE HISTORY OF A GEMINI WOMAN
Andie is 24, a Gemini, and married to Jeff, an Aries. They have twin babies.
"Our sexlife has gone downhill since we've had the babies, no doubt about it. But Jeff's also had a stressful time at work and gone right off sex. These days I feel he's just going through the motions once a week, and only interested in his own pleasure. Whereas before we were married, he was such a keen and considerate lover.

"My body's not what it was , I know that, and he just can't disguise the fact he's bored with me and our lovemaking. But he won't accept it's got anything to do with him. He's got a beer gut and a faceful of stubble, but he still thinks he's God's gift to women.

"I do make the effort sometimes with nice underwear and sexy talk, you know the sort of thing. But if he's not in the mood, I'm wasting my time. He's such a selfish lover now. It's sad but I suppose I'll just have to accept that."

STARWATCH
The survey results suggest women base their search for a suitable partner on different criteria to men. In the women's case, finding a particular starsign the least sexy does not seem to make them any less likely to end up with a partner from that sign. Perhaps traditional astrology does not go far enough in highlighting the male/female differences within each sign.

WHAT ATTRACTS PARTNERS TO EACH OTHER?
Men and women are attracted to different things—and the AstroSex Survey proves it. For women, for example, the eyes are the first feature they focus on, with 44% saying they are most important. But men rate a warm smile highest and give eyes second place.

But the main difference that emerges is that in general women initially go for attractive personalities, and men for attractive bodies. Men's overall top four are Warm Smile (43%), Nice Eyes (40%), Curvy Body (33%) and Great Legs (28%). While women choose a very different order of Nice Eyes (44%), Kindness (35%), Great Smile (35%) and Faithfulness (30%). And men are attracted to a slim body 21% of the time, while for women the figure is only 9%.

So much for the general figures. But examining initial attraction across the zodiac shows just how unique each starsign is in his, or her, approach.

WHAT FIRST ATTRACTS MEN?

Almost all the men replying place a warm smile at the top of their list of attraction features, with open, friendly Sagittarius and Taurus finding this most alluring of all at 46% each.

Only two male signs, in fact, did not rate the smile as number one. These are Leo, the starsign of sincerity—because 50% of Leo men rate nice eyes as their prime element of attraction. And earthy but image-conscious Virgo men are first attracted most to a good body (45%), followed by nice eyes (43%) and only then a nice smile (42%).

So it's no surprise to learn that Virgo men are also most likely of all male starsigns to go for a slim partner. 28% of Virgo men think this is vital, compared to just 16% of more easy-going Libra men. "I just don't find myself attracted to overweight women" says Sam, a 21-year-old Virgo man. "In fact, it's a real turn-off. I'm very fashion conscious and care a lot about how I look. And I expect a partner to do the same. What's wrong with that?"

Some survey findings in the first attraction section are exactly what traditional astrology might expect of each starsign. For example, active, gregarious Gemini rates shared interests (32%) higher than any other male sign does. And sensitive Cancer is keener on a kind nature, a gentle manner and good homemaking skills than any other man.

But this section has its share of surprises, too. Who would expect Aries man to be the one who rates homemaking skills the highest? Or notoriously non-committed Sagittarius to value faithfulness more than any other man in the zodiac? In both examples it may be a case of one rule for me, another for my partner.

Among the men, the starsign who is first attracted to the widest variety of features is Gemini. As long as he doesn't expect them all in one partner, that makes Gemini man the least exacting. He's followed closely by Virgo, and then Taurus. And the men who are most selective, and so attracted to the most limited range of factors, are Aquarius, Aries and Sagittarius.

WHAT FIRST ATTRACTS WOMEN?

The zodiac's women are virtually unanimous in what first attracts them to someone—11 out of 12 signs go for nice eyes and give these a total score of 44%, a full 9% higher than the next most popular category, kindness.

Only one starsign breaks this pattern, and that is Capricorn women, who prefer to give their tope vote to a great smile (42%) with nice eyes a close second at 41%. Of all the women, Capricorn casts the widest net to catch a potential partner. For this practical sign rates kindness, a great smile, faithfulness, confidence, height, muscular build, a good voice and being a good provider more often than any other female sign. But there is one area men can relax—Capricorn are next-to-least likely of all women to be attracted to nice eyes...

Traditional astrology would tend to expect this rather conventional starsign to seek a partner who can be a good provider (12%). Nor is it surprising that go-ahead Aries prefers to see confidence in a partner (26%) more often than any other woman. Or that talkative and perhaps slightly vain Gemini, Libra and Sagittarius all go for a good line in chat (13%).

CASE HISTORY OF A LIBRA WOMAN

Libra Sally, 30 years old and divorced, is "playing the field" at the moment

"I adore flirting—I can't get enough of it! It doesn't necessarily have to lead to sex, or even a date—in fact I think talking can be even better than sex. It's an undercurrent of attraction that electrifies a conversation.

"If a man can't talk. I don't want to know. I can tell within a couple of minutes if he's funny, interesting and fascinating to be around. And if he's not, there's no chance of him getting into my diary, let alone my bed.

"When I was younger I used to sit through some appalling chat-up routines, but not any more. I've got a good get-out line now. I say

'Well I never normally sleep with men I've just met, but in your case I'll make an exception.' Then I close my eyes and pretend to snore. That soon gets rid of them."

This section of the survey is far from all predictable, however. Who would expect emotional Cancer women to vote smart clothes more important than other women do, for instance (20%, or one in five, Cancer women look for that factor first). Or that Pisces, along with Leo, is keener than any other woman on a slim body (11%).

Taking a general view, Capricorn woman has by far the widest range of attraction factors when scouting for a partner. She's followed by Taurus and Aries women. But at the other end of the scale, as we found with men, it's Aquarius who is first attracted to the least number of things, along with Virgo and Cancer women.

STARWATCH
Aquarius is the starsign who loves and accepts everyone according to traditional astrology. Yet survey results prove both men and women born under Aquarius can be more specific than other signs when choosing partners.

WHAT KEEPS COUPLES TOGETHER?
When starsigns were asked what first attracts them to someone, the answers were very varied. But when the survey shifts to the more specific, quizzing men and women on what one quality matters most in a partner, different preferences really start to show.

The first major split is between men and women. For although the top few qualities follow the same general order of preference for both sexes—Loyalty, Kindness, Understanding How I Think, Sense of Humour and Sexual Attraction—5% more women than men rate kindness as most important, while more men than women vote for sexual attraction and sex skills as the one vital quality in a partner. Men are also keener on good looks, while women focus more on money and whether a partner is a hard worker. Equality hasn't quite reached some distant corners of the zodiac yet...

WHAT KEEPS MEN KEEN?

Loyalty is the number one quality for the majority of men, led by sensitive Cancer and Pisces, each with 29%. And next, perhaps surprisingly, comes cool Aquarius, whose "couldn't care less" attitude to commitment could just be a con trick...

There are a few exceptions to this general rule, however. Gentle Taurus and Scorpio, Sagittarius and Leo (which can be difficult signs to live with long-term) all put kindness in first place instead.

While livewire of the zodiac, Leo, also shows signs of that famous selfish streak by saying it's second most important a partner "Understands how I think." And 22% of Aquarius, 21% of Cancer and 19% of Sagittarius men also want partners who can tune into their innermost thoughts. Bottom of the league table for this category is Aries, with just 9%, compared to the average mark of 15%. Understandably, physical, not mental, compatibility matters more to act now, think later Aries.

Sense of humour scores high with all men, notching up a total of 14% of the votes. And out in front here are earthy Capricorn (18%) and Virgo (17%) followed by Leo and Sagittarius (both 16%). The male starsigns who rate sense of humour lowest? Cool air sign "thinkers" Aquarius (11%) and Libra (10%).

CASE HISTORY OF A CAPRICORN MAN

Gerry, a 47-year-old Capricorn, has lived with Monica, 43, a Virgo, for 20 years

"The first time Monica and I slept together, we could hardly make love for laughing. We'd borrowed a friend's apartment and he had a water bed—we kept sliding off it. But far from making the memory a bad one, it makes it better. Laughter is one of the great healers and the great helpers in life. And I could never be with a woman who didn't find the same things funny.

"Monica and I often play practical jokes on each other—it's an unspoken challenge to come up with more and more outrageous ones. But we draw the line at anything that would embarrass the other person. We giggle like a couple of kids in bed and like the same sort of comedy shows on TV. Sharing a good laugh together is almost as satisfying as sharing good sex. And it's just as healthy for our relationship..."

When it comes to the quality of sexual attraction, the starsigns really start to show their differences. For 19% of Aries men rate this as a partner's most vital element—over three times the number for perhaps less physical Aquarius males (just 6%). Other signs traditionally thought of as highly-sexed, Scorpio and Leo, also score high on this category (15% and 14% respectively). While Cancer (7%) and Sagittarius (8%) are next lowest after Aquarius.

Fun is rated most essential by 9% each of Aquarius, Scorpio and Gemini men—but by only a minuscule 1% of Taureans, who do tend to take relationships very seriously. The same tiny percentage (just 1%) of Virgo men vote for a partner who's a homelover—an unexpected result for the starsign traditionally considered conventional and domestic.

But sociable, outgoing (according to traditional astrology, anyway!) Gemini scores 7% in this section. Followed by Libra and Scorpio (both 4%). But for once staying true to his accepted star profile, Sagittarius man doesn't want his women to be home-loving AT ALL.

It's no surprise that the sex king of the zodiac, Scorpio man, rates sex skills in a partner more essential that any other male, at 5%. And no Capricorn or Cancer man rates them important at all. Perhaps these are more practical signs who realise sex can be improved if everything else is right.

Good looks come next in men's overall line-up—occasionally

vain, and certainly usually style-conscious, Libra man is tops in this vote, with 5%. "Yes, if I'm honest, I would have a one-night stand with an ugly woman—but it wouldn't go any further," says one Libra man. But for Taurus and Pisces men, good looks don't come into it at all.

Money only matters to a grand total of four male starsigns. And they're not the ones we might expect. Capricorn scores 3%, Aries and Sagittarius both 2% and Cancer 1%. It's charitable to suggest it's security the first and last signs are seeking, and assured independence for the middle two. But it could also be an easy life...

Finally, just three men want a woman who is a hard worker— Taurus (3%) and Virgo and Sagittarius (both 1%). Could the first two be trying to break away from their traditional image as strong, protective starsigns?

WHAT KEEPS WOMEN KEEN?

Like the men, the zodiac's women also rate loyalty high at 24%. But exactly the same amount, 24%, vote for kindness as a partner's most essential quality. That means almost one in two of all female starsigns opt for one or the other of these personal qualities first.

But, starsign by starsign, the order is slightly different. Leo woman, at 29%, looks for loyalty most, followed by Virgo (28%) and Libra (27%). While Aries is first to want kindness in a partner (29%), with Pisces next on 28%, then Taurus and Gemini (both 27%).

STARWATCH

Women's signs that can be aggressively independent, like Aries and Leo, obviously realise they need a kind, loyal and understanding partner if a relationship is to last. Here they show more foresight than astrology might credit.

The woman who most wants a partner to "understand how I think" is Gemini—but given that starsign's quicksilver mind, that may be a tall order. Aquarius also scores 20%, or one in five, who rate mental compatibility as vital—in this the result mirrors Aquarius men. And Cancer, again like the men, rates this high too, at 19%. Least keen of all women on having a partner on the same wavelength is Virgo, who scores 14%.

Who insist their man have a sense of humour? Sagittarius (19%), Aquarius (17%) and Scorpio (16%). Apart from Sagittarius, these show a different pattern to the men. Perhaps while men want women to share their own love of laughter, more serious female signs like Scorpio and Aquarius are consciously looking for a man to help them lighten up? But overall, slightly more women than men vote Sense of Humour essential—15% to 14%.

The next category shows a much bigger divide between the sexes however. For while sexual attraction is vital to 11% of men, it only counts for an average of 8% of women. But once again up near the top of the list is sexy Scorpio, with 11%. Next in line is Leo (10%), then Capricorn, Aquarius, Pisces and Aries, all 8%.

CASE HISTORY OF A SCORPIO WOMAN
Jean, 34, is a nightclub singer with three regular lovers. She is a Scorpio

"OK, so maybe I do like sex more than most women, but physical attraction, that sexy 'spark' is the first thing that attracts me to a person. And once that fades, or dies altogether, the relationship is over for me. I couldn't stay with someone I didn't fancy. It would turn my stomach.

"I have one long-term lover at the moment who I've lived with for ten years. We don't make love as often as we used to because he's away a lot—he's a musician—but when we do the attraction is definitely still there. I also have one other man, and one woman, in my life for what I call 'sexual friendships'. And though respect and liking comes into it, of course, sex is my main driving force.

"I love them all in different ways, and I think they love me—they certainly say they do. But sexual attraction isn't something we take for granted. We work at it—it's fun."

Still on the subject of fun, this is another partner factor that women rate less highly than men—5% of females across the zodiac say fun is a partner's most vital quality, compared to 7% of men. But slightly more unexpected is just who looks for fun in a partner—topping the ladies' list are Virgo and Taurus, with 8%, then Cancer and Capricorn who give it 6%. While the lowest score for fun comes from supposedly light-hearted Libra (3%).

Home lover is the next quality for the women's partners, with a total of just 2% going for this—but that's twice as many as vote for sex skills as a partnership must-have. Cancer and Taurus (both 4%) are the first to look for a home-loving partner, while least interested is out-going Libra (1%).

As with the men, however, Scorpio scores highest on sex skills (2%), though among the women this is equalled by Aquarius and Virgo. And though Aries men rate sex skills very low (and sexual attraction high)—not one of them opt for sex skills as a desirable quality in a mate.

Practical Virgo insists on money as a partner's essential quality 3% of the time, but idealistic Cancer discounts it altogether. And Virgo is also keenest of all women on a partner who's a hard worker (3%)! This time, at least, the starsign is matching up to traditional astrology's expectations...

In general a much wider spread of women vote for the categories money and hard worker than men do. So whatever new definitions of equality may mean, old-fashioned values still seem to apply.

But one element where women differ the other way from men is in good looks. Far fewer women than men say good looks are essential in a partner. Overall, just one in 100 rates a partner's physical attractiveness as the one thing that matters most. For men the figure is 3%. Of those women who do, Aquarius tops the list with 2%. But Gemini, Scorpio and Sagittarius women don't consider looks important at all.

DOES SEX GET BETTER WITH TIME?

The good news for those wondering if familiarity breeds contempt, or content, is that a substantial majority of those replying to the survey declare that a long-term relationship has made them more interested in sex.

The figure is slightly higher for women than for men, but there is a down side, too. For women are also considerably more likely to say long-term love has made them LESS interested in sex—17% do so, compared with just 10% of men.

MEN ON LONG-TERM LOVE

Looking first at the male starsigns, the man who finds long-term relationships the most satisfying is Cancer—56%, well above average, say they have become more interested in sex as a relationship progresses. Which could explain why Cancer is the zodiac's most-married man, too.

But Cancer is also more likely than any other man to say he's got less interested in sex long-term (19%) and least likely to say his interest hasn't changed at all (just 26%, way below any other starsign). Changeable sign of extremes, that's Cancer, all right.

Other men who feel sexier within a relationship are, surprisingly, laid-back Libra with 53%, followed by Sagittarius, who scores 51%. While the lowest score of all, 43%, is notched up by Aries man, prone perhaps to get bored more rapidly than most. "It's always great to start with but I soon find myself looking at other women and wondering, 'What If...' admits one 24-year-old Aries.

STARWATCH
Libra and Sagittarius the most keen on sex within a loving relationship? Perhaps these two starsigns are less keen on competition and variety than conventional astrology says.

Several signs do find long-term loving a turn-off, notably Cancer (19%), Scorpio (16%) and Aries (12%), who all admit their interest in sex has dwindled within a relationship. But by far least likely to say this is strong, steady Leo, with just 3% of Leo men saying sex has lost its sparkle. And Leo is also most inclined to rate sex drive unchanged by circumstances—at 52%. That's exactly double Cancer's score for this section of just 26%...

WOMEN IN LOVE
Just over one in every two women who replied to the survey say a long-term relationship has made them more interested in sex. And the list is led by Cancer again (54%), just as among the men. Next keenest on long-term love among the ladies is Aquarius (53%) and Aries (also 53%)—meaning Aries women are 10% likelier to get sexier within a relationship 10% more than Aries men (43%, lowest male score of all).

Least thrilled by established sex is Capricorn, 47%—and this exacting sign is also most likely to admit to losing interest in sex long-term (23%). That's a full 3% higher than the next starsigns on the list, Pisces and Taurus (both 20%). And almost double the lowest in this category, Leo woman, who loses interest in long-term just 12% of the time.

This general placing is the same as for Leo men—although Leo women do lose interest four times more than Leo men! But when it comes to saying sex drive has remained unchanged through the years, Leo lady—again like Leo men—is tops too, with 39%. Also still keen over the years are Scorpio (36%) and Gemini (35%) women.

CASE HISTORY OF A LEO WOMAN

Mary, a 28-year-old Leo, has just been divorced after seven years of marriage to an Aquarius man.

"We were together for a couple of years before we got married and had time to iron out any tiny problems in our sex life together. So there was no reason to get less interested in sex—I would say my sex drive did stay roughly the same.

"But I was surprised it didn't increase, if I'm honest, once we were sharing the same bed every night, and the same house every day. I suppose a couple reaches its own level of lovemaking and simply stays there.

"But if sex between us was fine, everything else wasn't. My husband had business and money worries and started to withdraw from me, emotionally and physically. When I found out he'd used our children's savings without telling me, that was the low point. But I still found him very attractive, and it was hard to leave. We still sleep together now occasionally, absolutely no strings. And it's still so good."

WHAT HAPPENS IF CHILDREN COME ALONG?

"Nothing changes" is the resounding reply from the survey partners when asked if having children together has any effect on a partner's sex appeal. But sex by sex and sign by sign, surprises lie in store...

FATHERS CONFESS

If you want a passionate partner—and a good father—look no further than Pisces man. For an astounding 33%, or one in every three, say having children together makes their partner seem more sexy to them. And this is closely followed by family-centred Scorpio who scores 30%, and loyal Taurus with 29%. Bottom of the list is Virgo man with just 16% saying partners seem more sexy after babies. And the reason many give is finding changes to a partner's body hard to accept.

Also scoring low here is Sagittarius—just 18% rate babies as a sex appeal boost—and this sign of substantial appetites is also most likely to say having children together makes a lover seem less sexy (27%).

CASE HISTORY OF A SAGITTARIUS MAN

Sagittarius Grant, 34, has two children aged two and four with his partner Nancy, 30 a Taurus.

"Saggy boobs and stretch marks—what red-blooded male is going to find these exciting? Get real here. Yes, I still love Nancy and I have great respect for her as a carer and a mother. But our sex life has nose-dived since the kids were born, and that's the truth.

"Perhaps I shouldn't have gone to the births, somehow I can't get them out of my head now. And every time we start to make love I remember Nancy in those stirrups being stitched. Any mystique sex had has evaporated completely.

"She's not put on a lot of weight or anything, her body's just different—and of course the children make so many demands on Nancy she doesn't have so much time for me. Yes, if I'm honest, I do feel neglected. Sometimes I feel like sex but then I look over at Nancy in bed and she's already sound asleep. A girl in the insurance office where I work is sending sexy signals my way and one of these days I might just take her up on it. Nancy wouldn't notice—she might even be pleased to get the pressure off herself..."

Capricorn man opts for children making a partner seem less sexy second most often at 26%, followed by Cancer at 24%. Could these signs have more difficulty than others digging below surface attraction to deep, hidden feelings?

As for accepting children into their life without feelings changing at all, most likely to do this is Gemini man—66%, two out of every three, say having kids has not changed their sexual attraction to their partner. Next is Virgo at 61% and Leo (59%).

DOES PARENTHOOD PUT WOMEN OFF SEX?

Even more women than men say having children together has made no difference to their partner's sex appeal—a grand total of 64% or almost two-thirds. Out in front here are Capricorn and Virgo women—71% of each starsign judge sex attraction unaffected by parenthood.

Which women find sharing the joys of motherhood a positive turn-on? Sexy Scorpio heads this list again, with over a quarter, 26%, finding a partner more sexy as a parent. Then come Aquarius and Pisces (both 25%) and Leo and Gemini (both 23%). "It's an extra bond drawing us together forever—this is a life we've created together and will carry on caring for. That's chased away any doubts I had about my partner and made him seem even more sexy to me, because now I know he's mine alone," says a Pisces mum of six months.

Scorpio isn't known as the sex queen of the zodiac for nothing, however—for as well as being most turned on by parenthood, Scorpio woman also finds it the biggest turn-off. 19% say having children together makes a partner less sexy, followed by 18% of Pisces (yes, again.) and 16% of Leos.

STARWATCH
The general rule for starsign women seems to be, each starsign either has no feelings at all on sex after children, or goes to real extremes.

THE 12 STARSIGNS' PARTNERSHIP PROFILES

ARIES MAN AND PARTNERS

*Most popular permanent partners for Aries man are Cancer (15%) Virgo (12%) and Pisces (12%).

*But he is least likely to end up with Taurus (4%) Sagittarius (5%) and Capricorn (5%). "I went out with a Capricorn once, but I didn't slot nicely into the pigeonhole she had marked 'Boyfriend'," says one Aries man.

*A slight narcissistic element makes Aries men overwhelmingly find other Aries partners the most sexy—23% do, a full 10% more than the next sexiest sign in Aries' eyes, Cancer, which scores 13%. And then comes Virgo, 11%.

*But it's Cancer again when Aries men vote for the starsign they've found least sexy! These are 13% Cancer, 13% Libra, and 11% Taurus. And the main reasons given are lack of spontaneity and unwillingness to experiment.

*Aries is first attracted to: Warm Smile (44%), Nice Eyes (42%), Curvy Body (34%), and Great Legs (28%). Then comes Kind Nature (24%), Faithfulness (23%), Shared Interests (20%), Slim Body (17%) and Good Homemaker (16%). Aries is more attracted than any other man to this talent! And his least popular three are Gentle Manner (15%), Attractive Voice (9%) and Sexy Laugh (9%).

*Which quality matters most to Aries man in a partner? Loyalty (22%), Kindness (19%), Sexual Attraction (19%, and the top score for any man in this category), Sense of Humour (13%). Then he rates Understanding How I Think (9%), Fun (7%), Home Lover (4%), Good Looks (4%), Money (2%) and finally Sex Skills (2%—lowest of all men, obviously enthusiasm and attraction matter more than experience.). No Aries is interested in a Hard Worker.

*Aries is least likely of all men to get more interested in sex within a long-term relationship, just 43% say they are. 12% are actively less interested, 45% the same.

*27% find having children together makes a partner seem more sexy. 22% vote for less sexy and 51% (second lowest of all men) say she seems the same. "How could things not be different after such a major life-changing event?" asks Jon, 32. "The challenge is to cope with it, not let it beat me...sorry, I mean us."

Aries man is influenced by physical first, personal second, when choosing and keeping a partner.

ARIES WOMAN AND PARTNERS

*The men she makes a future with most often are Aquarius (10%), Scorpio (10%) and Cancer (10%).

*And Aries woman is least likely to settle with Capricorn (7%), Sagittarius (7%), Taurus (6%) or other Aries (6%).

*Top "turn-on" factor is found in Leo (12%), Aries (11%) and Scorpio (10%). "It may not last, but they all make you feel like the most desired woman alive," is one comment.

*Thumbs down for the least sexy starsigns? Aries gives it to Cancer and Taurus, both with a score of 12%.

*In order of preference, Aries woman is first attracted by: Gorgeous Eyes (47%), Kindness (37%), Great Smile (32%), Faithfulness (31%), Confidence (26%—top vote of all women in this category), Height (17%), Smart Clothes (16%), Muscular Build (16%), Good Voice (14%), Good Line in Chat (10%), Good Provider (8%) and a Slim Body (7%).

*But when it comes to sticking with a partner, the qualities she rates highest are: Kindness (more than any other woman at 29%), Loyalty (24%), Understanding How I Think (15%), Sense of Humour (14%) and Sexual Attraction (8%). Then comes Fun (5%), Home Lover (3%), Money (1%), Hard Worker (1%) and Good Looks (1%). The only quality no Aries opts for is Sex Skills. "I'm the best teacher of that, anyway" says Debbie-Sue, 26.

*53% have grown more interested in sex in a long-term relationship, second highest of all women. 17% are less interested, 31% say interest hasn't changed.

*Having children together has made 21% of Aries' partners seem more sexy, 14% seem less sexy and 64% stay the same.

Aries woman looks for kindness and confidence in a partner—and sex gets better as time goes by.

HOW DO THE SEXES COMPARE?

Less than half as many women as men rate sexual attraction as a partner's most vital quality (8% women, 19% men). But Aries men and women alike find the same signs unsexy, and bad bets long-term. And though both do fancy each other, it's slightly one-sided—23% of Aries men vote Aries women most sexy, less than half the women (11%) return the compliment. While Aries man is amongst the least likely to enjoy sex more within a long-term relationship, Aries woman is one of established love's biggest fans.

TAURUS MAN AND PARTNERS

*Taurus man most often ends up with Aquarius (13%), Aries (11%) and Taurus (11%—one of the few men to make a go of love with the same starsign).

*Who are his least favourites? Pisces (6%), Scorpio (5%), and Sagittarius (just 2%).

*Top vote for the sexiest starsign gives equal first place to Virgo, Gemini and Taurus, all scoring 12%.

*Warm Smile is way ahead in the league of first attraction factors—46% of Taurus men vote for this, more than any other male sign. Next is Curvy Body (39%), Kind Nature (37%—again way ahead of the others, 7% more than the nearest sign), Shared Interests (29%), Faithfulness (27%), Attractive Voice (19%), Gentle Manner (17%), Sexy Laugh (17%), Slim Body (16%) and Good Homemaker (14%). "Yes, home is where the heart is for me, I don't mind admitting it," says one Taurus.

*Once he's won his woman, Taurus judges the following to be her most important qualities: Kindness (26%, the number one score), Loyalty (23%), Understanding How I Think (18%), Sense of

Humour (12%), Sexual Attraction (9%), Sex Skills (4%), Home Lover (3%), Hard Worker (3%—of just three men who voted for this category, Taurus gave the highest score!), and Fun (at just 1%, Taurus man rates fun in a relationship far lower than any other man in the zodiac). But he doesn't think Good Looks or Money are important at all.

*49% say they're more interested in sex within a long-lasting relationship, 9% that their interest has lessened, 42% that it has stayed the same.

*Having children has made their partner seem sexier for 29%, less sexy to 18%, and unchanged to 52%.

Kind and cuddly Taurus man wants 50-50 commitment—and fun is optional.

TAURUS WOMAN AND PARTNERS

*Who does Taurus woman take as her partner most often? Other Taurus (12%), Aries, Libra, and Capricorn (all 10%).

*She's least likely to end up with Pisces (6%) and Sagittarius (5%).

*Taurus partners win her vote as the most sexy, too, at 11%—one of the few signs who actually pair off with the people they fancy most. She also goes for Libra (11%).

*But another 11% of Taurus women find Libra a turn-off, along with Aries (12%).

*She likes Gorgeous Eyes best (41%, although less than any other woman), then Kindness (39%), Great Smile (38%), Faithfulness (33%), Confidence (21%), Smart Clothes (18%), Height (18%), Muscular Build (16%), Good Line In Chat (12%), Good Provider (11%—"If he can't keep me in champagne and roses, let alone bread and milk, then no thank you," says one luxury-loving Taurus). A Good Voice and Slim Body bring up the rear (both 10%).

*To let a partner stick around, however, Taurus woman looks for Kindness (27%), Loyalty (20%), Understanding How I Think (18%), Sense of Humour (13%), Fun (8%—highest score of all women), Sexual Attraction (6%—lowest score of all women),

Home Lover (4%), Money, Good Looks and Sex Skills (all 1%).

*An average 51% find sex drive increases within a relationship. But 20%, in the high range, find it decreases, and a below average 29% say it stays the same.

*For 22%, the arrival of children makes their partner seem more sexy. 14% say he's less sexy, and 63% that he's the same. "Well, he was last time we had sex, but that was a while ago." says Sharon, 36.

Love actions speak louder than words for Taurus woman— she'll choose security over sexuality in a partner.

HOW DO THE SEXES COMPARE?
Both men and women from this starsign find each other the most sexy and—lucky lovers—they're also most likely to settle down with other Taureans. Both sexes also partner the same starsigns the least—Sagittarius and Pisces. But Taurus women are eight times more insistent a partner should be fun than Taurus men.

GEMINI MAN AND PARTNERS
*Most likely choice of partner for Gemini man is Virgo (13%), Aries (12%), Cancer and Libra (both 11%).

*He's least inclined to settle down with Taurus, Capricorn or Aquarius (all 5%).

*Lucky for him, he also finds Virgo one of the sexiest starsigns, scoring it at 14%. Next is Aries at 12%, but best of all are fellow Geminis, 15%.

*When it comes to nominating the least sexy starsign, Gemini man plumps for Taurus (15%), Capricorn, Pisces and Cancer (all 11%). "They wouldn't know a fantasy if it slapped them in the face," grumbles Gemini Jake, 48.

*Warm Smile tops his scale of first attraction features, with a score of 41%, but that's the second lowest among the men. Then comes Nice Eyes (40%), Great Legs (35%—highest vote of all men!),

Curvy Body (33%), Shared Interests (which Gemini rates highest of all men, at 32%). "Opposites may attract, but what will keep them together?" asks one Gemini. Next comes Kind Nature, Slim Body and Faithfulness (all 28%), Sexy Laugh (20%, again more popular with Gemini than any other man), Gentle Manner (19%), Attractive Voice (15%) and Good Homemaker (12%).

*But what keeps Gemini with a partner? 20% vote for Loyalty, 17% for Understanding How I Think, and 15% for Kindness. Then comes Sexual Attraction (13%), Sense of Humour (12%), Fun, at 9% the highest vote of the zodiac's males, Home Lover (7%), and finally Sex Skills and Good Looks, with 4% each.

*Interest in sex has increased within a bond for 46%, decreased for 8% and stayed the same for 46%.

*And once they have children together, 22% of Gemini men see their partner as more sexy. 12% (lowest overall) say less sexy, 66% or two in three (highest of all men) say it makes no difference.

Find him a lively mind in a lovely body and Gemini man will meet his perfect match.

GEMINI WOMAN AND PARTNERS

*Gemini woman's most favoured partners are Cancer (11%), Virgo (10%), Libra (9%) and Aries (also 9%).

*She's least likely to stick with Leo (7%), Sagittarius (7%) and Gemini (7%).

*Who does she find most sexy? Aries is ahead here on 12%, followed by Taurus, Libra and Scorpio, all on 10%.

*Yet 12% of Gemini women also find Aries the least sexy sign of all, along with Capricorn and Pisces, both 10%.

*Gemini woman is drawn to Gorgeous Eyes (43%), Kindness (38%), Great Smile (37%), Confidence (25%), Faithfulness (23%—lowest vote of all women), Smart Clothes (20%—highest vote of all women!), Muscular Build (15%), Height (13%), Good Line In Chat (13%, again highest of all women), Good Voice (12%), Good Provider (8%) and Slim Body (7%).

*In a permanent partner, however she opts for: 27% Kindness, 21% Loyalty, 20% Understanding How I Think (the zodiac's top score for communicative Gemini), Sense of Humour 14%, Sexual Attraction 7%, Fun 5%, Home Lover and Money 2% and Sex Skills and Hard Worker both 1%.

*A total of 52% have got more interested in sex within a long-term relationship, 14% are less interested, and 35% remain the same.

*Having children together makes a partner sexier in the eyes of 23% of Gemini women. "And everyone else, judging by the number of women chasing him!" comments Carla, 31. 14% find their partner less sexy, and for 63% he's no different.

Smart clothes and smart moves matter more to Gemini woman than fidelity

HOW DO THE SEXES COMPARE?

Both Gemini men and women choose permanent partners from the same top four starsigns, and value mental qualities like conversation and communication more than conventional partnership factors. But Gemini women are less interested in fidelity than men (23% compared to 28%), while this starsign's males are bigger fans of fun in a relationship. Looking long-term, more women than men feel sexier within a relationship—yet almost twice as many feel LESS sexy too. Women's sex appeal to men is less affected by having a family than vice versa.

CANCER MAN AND PARTNERS

*Leo (16%), Aries (12%) and Cancer (11%) are Cancer man's most likely matches.

*And he's least inclined to choose a partner who is Virgo (4%), Sagittarius (3%) or Libra (2%).

*He gives the most sexy starsign vote to Cancer (17%), Pisces (13%) and Taurus (12%).

*And Cancer's least sexy starsign? That's Aries (16%), Pisces (13%) and Virgo (10%).

*Order of first attraction features runs as follows for Cancer men— Warm Smile (44%), Nice Eyes (43%), Kind Nature (30%, and second highest of all men), Curvy Body (27%), Great Legs (24%), Shared Interests (23%), Faithfulness (21%, perhaps surprisingly, second lowest of all men.), Gentle Manner (19%, meaning more Cancer men vote for this than any other male sign), Sexy Laugh (19%), Slim Body (18%), Attractive Voice (16%), and Good Homemaker (16%).

*In a long-term partner, however, the qualities Cancer looks for are Loyalty (29%, top score of all men), Understanding How I Think (21%), Kindness (20%), Sense of Humour (13%), Sexual Attraction (7%, second lowest score overall),Fun (also second lowest) at 6%, Home Lover (2%) and Good Looks and Money (1% each). Cancer Man gives a zero vote to Sex Skills and being a Hard Worker. "Who wants a woman who gives all her energy to work and none to you?" asks one Cancer man.

*He's the man most likely to be more interested in sex within a relationship—56% answered positively to this question. "I won't let myself really relax until I know things are serious," confesses Royce, 26. "I've been hurt too many times before." But he's also the man most likely to be LESS interested in sex in a long-term bond, at 19%. Just 26%, lowest score of all men, say sex stays the same.

*What about having children? For 21% it makes a partner seem more sexy, for 24% less sexy and for 55% makes no difference.

Cancer man—treat him kind, keep him keen. But partnership can be all or nothing...

CANCER WOMAN AND PARTNERS

*Who does Cancer woman choose for a lifetime together? Pisces (12%), Capricorn and fellow Cancer (both 10%).

*But she gives the cold shoulder to Aries and Taurus (7% each), Virgo (6%) and especially Libra at just 5%.

*There's no question who she finds the sexiest starsign—Scorpio is

way out in front with 17% of the vote. Next comes Pisces with 14%.
*And almost as high a score the other way goes to Aries partners—16% of Cancer women vote them the least sexy of all. Taurus and Gemini don't do much better on 10% apiece.

*Cancer women are first attracted to Gorgeous Eyes 46% of the time. Then comes Kindness (34%), A Great Smile (30%, lowest of all the women), Faithfulness (30%), Smart Clothes (20%, or one in five rate this, that's the joint highest score overall), Confidence (16%) Height (15%), Muscular Build and Good Voice (12% each). Good Line In Chat, Slim Body and Good Provider bring up the rear with 9% each.

*Looking at a partner's most vital quality, one in four, 25% of Cancer women choose Kindness. 23% opt for Loyalty, for 19% Understanding How I Think matters most, while 13% plump for a Sense of Humour. 7% rate Sexual Attraction, 6% vote for Fun, 4% for Home Lover, 1% each for Sex Skills, Good Looks and a Hard Worker. The only attribute that leaves Cancer cold is cash. "Money shouldn't come into love at all—it's irrelevant," says Sadie, 18.

*54% of Cancer women, more than any other sign, find they are more interested in sex within the security of a relationship. 17% are less interested, 29% stay the same.

*After having a family together, a low 18% rate a partner as more sexy, 15% as less, and 67% say there's no change.

  Strong ideas under a gentle surface—Cancer woman knows who she wants and how to keep him.

HOW DO THE SEXES COMPARE

Cancer men and women are the most likely in the zodiac to get more interested in sex within a relationship. Unusually, once kids come along, Cancer women are less inclined than men to find a partner's sex appeal increases. But men also find a partner less sexy after a family far more than women (24% to just 18%)! Male and female choice of popular partners are very

different, but they do agree on one major point—that neither fancies Aries. Views on need for sexual attraction and fun are identical, too.

LEO MAN AND PARTNERS

*Leo man lasts the course with Capricorn (13%), Taurus (12%) and Virgo (11%) partners.

*But he's less likely to make a go of love with Sagittarius (5%), Libra (4%) and Pisces (3%).

*Sex bombs of the zodiac, in Leo's opinion, are Gemini and Taurus on 13% each, and fellow Leos, scoring 12%.

*But don't ask him to sleep with a partner from starsign Cancer. An amazing 25%, or one in four, vote Cancer the least sexy sign of all. But Taurus gets a negative vote too, at 13%, with Scorpio on 11%.

*More than any other man, Leo wants to look deep in a partner's eyes —exactly half (50%) say Nice Eyes are what first attracts them to someone. But a Warm Smile is important, too, at 45%, followed by a Curvy Body (37%), Great Legs (30%), Shared Interests (28%), Faithfulness (25%) and Slim Body (21%). Leo is less keen than other men on a Kind Nature, awarding it just 19%. Sexy Laugh scores 18% with Leo man, Attractive Voice 15%, Gentle Manner 11%, and the talent that attracts him least is Good Homemaker at 8%).

*Listing the qualities that matter most in a partner, Leo goes for Kindness first (19%), then Understanding How I Think (18%), Sense of Humour and Loyalty (both 16%), Sexual Attraction (14%), Fun (7%), Sex Skills and Good Looks (both 4%). But he rates being a Home Lover lower, at 3%. "I don't stay in, why would I want my partner to do it?" ask Graeme, 34. And Money and Hard Work don't get a score at all.

*Time together isn't always a turn-on for Leo man—just 45%, below average, say they've grown more interested in sex within a relationship. But 3%, the lowest score of all, say they're less interested. And 52% of loyal Leos say their interest has stayed at the same level.

*Having children together has made a partner seem less sexy to only 15%, the second lowest number of all. "Yeah, things are very different, but they're not worse—just different," says one 27-year-old father of four. 26% say she's more sexy now, 59% that having children has made no difference.

The eyes have it for Leo man, but home is where his heart isn't when choosing a lover.

LEO WOMAN AND PARTNERS

*Looking long-term, Leo woman ends up most often with Libra (12%), Pisces (11%) and Taurus (11%)

*And her worst bet for long-term togetherness are Aquarius, Capricorn, Scorpio and Gemini (all scoring 7%).

*Leo lady's vote for sexiest starsign goes to Leo (13%), Taurus (13%) and Aries (11%)

*But she's least enthusiastic about Cancer (15% say the water sign is least sexy of all—"About as exciting as a bath of ice-cold lumpy porridge," as one Leo lady puts it.) She doesn't rate Virgo (12%) either.

*What first attracts Leo ladies? Gorgeous Eyes (43%), Great Smile (34%), Kindness (32%), Faithfulness (30%), Confidence (19%), Smart Clothes (16%), Muscular Build (16%), Height (15%), Good Voice (12%), Slim Body (11%, the only category where Leo women have the highest score), Good Line In Chat and Good Provider (both 9%).

*Loyalty is the thing that matters most in a partner, says Leo—and how. 29%, above any other female sign, place this first. Kindness scores 24% of Leo's vote, while Understanding How I Think gets 17%. Sense of Humour scores 11%, Sexual Attraction 10% (second highest score overall), Fun 4%, Home Lover 2% and Sex Skills, Hard Worker, Money and Good Looks 1% each.

41

*Exactly half, 50% of Leo women find they are more interested in sex in a long-term relationship, that's slightly below average. Like the men, they're least likely to say they've got less interested—12% do so. And again like Leo men, they're most inclined overall to declare interest hasn't changed (38%).

*Having children together makes a partner more sexy to Leo women in 23% of cases, less sexy 16% of the time—and the same, 61%, putting her in the middle range.

Give Leo lady good looks, loyalty and unlimited sex and she will make sure a relationship last...

HOW DO THE SEXES COMPARE?
The two sexes within starsign Leo agree on who they find sexy, but disagree on which signs to settle down with. But neither finds Cancer sexually exciting, men even less than women. Kindness and fidelity matter far more to Leo women than men—but neither sets much store by domestic talents in a partner. Both are least likely overall to lose sexual interest within a long-term relationship, although at 12%, Leo women are four times as likely to go off a partner than Leo men (3%).

VIRGO MAN AND PARTNERS
*Settling down material for Virgo man is provided mostly by Capricorn and Gemini partners (both score 13%), and Sagittarius, (10%).

*He's least likely to live happily ever after with Leo (7%), Cancer and Aquarius (3% each).

*Starsigns voted the sexiest are Gemini (14%), other Virgos (13%), and Leo (13%).

*But least sexy in Virgo man's opinion are Taurus (18%), Aries (16%), and Gemini again at 15%. "The only Gemini I've ever slept with just didn't know how to take her time in bed—each time seemed to be more of a rush than before," admits Virgo Al, 41.

*Asked what first attracts him to someone, Virgo man differs from every other male by putting a Curvy Body in first position, with a total score of 45%. "People seem to think being a Virgo means you're more interested in women's morals than their bodies. Well, I can assure you this isn't the case," announces one 21-year-old Virgo.

Next is Nice Eyes (43%), Warm Smile (42%), Great Legs (30%), Slim Body (again he's keener on this than other men, awarding it 28%), Kind Nature (27%) and Faithfulness (24%). Shared Interests scores 24%, too, then comes Attractive Voice, which Virgo rates more than other men do (23%). He gives Gentle Manner a 19% vote, again highest overall, Sexy Laugh 15% and Good Homemaker 9%.

*Like most men, however, Virgo thinks Loyalty is a partner's most vital quality, and scores it 26%. Kindness gets 20%, Sense of Humour 17% (second highest overall), and Sexual Attraction and Understanding How I Think 12% each. 5% of Virgo men think Fun matters most, while 3% each go for Sex Skills and Good Looks. And just 1%, surprising for supposedly domesticated Virgo, vote for a partner who's a Home Lover. The same tiny percentage want a Hard Worker—and no Virgo man at all is interested in a partner's money prospects.

*For 47%, sexual interest has increased long-term in a relationship, and for 10% it's decreased. 43% report no change. That places Virgo in the middle range.

*A partner is sexier after children for 16%—lowest of all men overall. 23% say they actually find her less sexy, while 61%, second highest overall score, note no change in sex appeal.

Sense of humour, and sexy shape, are Virgo man's vital statistics for a partner—he doesn't care about cash.

VIRGO WOMAN AND PARTNERS

*Virgo woman's lasting mates most often are Cancer (12%), Gemini (11%), Leo and Libra (both 10%).

*But her partner is least likely to come from starsigns Aries (7%), Taurus (6%) or Sagittarius (5%).

*Sexiest signs, she says, are Cancer (11%), Gemini (10%) and Leo (10%) and her least sexy vote goes to Pisces (13%) and Aries (10%).

*What is it that draws her towards someone initially? Gorgeous Eyes for 43%, a Great Smile (34%), Faithfulness (32%), Kindness (31%), Confidence (17%), Smart Clothes (16%). 16% also like a tall man, 15% a Muscular Build, while 9% of Virgo women like a Slim Body in their men. Good Line In Chat sways 8%, 7% prefer a Good Voice and just 6%, second lowest of women overall and not expected of "conventional" Virgo, are attracted towards a Good Provider. "I'm perfectly capable of providing for myself—what I want from a man is all the things I can't give myself, like back rubs, hugs, surprises and unquestioning support," says Lesley, 39.

*For Virgo, the one quality that matters most in a partner is Loyalty (28%), followed by Kindness (20%), Sense of Humour (15%), Understanding How I Think (14%) and Fun, which Virgo women vote more vital than any other woman at 8%. Sexual Attraction matters most to 7%, 3% each go for Money and a Hard Worker, 2% value a Home Lover and Sex Skills and Virgo awards her lowest mark, 1%, to Good Looks.

*An average 51% of Virgos find interest in sex increases within a relationship. For 17% it gets less, and 32% find it stays the same.

*Like the men of this starsign, Virgo woman is least likely to see a partner as sexier after children come along—just 16%, well below average, do so. But 13% say a partner is actually less sexy—and for the highest score overall, 71%, there's no change in attraction.

Virgo girls just want to have fun—and are less interested in security than is usually supposed!

HOW DO THE SEXES COMPARE?

Virgo woman may rate fun in a relationship higher than any other woman, and not seek a good provider—but she still insists on faithfulness far more than Virgo men—32% of women compared to just 24% of men. Virgo men's initial interest is

extremely physical, but for women looks just don't come into it—three times as many men vote good looks as a partner's most essential quality. Neither sex finds their sexual interest is affected much by long-term love, though both Virgo men and women are the least likely in the zodiac to find a partner more sexy after having a family together (just 16% each).

LIBRA MAN AND PARTNERS

*Libra man's top three partners are as follows: Sagittarius (14%), Scorpio (13%) and Taurus (11%).

*He is least likely to look for a long-term bond with Gemini (6%), Aquarius (4%) and Virgo (4%).

*Where physical attraction is concerned, however, Libra man finds his own starsign, Libra, sexiest at 15%. "It's the way Libra women have of tuning into your secret desires—the things you'd like to try but don't dare suggest," says Trent, 27. Then comes Gemini (12%) and Aries (11%).

*Least sexy starsigns in his view are Pisces at 13%, Aries and Taurus, both 12%.

*Top attraction power for Libra man lies in a Warm Smile at 43%. Then he likes Nice Eyes (40%), a Curvy Body (36%), Great Legs, Kind Nature and Faithfulness (all 28%), Shared Interests (21%), Attractive Voice (20%), Slim Body (16%), Sexy Laugh (13%), Good Homemaker (11%) and Gentle Manner (only scoring 8% here makes him less keen on this than other men). One Libra man speaks for many when he declares, "I want a real woman in my life, not a wimp."

*In a partner Libra rates the most essential quality as Loyalty at 26%. Next equal are Kindness and Understanding How I Think at 18%, then Sexual Attraction at 11%, Sense of Humour (10%) Fun and Good Looks (5% each—he's more attracted by good looks than any other male sign), Home Lover 4% and Sex Skills 3%. Money and Hard Work mean nothing to Libra man.

*An unexpectedly high 53% of Libra men report they're more interested in sex within a long-term relationship. Just 8% are less interested, 39% say there's no change.

*A below average 20% find a partner sexier after children come along. 22% say it makes her less sexy, while 57% have unaltered feelings.

Libra man longs for a partner who knows her own mind, her own body—and his.

LIBRA WOMAN AND PARTNERS

*Long-term, Libra woman lands up with Cancer and Leo (both 11%) and Gemini and Capricorn (both 10%) most often.

*Her least popular partner choices are Pisces, Aquarius, Sagittarius and Taurus, all scoring 6% each.

*Sexually, she's inspired most by Scorpio at 12%, Leo (also 12%) and Libra (11%).

*But the signs that turn her off are Virgo (12% vote this the least sexy sign of all), Aries (11%) and Taurus (11%).

*Ms Libra knows what she likes in a potential partner—first on the list of attractiveness plus points are Gorgeous Eyes (42%), then Great Smile (37%), Kindness (36%), Faithfulness (32%), Smart Clothes (19%), Confidence (17%), Muscular Build (16%), Good Voice (14%), Tall (13%) and Good Line In Chat (at 13%, Libra ladies like this more than other women). "You can tell what a man's going to be like in bed by talking to him," explains Libra Lynne. "If he hogs the conversation, doesn't listen to a word you say, and is constantly looking to see if anyone more interesting is around, then why should his behaviour be any better between the sheets? But if he's thoughtful, generous, and really cares how you feel, well, say no more..." Last on free-thinking Libra's list is Slim Body (7%) and Good Provider (5%—lowest score overall).

*In a permanent partner, Libra likes to see Loyalty most often, at 27%. Many stress how they cannot stay in a relationship unless they trust a partner 100%. And once shattered, that trust is very hard for Libra woman to rebuild. 25% choose Kindness, 16% Understanding How I Think, 15% Sense of Humour, 6% Sexual Attraction, 3% Fun (surprisingly, the lowest female rating in the zodiac), 2% want a Hard Worker and 1% each vote for Home Lover, Sex Skills, Money and Good Looks.

*Just above average 52% of Libra women feel more keen on sex within a relationship. 18% feel the opposite—"The harder I try to be spontaneous, the more predictable I seem to become," laments one Libra lady—and 29% don't notice any difference.

*Does having children affect sex drive? Yes, for 22% who find a partner sexier afterwards—and 13% who say they perceive a partner as less sexy. But no, for the 65% whose feelings don't change. This places Libra woman in middle range.

Sparkling chat and loyal heart win Libra woman's love, but practical qualities leave her cold...

HOW DO THE SEXES COMPARE?

Neither men nor women born under Libra are mercenary in their approach to love—a partner's cash profile matters far less than physical, and mental, compatibility. Both sexes want a partner who's their equal, and value loyalty higher than any other quality. But Libra men go for good looks five times as often as Libra women and a slim body more than twice as often, while a full 5% more of Libra women than men rate a sense of humour as essential. Female Librans frown on infidelity more than men, but surprisingly it's Mr Libra who more often finds that sex drive flourishes within a relationship. But men from this starsign are also more inclined to go off a partner after starting a family...

SCORPIO MAN AND PARTNERS

*Scorpio's most popular partners are selected from Libra (14%),

Virgo (11%), Cancer and Taurus (10% each) starsigns.

*But he's not so well matched with Aries (6%), Capricorn or Aquarius (4% each).

*Who does he find most sexy? An astounding 24%, roughly a quarter, of Scorpio men find partners who are also Scorpio the sexiest. "There aren't many women who can keep up with me in bed, but I've always found Scorpio women not only keep up, they leave me standing," says Lee, 29. But Virgo and Cancer get a mention too, with 11% vote each.

*Scorpio man is equally positive who he doesn't find sexy—with a 27% negative vote going to Aries partners. Too bossy, too selfish and too scared to reveal feelings or weaknesses are the most common reasons given by Scorpios. Then it's Taurus and Leo, both on 10%.

*On the subject of initial attraction, Scorpio goes first for a Warm Smile (42%), then Nice Eyes (40%), Great Legs (31%) Curvy Body and Kind Nature (30% each), Faithfulness (27%), Shared Interests (21%), Gentle Manner (19%—of all men he likes this best), Slim Body (16%), Sexy Laugh (13%), Attractive Voice (12%) and he's least interested of all men overall in a Good Homemaker (7%).

*A partner must possess Kindness first, says Scorpio man (18%), followed by Loyalty (also 16%) and Understanding How I Think (also 16%). Then he looks for Sexual Attraction (15%, second highest score overall), Sense of Humour (12%), Fun (he's joint keenest on this at 9%), Sex Skills (also ahead of other men at 5%), Home Lover (4%) and Good Looks (3%). But Scorpio man's partner needn't worry about Money or Hard Work.

*An average 48% of Scorpio men report a greater interest in sex within a relationship. But 16% say their interest has lessened, and that's well above average. For 37% it's stayed unchanged.

*What about babies? Good news here, for 30%, the second highest number overall, vote their partner sexier after children together, 18% opt for less sexy, and 52% report no change.

Once the chemistry's right with Scorpio man, kids make no difference—but complacency might.

SCORPIO WOMAN AND PARTNERS

*Virgo (11%), Taurus (11%) and Leo (10%) are Scorpio woman's most popular long-term partners. "Leo is strong and steady yet still has the ability to surprise," says Scorpio Susie, 35.

*She's least likely to grow old with Pisces (7%), Cancer (7%), and Sagittarius (6%).

*Mirroring Scorpio men, she overwhelmingly finds her own sign sexiest—one in four, 25%, vote for Scorpio as the sexiest sign in a partner. Then it's Taurus on 10% and Cancer (9%).

*Her least favourite sex-wise is, again like Scorpio men, Aries. But the women aren't quite so anti-Aries, with just 15% voting Aries the least sexy sign. Taurus doesn't do so well either, with a 12% share of the negative vote.

*What first attracts Ms Scorpio to someone? More than any other woman, she likes Gorgeous Eyes (48%), then Scorpio woman goes for Kindness (35%), a Great Smile (33%), Faithfulness (29%) and Muscular Build (20%, and more than any other woman). She then chooses Confidence (19%), Smart Clothes (17%) and Height (17%), while less popular with Ms Scorpio are a Good Voice (13%), Good Provider (although at 12% she still rates it higher than any other female sign). "I want men to be men and women to be women, and that means a partner providing for me and any children," explains Carly, 26. "I just see that as a man's role." Finally, Slim Body scores 9% and a Good Line In Chat 8%.

*The quality that matters most to Scorpio women in a partner is Loyalty (24%), followed by Kindness (21%), Understanding How I Think (18%), Sense of Humour (16%). She's keenest female sign overall on Sexual Attraction (11%), gives Fun a 5% vote, Home Lover and Sex Skills 2% each, and Money and Hard Work 1% apiece. But Good Looks don't count with her at all.

*Just below average 50% reveal they're more interested in sex within the security of a relationship, 15% are less interested in lovemaking and 36%, second highest score, say nothing has changed. *But when children come along it can be a boost to Scorpio's sex life—26%, most overall, say a partner seems sexier when they've had children together. But she's also most prone to swing the other way—19%, again highest figure, say a partner is now less sexy. Just 55%, lowest overall, say kids change nothing.

Scorpio woman seeks strong muscles in strong men—but family life may make or break her sex drive.

HOW DO THE SEXES COMPARE?

They may not end up together, but Scorpio men and women should certainly enjoy a fabulous fling—each clearly votes the other as sexiest sign in the zodiac (24% men, 25% women). And both give Aries the sexual thumbs down, too, although men (27%) are even less keen on Aries partners than women (15%)! Both Scorpio sexes place high value on sexual attraction as the spice of a relationship, although getting down to the nitty gritty, Scorpio men rate actual sex skills (5%) higher than Scorpio women do (3%). And while Scorpio women want loyalty most in a partner, Scorpio men seek kindness. Long-term, men and women are both more likely than average to lose interest in sex. But the good news is producing a family together can make a partner seem sexier, for 30% of Scorpio men and 26% of Scorpio women.

SAGITTARIUS MAN AND PARTNERS

*Sagittarius man's best bets for a permanent partnership are Libra (12%), Virgo (10%), Taurus (10%) and Aries (10%).

*And he's least likely to make a match with his own sign Sagittarius or Capricorn (both 6%) or Leo or Scorpio (both 5%).

*Aries gets Mr Sagittarius' vote as the sexiest starsign of all, with 16% score. Then he rates Libra (14%) and Pisces (10%).

*Up front in the least sexy stakes, however, is Pisces again (14%) and Taurus (13%).

*Work at that Warm Smile, to find the best way to win Sagittarius man's heart—46%, top equal score of men overall, vote for this attribute as most attractive. "The smile can't lie—it shows a woman is either sincere or not," says 41-year-old Sagittarius Jamal. Then comes Nice Eyes, with 32%, and, astonishingly for carefree Sagittarius, Faithfulness, which scores a total of 30%, more than for any other male sign.

*Shared Interests rates high on 27%, then Slim Body, Curvy Body and Kind Nature all merit 25%, and he's least keen of all men on Great Legs (20%). 16% vote for a Gentle Manner, 15% for Attractive Voice, and 12% each opt for Sexy Laugh and Good Homemaker.

*To keep him keen, show Sagittarius man plenty of Kindness—22%, second highest overall for men, rate this as a partner's most important quality. 21% choose Loyalty, 19% Understanding How I Think, 16% Sense of Humour and 8%, on the low side, Sexual Attraction, 5% reckon Fun is what a partner must have, 3% Sex Skills, 2% each Good Looks and Money and 1% Hard Worker. Sagittarius certainly isn't interested in a Home Lover—not one man from this starsign voted for that.

*Believe it or not, an above average 51% of Sagittarius men are more interested in sex in the context of a long-term love, below average 8% are less interested, and 41% haven't changed. "Yes, I've had a lot of girlfriends in my life, but when I'm in a relationship then that particular woman, and the lovemaking we share, means everything to me," says one Sagittarius. "I become almost obsessed—maybe that's why my affairs burn out so quickly."

*But more Sagittarius men than any other sign say partners seem less sexy to them after having children together—a substantial 27%. Only 18%, second lowest of all, reckon partners are sexier, 55% say no change at all.

More faithful and less frisky than he seems, Sagittarius man thrives with the right partner—but beware the happy families rut.

SAGITTARIUS WOMAN AND PARTNERS

*Capricorn (12%) and, unusually, her own sign of Sagittarius (10%) are this lady's top two partnership choices.

*But she has a long list of least likely—Aries, Taurus, Gemini, Cancer, Libra and Pisces all only score 7% with Ms Sagittarius.

*Who does she find most sexy sign of all? Aries (13%), Gemini (10%), Leo (10%) and Scorpio (10%).

*And Sagittarius woman is least turned on by Aries (11%), Virgo (12%) and Leo (11%). "Only one person can be in charge in my bedroom, and that's me," confesses Clarrie, 30. "And I have to be the centre of attention. So while Leo and Aries men are great for energy and ideas, they do tend to take over..."

*Prime attraction feature is Gorgeous Eyes, she scores first equal on this, at 48%. Then she looks for Kindness (36%), Great Smile (31%), Faithfulness (29%), Confidence (18%), Smart Clothes (17%) and Height (17%), Muscular Build (15%), Good Line In Chat (13%—equal most votes in this category), Slim Body (10%), Good Provider and Good Voice just 8% each.

*In a permanent partner Ms Sagittarius must have Kindness (24%), Loyalty (20%), Understanding How I Think (19%) and Sense of Humour (also 19%). Then Sagittarius woman rates Sexual Attraction (7%), Fun (4%), Home Lover (3%), Hard Worker (2%), and Sex Skills and Money 1% each. She doesn't care at all about Good Looks.

*In a relationship, 52% say their sex drive increases, 17% that it decreases, and for 31% it stays the same. So Sagittarius sticks in the middle range. But several do express doubts that they will be able to make love with just one person for the rest of their lives.

*When children come along, only 17%, second least overall, say a partner seems sexier. 13% actively vote for less sexy. 70%, above average, reckon there is no change.

Sagittarius woman wants to listen, touch and laugh rather than look when choosing a lover.

HOW DO THE SEXES COMPARE?

Both men and women born under Sagittarius want warm and genuine partners—they value kindness higher than any other lover's quality. And, contrary to their footloose and fancy-free zodiac image, women (29%) and men (30%—highest overall) are attracted to faithfulness in a partner first. Both also place less emphasis on sexual attraction than we might expect. But Sagittarius women are keener on home sweet home than their male counterparts—although only 3% of women voted this essential, not one man did so. She is also more attracted by a sense of humour (19% of Sagittarius women judge this essential, but only 16% of men). But in general the men of this starsign are more likely to see sex drive increase within a relationship.

CAPRICORN MAN AND PARTNERS

*Capricorn pairs off with Pisces and Leo (12%) or Virgo and Aries (11%) partners more often than any other.

*And Sagittarius (5%), Capricorn (5%) and Taurus (3%) least often of all. "It's tempting to be impulsive and opt for someone you love but who doesn't suit you," says Capricorn bachelor Arnie, now 51. "I prefer to get all the right qualities in the right person, and that's worth the wait. Mind you, I didn't expect to wait quite so long."

*Maximum sex appeal for Mr Capricorn comes from Gemini (14%), Aries and Capricorn starsigns (both 12%).

*He's least sexually aroused by Taurus (15%) and Aries again at 12%.

*A Warm Smile attracts him first (44%), then Nice Eyes (39%),

Great Legs (29%), Curvy Body (27%), Shared Interests (26%), Faithfulness (30%) and a Kind Nature (22%). He's second most keen of all men on an Attractive Voice (21%). "I first spoke to my girlfriend on the telephone when I rang up to order a pizza," says one Capricorn. "Her voice was so husky and sexy I couldn't get it out of my head. I ordered pizza every night for a week before I plucked up courage to ask Kim out." Capricorn then rates Slim Body (18%), Gentle Manner (17%), Sexy Laugh (12%) and Good Homemaking Skills (10%).

*In permanent partners Capricorn wants Loyalty first and foremost (21%). Then give him a Sense of Humour and Kindness (18% each), Understanding How I Think (16%), Sexual Attraction (12%), Fun (5%), Good Looks (4%), Money and a Home Lover (3% each). But he doesn't value Sex Skills or Hard Work at all.

*Below average 45% of Capricorn men are keener on sex within a relationship. 7% are less interested, again in the lower range—but an above average 49% say their interest hasn't changed.

*Does having children together affect Capricorn's view of his partner? 21% say she is more sexy, but an upper range 26% opt for less sexy, second highest of all men. 53% reckon she's the same. **Capricorn man is attracted by lust before trust—but needs both long-term.**

CAPRICORN WOMAN AND PARTNERS

*Most likely to stick with Capricorn woman are Taurus (12%), Gemini (11%) and Cancer (11%) partners. "I'm on my third Taurus boyfriend in a row and I'm being thoroughly spoiled," says Capricorn Michelle, 26. "Weekends away, champagne, silk sheets, shared showers—he somehow knows just what I like best. And isn't that what love is all about?"

*Ms Capricorn's least popular partner choices are Sagittarius (6%), Libra (5%) and Capricorn (4%).

*Sexiest starsign vote for Capricorn goes to Taurus (13%), Virgo (12%) and Aries (10%).

*While Cancer, Aries and Leo all get 12% of the "least sexy" vote.

*Number one attraction point for Ms Capricorn is a Great Smile—at 42% she rates this higher than any other woman. And the same is true for Kindness (40%), Faithfulness (33%), Confidence (26%), Height (22%), Muscular Build (20%) and Good Voice (15%). But giving Gorgeous Eyes 41% makes it the second lowest score for a woman. Smart Clothes gets 18% vote, Good Provider 12% (again tops among all the women), Good Line In Chat and Slim Body, 10% each.

*When Capricorn's loving for keeps though, she looks for Loyalty in a partner (26%), then Kindness (23%), Understanding How I Think (17%), Sense of Humour (16%), Sexual Attraction (8%), Fun (6%) and Home Lover (2%). Sex Skills, Money, Hard Worker and Good Looks are all awarded 1% each.

*On the negative side, she's least likely of all women to become more interested in sex in a long-term bond, just 47% say they have. And the highest total of all starsigns, 23%, have actually seen interest lessen. "It's all too cosy now—give me a good book and a warm quilt rather than hot sex any day," says one Capricorn in her 10th year of marriage. 31% have noted no change.

*Children coming don't affect Capricorn woman too much, however. A less-than-average 19% say they see a partner as more sexy when they've found a family together. 11% opt for less sexy, but 71% (joint highest score) report no change.

She's open to all sorts of offers, but partners must be prepared to work at keeping Capricorn woman's interest.

HOW DO THE SEXES COMPARE?

Capricorn woman is the most open-minded in the zodiac when it comes to partners—she is more attracted to more features than any other starsign, including Capricorn man! But the two do have much in common—both are first attracted to a warm smile most of all, and rate loyalty as of prime importance in a partner. Surprisingly for this "stable" sign, neither men nor

women born under Capricorn seem certain to thrive in long-term relationships. Just 45% of men and 47% women (lowest female score of all) say they've got more interested in sex in a long-term partnership. And for Capricorn women the outlook is even worse. 23%, or almost one in every four, say they've become less interested in sex within a relationship. For the men it's kids that call a halt to fun—26%, second highest of all men, say their partner seems less sexy after having children together. But Capricorn women (just 11%) cope with this change better.

AQUARIUS MAN AND PARTNERS

*Most often Mr Aquarius picks a permanent partner who is a Taurus (15%), Aries (14%) or Cancer (12%).

*But bottom of his partner preferences are Capricorn, Sagittarius and Libra (all 5%), Scorpio (4%) and Pisces (3%).

*His sexiest starsign vote goes to Gemini (14%), Aquarius (11%), Taurus, Aries and Cancer (10%)

*And least sexy, says Aquarius man, are Virgo (15%), Gemini (11%) and Aries (11%). "They all seem to want constant reassurance before they can relax, and I'm just not prepared to give it," says one single Aquarius with two girlfriends.

*Warm Smiles are what first attract Aquarius, with a 41% total vote. Then he goes for 36% Curvy Body, 32% Nice Eyes, 25% Kind Nature, 23% Great Legs, 22% Slim Body and 23% Faithfulness. "If an emotional bond between two people is good, then purely physical infidelity won't break it," suggests Ged, who's had an "open relationship" with Edith for five years. "It might even grow stronger as a result. But the danger comes when emotions get involved and it's a 'love' affair. That's a different matter altogether." Shared Interests and Gentle Manner also score 18%, Good Homemaker scores surprisingly high at 14%, while Attractive Voice and Sexy Laugh bring up the rear on 10% each. Of all the zodiac's men, Aquarius is attracted to the least number of factors, making him the hardest to please.

*Loyalty (28%) matters most to Aquarius in a partner, followed by Understanding How I Think (22%)—which he thinks more crucial than all other men do. Kindness rates 16%, Sense of Humour the second lowest in the zodiac at 11%. He's joint keenest, with Gemini man, on Fun at 9%, while Sexual Attraction scores an exceptionally low 6%. Sex Skills add up to 4%, Good Looks and Homelover 2% each. And like many men he doesn't rate Money or Hard Work.

*48%, around average, have become more interested in sex in a long-term bond, 9% are less interested and 43% haven't changed.

*Starting a family together makes partners seem more sexy to 24% of Aquarius men, less sexy to 19%—and no different to 57%. That places Aquarius in the middle range.

Choosy Aquarius man wants someone to share his thoughts first, then his sheets.

AQUARIUS WOMAN AND PARTNERS

*Her preference for partners is as follows: Aquarius (11%), Gemini (11%) and Libra (10%).

*Least often she lands up with Pisces (6%), Capricorn (5%) and Virgo (4%).

*Most sexy starsigns for Ms Aquarius are, first equal, Gemini and Scorpio, both on 11%

*But Aries (14%), Gemini (9%) and Virgo (9%) don't do much for her. She rates them least sexy.

*She's first attracted by Gorgeous Eyes (43%), a Great Smile (32%), then Faithfulness and Kindness (both 28%—she rates kindness lower than any other woman). Smart Clothes merit 17%, Confidence 16%, Height 15%, Muscular Build and Good Voice both 12% and Good Looks, Slim Body and Good Provider 8% each. Overall, Aquarius woman is the least open to different attraction factors in the zodiac, in this reflecting Aquarius man's results. "I just know what I like and what I want from love and sex—what's so awful about that?" asks Aquarius Jennie, 32.

*Her ideal partner shows Loyalty (25% want that) and Understands

How I Think—20%, one in five and most of all women, place this quality first. 18% opt for Kindness (lowest score overall), 17% say a Sense of Humour is vital, and 8% say Sexual Attraction. Fun gets a 4% vote, Home Lover, Sex Skills, Hard Worker and Good Looks 2% each, while Money scores lowest at just 1%. "Anyone who bases their love life on cash considerations doesn't deserve to be happy," is a common Aquarius statement.

*Surprisingly, an above average 53% of Aquarius women are more interested in sex within a relationship. 16% are less keen and 31% haven't changed.

*Having children together has made the second highest women's score, 25%, find their partner more sexy. And among Aquarius women the lowest overall mark (10%) say their partner is less sexy now. For 65% he's the same.

Aquarius woman takes her time selecting the perfect partner—but when she does decide, it's for life

HOW DO THE SEXES COMPARE?

More alike than many starsigns, Aquarius men and women both expect loyalty and insist a partner understands how they think—and neither sets much store by kindness (scoring second lowest of all men and lowest of all women). Both sexes are also the zodiac's least easily pleased when it comes to initial attraction. And although who they settle down with is less similar, neither sex is in any doubt which starsigns they find least sexy—Aries, Gemini and Virgo. There are several points where Aquarius men and women differ however. Unusually, women are more enthusiastic about sense of humour (17% women, 11% men) and sexual attraction (8% women, just 6% men). And though both sexes are better bets long-term than astrology might expect, it's Aquarius women who resoundingly enjoy sex more both within a relationship (53%) and after having a family with a partner (25%).

PISCES MAN AND PARTNERS

*Who does Pisces pair off with most often? Alone among men, it's his own starsign Pisces—16% have Pisces partners. "Once I'd had one Pisces lover I was hooked," admits Spencer, 32. "Now I go through a special astrological dating service to save time. I've never met a Pisces partner yet I didn't feel affinity for immediately." But Leo is also a popular choice at 15%.

*Pisces man's least preferred partners come from starsigns Taurus, Cancer, Libra (all 6%), Virgo (4%) and Capricorn (just 3%).

*Again, Pisces doesn't look too far for his sexiest sign—an astounding one in five (20%) say other Pisceans are most sexy. Followed by Sagittarius at 12%.

*He's least sexually satisfied by Taurus and Leo (both 13%) and Libra (11%) partners.

*Pisces is drawn towards a Warm Smile first (43%), then Nice Eyes (39%) Great Legs (32%) and a Curvy Body (31%). Next most attractive is a Kind Nature (26%), Faithfulness (25%), a Slim Body (23%), Shared Interests (17%), Gentle Manner (16%), Sexy Laugh (15%), Attractive Voice (14%) and Good Homemaker at 13%.

*When it comes to a long-term partner, Pisces puts Loyalty top of his list of must-haves—higher, in fact, than any other male starsign, with a 29% vote. Kindness rates 18%, Sense of Humour 15%, Understanding How I Think 13% and Sexual Attraction 10%. 8% of Pisces men think Fun matters most, while 4% go for Sex Skills and 2% a Home Lover. But no Pisces man rates Good Looks, Money or Hard Work! "Or at least, if we do, we're not going to say so," admits one. "Who wants to be branded as a sexist gold-digger?"

*Long-term love makes 49% more interested in sex, 8% less interested and 42% the same. That's slightly above average.

*Having a family together leaves more Pisces than any other man fancying his partner more—one in three, 33%, say their partner seems more sexy after children. 22%, also in the upper range, say the opposite and 45%, lowest male mark overall, say attraction is unchanged.

Pisces man wants a partner with lots in common—preferably everything.

PISCES WOMAN AND PARTNERS

*Ms Pisces is most likely to match up with Taurus (11%), Aries, Gemini and Scorpio (10%).

*But Libra (7%), Aquarius (6%) and Leo (5%) are her least likely partners.

*Sexiest starsign by far for Pisces woman is Scorpio, scoring 15%. Taurus is next with 11%. "Scorpios don't stand for inhibitions or shyness—I had a Scorpio lover once who had me doing things I'd never dreamt of. And it was fantastic," says Pauline, 41.

*Aries (12%) gets her vote as least sexy, along with Taurus again on 11%.

*Gorgeous Eyes (44%), Kindness (37%), Great Smile (36%), and Faithfulness (31%) are the top four things that attract her first, followed by Confidence (16%), Height (15%), Smart Clothes and Muscular Build (both 12%), Good Voice and Slim Body (both 11%), Good Line In Chat (10%) and Good Provider (8%).

*Once in a relationship, she reckons what matters most is Kindness (28%, second highest female score), then Loyalty (20%), Understanding How I Think on 18% and Sense of Humour, 16%. 8% of Pisces women think Sexual Attraction is of prime importance, 2% rate Fun, 2% each Home Lover and Money and 1% each Sex Skills and Good Looks. But as for Hard Work, no thanks.

*A below average (for women) 49% find themselves more interested in sex in a long-term relationship—20%, second highest overall, find they're less interested. 31% have stayed the same.

*Making a family together has positive effects on Pisces however— 25%, one in four, find their partner sexier afterwards. But an also above average 18% say he is less sexy now. For 57% their feelings haven't changed at all.

Pisces woman—changeable lover seeks sexy, steady other half.

HOW DO THE SEXES COMPARE?

Unique in the survey, Pisces man both fancies, and marries, Pisces woman most. But unfortunately she doesn't return the compliment and chooses Pisces neither as her favourite soulmate, nor her favourite bedmate. In fact he doesn't even make the top three. But in other areas the Pisces sexes are more in tune. Both agree, roughly, on the importance of sexual attraction and sense of humour in a relationship. And both find a partner sexier after having children together—but again men (33%) are even keener than women (25%). Pisces women value kindness in a partner 10% more than Pisces men, but the males of the starsign are four times more interested in fun (8% men to just 2% women). Numbers who grow more interested in sex long-term are identical (49%) but for women this works out at below average and for men, above average.

2
Sex In Action

* WHAT PUTS PEOPLE IN THE MOOD FOR MAKING LOVE * WHICH STARSIGNS ARE THE MOST SEXUALLY ADVENTUROUS— AND WHO WANT TO TRY MUCH MORE * WHERE — AND HOW —SEX CAN BE MOST EXCITING * HOW LONG EACH STAGE OF LOVEMAKING LASTS * WHICH STARSIGNS HAVE MOST ORGASMS, WHO HAS NONE, WHO FAKES THEM * INTIMATE MOMENTS AND SEX FANTASIES REVEALED * THE 12 STARSIGNS' SEX IN ACTION PROFILES

A fast five minutes of hottest passion, or hours of gentle lovemaking? Experimental or conventional? The answers to the most intimate questions in the AstroSex survey rip through a lot of accepted astrological views about the sexuality of each of the starsigns. And men, and women from the same zodiac can have very different sexual tastes, behaviour, and desires.

WHAT PUTS PEOPLE IN THE MOOD FOR LOVE
Women are more easily turned on than men—or to be more exact, a wider variety of factors put them in the mood for love. For while both sexes are in agreement about what turns them on the most—a slow, sensuous massage is tops with 80% of males and 76% of females in the survey—after that their ratings do start to differ significantly

While women like shared, non-overtly sexual pleasures like slow dancing (71%), a romantic meal (68%) or listening to music in a softly-lit room (64%), men prefer the more direct approach of a sexy movie (77%), shared bath (73%), shared shower (71%) or being caressed on their thighs (65%).

Female partners do need reassurance, too—almost 10% more women than men slip into a sexy mood with the words 'I love you', and 35% of women respond to compliments, compared to just 27% of men. But the zodiac's males are far more turned on by playing sport. "My girlfriend meets me from my Sunday morning racketball game wearing just a raincoat and no panties," says Fred, a 27-year-old Leo. "There's a deserted alley behind the sports centre where we've had some of our moments of hottest, hardest passion."

GETTING THE MEN GOING

Sport, however, is towards the end of the men's list of turn-ons. At the top, it is massage that makes most men feel in the mood—80%, in total. And Libra is most in favour of the hands-on approach, with 88% of Libra men finding massage a sure-fire arousal route. Traditional astrology might have expected to find a more physical, sensuous sign, like Taurus in the first place.

Watching a sexy movie is next, at 77% average score (tops with Cancer men who give it 84%), then a shared bath (76%—and 80% top score from Taurus).

Sharing a shower earns 71% of the zodiac male vote—and is a special favourite with all-action, no-nonsense Sagittarius men. Then men thrill to having their thighs caressed (65%, and biggest fan of this is Libra man with 74%). Followed by the Taurus favourite, slow dancing (61% total vote) and caresses on the chest (60%). Two out of three Aquarius men like this—that's more than any other sign.

CASE HISTORY OF AN AQUARIUS MAN

Leonard, 48, is an Aquarius. He is not in a relationship at the moment but frequents singles bars.

"Men's locker-room talk does sometimes turn to what we find sexually arousing, but I never join in because I've never met anyone else who liked the same as me—having my chest caressed and my nipples fondled and sucked. Just thinking about it gets me going!

"I once met a woman in a singles bar who promised me the time of my life if I'd let her do what she liked, and she was right. As a prelude to sex she shaved my chest hair and rubbed warm musk oil all over. Then she dipped her tongue in iced water and circled my nipples, tugging each one gently with her teeth. I was erect immediately and stayed that way for hours. It was incredible."

Female favourites like a romantic meal, music and soft lights, or the words 'I love you' rate rather lower with the males. In fact a full 9% less are put in the mood by declarations of love. Men are much less influenced by compliments, too (27% men to 35% women).

Their least favourite stimulants are having their feet caressed— just 19% like this, although one in four Pisces find it a turn-on. And an average of 19% feel sexy after playing sport—led by energetic Aries on 26%. But men's least likely turn-on is a gift of flowers, with an average rating of just 7%. Still it's almost twice as popular with romantic Cancer men who award this category 12%.

Which male starsigns are most easily aroused? Taurus, Aries and Pisces are the top three. But among the men Scorpio is third most difficult to get in the mood, after Capricorn. And by far the most difficult man to turn on is Gemini.

STARWATCH

Not for the first time, Mr Scorpio does not quite match up to his traditional star profile of a sex machine (despite being a star

**pick by females of all starsigns). But the same can't be said for
female Scorpios.**

WHAT AROUSES FEMALE STARSIGNS?

The women of the zodiac are most turned on by a mixture of sensual
touching and romantic togetherness. For it seems their brains need
to be engaged at the same time as their bodies. Most popular of all
as a prelude to love are, first equal, massage and being caressed on
the breasts, each with a total 76% score.

But while occasionally uptight Virgo is most keen on massage
(81%), it's more sensual Scorpio who votes highest for having her
breasts fondled (79%).

Next in line, with a 74% total vote, is watching a sexy movie— and
here the starsign of fantasy and imagination, Pisces, scores highest
on 78%. And women vote next for slow dancing (71%), a shared
bath (69%), a romantic meal (68%), being caressed on the thighs
(66%) and listening to music in a softly lit room (64%).

Earthy Capricorn women are keenest on slow dancing and shared
baths, sociable Libra is most aroused by a romantic meal, and Ms
Scorpio scores highest again on both thigh caresses and music. Two
out of three Scorpio women find a shared shower puts them in the
mood for love, too that's also the highest of all female signs.

CASE HISTORY OF A SCORPIO WOMAN

*38-year-old Rhonda, a Scorpio, is married to Neil 25, whose
starsign is Aries. He is her third husband.*

"My other two husbands were much less adventurous than Neil—
he's a different generation and there's nothing he won't try. Lucky
me...

"Sharing a shower together is a favourite way we have of getting
in the mood if we're both tired after work. As soon as the warm
water starts caressing my body, followed by Neil's soapy hands, I'm
ready for sex. But he always makes me wait, using the shower spray

to seek out secret places, at first gentle— then a stronger jet of water. I have my first orgasm like that, then he lifts me against the cold tiles and I wrap my legs around his warm, wet body.

"We do come out of the shower eventually—but only when he is ready to make love all over again."

A holiday in the sun turns more than half of all starsign women on—but Capricorn likes this best at 56%. And the words 'I love you' are arousing for 52% of women in general—and 59% of seemingly confident but secretly insecure Aries women.

Turning to what the women of the zodiac find least exciting— being caressed on the feet rates only a 23% total vote, as does a gift of flowers. Leo is the lady who likes her feet fondled the most, while luxury lover Libra is most appreciative of a bouquet. But playing sport only rates 9%—although it does get 13% from sexy Ms Scorpio.

So it's no shock to discover that of all the signs, Scorpio women are most turned on by the widest range of factors. Next easily aroused are Libra, Taurus, Aries and Pisces. While the starsign that's most difficult to put in the mood is Cancer, followed by Virgo and Aquarius. With Leo, Gemini, Sagittarius and Capricorn mid-range.

STARWATCH
This section shows surprising similarities between women of the zodiac, as well as differences. For each female starsign follows roughly the same pattern of preference. And dynamic Aries, for example, who traditional astrology might expect to be turned on by playing sport or getting a sexy call at work, falls firmly in the lower range for these categories.

WHICH SETTING IS SEXIEST?

Given a choice of four settings and asked to select the sexiest, men and women's responses are broadly similar. But men, in general, tend to go more for the less conventional places...

MEN'S SITES FOR EXCITEMENT

Way ahead as sexiest love setting is a luxury hotel with a round bed and satin sheets, that's the view of 42% of the zodiac's men. Led by stylish, luxury fan Libra who gives it 49%. But opulence doesn't go down so well with Virgo men, only 27% find this a sexy setting.

Next, most men would choose a warm, deserted beach at sunset (34% overall). This is very popular with water sign Cancer (41%), but least liked by fellow water sign Pisces (27%). A secluded moorland is third favourite with the men of the zodiac, with 21% overall voting it the sexiest setting. Top of the voters here is Virgo with a stunning 31%, well above average, savouring rough grass on their skin and wind in their hair. But Taurus men do like their comfort—only 15% want to make love on the moors. "I tried it once and couldn't relax—the bracken scratched my knees and I could just imagine my butt in the sights of some hunter's rifle." laughs Taurus Adrian, 24.

Finally, least rated as a sensuous place by men is a private flat with black walls and candles—this scores just 12% on average. But again, Virgo men are keenest on this setting (16%), along with Pisces (also 16%). Capricorn, lover of familiar places, gives this exotic environment just 6%, lowest of all men.

STARWATCH

Supposedly staid Virgo men are keenest by far on both sex on a wild moorland and in an erotically-decorated flat. This does reshape conventional astrology's view of him.

WOMEN SET THE SEX-SCENE

Like the men, the women vote the sexiest setting as a luxury hotel room with champagne and satin sheets (42% for women, and men). Comfort-loving Capricorn scores the highest here amongst the women however, with 51%. While Cancer likes the idea of a hotel least (33%).

CASE HISTORY OF A CANCER WOMAN

Therese is 25 and was born under the sign of Cancer. She has lived with her lover Raoul, a Scorpio, for 18 months.

"A friend who works on reception in a famous hotel once told me they used to play this game of calling up guest couples on the phone just after they'd checked in. Because nine times out of 10 they'd be already having sex.

"I don't want to be that predictable—I think sex in hotels, however glamorous the hotel, is always a bit seedy. In the room, anyway. Raoul and I did once dash into the ladies room of a big hotel and made love in a cubicle, and that was pretty special.

"But when it comes to a sexy setting my ultimate fantasy is to be inside a harem with dozens of beautiful women to get me ready for love with oils, hands and tongues. Then hand me over to their master who wants only me ... I would have the power to please him in every way."

As well as the luxury hotel however, romantic women are equally keen on a warm, deserted beach at sunset, and give this 42% of their vote, too—compared with just 34% of men. Outdoor fan Sagittarius gives the beach top marks with 49%, but only 37% of Capricorn and Gemini women agree.

A secluded moor is sexiest for 16% of women, 5% less than for the men. Perhaps surprisingly, this outdoor setting scores highest with Cancer women (21%), who are known to have a taste for the exotic in sex...

A private flat with black walls and candles is even less popular with female than male starsigns. Only a total of 8% rate it a sexy setting. But Scorpio is way out in front on 11%. And Virgo and Libra (both 6%) like it least.

WHO HAS MADE LOVE WHERE?

A total of 96% of men and 97% of women have made love in bed, that's the big majority we would expect. But the question that must be asked is, what about the 4% of men and 3% of women who haven't. Either they must have very adventurous sex lives, or perhaps they are like teenage Gemini couple Russell and Sue, who are both living with their parents for now. "Neither family is happy for us to have sex under their roof, and they watch us like hawks. So we get it together wherever we can. That includes an empty train compartment and Sue's parent's camper van. We dream of the day we can become staid and normal and sleep in a bed together" says Russell.

As a general rule, the survey results reveal more women than men have made love in different—but not too different—locations, like on the floor, in the bath, in the car, the kitchen, on a chair or table. It seems the female side of the zodiac is happy to experiment as long as she can stay close to home.

But when it comes to love in the outside world, men take the lead. Almost three times as many men as women have had sex in the office (22% men to 8% women) and twice as many have made love in a train or swimming pool. Plus men are more likely than women to list more exotic changing cubicles, buses, cinemas and planes as past love-places.

WHERE HAVE MEN MADE LOVE?

Men's top six places for sex are Bed (96% total), Floor (91%), Sofa (90%), Car (63%), Bath (62%) and Chair (58%). Bed is most popular with Libra men, every single one of them has had sex between the sheets. But significantly less Scorpios and Aquarius have done so—just 93% of these experimental signs answer yes.

More Libras than any other male sign also choose the floor to get down on, at 97%, while comfort-keen Capricorn is most bored by boards on 84%.

The sofa scores highest with Aquarius men (94%) and lowest with Sagittarius and Cancer (both 86%). Adventurous Leo likes love on the move in the car (71%), but Gemini and Virgo don't (54%). Slightly lazy Sagittarius favours a sexual variation where he doesn't even have to leave his chair, on 63%, and Libra is equally keen on this.

Working down the rest of the list of hotspots, Pisces men have had sex most often in the shower, on the beach and in a train. Libras are ahead of the game when it comes to kitchen loving, and they're also the men who've made love in the park most often, plus in the swimming pool and plane.

Aquarius has had sex on tables more than other men, Aries men are most likely to have got down to it in the office. As for a changing cubicle, that's Cancer country, and one in ten Cancer men have also made love on board a bus. Finally, who else but dramatic Leo would have got passionate most often in a cinema?

The starsign who finds most spice in a variety of passion places is Libra man. And the least adventurous overall is Virgo. Which backs up the view that he has plenty of exciting passion plans but never turns them into reality...

CASE HISTORY OF A LIBRA MAN

Trevor, 29 and a Libra, challenges himself and his lover Grace, also a Libra, to make love in ever more bizarre places.

"Yes, it's often me who has the ideas for where we make love, but Grace does too—the stationery cupboard at her office was one of hers. She had to smuggle me in one lunch hour and we had sex in the pitch black while her boss ate his sandwiches on the other side of the wall.

"That was good, but the ghost train was even better. Grace didn't wear any underwear and sat on my lap as the car started to move.

Neither of us ever takes longer than a couple of minutes to climax in these situations because the build-up is so exciting. We can't wait for the next time the fair comes to our town.

"At the moment we are planning passion sessions in the library, a flotation tank, prison cell (don't know how we will swing that one), and car wash. It's the mental as well as physical challenge we enjoy, pulling it off without getting caught! But it does make ordinary sex seem a bit of a non-event."

WHERE DO WOMEN PICK FOR PASSION?

Women's first half-dozen love locations are exactly the same as men's, but there are two important differences. Firstly, that more women than men have made love in all six of them. And secondly, that the order is slightly different, in that more women have had sex in the bath than the car, while with men the opposite is true.

An overall 97% of women have made love in bed, with the top score here going to Sagittarius (99%)—a starsign that, as we shall see, seems to be far more conventional than traditional astrology would expect. The floor is top spot for Capricorn, Libra and Virgo ladies (all 94%), and scores an average 93% across the zodiac. Then comes the sofa, with 92% of women having got closer on the couch. Led by Libra (again) and Pisces (93%).

Next favourite for women's intimate moments is the bath (67%). 72% of water sign Cancer women have tried this, but Sagittarius likes it least of all (59%). As for getting horizontal in the car this has been tried by 65% overall, almost one in three, but most often by Taurus (69%). And the chair is the favourite seduction site for Virgo women on 63%—and by 60% of all women.

Aries women are keener than others on two very different places, the kitchen (55%) and the cinema (3%), while Gemini women have made love more often than most in the office (11%). Cancer and Leo ladies like love on the tracks (9%), and Leo is also most likely of all women to have had sex in a changing cubicle (8%). And Libra and Pisces head the small list of women who've had sex on a plane.

71

But sex queen yet again is Ms Scorpio—she has made love more than any other woman on the floor (94%), in the bath (72%), in the shower (54%), on the table (45%), in the park (42%), on the beach (34%), in the swimming pool (12%), on the bus (7%), and (jointly, this one) in the cinema (3%).

So as well as being the easiest to arouse, Scorpio is also the most adventurous of the female signs when it comes to location. The least adventurous sign is more shocking however—Sagittarius is least likely of all women's starsigns to have had sex in the bath, in a car, on a chair, in the kitchen, on a table, in the park, on the beach, in a swimming pool, in the office, or in a cinema.

STARWATCH
Could Sagittarius be less danger-driven and more conventional than astrology has always assumed—until now? These results say, yes .

WHICH POSITION IS MOST EXCITING?
Given the same selection of possible sexual positions, men and women show very different preferences—and so do different signs within the same sex.

WOMAN ON TOP—WINNER FOR MOST MEN
There's no competition where men are concerned—60% vote for Woman On Top as the most exciting position for sex. And Aquarius scores this highest of all, with 72%. Aquarius is also least keen of all men on being on top himself for sex.

The only male starsigns who don't find it most exciting to have the woman in dominant position are Gemini, Cancer and Pisces, who all prefer Oral Sex, and Virgo who alone among men prefers his woman on hands and knees. 66%, or two out of three Virgo men, a full 10%

higher than the next sign, say this is the most exciting sexual combination.

"I love to caress a woman's buttocks, and know I can reach round and touch her breasts or her clitoris comfortably," says Virgo Hal, 40. "It's somehow very exciting to have a body but not a face. And when a woman is on all fours, the sensations during penetration can be varied so much more. I think it's a natural way to have sex.

In general, oral sex is the position men find second most exciting (56% overall), and then it's the woman on hands and knees (53% overall).

Next most popular position for men is with the woman face down, with an overall total of 31%. This is most favoured by Libra (41%) and least liked by Leo (just 25%). "Getting in is all right, it's staying there that's the problem," grumbles Leo Doug, 28.

Libra is also keener than other men on lovemaking on each other's laps (32%, joint highest score with Scorpio). And Taurus finds this position least exciting (20%).

Man on top gets the top vote from tradition-respecting Capricorn males at 32%, and lowest scores from perhaps more experimental Aquarius and Pisces (18%). The overall total for this position is 25%. So only one man in four finds it most exciting.

Cancer man is keenest on sex with both partners lying on their sides, the ultimate in closeness, yet this scores lowest with normally tender Taurus (16%), and manages a total of 23%. Manual sex is more exciting for Sagittarius than any other man (26%). Perhaps because it's quick and involves purely physical rather than emotional involvement?

Who likes to make love standing up? 23% of Virgo men, but only 13% of Aries. At 19% overall, this is the position men in general find least exciting.

WAYS TO DRIVE WOMEN WILD

The women of the zodiac have two sexual positions they like best—and neither of them are the same as the male favourite! For first equal in the female vote for most exciting sexual technique are oral sex and man on top, both scoring 43%. So it seems both men and women find it more exciting to be in a passive rather than active position.

Capricorn women are keenest of all on both oral sex and lovemaking with the man on top (both 51%). Sagittarius likes oral sex least (39%) and Pisces gives the lowest rating to man on top sex (37%).

But looking at the results individually, several starsigns do find the men's favourite position, woman on top, most exciting. These are Gemini, Scorpio, Sagittarius and Pisces, all 42%—and all signs, perhaps, who prefer to control rather than be controlled? Meanwhile Capricorn, so enthusiastic about the first two categories, is least interested in being on top herself, at just 34%.

CASE HISTORY OF A CAPRICORN WOMAN

Roslyn, a Capricorn, is 51 and recently divorced after 26 years of marriage to a Taurus.

"I know my kids think their mother has hardly ever had sex, and if she did must have gritted her teeth throughout. But if only they knew the truth.

"I tried everything there was to try with my husband who was a Leo, we must have gone through the Kama Sutra a dozen times. But I'm a very straightforward person really and I always come back to the one position I liked best, man on top. I did try being on top myself, of course I did. But I just never felt really comfortable, and that's the whole point, isn't it? I want a man to give me pleasure, not take it myself. Contrary to what most experts seem to say, the missionary position is the only one I've been able to achieve orgasm in through penetration alone.

"Yes, I do find oral sex wonderful, to be so selfishly given pleasure. We used to play with silk scarves as blindfolds and to tie each other up, and I found that so erotic."

Next most exciting for women, is being on her hands and knees, although only 37% of women rate this, compared to 53% of men. Most turned on by this position is Aquarius (41%), but it leaves Cancer (33%) rather cooler. Laziness could be a factor in the women's next favourite, sex sitting on each other's laps. For two notoriously laid-back signs, Sagittarius and Libra, have the highest rating for this (30%)—overall it's a good bet for 25%, a quarter of all women.

Capricorn (again) likes the cosiness of both partners on their side (30%), but Aquarius (18%) doesn't. And 26% of try-anything Scorpios like to lie face down themselves whereas for Virgo and Taurus the figure is just 18%. Aquarius and Libra (both 23%) are most excited by the slightly impersonal, but immediate, pleasure of manual sex—romantic Taurus only gives it a 14% mark. "It reminds me of being a schoolgirl again, fumbling in the back row of the cinema. No thanks!" says Taurus Simone, 35. And both partners standing is favoured by Scorpio (18%) before all other starsigns.

STARWATCH

Female starsigns seem to want sex that lets them be the opposite of their ordinary selves. So capable Capricorn prefers to let the man take charge, yet gentle Pisces likes to be dominant herself. And so-sensual and intense Scorpio is keener than any other woman on lying face down, away from her lover. So is traditional astrology mistaken to assume female starsigns love lives always reflect their personality?

WHAT CARESS SPELLS SUCCESS?

Slowly and lovingly or fast and passionately? Both men and women from all starsigns are in no doubt which sort of caress they like best. 83% of men and 81% of women prefer a lover to take his or her time, with both Virgo men (88%) and women (85%) keenest on the slow and sensuous approach.

Perhaps the most surprising result in this section is that slightly more women (19%) than men (17%) prefer caresses to be fast, firm and passionate. And heading the women who do favour rough stuff is, amazingly, Pisces on 22%, followed by perhaps more expected fans of speed, Aries and Sagittarius, both on 21%.

Among the men, meanwhile, supposedly sensitive Pisces is also the man most likely to want firm, no-nonsense touch—26%, or more than one in four, find this more exciting than slow gentle caresses. Second place here goes to Aquarius (22%), followed by Scorpio (21%).

STARWATCH
Again, Pisces' liking for firm treatment suggests starsigns show a completely different side of themselves in sex.

FOREPLAY—FAST FIVE MINUTES OR LONG HOURS OF LOVE?
The survey asked how long each starsign would like to spend on foreplay—but who would have predicted that men, supposedly fans of wham bam instant sex, would consistently quote longer foreplay times than women? In fact the average time men would like works out at 31.3 minutes of foreplay. For the women of the zodiac, the figure is only 27.8 minutes. More men vote for half an hour as ideal than any other length of time—while the majority of women choose just 15 minutes. And while 28% of men want it to last hours, only 22% of women agree.

Breaking each sex down into separate starsigns throws up many more interesting factors.

MEN LEADING UP TO LOVE
Long, lingering moments of foreplay aren't favoured by Mr Virgo— not only does he have the lowest male average overall (28.2

minutes), but he's also most keen of all men on no foreplay at all (5%) and on just five minutes' worth of love games (18%, a clear 6% more than the next sign along). And Virgo men are also decidedly less keen than most on foreplay that stretches past the 15 minute mark.

At the other end of the scale, Taurus men like the most foreplay—32.7 minutes on average. 38% would appreciate half an hour or more, and 29% want to keep going for hours. Meanwhile, just 5% of Taurus men think five minutes is enough. Overall, the men next keen on foreplay are Aries (32.1 minutes) and Sagittarius (32 minutes). Hardly what traditional astrology might expect from impatient, "insensitive" fire signs.

CASE HISTORY OF AN ARIES MAN

Aries James, 57, has been married 30 years to a Taurus but also has a younger Gemini mistress.

"It's rare for my lover Dee and I to get much time alone, so sex is often a hurried affair. But when we do manage to sneak some time I love to make foreplay last for ages and take us both to the brink and back again several times.

"We usually start with a scented bath and sharing some ice-cold champagne and smoked salmon. Then we massage each other and talk about our fantasies. Dee's latest one is linked to a threesome with another woman in the office where we both work. We both find that very arousing. Caresses gradually get less general and more specific, we have oral sex, maybe to orgasm for Dee. Or we may get out one of the toys we've bought together, like a vibrator. When she slips that inside me it's the most amazing feeling.

"She is so young and responsive I could make love to Dee forever. My wife has never been too interested in sex and I always had to have extended foreplay with her just to get her lubricated enough. So I've had enough practice."

Libra and Capricorn men are among the zodiac's more generous lovers—they are the only ones who give a zero vote to no foreplay whatsoever. 32%, almost one in three, of Sagittarius and Capricorn men reckon 15 minutes is the ideal time. Both are starsigns who don't believe in wasting time—but for different reasons.

A total of 38% Taurus and Capricorns also opt for 30 minutes. But the man who is most keen on love that lasts hours and hours is Leo—one in three, more than for any other category, vote for this one.

The complete picture for men is as follows: 2% want no foreplay at all, 10% reckon five minutes is enough, 27% vote for 15 minutes, 32% for 30 minutes, and 28% would most like it to last hours...

STARWATCH

Two earth signs at odds again—sensuous Taurus likes most foreplay, but supposedly slow-to arouse Virgo likes least. And Aries and Sagittarius, traditionally considered selfish and impatient starsigns, also break away from their astrological profile. But perhaps we should remember this is how much foreplay these signs say they would like—not how much they actually have.

WOMEN WARM UP FOR SEX

"There's nothing more exciting than feeling sexy on the way home from work in the train, grabbing my boyfriend in the hall and having sex there and then with all our clothes on. But if I'm feeling less in the mood, or just feeling affectionate, I like lots of foreplay, caressing each other and whispering 'I love you' as a slow start builds to something more urgent..."

Danielle, a 28-year-old Gemini woman, finds how much foreplay she likes differs according to the circumstances—and in this reflects the rest of her starsign accurately. For Gemini woman is the one who sets the pace for the rest of the zodiac. She is keenest of all on no foreplay at all (5%) and yet the most enthusiastic about hours of love games (26%). And her scores average out to give her the highest female average time overall, of 29.1 minutes of foreplay.

But Leo ladies are close behind—with the joint highest score for zero foreplay (5%), and second highest for "hours" of 24%. Also in the upper range in general are Cancer, Libra and Aquarius women.

Capricorn has the lowest average time of 25.7 minutes. Only 15% of Capricorn women want foreplay to last "hours", by far the lowest of all female signs—and a good 5% lower than the next one on the list.

Who would have expected women to vote for less foreplay, in general, than men do? The exceptions to this rule are No Foreplay At All which appeals to 3% of women but only 2% of men, and 15 minutes' worth, which wins a 35% share. 10% of women, the same as for men, think five minutes is ideal, while 29% vote for half an hour and 22% want foreplay that lasts hours (6% less than the men).

Scorpio and Cancer women are keenest on just five minutes fooling around before sex (14%), compared to Ms Sagittarius, who gives this only 4%. But she is by far the biggest fan of 15 minute foreplay sessions, scoring 41%. And despite having the lowest total overall, Capricorn women are the most interested in loveplay that lasts 30 minutes (39%). While only 25% of Aries lovers want to keep going that long...

STARWATCH

So the starsign usually considered fast, Gemini, would like most foreplay—and the sign thought of as slow, Capricorn, would like least? As Aquarius and Libra also want more foreplay than average, the common factor may be their tendency to operate first on a mental plane rather than a physical one.

PENETRATION—HOW LONG DOES IT LAST?

Men may be more keen on foreplay—but they also spend longer on penetration—or so they claim in the AstroSex survey! The averages overall are 22.3 minutes of penetration for men and 20.9 minutes for women. But this time there are less obvious gender differences in the answers for each section—although still striking variations from sign to sign.

WHAT SATISFIES MEN?

Lovers of Aquarius males should settle in for a marathon session—as this male starsign has the highest average penetration time of 26.6 minutes. Next along is Aries on 23.4 minutes, then Gemini, 22.9. And 10%, or one in 10, of men belonging to each of these signs, requires penetration that lasts over an hour.

Least long-lasting lover is Capricorn, who only performs 19.8 minutes penetration on average. But Mr Virgo doesn't fare too well again—he is by far the most likely man to say penetration lasts less than five minutes—21% do so, a full 6% more than the next starsign along.

Cancer men opt most often for penetration of six to 10 minutes—and they're least likely overall to be thrusting between half an hour and an hour. Between 11 minutes and 15 minutes is Scorpio's ideal (32%), while Taurus favours 16-30 minutes. And Mr Libra is out in front for lasting 31-60 minutes—this is favourite with one in five, 20%, of the air sign's men. Yet Libra, along with Taurus, is also least likely of all men to seek penetration of over an hour (just 3%).

"The truth is, after more than half an hour I get a bit bored with repeating the football league tables to myself to stop my orgasm," admits Stuart, a 40-year-old Libra. "So if my partner still hasn't had her orgasm by then I prefer to climax myself and see to her pleasure afterwards."

The general pattern for men is as follows: 12% want penetration of less than five minutes, 21% vote for six to 10 minutes. 20% say 11-15 minutes is ideal, while 28%, more than any other category, opt for a sex act that takes 16-30 minutes. For 31-60 minutes the average is 14%, and 7% of all men want to keep going for an hour or more.

HOW MUCH SEX DO WOMEN WANT?

Less than the men, was the general response when AstroSex asked women how long penetration lasts. Perhaps they're just not as keen on timing it. Yet again, the exception is Scorpio women, who say penetration lasts an average of 24.2 minutes, highest of all women, and also higher than Scorpio men (21.1 mins). Ms Scorpio is least likely to have sex lasting under five minutes (10%). But she's most in favour overall, of penetration of 31-60 minutes (21%) AND of over an hour (7%). Add these two figures together and it means 28%, more than one in four, Scorpio women expect men to keep going for over half an hour...

Virgo (21.3 mins average) and Capricorn (20.9 mins) are next in the line for longer-lasting sex. But Virgo women, like Virgo men, are still first in line for the fast and furious approach—15% say penetration endures less than five minutes. Taurus ladies like 6-10 minutes best (26%), while 25% of Sagittarius females opt for 11-15 minutes. Pisces is keenest on 16-30 minutes (27%).

CASE HISTORY OF A PISCES WOMAN

Marion, 25, is a Pisces, who lives with Ken, 31 and a Cancer, but also has sex with her ex-husband Liam, 29, a Scorpio.

"People say size doesn't matter, but to me there's nothing better than feeling my man inside me, filling me completely. That's my favourite way to have an orgasm because I completely lose control. But it may take a while to work up to, with lots of different positions.

My ex-husband Liam understood that and could keep going for hours—he was also better endowed than Ken, who hasn't managed to satisfy me with penetration alone yet. That could be why I still get it together with Liam occasionally, although there's nothing left between us except sex. It's comfortable and uncomplicated—and I can relax and know Liam will get me there.

"But Ken is the one I love, and he has other ways of bringing me to orgasm. If only he could manage it the way I like best, everything would be perfect."

Totals for the zodiac's women are: 13% have less than five minutes penetration, 23% say six-10 minutes, 21% vote for 11-15, 24% for 16-30 minutes, 13% choose 31-60 minutes and for 6%, penetration takes up one hour plus.

WHO IS HAVING MOST ORGASMS?

Women may want to spend less time on sex than men, but they do get better results, if only just. For while men average 1.8 orgasms per session, women manage 1.9. And women are twice as likely as men (8% to 4%) to have four or more orgasms during a bout of lovemaking.

MEN COUNT CLIMAXES

Admirable self-control or inability to let go fully? Whatever the reason, 7% of Aquarius men don't expect to have any orgasms during a sex session. And fellow air sign Gemini is next highest, on 5%. But Aries, Libra and Pisces men have no such problems, they say—they never fail to climax at least once during sex.

The majority of men (42%) can count on one climax, and top of the "singles" list is Libra, on 54%. Lowest is Leo men, only one in three (33%) expect to climax only once. And 44% of Leos, highest of all zodiac males, expect to climax twice. Scorpio is out in front in the triple challenge—17% climax three times... and Gemini (6%) is first at going for number four.

Sensitive, caring Cancer is the zodiac's luckiest man in this section, however—7% of Cancers have more than four orgasms per session. Followed by 6% of Sagittarius men. But only one in 100 Virgo and Libra men are so fortunate. "More than one orgasm per session? I think that would kill me," says Virgo Eric, 46. "I already feel like I've had a mains current shot through my body with just one."

Overall, 2% of all men don't climax at all, 42% enjoy one orgasm. The earth moves twice for 37%, three times for 12%, four times for 3%. And 4% of men overall have more than four climaxes.

STARWATCH
Cancer man confounds sex experts - over one in 10 climaxing four times or more per session. Could this starsign be more physical and less emotional than traditional astrology has always assumed?

CLIMAX POINT FOR WOMEN
Women may be more likely than men to have more than four climaxes in a sex session, but they are even more likely not to orgasm at all—overall, 7% of women who replied to the survey do not expect to climax, compared to just 2% of men. Capricorn and Pisces women are most inclined of all (9%) not to reach final release. But more confident and demanding Aries and Scorpio women score lowest in this section, at 5% each.

When Pisces does reach orgasm, it's likely to be just once—45% of Pisces women expect just one climax, more than any other female starsign. One in three (33%) of Virgos go for double pleasure, and that figure is the same for Aries. For Geminis, three's the lucky number—highest total overall, 15%, usually climax three times during sex. Libra is tops for number four (6%), while an astounding 10%, or one in 10 of Scorpio females count on more than four helpings of ecstasy.

This helps give Scorpio, on 2.1, the highest average number of orgasms of all women, followed by Aries, Gemini, Virgo and Aquarius, all on two. Lowest are Pisces and Capricorn (1.8).

The women's general league table is like this: 7% don't climax at all, 40% expect one orgasm, 28% come twice, 12% reach the heights three times. For 5%, four is the magic number, and 8% can come more than four times.

CASE HISTORY OF AN ARIES WOMAN
Aries woman Anna, 30, has been married for eight years to a Sagittarius and recently "stumbled upon" multiple orgasms...

"I can't believe I've been making love all these years and never realised such a thing existed—now my husband Alex is worried I'm not going to be happy with two or three and want dozens of orgasms every time we make love. Well, why not? Once you've had multiple orgasms, who'd ever settle for just one again.

"How did I discover this delicious secret? Well usually Alex holds back and waits for me to come, then when I do he immediately lets go himself. And that's that. But this time for whatever reason—stress at work, he reckons—Alex didn't come immediately. And as my first climax died away I felt another starting to build. And then another—each one more powerful and lasting longer than the one before it. It was fantastic."

MAKING IT—OR FAKING IT?
Who fakes orgasm? Women are far more likely to do so than men (30%)—but the interesting thing is how many men do actually pretend (11%). And way ahead of the rest are Cancer men—15% of them admit to faking sometimes.

CASE HISTORY OF A CANCER MAN
Colin, 33, is a Cancer who is a self-employed artist. He lives with Lee, 40, a Virgo.

"Sometimes I'm just not in the mood, but I know Lee gets so hurt if I don't come, so I pretend. We use condoms, so it's a matter of whipping it off and rushing to flush it away before she notices. By the time I get back in the bedroom my erection has gone anyway. Yes, it's dishonest—but it doesn't happen often and I only do it to spare Lee's feelings."

Capricorn is least likely of all men to put on an act, but 8% still do so...

Turning to the women, 35% of Pisces women do resort to faking their climax, that's more than any other female starsign. Perhaps because this caring sign puts everyone else's happiness before their own?

Capricorn scores 34% here and Leo—surprisingly for this strong and honest sign—32%. "I never have an orgasm, but my husband doesn't know—he thinks I come noisily and wonderfully every time we make love," says Leo Kelsey, 24.

"It all started when we first met. I was very inexperienced sexually but I pretended to be a redhot sexpot—and that included climaxing at the drop of a hat. I've watched a few porno films in my time so I know how to fake it. But it's all gone too far now and I don't know how I'm going to get out of this situation."

At the other end of the women's scale, unsurprisingly, as least likely by far to fake it is... Ms Scorpio, at just 23%.

WHO HAS TRIED WHAT?

Men have had more oral sex and watched more erotic videos—but women wear sexy undies and rubber and use sex toys more often. And though roughly the same numbers of each sex have tried licking food off bodies or spanking, for instance, men are more than twice as likely to have taken part in a threesome or swapped partners, and seven times more likely to have paid for sex...

VARIETY BY MALE ORDER

91% of men across the zodiac have tried oral sex. Most likely to have sampled this sex variation is Libra man on 96%—meaning only four out of 100 Libras haven't tried it. Least likely is Scorpio, where 16%, four times as many, haven't experienced oral sex.

Erotic videos are the next most common stimulant for men, and 76% have watched them at some time. Most often is Taurus, on 81%, but Sagittarius likes them least (70%). 75% of men know what sensual massage feels like—82% of Virgos, but only 68% of Capricorns. And while almost half, 49%, of Libra men have experimented with sex toys, only about one in three (34%) of Geminis have done the same.

Sexy undies have been worn most by Taurus men (49%) and least by Virgo and Libra (34%)—overall their rating is 40%. And notoriously food-loving Taurus is also the man who's eaten food off bodies most, with 51% having done so. Yet for Leo men the total is a full 20% lower, on 31%. Overall, 40% of men have done this.

Almost a quarter of men have tried bondage—Scorpio is most likely to have done so, on 28%. Spanking rates a 19%, and telephone sex 16% vote overall, but adventurous Taurus gives both a 26% score. Libra man has taken part in the most threesomes (21%), but only 9% of Geminis have. And while 17% of Sagittarians have paid for sex, loving Cancer, to whom relationships are so vital, gives a response of only 7%. Overall, 14% of men have paid for sex at some time.

Almost 7% across the zodiac have swapped partners, led by 10% of Aries men—but only 3% of Taureans. And though wearing rubber is joint least favourite with all men, it's a hit with Scorpio—14% of Scorpios have tried rubber, compared to an overall average of exactly half that, 7%.

STARWATCH
Most sexually adventurous man in the zodiac is Taurus—traditionally considered a bit of a stick in the mud. And Gemini, the livewire of astrology, is the man who's tried least. Yet again, the AstroSex survey rewrites the rules of astrology.

WHAT WOMEN DO
Oral sex has been tried by 87% of women overall—and by 91% of Sagittarians, the top score. But next most common variation among

the female starsigns is sexy undies—84% overall have worn them, and they're most popular with Libra and Scorpio (87% each). But Cancer is least keen on sexy underwear (80%).

Down-to-earth Virgo is the biggest fan of sensual massage (77%) and massage earns 72% average score from all women. 67% have watched erotic videos—Capricorn and Pisces watching most (70%), and Sagittarius watching least (63%).

The next few sections are where sexy Scorpio comes into her own again, for Scorpio women, more than any other starsign, have tried: sex toys (53%, average 43%), eating food off bodies (43%, average 38%), bondage (30%, average 22%), spanking (28%, average 20%), and telephone sex (14%, average 11%). 5% of Scorpio women have also swapped partners, that's more than any other woman too.

CASE HISTORY OF A SCORPIO WOMAN

Gill is a 37-year-old Scorpio who belongs to a wife-swapping club. She is married to a Taurus man.

"I think my husband John and I had tried everything we could, just the two of us. I particularly like John to spank me with some soft kid gloves, then put them on and caress my breasts....

"The swapping started when we were on holiday with a couple we'd known for ages, in a cottage in the country. One night we'd all had a bit to drink, when the man said to us, 'Just what do you get up to in your bedroom at nights? We've heard all the noise.'

"And I said, 'Why don't we show you?' and unzipped John's trousers there and then and started sucking him to get him hard. He got the gloves out of his pocket and lifted my skirt to spank me. But I looked at the other man instead and said, 'Would you like to ...?'

"That night we each ended up with each other's partner and it was fantastic. The thrill of the unknown, yet the safety of my own husband to go back to afterwards. When we got home all four of us joined a club I read about in the small ads. And we go swapping regularly.

"When the keys are thrown on the table and selected to see who pairs off with who, I can feel the heat and wetness between my legs start. Yes, I've had some ugly, fat, smelly men. But even that is exciting in its own way. It works because I want to do it, my husband wants to do it."

At the opposite end of the scale to Scorpio, Sagittarius shows least interest in sex toys (35%) and eating food off bodies (31%), Taurus is least likely to have tried bondage (17%), while Capricorn has attempted spanking and telephone sex less often than the other signs (14% and 7% respectively). But Capricorn is still the female starsign who has taken part in threesomes and worn rubber most often.

Only one in 100 Sagittarius women have swapped partners, or paid for sex, lowest scores in both sections. But at 3%, Leo ladies are the ones who have parted with money for lovemaking most.

...AND WHO WOULD LIKE TO TRY WHAT?
Men are keenest on threesomes, followed by sensual massage. But the one thing women want to try most is eating off their partner's bodies.

MEN'S SECRET DESIRES
What would men like most to try? The overwhelming answer is a threesome, with 42% of men opting for this, 10% more than the next popular choice, sensual massage.

But Virgo man is even keener on a threesome than average—over half, 53% of Virgos secretly long to go to bed with more than one person. "But the only time I've ever dared to bring the subject up, my girlfriend went spare and threatened to leave me," is a very common comment. Three-in-a-bed sex appeals least to straightforward Sagittarius, who scores just 32%.

Earthy Capricorn would like to try massage more than other men, on 46%, but he is also least likely to have tried it already (see above).

A total of 29% of men want to try eating food off their partner's bodies. And if AstroSex replies are anything to go on, the food they have in mind ranges from whipped cream to a pint of Guinness. "Pour it on cold then lick it off warm, drop by drop," says Rory, 25. "Sheer ecstasy."

Sex toys are something Gemini men have tried least—and would like to try most (34%), a surprising result for this starsign thought to be so fond of variety. And although 90% of Aries men earlier claimed to have tried oral sex, 30%, more than any other sign, say they'd like to give it a go. So who's telling the truth here?

This does seem to be the section where starsigns express their darker, hidden side. So Scorpio, for once matching his supposed star profile, is keenest on swapping partners (28%) while supportive Pisces hankers after bondage (29%). For normally macho Leo a turn on is sexy undies (23%), while Libra fancies spanking (18%) more than any other man.

CASE HISTORY OF A PISCES MAN
Pisces Jim, 39, is a househusband, looking after his, and Cancer-born wife Terri's, two children.
"My life is all give, give, give and trying to make allowances and be flexible. So when it comes to sex I'd like to ditch all that responsibility. I get so fed up being a new man, in bed I want a chance to control and be controlled. That's what bondage, to me, offers.

"I'd love Terry to tie me up and do what she wants with me. Scratch and slap me, even use a whip. But the odds are against it. Terri won't even wear stiletto heels or suspenders in bed because she thinks they're 'dirty'."

A complete run-down of men's fantasies goes as follows: 42% would like to try a threesome, 32% sensual massage, 29% eating food off bodies. For 28% sex toys would be a welcome treat, 24% feel the same about oral sex. 24% want to watch erotic videos, 22% swap partners, 18% try bondage, 16% wear sexy undies. Another

12% say spanking is what they'd like to try, 11% vote for rubber, 10% for paid-for sex and 9% telephone sex.

Virgo is the male starsign who would like to try most. And Pisces wants to try least.

STARWATCH
What men want to try sexually matches their traditional starsign profiles more closely than what they have actually tried.

WHAT WOULD WOMEN LIKE TO TRY?
Eating food off their partner's bodies is top of the must-try table for the zodiac's women—34% on average want to attempt this, led by a staggering 41% of Aries women. And foods women would choose often reflect a sweet tooth—like chocolate mousse and ice-cream.

Capricorn women dream most of sensual massage, with 36%, or over one in three wanting to try it, while Libra longs to give sex toys a go (27%) and the same number of Cancer women want to wear sexy undies (sometimes shy Cancer is least likely of all ladies to have tried this already—as in the previous case history).

Bondage is the next thing women in general fancy—and Taurus in particular, on 26%. While 22% of Leos and Libras long to switch on to erotic videos. Virgo is the female sign who'd most like to be part of a threesome, while one of Leo's secret desires is oral sex. Scorpio (surprise, surprise) fantasises most about wearing rubber (21%) and swapping partners (13%)—even though she has already tried this more than any other sign.

Taurus shows a tantalising side by dreaming of telephone sex most (15%). "Sex for me has always been a very physical thing, so I'd like the chance to use words instead," says Taurus Joanne, 28. "I have got as far as ringing my boyfriend at work and trying to talk dirty to him, but I feel so silly. I decided to write him a dirty letter instead and he loved it. So that's given me courage to try talking on the phone again."

Least appeal for women in general is offered by paid-for-sex. Leo is the lady who wants to try most things, and, the exact opposite of the men's results, Virgo wants to try least.

STARWATCH
While men's secret desires match their conventional star profile, women's are often the opposite. They want to do things traditional astrology would judge completely out of character.

SHOULD A PARTNER TALK AND MAKE SOUNDS OF PLEASURE DURING SEX?

Yes, is the resounding reply from both men and women across the zodiac—but men appreciate aural sex more than women! 93% of men overall welcome a partner making a noise during sex, while for women the figure is 88%.

Aquarius and Taurus men (both 97%) are keenest on self-expression, perhaps partly as a boost to their own self-esteem. Both these signs like reassurance they are on the right track.

But surprisingly, normally communicative Gemini is least keen on hearing a lover's sounds of pleasure, just 88% of the air sign answered yes to this question. Perhaps this talkative man prefers a one-way system of communication...

Among the women, however, it's Gemini and Pisces, who are the starsigns keenest on hearing a partner's feelings—good or bad. Both answer yes 91% of the time to this section. And Leo ladies are least likely to appreciate a partner's comments. Do they like to be star of the show, or simply dislike distraction from their performance?

WHO IMAGINES A PARTNER IS SOMEONE ELSE DURING SEX?

Extreme honesty on all sides was called for in this survey question, which asks if men or women ever close their eyes and fantasise their partner is someone else. And if so, who? Here the answers range from Kim Basinger and Kevin Costner through various pop stars and public figures to "My wife's sexy sister" and even "the insurance salesman."

But the majority of both men and women are in no doubt—they definitely do NOT imagine their partner is someone else, say 51% of men, and 68% of women. So once again, if fantasising is taking place, it's more likely to be inside male brains than female.

Which woman does imagine her lover is someone else? It's no surprise to discover it's Scorpio again (36%), she who seems to lead the richest and most varied sexlife of the whole female zodiac. But joint equal is fantasy starsign Pisces (36%) who can sometimes have trouble living in the real world. But next comes a sign not known for vivid imagination, Sagittarius.

CASE HISTORY OF A SAGITTARIUS WOMAN

Trudy, a 26-year-old Sagittarius, leads a rich and varied fantasy life with a Capricorn boyfriend...

"Of course I love my boyfriend Hugh, and of course sex with him is wonderful. It's just sometimes even more wonderful when it's with my bank manager, who's a very sexy, sporty older man who's made it plain he fancies me. I don't want an affair, but with imagination, who needs one?

"Another favourite fantasy lover of mine is a priest in the local church who has gorgeous dark eyes and long eyelashes—forbidden fruit there, I suppose.

"I use my fantasies a lot when I masturbate, but also sometimes when making love. Fantasies are just a sex aid like any other. But no, I haven't told Hugh. You know how men are, he'd only feel

92

threatened and less of a man. And I don't know how I would feel
if he told me he was mentally swapping me for some sex symbol."

Among the men too, Pisces is most likely to change a lover to
someone else (49%), and Cancer is close behind on 48%.

But who are the starsigns happy with their lot—or simply lacking
in imagination? Least likely to fantasise a partner is someone else
are Libra women (72%, almost three out of four, answer no). While
Virgo, Scorpio and Sagittarius are the men who prefer the real thing
(62% each). But here, as in many other sections of Sex In Action,
male scores are significantly higher than female.

THE 12 STARSIGNS' SEX IN ACTION PROFILES

ARIES MAN AND SEX

*Top three turn-ons for Aries man are massage (79%), watching a sexy movie (77%) and sharing a bath (also 77%). But this action man is also keenest among male signs on a shared shower (75%) and playing sport (26%). What does he like least? Having his feet caressed (18%) and a gift of flowers (7%). "I just get irritated, not aroused when my partner touches my feet," says Tony 41. "And as for toe-sucking—it's ludicrous."

*Sexiest setting for Aries is a luxury hotel with round bed and satin sheets, say 41%.

*He's most likely of all men to have made love in the office (22%), and second most keen on the bed (98%). But the Aries man is least likely to have been passionate in the kitchen (40%), or on a table (29%). Beaches, floors and cinemas aren't big hits either.

*52% find woman on top most exciting, and Aries gives the same score to oral sex—both firmly in the lower range. And he's also less excited than other men by woman on hands and knees, woman face down, manual sex and both standing. Perhaps Aries would rather invent his own positions...

*82% prefer slow, gentle caresses—only 18% want passionate speed. That's slightly below average.

*Average time he'd like for foreplay is 32.1 minutes, second highest of all men. 2% vote no foreplay at all, 8% for five minutes, 31% say 15 minutes, 28% half an hour and 31% want loveplay to last hours.

*Aries is second highest again in average length of penetration— 23.4 minutes total. Most popular penetration time is 16-30 minutes, but one in 10 Aries men, most of any sign, keep going over an hour. "I refuse to give up until she has an orgasm," is a common remark.

*He never has sex without an orgasm, and averages out at 1.8 per session. 44% come once, 36% twice, 16% three times and 5% four times or more.

*10% fake orgasms, just below average.

*He's among the men most likely to have tried eating food off bodies and wearing sexy undies—and, at 10% score, the one who's swapped partners most often!

*And what would he like to try? 30%, most of all men, want to sample oral sex, while 27% fancy erotic videos. But like almost every other male sign, what Aries fancies most is a threesome. "Ideally me, Julia Roberts and Kim Basinger. But don't tell my wife." Spanking (just 7%) appeals less to him than any other man.

*93% like a partner to make sounds of pleasure during sex.

*44% do imagine their partner is someone else while making love. That's slightly above average.

ARIES MAN is more considerate and less experimental than he may claim—but he can be difficult to satisfy.

ARIES WOMAN AND SEX

*She is put in the mood most by massage (73%), having her breasts caressed (74%) and watching a sexy movie (75%). And more than any other woman, Aries is turned on by the words, 'I love you', and by hot dancing. "The smell of sweat and bodies that occasionally rub together, with all the time that pounding beat... it's great," says Marsha, 32. Her least likely turn-ons are having her feet caressed and a gift of flowers (24%) or playing sport together (just 9%).

*Sexiest setting for 44%, is a luxury hotel with satin sheets and a round bed.

*The opposite of Aries man, she's the woman MOST likely to have made love in the kitchen (55%) or cinema (3%). She also quite likes the park and the bus. But she votes in the lowest range when it comes to the floor and the beach.

*Which position excites her most? Perhaps surprisingly, it's the missionary, or man on top (49%). Then she likes oral sex (48%) and woman on top (41%). She's in the middle to upper range for all other positions, from manual sex to both partners on their side.

*21%, second highest score, prefer fast, firm and passionate caresses.

*She would like the second lowest amount of foreplay on average, just 25.8 minutes. 3% vote for none at all, 13% say five minutes, 39% go for 15 minutes, 25% for 30 minutes and 20%, one in five, look for foreplay to last hours.

*Penetration time is in the lower range too, at 20.6 minutes average. "If nothing's happened by then, it's never going to," says one Aries.

*She manages an above average two orgasms per session. 5%, second lowest female score, have none, 36% come once. She's most likely of all women to come twice— one in three say they do. 13% manage three climaxes, and 13% four or more.

*31% above average, do fake orgasm.

*Aries is more likely than most women to have tried rubber and paid-for sex. But she's second least likely to have eaten food off her lover's body. What has she tried most? Oral sex (85%), wearing sexy undies (82%) and sensual massage (70%).

*When it comes to what she'd like to try, there's no competition— more than other female sign, Aries wants to try eating food off bodies (41%). She's also quite keen on wearing rubber and swapping partners. But sex toys, telephone sex and spanking leave her ice-cold. "Pain, even inflicted for fun, has no place in love-making in my opinion," more than one have commented.

*Below average 87% like a partner to express pleasure through sound. That's second lowest of all zodiac women.

*30% imagine a partner is someone else during sex. That's second lowest again.

Sex for Aries woman is fast food rather than a leisurely feast, but she'd like to extend her menu.

HOW DO THE SEXES DIFFER?

Aries woman has tried more—and would like to try even more—than the Aries man. Except when it comes to eating off bodies ... She also sets about sex in more of a rush, and wants it more rough and ready. She has more orgasms—but is three times as likely to fake it too.

TAURUS MAN AND SEX

*Overall Taurus is the man turned on by most things. His top three are massage (82%), a sexy movie (76%) and shared bath (80%—highest score of all men). But he also gets in the mood more than other men by slow dancing (68%), a holiday in the sun (57%), the words 'I love you' (50%), and a sexy call at work (51%). And he's second most turned on by a romantic meal (63%). But don't caress his hair—he likes that less than any other man. Least favourites of all are playing sport (22%), caresses on the feet (19%) and a gift of flowers (6%).

*He chooses a luxury hotel and satin sheets as the sexiest setting (41%) but a close second is a deserted beach at sunset (40%). "I do like my comfort—and I don't like the thought of someone stumbling over us having sex in public," admits Lance, 25.

*The majority of Taurus men have made love in most places—but the only locations he seems to favour more than most men are the bath (69%), the park (43%), the beach (39%) and changing cubicle (13%). He's not keen on the shower or chair.

*His favourite positions are woman on top (60%), oral sex (53%) and woman on hands and knees (50%). "Because I like to look as well as feel," is the reason given by most Taureans. But he's also second most excited by traditional man on top sex. He definitely doesn't like both partners on their side, manual sex, both standing or sex sitting on laps as much as other men.

*81% prefer to be touched slowly and gently.

*Of all men, he would like the longest foreplay allocation, 32.7 minutes on average. 38% of Taurus men want to fool around for at least half an hour, and he's least likely of all to settle for just five minutes (5%).

*Penetration times are shorter, though—22.2 minutes average. 14% say less than 5 minutes, 15% vote for 6-10 minutes, for 17% penetration takes from 11-15 minutes. 32% (highest of all men) vote for 16-30 minutes, 19% for 31-60 minutes and just 3% last for hours.

*He averages 1.8 orgasms per sex bout, but 2% of Taurus men don't usually climax at all. 38% come once, 42% twice, 13% three times and 4% four or more.

*He's the man second most likely to fake orgasm (13%). "I just couldn't let my partner blame herself—after all sex is about sharing," says Franco, 36. "But each time I do fake it I feel guilty for weeks afterwards."

*He's tried more sexual variations than any other man. These include erotic videos (81%), sexy undies (49%), eating food off bodies (51%), spanking (26%), telephone sex (26%). And for most other things he falls in the upper range, too, except oral sex and swapping partners (just 3%, lowest of all zodiac, have tried this).

*But he would LIKE to try it—26%, third highest score overall, say they'd like to swap partners. Taurus is also more interested than other men in paid for sex (14%) and wearing rubber (18%). Perhaps in an effort to escape his "nice guy" image? But he's the man least keen on sampling oral sex (just 18%).

*A massive 97% more than any other male sign, like a partner to make lots of noise during sex.

*Only 39%, well below average, imagine a partner is someone else when making love.

A caring, sharing lover with few inhibitions, the Taurus man secretly longs to let his darker side show...

TAURUS WOMAN AND SEX

*Massage gets 77% in the mood, caresses on the breasts work for 75%, while 72% are turned on by a sexy movie. Ms Taurus is also the woman most aroused by a romantic meal (68%), having her throat caressed (53%), and compliments (39%). "Yes I like love making to be a complete event, not just a physical release," remarks Tracey, 18. Only a couple of things turn her on markedly less than average—a shared bath, touching her stomach and fondling her feet.

*Sexiest setting, say 43% is a warm deserted beach at sunset. "Straight out of a romantic movie ... lovely," says one Taurus. "Even if the reality is sand in all your most tender places and a salt water rash."

*Bed, floor and sofa are the places she's made love most—but Taurus woman also beats the rest of the zodiac when it comes to passion in the car—69%, most of all female signs, have tried this. And she's had sex in the office second most often, too. Compared to other women, she's made love less in the shower and the bath—and on trains.

*Man on top is traditional Taurus' most exciting sexual position (45%) followed by oral sex (44%) and woman on top (40%). She's least excited of all women by manual sex, and by both standing and woman face down.

*80% prefer slow, gentle caresses.

*When it comes to ideal foreplay time, she falls in the middle range with an average of 27.9 minutes. 2% of Taurus women want no foreplay at all, 10% prefer five minutes. 15 minutes is chosen by another 35%, while 33% opt for half an hour and 21% want to go on for hours.

*Six-10 minutes penetration is the time most Taurus women manage (26%), but her average time is around 20 minutes.

*7% have no orgasms, 42% have one, 27% go for the double, 10% the triple and 13% in total climax four or more times.

*31%, just above average, admit to faking orgasm sometimes.

*Overall, she's tried second least sexual variations of all women. Her top three are oral sex (89%), sexy undies (82%) and sensual massage (70%), but she's also tried swapping partners and paid-for sex more than most women. At just 17%, however, her score for bondage is lowest in the zodiac...

*... and bondage is just what she'd like to try, more than any other female sign. 26% of Taurus women fancy attempting bondage, and 37% (second highest number) want to eat food off bodies, too. She's

also fascinated by telephone sex but is less keen than average on erotic videos and paid for sex. (But then, she is one of the most likely to have already tried it!).

*89% like a partner to make sounds of pleasure during sex.

*One in three, 33%, occasionally fantasise a lovemaking partner is someone else. "The main danger is getting so carried away you call out the wrong name at the moment of truth," says Carole 28. "Luckily we're usually both so excited by then it doesn't register." **Taurus woman likes sex with all the trimmings—and struggles to control a wild imagination.**

HOW DO THE SEXES DIFFER?

In general, Taurus men have tried far more sexual variations than women, but the female members of this starsign do seem to have experienced some things the men don't dare, e.g. swapping partners. Wearing rubber appeals much more to men than women, telephone sex vice versa. Both sexes have roughly the same orgasm level, but men like more foreplay and penetration. While she prefers sex with man on top, he wants woman on top...

GEMINI MAN AND SEX

*Gemini man is the least easy to arouse in the zodiac. But his first choices for getting in the mood are massage (79%), a shared bath (74%) and watching a sexy movie (73%). There's no stimulus that turns him on more than other men, but plenty turn him on less— these include thighs caressed, slow dancing, stroking his chest, soft music and lights, a sexy call at work, having his face fondled, compliments, caresses on the throat and on the feet.

*Sexiest setting, in Gemini's view is the five-star hotel with satin sheets.

*He's least likely of all men to have made love in the bath (54%) or shower (40%), but most likely to have had passion experience in a cinema or on board a bus. Like most men, he's had sex most often in bed, on the floor or the sofa.

*Oral sex is the position that excites him most (65%, more than any other man), but unlike other signs, there's no variation that leaves him completely cold. "I'm open minded to any suggestions," says one Gemini. "The more unusual the better..."

*87%, second highest overall, like to be caressed in a gentle, loving way.

*His ideal foreplay time is slightly below average on 30.2 minutes. 2% vote for no foreplay at all, for 12%, five minutes is easily enough. 25% opt for 15 minutes, 36% choose half an hour, and 25% want to carry on for hours and hours...

*He's third highest in the staying power tables—average penetration time for Gemini is 22.9 minutes. But 15% do opt for less than five minutes, second highest of all men.

*He averages 1.8 orgasms per sex session. But 5% of Gemini men don't have any at all. 39% orgasm once, 38% twice, 8% three times. But Gemini is the man most likely to orgasm four times—6% say they do, and do, and do, and do... And a further 5% score more than four. "But it depends how long a sex session is," comments Tim, 35. "Are we talking half an hour—or a long weekend without the kids?"

*10%, slightly below average, have faked an orgasm on occasion.

*Gemini is the zodiac's least adventurous man—things he has tried less than other men include sex toys (34%), spanking (14%), telephone sex (11%), and threesomes (9%). And the only variations he's tried more than most are bondage and swapping partners.

*But what would Mr Gemini like to taste? Sex toys and sexy undies are his personal preferences, but like most other men his number one secret heart's desire is a threesome (39%), then sensual massage (32%) and eating food off bodies (31%). "Why do I like the sound of sex toys? It's the idea of a hard object combined with soft bodies, also giving pleasure over to a third party—and yes, perhaps investing sex with less emotion," says one Gemini candidly. "The only trouble is, shops and catalogues that sell the things seem so seedy to me." The games Gemini is least inclined to try are spanking (8%), paid-for sex (7%) and telephone sex (also 7%).

*Silence is golden to more Geminis than any other man. 12% say they do NOT like a partner to make sounds of pleasure during sex.

*41% do sometimes imagine a sex partner is someone else. That's just below average.

Gemini man knows what he likes in sex—and certainly knows what he doesn't.

GEMINI WOMAN AND SEX

*77% are put in the mood by massage, 70% by slow dancing and 70% by a shared bath. But in general Gemini women find a variety of actions, settings and caresses arousing—yet are not extremely turned on, or off, by any of them. Except perhaps the words 'I love you', which only puts less than half (49%) of Gemini women in the mood, second lowest of the zodiac. "I always find myself thinking, he's only saying that to get his leg over—does he really mean it? I'll show him. So it has the opposite effect," says Kay, 40.

*Sexiest setting, for Gemini woman, is a top flight hotel suite complete with champagne and satin sheets. She's least interested of all women in a deserted beach, but above-average keen on a deserted moorland.

*Bed, floor and sofa are her most common love-locations. But she's also the female sign most likely to have got carried away in the office (11%). She's pretty keen on the kitchen and the shower, too—but not on changing cubicles. "It's OK with a big strong man to hold you up, but my boyfriend weighs less than I do. How else, short of hanging from the coat hooks, can you keep your feet above the gap at the bottom of the cubicle?" asks one Gemini.

*Preferred sexual position for Gemini is oral sex, 44% say this is most exciting of all. But 42%, top score of all female signs, also vote for woman on top. And 40% say they like the man to be on top. Gemini is also second most excited by lying face down herself. And unlike the men, there's no position she finds markedly less stimulating than other signs.

*84% want to be touched in a slow and gentle way.

*More than any other woman, Gemini likes instant sex—5% vote for no foreplay at all in an ideal world. Yet overall she likes the most of all women, with an average time of 29.1 minutes. 9% of Gemini women want five minutes foreplay, 32% would prefer 15 minutes, 28% say 30 minutes and 26%, again highest score overall, opt for foreplay that lasts for hours...

*She likes penetration to last 20.7 minutes, slightly below average.

*She reaches exactly two orgasms per session and is the one woman most likely to manage three (15%). 6% don't climax at all, 39% once, 28% twice, and 12% four times or more. This puts Gemini well into the upper range.

*She's the second least likely to fake it too—only 25%, one in four, do. "I can't lie to my partner in any other situation, so what makes sex any different?" comments 22-year-old Fiona. "I think it wouldn't solve anything, just create more problems."

*Gemini woman has had a go at most sex games, but especially wearing sexy undies, eating food off bodies, telephone sex and wearing rubber. Things she has tried less than average are erotic videos, sex toys, and spanking. In common with most women, only two in 100 Geminis have swapped partners, and only half that have paid for sex.

*There's no one sexual variation she's longing to try, either— overall, Gemini scores second lowest on secret desires. And she's less interested than other women in sex toys, sexy undies and swapping partners. But she does show above-average interest in spanking, paid-for-sex and threesomes.

*91%, more than any other woman, want a partner to express pleasure through sounds.

*32%, exactly average, do sometimes imagine a partner is someone else while making love.

Gemini woman likes sex fast, slow, hot, cool, clean, dirty—but always noisy.

HOW DO THE SEXES DIFFER?

Both men and women born under Gemini get more than their share of orgasms in general—yet almost as many men (5%) as women (6%) have none at all! Gemini females are more keen on quickies than males, and they're also attracted to a wider range of sexual variations. And they've got more experience too. While Gemini men are most likely to want silence during sex, Gemini women can't get enough noise...

CANCER MAN AND SEX

*What puts Cancer men in the mood for love? 84% (more than any other man) say a sexy movie, 82% vote for massage, and for 75% a shared bath is a turn-on. But Cancer is aroused by a gift of flowers more than any other male starsign (12%) and second most excited by playing sport (23%). Things he finds put him less in the mood than most men include stomach caresses, and hot dancing. But overall he scores around average on each category in this section.

*Sexiest setting for love? Like most men, Cancer goes for the luxury hotel, champagne on ice and satin sheets on a round bed (42%). But he's also more interested than other men in a warm deserted beach at sunset (41%).

*Bed, floor and sofa, in that order, have witnessed his passion most often. But he's still least likely of the zodiac's men to have had sex on the sofa. Unexpectedly, he's made love most often in changing cubicles (17%) and on buses (10%) and 57% have tried the shower too. Least popular love-places are the cinema (7%) and on a plane (3%). "I'm concentrating so much on not being afraid of flying, I don't think I could relax enough to get an erection," says Gregory, 38.

*Oral sex is the position Cancer men find most exciting, at 61%. Then he likes woman on top at 55% (although second lowest score of all men) and woman on hands and knees, 52%. But most of all the zodiac's males, he likes sex with both partners lying on their side. "Making love like spoons is a lovely way to wake up together in the morning. It's cosy and slow, but so exciting too," says one Cancer husband.

*84% like to be caressed slowly, gently and lovingly.

*Slightly less foreplay than average is preferred by Cancer—30.7 minutes. 3% like no loveplay at all, 8% want five minutes, 30% say 15 minutes while 31% opt for half an hour. And 27% could go on for hours.

*20.6 minutes is his average penetration span—that's in the lower range. Cancer man is most likely to last six-10 minutes (32%), and least likely to make it 31-60 minutes (9%).

*He manages 1.9 orgasms per session, in the upper range. Only 1% don't climax at all, 45% have one orgasm, 33% have two, 10% three and 4% four. But a lucky 7% of Cancer men come more than four times—most of all men in the zodiac.

*He's also tops in a very different table, as more Cancer men than any other sign fake their orgasm (15%). Could he possibly be faking it more than four times?

*He's one of the least adventurous signs, but has tried oral sex (91%), sensual massage (77%), and erotic videos (76%). He's the man least likely to have had a bash at bondage or paid for sex.

*More than any other man, sensual Cancer would like to lick food off a lover's body (35%), and even more are tempted by a threesome (38%). Cancer is also the man who would by far most like to try paid for sex (23%) and telephone sex (13%). "Sex is so tied up for me with love and relationships, I'd give anything to do it for money, where all that mattered was my pleasure alone." But sexy undies certainly do nothing for him (just 9%).

*92%, in the middle range, like to hear a partner's sounds of pleasure in sex.

*48%, second highest of all men, sometimes imagine a sex partner is someone else.

Cancer is the man most likely to make it—and fake it—in the zodiac.

CANCER WOMAN AND SEX

*76% get in the mood with massage, 70% with a sexy movie and 68% by having their breasts caressed. Cancer woman is least keen of all female signs on all kinds of dancing, and thigh caresses, as a prelude to passion. Touching her hair or throat don't do much for her either, nor paying her compliments....

*A warm deserted beach at sunset, lying half in, half out of the water, is Ms Cancer's idea of sexy heaven. She's the woman least likely to choose the more conventional luxury hotel and satin sheets (33%), but most keen on a secluded moorland (21%). "Any sex outdoors is more exciting than inside, if you ask me. It's the sensation of scratchy sand or grass, the feel of warm water or cool breezes on bare skin...need I say more?" says Katrina, 31.

* She's the woman who's made love in bed least, and in the bath most (72% of water loving Cancers). 9% of Cancer women, more than any other sign, have also had sex on a train, and 3%, joint highest female score, in a cinema...

*She finds man on top and woman on top equally exciting positions (41% each), followed by oral sex which rates a 40% vote. And Cancer is least keen of all women on being on her hands and knees (33%). "I shouldn't say so but I find it degrading—I like to see my lover while we're having sex," says one. Her least favourite of all is manual sex (15%), with sex standing up next in line on 16%.

*80% like slow, gentle caresses rather than fast passionate ones.

*She would like the second longest foreplay, of 28.8 minutes overall. 2% are happy with none, 14% reckon five minutes is enough, and 31% say 15 minutes. 29% opt for half an hour, 24% for hours and hours...

*On average, penetration lasts 20.8 minutes, in the middle range. But 7% of Cancer women keep going for over an hour, more than any other female sign. Many comment once they get going they could carry on all night.

*Perhaps because 8% of Cancer women have four or more orgasms per lovemaking bout. Her average is 1.9, but 7% don't climax at all.

*31%, just above average, have faked orgasm at some time. Most common reasons are tiredness, not being in the mood and even wanting to get on with reading a book.

*Cancer woman is in the lower range when it comes to sexual experience. But like the majority of women she's most likely to have tried oral sex (87%), sexy undies (80%) and sensual massage (73%). She has below average experience of sex toys and three-somes—and above average of bondage, spanking, swapping part-ners and paid-for sex. So although she may not have tried a wide variety of sexual variations, she's tried some that other women wouldn't dare.

*What would Cancer woman like to try? Sex toys, sexy undies and (even more) spanking. But she's not drawn towards sensual mas-sage or erotic videos.

*88%, exactly average, like a partner to make sounds of pleasure during sex.

*30%, slightly less than average, have fantasised a lover is someone else.

Give her exotic locations and erotic suggestions and Cancer woman will supply everlasting love.

HOW DO THE SEXES DIFFER?

Both like outdoor sex, and like unusual passion places—though not the same ones! Nor does Cancer woman share Cancer man's fondness for sex lying on the side. More women than men like penetration for longer than half an hour, but the males of this sensitive sign do favour more foreplay. Well matched in climax power, 7% of men and 8% of women orgasm over four times during sex. And both sexes average the same amount, 1.9. But while Cancer women are among the least likely to fake, Cancer man, at 15%, pretends most often of any male.

LEO MAN AND SEX

*Leo lands in the lower range of turn-on-ability, but the one thing that arouses him most is watching a sexy movie (77%), then massage and a shared bath (both 76%). As might be expected of a sign ruled by the sun, Leo does get in the mood on exotic holidays, and he's the third most likely man to respond to having his ego flattered with the words, "I love you." But he's less keen than anyone else on slow dancing, having his face caressed, and gifts of flowers.

*Sexiest setting, in Leo man's opinion, is a luxurious hotel complete with champagne and satin sheets.

*More impulsive Leos have made love on the floor (95%) than in bed (94%). And he's keen on the sofa, too (92%). Leo is the man most likely to have had sex in the car (71%, almost three out of four say they have) and in a cinema. But he's least likely to have experienced passion in a swimming pool.

*Woman on top is the sex position that excites Leo most, followed by oral sex, then woman on hands and knees. But he's less excited than other men by making love to a woman who's lying face down. "I just can't get adequate penetration that way to satisfy me," says Yuri, 33.

*85% prefer caresses that are slow, subtle and loving. So 15% don't.

*He likes an above average amount of foreplay—31.8 minutes. But Leo is the one man who most likes loveplay to last for hours on end (33% do). 4% are happy with none at all, 12% settle for just five minutes. 24% would ideally like 15 minutes foreplay, while 25% (lowest of all men) say half an hour.

*Again, Leo comes in just above average in the penetration time he likes—22.7 minutes.

*Two is Leo man's lucky number—44% of this starsign's men usually have two orgasms during sex. "I'm living proof men can climax without ejaculating—but I don't think my body could take more than two orgasms at a time," says one happy Leo. 3% never climax at all, 33% (lowest of all signs) manage once, 12% orgasm three times and 7% four times or more. Overall, he averages 1.9, joint top score for men.

*Only 9% of Leos admit to faking orgasms, second lowest of all signs.

*He's tried oral sex most (90%), followed by sensual massage (78%) and erotic videos (77%). But he's least likely of all men to have experienced eating food off bodies, or spanking.

*What would Leo like to try? A threesome, in common with every other man, also swapping partners (27%) and bondage (24%), but especially wearing sexy undies (23%). "The feel of cool silk on warm skin is so exciting," says one Leo. He's less interested than any other man in sex toys and paid-for sex.

*90%, the second lowest overall, like their partner to talk and make sounds of pleasure during sex.

*40% do sometimes imagine a partner is someone else while making love.

Leo men take time to warm up, but he's worth the wait.

LEO WOMEN AND SEX

*She's turned on most by sensual massage (75%), but a close second is having her breasts caressed at 73% and slow dancing (68%). Ms Leo is the woman who most likes hot dancing and having her feet caressed. But she's less enthusiastic about a lover touching her face. She's also the woman who gets in the mood second most often by playing sport.

*The winning sexy setting for Leo is a luxury hotel (45%) followed by a warm deserted beach at sunset (40%).

*She's made love most often in bed (97%), on the sofa (92%) and on the floor (91%). She's the woman most likely to have had sex in a train or changing cubicle, but least likely to have canoodled in the kitchen. "What's exotic about the kitchen—all those dirty dishes everywhere" comments Claire, 28.

*She finds oral sex the most exciting position (41%), then man on

110

top and woman on hand and knees (both 40%). Woman on top gets a 39% vote. But Leo shares the title of woman least interested in making love standing up.

*85%, top score for all women, prefer a lover's caresses to be slow and gentle.

*Above average foreplay is her ideal—exactly 25 minutes. Yet 5% of Leo women, highest score overall, would ideally like instant sex with no foreplay at all. 12% want five minutes, 33% opt for 15 minutes. 26% say half an hour would be adequate, and 24% want foreplay to be hours long.

*Average penetration time is 20 minutes and that's in the middle range. But Leo is the woman least likely to last for 16-30 minutes.

*Middle range again for Leo's orgasms—an average of 1.9 per sex bout. And she's second most likely to have more than four (9%). 8% climax not at all, 41% once, 26% twice, 12% three times and 4% manage four.

*Almost one in three (32%) fake, or have faked, orgasm at some time.

*In the middle range when it comes to experimentation, the only thing Leo has tried more than other women is paid-for sex. "Sex without strings, it can be addictive," comments one. 85% have tried oral sex, 82% sexy undies and 72% sensual massage. And Leo is second most likely to have been part of a sex threesome too.

*But when it comes to wanting to try new things, Leo takes the lead in the female zodiac. She would most like to try watching erotic videos (22%) and oral sex (21%), while one in three dream of eating food off bodies and one in four of playing with sex toys. She's also keener than most women on wearing rubber and spanking, too.

*85%, least of all women, like a partner to make sounds of pleasure while making love.

*30%, below average, admit they sometimes fantasise a love-partner is someone else during sex.

Pandora's box of passion ideas, but Leo woman likes her loving less hectic than her life.

HOW DO THE SEXES DIFFER?

Leo woman needs her ego (and her body) massaged less than Leo man to get in a sexy mood, and she's not so keen on passion on four wheels. Leo man, meanwhile, likes lots more foreplay—one in three men want it to last hours, but only one in four women! Men of this starsign are more likely than women to have two orgasms per session, but overall both sexes average 1.9. Ms Leo wants to try more sexual variations than her male counterpart, but both enjoy wearing sexy undies, and are among the signs least likely to like a partner making noise during sex...

VIRGO MAN AND SEX

*What puts Virgo man in the mood for love? For 83% it's a sensual massage, for 77% a sexy movie and for 76% a shared bath. But there is no specific turn-on factor that arouses Virgo more than any other, except perhaps having his feet and/or chest caressed. He's least excited by playing sport (19%) or a gift of flowers (6%).

*Alone among men, Virgo votes the sexiest setting as a secluded moorland, with rough grass on bodies and cool wind on skin (31%). But he's also the one man keenest on a private flat with black walls, lit with candles (16%). Is this hidden Virgo daring shining through?

*He's made love in less places, or less often when he has, than most men. For example, Virgo is the man who's had sex least in the car, bath, park, office, changing cubicle, bus and cinema. His top three love locations are the bed (95%), floor and sofa (both 92%). But only one in 100 male Virgos have made love on a plane.

*Woman on hands and knees is the position that excites Virgo most—two out of three (66%), vote for this variation. Next is woman on top (65%)—and Virgo is the man who enjoys oral sex the least. "Well I don't mind getting it but I'm not into giving it," says one. "I can't shake off the idea it's dirty." He's also very keen on sex when both partners are standing.

*88%, more than any other starsign, vote for slow, gentle and loving caresses.

*He likes the lowest foreplay time of all men—just 28.2 minutes on average. And Virgo is most likely to opt for none at all (5%) AND for just five minutes (18%, a full 6% higher than the next sign down). "Most arousal takes place in the brain before the body is even touched," says Steven, 27. "So I like to get straight into the fun part." 23% (lowest of the zodiac) like 15 minutes, 28% half an hour and 26% want foreplay that lasts for hours. More Virgos than any other male sign last less than five minutes (21%, more than one in five!). But overall his time, 22.3 minutes is exactly average.

*He has the lowest orgasm average for men, 1.7 per sex session. At either end of the scale, just one in every 100 Virgos don't climax at all, while the same number orgasm four or more times. 44% have one orgasm, 39% two, 12% climax three times and 3% manage a fourth.

*10% have been known to fake it, slightly less than average.

*Virgo has tried sensual massage more than any other sign (82%, and it's his second favourite overall, after oral sex 91%). On the other hand he's the man least likely to have worn sexy undies (34%). He's experienced less than average sex toys, bondage and partner-swapping—but more than average telephone sex and erotic videos.

*Of all men, he would like to try most sexual variations—over half all Virgo men (53%) want to be in a threesome, while he's also most interested in eating food off bodies, oral sex, erotic videos, spanking and paid-for sex. But rubber has less fascination for Virgo than all other male signs.

*92% appreciate a partner's sounds of pleasure and conversation during sex.

*He's least likely to imagine a partner is someone else (just 38% say yes to this question).

Virgo man—no-nonsense lover who toughly resists temptation, then kicks himself for doing so.

VIRGO WOMAN AND SEX

*Second hardest to arouse in the female zodiac overall, Virgo woman is still most turned on by massage (81%). Then she likes having her breasts caressed (75%) and slow dancing or a shared bath (both 69%). She shows well below average response to soft music and lights, a romantic meal, sexy call at work, touching her face, compliments or having her feet caressed... But least arousing of all for Virgo is playing sport—just one in 10 find this does anything for them.

*As sexiest setting, she's the woman who is second most positive about a room in a luxury hotel. But she's most negative towards a private flat with black walls, lit by candles.

*Floors, chairs and cinemas must get Virgo going—she's made love in all these more than other women. But bed is her number one choice (98%). She's had less than average experience of sex in the car, on the table, on the beach and in a changing cubicle. "I can happily experiment within my own home, but I get nervous outdoors or in public places," admits Irene, 43. "Yes, I might like to make love in the car—but only if it was in the garage.

*45% prefer the position of man on top, that's Virgo's number one choice. Next is oral sex (42%) and woman on top (41%). She's also keener than average on both standing and both lying on their side. But being face down or on hands and knees herself is a no-no.

*85%, joint top score for women, like to be caressed slowly and lovingly. "My boyfriend teases me with a feather until all my nerves are screaming for release," confesses one Virgo.

*27.5 minutes, just below average, is the amount of foreplay Virgo would prefer. 4% settle for none at all, 10% want five minutes, 38%, 15 minutes, 25%, 30 minutes and 23% hours and hours.

*But she does like the second longest penetration time of all women, 21.3 minutes. Yet 15% of Virgos, more than any other female sign, also make penetration last less than five minutes.

*At an average of two orgasms per lovemaking period, Virgo is in the upper range. 7% don't climax at all, 35% once, 33% twice, 10% three times and 13% four or more.

*26%, easily less than average, admit to faking orgasm on occasion.

*She's most likely of all women's signs to have tried sensual massage (77%). And second most likely to have sampled oral sex (89%). What has Virgo tried least? Threesomes and rubber (both 6%), partner-swapping (2%) and paid-for sex (1%).

*Ask what she'd like to try and the answer is the opposite of Virgo men—not a lot. Although Virgo is the woman most intrigued by threesomes (21% would like to try), she's least interested of all women in: sensual massage, sex toys, bondage, telephone sex, spanking and paid-for sex.

*88% do enjoy it when a lover expresses pleasure through sound. "But I do find it so hard to make a noise myself—it makes me so self-conscious," many comment.

*Exactly one in three, 33%, sometimes fantasise a partner is someone else.

Limited experience for the most traditional of signs—but Virgo woman likes love that way.

HOW DO THE SEXES DIFFER?

Although neither Virgo man or woman is overly adventurous, the men would like to try almost anything, while the women are happy as they are. Both prefer foreplay and penetration to last as little time as possible, and have a penchant for standing up sex. But Virgo females don't share the male sign's obsession with making love on the moors, nor do they get too enthusiastic about his favourite position, woman on hands and knees. And she still manages to have more orgasms...

LIBRA MAN AND SEX

*He's the man who likes massage best as a prelude to sex (88%).

Next best at getting Libra in the mood is a sexy movie (83%), then a shared bath (78%). But he also shows a definite preference for having his thighs, stomach and hair caressed! Libra is much less influenced by the outside trappings of seduction like a romantic meal or soft music and lights—and the words 'I love you' don't do too much for him either. But the hands-on approach works every time.

*When it comes to choosing a sexy love setting, however, Libra's well-known love of luxury does show. 49%, biggest vote of any male sign, is awarded by him to a top hotel with chilled champagne and satin sheets.

*He's made love in bed most of all men—100% answer yes to this section. And he's got passionate on the floor the most, too, on 97% yes. But Libra doesn't stop there. As the man who's road-tested the most love-locations, he's also ahead of the field in the bath, on a chair, in the kitchen, the park, the swimming-pool and on a plane. 7% of Libra men claim to have joined the mile-high club, easily more than any other sign. "Once you've done it once, you have to do it on every flight. It's certainly cured my air-sickness," comments Ricky, 32. And overall, there's nowhere that seems to dampen Libra's ardour...

*Woman on top is the most exciting position for 63% of Libra men, 62% like oral sex best and 51% woman on hands and knees. But compared to the other men in the zodiac, Libra has a definite penchant for woman face down, and sex sitting on each other's laps.

*85% like slow, subtle caresses.

*Instant sex is out for Libra—not one man from this sign who answered the survey said he prefers no foreplay at all. And with an overall average of 31.9 minutes, Libra is in the upper range. 11% opt for five minutes, 28% for quarter of an hour, 32% for half an hour and 29% want foreplay that goes on for hours.

*For penetration, however, Libra is in the lower range—his average is 21.3 minutes, a full minute less than the overall average. But one in five Libras (20%) does last between 31 and 60 minutes and that's more than any other man for this time band.

*1.7 orgasms per session, in the lower range is Libra's norm—but, lucky man, he NEVER fails to climax. He has the highest total for a single orgasm, 54%, then 30% for double ecstasy, 13% climax three times and just two in 100 four times or more.

*He's less likely than average to fake orgasms—just 9% of Libras admit they do. But since he already claimed he never fails to orgasm, someone is bending the truth somewhere...

*He evens out as the second-most adventurous sign in terms of what he's already tried. More oral sex than any other man, for starters (96%), more sex toys AND the most threesomes. The two sexual variations that have done least for him so far are wearing rubber and sexy undies.

*But even though he does have an above-average interest in trying these, Libra is in no doubt what his secret sex ambitions are—more than any other man, he longs to enjoy erotic videos and spanking. And even though he's already tried threesomes more than most, this is the one thing most Libra men dream of experiencing. The only thing on offer Libra definitely doesn't fancy is paid-for sex. "Maybe once, for novelty value, but I'd spend so long worrying whether I'd caught something it would spoil whatever pleasure I did get," says a 45-year-old Libra.

*93% like a partner to make sounds of pleasure during sex.

*44% have fantasised that a lover is someone else in the course of a sex act.

Anywhere, anyhow, but not just anyone—that's high-flying Libra man's love motto.

LIBRA WOMAN AND SEX

*Unusually among women, Libra's top turn on of all is having her breasts caressed (78%), followed closely by massage (77%) and a shared bath (72%). But the other things which work better for her than other women are: a romantic meal, holiday in the sun, sexy calls at work, compliments, hot dancing and a gift of flowers (28%, more than any other female sign, vote for this). "I never feel sexier than when I am on a pedestal, adored by a man who'll do anything to prove how he cares. It's the power of it, I guess," says Cara, 31.

*Sexiest setting? Yes, the luxury hotel again, permitting Libra to play the star for a day (or a night).

*She's the top woman for making love on the floor and the sofa—and on planes. But Libra also has more than normal experience of the bath, chair, table, park and swimming pools.

*Oral sex and man on top (both 46%) tie for most exciting sexual position in Libra's opinion. Next most thrilling is woman on top (37%). But she's also keenest of all women on manual sex and sex sitting on laps. Least popular with Libra is both partners standing up.

*83% prefer a lover's touch to be slow rather than firm and passionate.

*An ideal foreplay time of 28.7 minutes puts Libra in third place overall. 3% like none at all, 6% prefer five minutes, 38% 15 minutes, 29% half an hour, and 23%, just above average, opt for hours.

*For penetration time, however, she's third lowest, averaging 20.3 minutes. One in four Libra women go for 16-30 minutes, only one in 20 for over an hour.

*At 1.9 per session, her orgasm average is in the female middle range. 6% don't climax at all, 43% manage once, 23% twice, 14% three times and four is her lucky number—6%, more than any other female sign, achieve this many. Another 8% score more than four, too.

*31% answer yes when asked if they ever fake orgasm. That's more than average. "Mind you it can be harder work faking it than having the real thing," says one down-to-earth Libra woman.

*Libra's tried more sexy undies and love toys and less sensual massage and threesomes than other women. 87% have had oral sex, but only 2% have swapped partners, and half that have paid for sex.

*But she does enjoy sex toys—because that's one of the things Libra wants to try most. She also has the biggest attraction towards erotic videos, sensual massage and paid for sex, two of the areas where she has below-average experience. But a couple of things she definitely doesn't want to attempt are bondage and wearing rubber.

*87%, in the lower range, like to hear noise from a partner while making love.

*Only 28%, lowest score of all women, ever imagine a partner is someone else during sex.

Adore her, but never bore her, and Libra woman will share her adventurous love spirit.

HOW DO THE SEXES DIFFER?

Male and female Libras have more in common than many signs, including a liking for many and varied love-sites—and sex sitting on laps. But he goes for direct physical foreplay, while for her, setting the scene properly is the most vital first step. She is far more influenced by gifts and compliments. But both are the zodiac's leaders when it comes to passion on planes. Libra men and women are most intrigued by erotic videos, but three times as many men as women want to try spanking, while more females from this sign fancy paid-for sex than males do! That's very unusual.

SCORPIO MAN AND SEX

*Scorpio's not the easiest of men to arouse—the atmosphere must be right. More than any other man, he gets in the mood listening to soft music in a subtly lit room. Watching a sexy movie is his biggest turn-on of all (79%), then a massage (74%, but still lowest male score) or shared bath (73%). But chances of seduction success are above average with a shared shower, slow dance, and romantic meal, too.

*Luxury hotel is his idea of sex heaven.

*He's made love in bed the least of all men, just 93% say they have. So what about the other 7%...? In fact, Scorpio has had sex on the floor as often as he has between the sheets (also 93%). And another 91% have made out on the sofa "At a lunch party where everyone ended up diving into the pool, my boyfriend slid into me without bothering to do more than pull the crutch of my swimsuit to one side, we reached orgasm together while people around us threw a ball around," says one Scorpio. The car, kitchen, park, beach, and bus have also seen above average Scorpio lust scenes and he's had sex in swimming pools the most (18%) of all male signs.

*Woman on top gets Scorpio's vote for most exciting position (60%), then oral sex (55%) and woman on hands and knees.. But he also has a special liking for sex with a woman sitting on his lap...

*He likes fast, firm and passionate caresses more than most men—21%, over one in five, prefer the less-subtle approach.

*In an ideal world, Scorpio would get 31.6 minutes of foreplay, just slightly more than average. 2% want none, 11% ask for 5 minutes, 24% would like 15 minutes, 35% half an hour and 28% look for love build-up that takes hours.

*But it's a below-average time for penetration for Scorpio, of 21.1 minutes. Almost one in three Scorpio men keep going 11-15 minutes, more for this time band than any other sign.

*His orgasm count works out at 1.9 per time of love-making, that's joint highest of men overall. 3% have no climax, 42% one only, 30% have two and 17% (highest of all signs) achieve a triple. A further 9% come more than four times.

*10% fake orgasms sometimes.

*Scorpio isn't afraid to try new things in his sexlife—although he's the man least likely to have experienced oral sex (84%). Perhaps because his tastes are slightly more exotic—he's most likely to have tried bondage and wearing rubber. Plus Scorpio has above-average experience of sex toys, sexy undies and threesomes...

*More than any other man, Scorpio would like to swap partners, and he's also keen on spanking and erotic videos! But overall he's the man least interested in licking food off a lover's body. And most other possibilities hold less fascination for him than other men.

*93% like it when a partner's pleasure erupts into noise during sex.

*He's least likely of male signs overall to imagine a partner is someone else—just 38% say they do.

His taste for the unusual means Scorpio man may not settle for everyday sex.

SCORPIO WOMAN AND SEX

*When it's time to get in the mood, Scorpio is second most keen of all women on massage (80%), and most enthusiastic of all about her breasts being fondled (79%). But as the zodiac's most responsive female, she also thrills more than others to having her thighs caressed, soft music and lights, a shared shower, sexy phonecalls at work, touching her face, and playing sport. The only things that arouse below-average desire within Ms Scorpio are: a romantic meal, the words 'I love you', caresses on the hair, and a gift of flowers.

*Sexiest setting for Scorpio is a warm, deserted beach at sunset, lying half in the water. But she's also the woman who most would like a private apartment with black walls and candles everywhere.

*She's the woman who's made love in most places—by far. For Scorpio's had more experience than anyone else of sex on the floor, in the bath, in the shower, on the table, in the park, on the beach, in the swimming-pool, on the bus and in the cinema. The most surprising result in this section is that she is one of only three female starsigns who haven't had sex on a plane... This is one of only two locations listed where she's had sex less than average. The other? On the sofa. "Sofas are OK for teenagers, but if you're going to experiment, you may as well do it properly. Now a sofa in a furniture showroom, that would be worth trying..." says Lisa, 24.

*Number one sexual position for excitement is woman on top, says Scorpio, and gives it a 42% vote. Next most exciting is oral sex (40%), then man on top or woman on hands and knees (both 38%).

She's also more enthusiastic than other women about woman face down (26%) and sex when both partners stand (18%). But overall she likes sitting on her man's lap less than other female signs do. *81% prefer slow, loving caresses.

*4% like no foreplay at all, 14% (most of any female starsign) prefer just five minutes. For 33%, exactly one in three, 15 minutes is ideal, and another 29% opt for half an hour. But sexpot Scorpio can't wait to get on to the real thing—only 20% want foreplay to last hours. Her average time is third lowest overall, at 26.5 minutes.

*Penetration, though, is different—here Scorpio likes MORE than any other woman—three minutes more, in fact, than the next sign along—24.2 minutes in total. She's keenest of all women on 31-60 minutes penetration (20%) AND one hour plus (7%), and least enthusiastic about less than five minutes.

*So it's not surprising she has the most orgasms—an average of 2.1 per session. And one in 10 Scorpio women climax more than four times in a row. 5% don't orgasm at all, 35% climax only once, 31% twice, 13% three times, and 5% four times.

*She's least likely to fake it, too—only 23%, lowest score of all women, do so.

*She's tried by far the most sexual games and variations—more than any other woman, Scorpio has experimented with sexy undies, sex toys, eating food off bodies, bondage, spanking, telephone sex, and partner-swapping. In fact, the only thing she has tried less than average is wearing rubber.

*Rubber is just one of the things Scorpio shows above-average interest in trying, however—in fact, she is the woman who wants to try it most (21%). She'd also like to swap partners more than any other female sign, and has a relatively high attraction towards bondage, threesomes, oral sex and spanking. Given how much she's already done, however, it's no surprise Scorpio is the starsign least inclined to try eating food off bodies or watching erotic videos...

*88% like partners to put pleasure into sound, or to talk during lovemaking. That's right in middle range.

*36%, more than any other female sign, do fantasise their lover is someone else during sex.

Free and uninhibited Scorpio woman could have invented sex— but she never stops improving on it.

HOW DO THE SEXES DIFFER?
Both men and women born under Scorpio have an almost obsessive fascination for sex—but almost without exception it's the females of this sign that turn it into reality most often, and in most ways. Ms Scorpio is more easily aroused than her male mirror, has made love in even more places and more positions. She likes less foreplay and more penetration than Scorpio man, and has more orgasms. But unusually, both Scorpio sexes do agree on the position they find most exciting—woman on top...

SAGITTARIUS MAN AND SEX
*Looking at men across the zodiac, Sagittarius is more turned on by a shared shower (75%), and having his hair caressed (48%) than any other sign. He's second most keen on a sexy call at work and a gift of flowers, too. But number one trick to get him in the mood is to show Sagittarius a sexy movie (76%). "My own imagination is a bit limited, but when I get a 'start' with an erotic film, well, it makes all the difference. I can't wait to copy what I've seen," says one long-married Sagittarius.

*As his idea of the sexiest setting, he opts for a luxury hotel with all the trimmings.

*He's made love in more chairs than other men (63%). Because he finds it particularly erotic or because he's too lazy to move? But like almost everyone else Sagittarius has had sex most between the sheets (98%), followed by the floor (88%) and sofa (87%). Of all men, he's the one who likes the beach least, and he's less keen than most on swimming-pools and cars, too.

*Woman on top is the position he rates most exciting (61%), then woman on hands and knees (58%) and oral sex (57%). He's below-average in favour of being on top himself, but is the male sign most excited by manual sex. "It's fast, uncomplicated and doesn't involve thinking about anybody else," admits Ralph, 42.

*84% like caresses to be loving and slow rather than firm and passionate. That's slightly higher than average.

*He appreciates 32 minutes of foreplay on average, the third highest score among the men. Only one in every 100 Sagittarius men wants none—an unexpected result for the starsign always considered impatient. 6% prefer five minutes, 32% want quarter of an hour, and the same amount opt for half an hour, while 29% of Sagittarius men would like loveplay to last hours.

*Penetration, at 22.3 minutes is exactly average. But 11-15 minutes is the time band most Sagittarius men prefer.

*He averages 1.8 orgasms per session, but is the least likely of all men to manage three. 2% don't climax at all, 43% climax once, 39% twice and 7% three times. A further 2% orgasm four times and 6% even more.

*11%, in the middle range, have faked orgasm at some time.

*Sagittarius is not one of the zodiac's most experimental signs, but he has tried paid-for sex the most of any man! And he has above-average experience of spanking, telephone sex and wearing rubber.

*What would he most like to try? Even more spanking, it seems— 18%, most of any male sign, of Sagittarius want to give that a go. And he shows more than a middling interest in wearing sexy undies, oral sex and erotic videos, too. But Sagittarius is less intrigued than other men by threesomes, partner swapping and bondage.

*90%, second lowest score, like a partner to make sounds of pleasure while making love. "As long as it's my name she's calling," say many.

*38%, joint lowest male score, do sometimes imagine a partner is someone else while having sex.

Sagittarius man is less emotionally detached than he thinks—but still likes sex without strings sometimes!

SAGITTARIUS WOMAN AND SEX

*Like most women, Sagittarius gets in the mood most with massage, then caresses on the breasts and thighs. But like the men of her sign she likes to have her hair caressed (53%—more than any other woman), and she's top of the table for stroking of face and stomach, too. Compliments, the words 'I love you' and a holiday in the sun are some of the things that arouse her less than average.

*She overwhelmingly votes for a deserted beach at sunset as the sexiest setting imaginable (49%) and likes this location better than any other woman. But though Sagittarius is traditionally thought of as the outdoors sign, she's least keen of all females on a windswept moorland as a scene for love. "Too cold—the least you can be when you're making love is warm enough," shivers one comfort-loving Sagittarius.

*She's made love in bed more than any other woman (99%), but that's about the stretch of Sagittarius' adventurousness. For she's had sex less than any other women in the bath, the car, a chair and the kitchen, on the table, in the park, on the beach, in the office or a swimming-pool, on a train and in a changing cubicle or cinema. "I guess I'm all talk and not so much action," admits Jasmine, 21. "I do often pretend I've had more experience than I have, and though I like the idea of new places and techniques, I somehow end up doing the same old things..."

*Independence does shine through in Sagittarius' choice of most exciting position, however—she prefers to be on top herself (42%), then man on top (40%) and oral sex (39%—she likes this least of all women). But she is more enthusiastic than any other sign about sex sitting on her man's lap (30%).

*She's one of the women who likes fast, firm, passionate touching best—21% vote yes to this.

*28.6 minutes foreplay, above average, is her ideal. 4% go for no foreplay at all, and the same for five minutes while 41% (most of all women) opt for 15 minutes and 28% say 30 minutes. But another 23% would like to go on for hours.

*Penetration, however, on 20.7 minutes works out slightly below the female average. But one Sagittarius woman in every four lasts 11-15 minutes.

*She has an average amount of orgasms, 1.9 per love-making episode. 8% have none, 42% one, 26% two, 13% three, and 12% four or more.

*31% fake orgasms sometimes.

*She's tried the least sexual variations of all women, but the most oral sex. Erotic videos, sex toys, eating food off bodies and swapping partners have all been attempted by Sagittarius least across the whole female zodiac.

*But there's not that much Sagittarius wants to try, either! Though she does have a higher-than-average interest in threesomes,

telephone sex, swapping partners—AND she's the woman who would most like to try paid-for sex. But most other options do very little for Sagittarius woman.

*89%, in the middle range, like a partner to make sounds of pleasure in sex.

*34%, above average, do sometimes imagine their partner is someone else.

Not as sexually confident as she may seem, Sagittarius woman's hang-ups can come back to haunt her.

HOW DO THE SEXES DIFFER?
Men born under Sagittarius take more risks and are more adventurous than the women—but that wouldn't be difficult. But both sexes are more turned on than anyone else by having their hair touched and have a secret passion for sex sitting down. Both cite woman on top as their favourite position for excitement, but women find manual sex less fascinating than the men do. They like less foreplay, less penetration, but have slightly

more orgasms. And both Sagittarius sexes are the keenest in the zodiac to try paid-for sex.

CAPRICORN MAN AND SEX

*Capricorn is the second most difficult man to get in the mood. But his favourite turn-on triggers are massage (82%), then a shared bath (75%) and shared shower (74%). He also has above-average interest in slow dancing, having his thighs caressed, a holiday in the sun and the words "I love you." And surprisingly, he's the one man who gets most aroused by hot, fast dancing. But a sexy call at work or shared romantic meal does less for Capricorn than other men.

*Sexiest setting, votes Capricorn, is the luxury hotel with round bed.

*When it comes to trying different love locations, Capricorn finds himself in middle to lower range—and he is the only man who has never had sex on a plane. (Or is he the only one who's honest about it?) He's made love in bed most, then on the sofa and the floor. And Capricorn chooses chairs and trains as passion places less than any other starsign. The kitchen, park, table and bath are some of the places he has tried more than average.

*Most exciting position for him is woman on top (63%), then Capricorn likes woman on hands and knees (58%) and oral sex (57%). But traditional Capricorn is also the man most enthusiastic about being on top himself. "Why do I like it? Because it's easy, I suppose, and it's what I've always done," says Capricorn Ted, 61. And 32%, almost one in three, of all Capricorns agree. Another 24% are most excited by manual sex.

*86% say slow, gentle caresses are best.

*He likes an average of 30.5 minutes foreplay, that's below average—and Capricorn, least of all men, likes foreplay to last "hours." But no Capricorn admits to liking instant sex with no prelude, either. 6% opt for five minutes foreplay, 32% like 15 minutes, and 38% half an hour. "I'd need an oxygen mask to keep going that long," jokes Simon, 41.

*Of all men, Capricorn keeps up penetration the least time—19.8 minutes overall. And only four in 100 last longer than an hour.

*He averages a lower range 1.7 orgasms per love-making period. Just 1% of Capricorn men don't expect to climax at all, 45% count on once, 41% twice, 8% three times and just 4% four or more.

*He's the least likely man to fake orgasm (just 8%, compared to an overall average of 11%).

*In terms of adventurousness, Capricorn isn't a trailblazer, although he has had above-average experience of erotic videos, sex toys, telephone sex, and swapping partners. But he's also the man least likely to have tried sensual massage. Threesomes, spanking and bondage appeal to him less than others, too. Many Capricorns explain this by saying sex should be special—so they resist any more "sordid" impulses.

*What would Capricorn man like to try most? Sensual massage, say 46%, more than any other male sign, then threesomes and eating food off bodies. And he's quite interested in sex toys, oral sex, and phone sex (13%, highest score of any male sign).

*96%, above average, enjoy it when a partner lets rip with moans and groans.

*42% have imagined a sex partner is someone else on occasion.

Capricorn man is a solid lover who mixes raunch with respect and makes every sex occasion special.

CAPRICORN WOMAN AND SEX

*Slow dancing (75%) and a shared bath (74%) are Ms Capricorn's sure ways to get in the mood—she responds more to these two than any other sign does. She's also the woman who most warms to music and soft lights, and a holiday in the sun. But she's least turned on of all by caresses on her throat or stomach. Playing sport is her most unlikely turn-on, it scores just 10%.

*When it comes to sexy settings, give Capricorn a luxury hotel room every time—over half (51%) opt for this, with satin sheets and chilled champagne, of course.

*She's had sex more often on the floor and in kitchens and trains than other women, and the least of all starsigns in the car or bus. "Once my husband hoisted me on to the kitchen sink and we made wonderful love right on top of the washing-up," says Dawn, 31. "But we've got a dishwasher now, so I don't suppose we'll repeat that experience..."

*Man on top and oral sex excite Ms Capricorn equally (51%—in both she exceeds any other sign's score). And Capricorn is the woman who most enjoys sex with both partners on their side. But she's least interested in being on top herself (34%).

*79% like caresses to be slow, subtle and loving, that's in the lower range.

*She likes the briefest foreplay allocation of any woman, at 25.7 minutes, and Capricorn is by far least likely to want it to last hours! 4% opt for instant sex with more foreplay, 13% choose five minutes, 31%, 15 minutes, 39% half an hour.

*But although Capricorn is the keenest starsign on less than five minutes penetration, she averages out at 20.9 minutes, third highest overall.

*She's the woman most likely not to experience orgasm (9%). "I've been almost there so many times, yet I just can't seem to let myself go enough to reach total abandonment," says Helen, 32. 41% climax once, 27% twice, 10% three times, and 12% four or more. Her overall average of 1.9 is in the lower range for women.

*Does Capricorn woman ever fake orgasms? 34% say yes, second highest number of all women.

*She's watched more erotic videos, taken part in more threesomes and worn more rubber than other women, but she's been spanked and tried telephone sex least.

*As for what she'd like to try, 36% choose sensual massage, followed by 35% eating food off bodies and 25% sex toys. But, maybe because she's already sampled it, Capricorn lusts after threesomes least of all women. "I don't think I could bring another woman into my sexlife with my boyfriend—what if he fancied her more than me? Another man, now there's an idea ... but it's just not in my nature to be unfaithful, even while my lover is there," says one 28-year-old Capricorn.

*90% like to hear a partner express pleasure through sound during sex.

*33%, exactly one in three, do occasionally imagine a partner is someone else. That puts Capricorn in the upper range here.

Wild fantasies under a businesslike front, that's Capricorn woman's sex style.

HOW DO THE SEXES DIFFER?

Neither male or female Capricorns are fans of marathon sex sessions—they're least likely of all signs to want foreplay to last hours. And both are far more enthusiastic than average about the missionary position and would like to experience sensual massage most. But while Capricorn men like hot sexy dancing, the women prefer to take it slow and sensual. And women fail to reach orgasm nine times more than men (9% to 1%), but they are three times more likely to climax more than four times, too (12% to 4%). Capricorn females are generally more adventurous than males, and have made love in a wider variety of places, including aeroplanes...

AQUARIUS MAN AND SEX

*Caress Aquarius man's chest and pay him compliments while sharing a steaming tub and he's sure to get in the mood for sex— these are the three turn-ons he likes better than any other male starsign. But he's second most keen on a massage as a love-taster, too. And, perhaps showing the vulnerability beneath that cool surface, 48% feel aroused when they're told, "I love you." But soft music and lights, a holiday in the sun, having his feet caressed and playing sport raise below-average interest.

*Sexiest setting, he says, is a luxury hotel with all the trappings. "Whatever your background, you can be anonymous somewhere like that, and that's really liberating," says Aquarius Bob, 36. And he certainly isn't interested in a rugged, windswept moorland as a love spot.

*But Aquarius is the man most likely to have had sex in a changing cubicle (17%), plus on the sofa (94%), (that's 1% more than say they've had sex in bed), and on the table (53%). And 5% have made love on a plane, second highest male score overall. "It's the spontaneity that matters—no place will be sexy if you sit down and plan it in advance," says one Aquarius man. "We could be in a changing cubicle a dozen times and nothing happens. Then one day we're both in the mood and ..."

*It's rare for Aquarius to show below average interest in any location—but he does favour the kitchen less than most ...

*By far his preferred sexual position is woman on top, almost three-quarters (72%) of Aquarius men find this most exciting. And he's least keen of all men of being on top himself (18%).

*22% prefer fast, firm and passionate caresses—still not a majority, but more than most other men.

*His ideal time for foreplay averages out at 31.8 minutes, that's in middle to upper range. 1% like none (in a changing cubicle, for instance), while 8% go for five minutes. For 26%, 15 minutes is the preferred amount, 37% like half an hour and 27% want foreplay to last hours.

*But Aquarius does like the most penetration of all men—26.6 minutes. And one in 10 Aquarius men claim they keep going for over an hour.

*Perhaps this is because he's also the man most likely not to climax—7% of Aquarius men say they don't have an orgasm at all. Reasons given vary, from being so interested in a partner's pleasure they sidetrack their own, to inability to "let go" completely because they fear loss of control. 39% orgasm once, 34% twice, 12% three times and 8% four times or more. Overall average is 1.8 per session.

*Aquarius is the man second most likely to fake it, too, on 13%.

*Bondage, partner-swapping, paid-for sex and telephone sex are some of the things Aquarius has tried more than most men. And the only variations he has below-average experience of are erotic videos, sensual massage, spanking and threesomes.

*What would he most like to try? A threesome (38%) and a sensual massage (34%), but compared to other male signs Aquarius is one of the most fascinated by bondage and wearing rubber, too. "I'd like to be tied up and at someone's mercy, that way I wouldn't be responsible for what happened," says one. Aquarius is least enthusiastic zodiac man about trying sex toys, however.

*More than any other man, he likes his partner to make sounds of pleasure during sex (97%).

*45% do sometimes imagine a lover is someone else.

Aquarius man needs help to focus on his own pleasure—but has a taste for the unusual.

AQUARIUS WOMAN AND SEX

*Her arousal pattern follows that of most women—she likes massage best (76%), then caresses on the breasts (74%) and a sexy movie (72%). She's least turned on of all women by a gift of flowers or playing sport, but does show above-average interest in foot fondling and having her stomach stroked.

*Sexiest setting is a luxury hotel, but a warm deserted beach comes a very close second (42% to 41%).

*Her love locations are varied, but no one place stands out as a hot favourite. In fact she's made love less than most women in almost all the suggested places, except swimming-pools. And she's one of the three female signs who have never got aboard a plane. "While I like the idea of sex in different places, I just can't seem to cope with the reality," says Heather, 21. "I worry about looking silly or it being a disaster."

*She chooses man on top as the position that most excites her (42%)—but only just! For a close second comes woman on hands and knees (41%) and oral sex (also 41%). Of all women, Aquarius is most enthusiastic about the all-fours position—and about manual sex (23%). And she's the female sign who least likes both partners lying on their sides.

*82% prefer slow, gentle, loving caresses.

*She likes 28.7 minutes foreplay, third longest of the zodiac. And almost one in four (24%) want foreplay to last hours. 2% would ideally like none at all, 9% choose five minutes, 38% opt for 15 minutes and 27% half an hour.

*But for penetration she ends up with the second lowest overall time, 20.1 minutes. And, at just 4%, Aquarius women have the most negative view of penetration that endures for hours...

*7% have no orgasm, 39% one, 27% two, 14% three and 13% four or more. At two climaxes per session, Aquarius falls in the upper range.

*29% do sometimes fake it, that's below average for women.

*She's third most daring woman overall in terms of what she's tried—the only sexual variations she's experienced less than average are wearing rubber, oral sex and paid-for sex. But she's one of the biggest fans of sensual massage, bondage, spanking and swapping partners.

*There's nothing she is desperate to try compared to other female starsigns, but Aquarius does show a decided interest in erotic videos and wearing rubber. "I think it must be a sensation unlike any other, and to feel it all over your body..." says Jean, 40.

*87% like a partner to make sounds of pleasure, in the lower range.

*One in three, 33%, occasionally fantasise a partner is someone else.

Image versus imagination can be a constant passion battle for Aquarius woman.

HOW DO THE SEXES DIFFER?
Aquarius men have sampled sex in more unusual places than women, but it's the females born under this sign who long to try the most new things sexually. But their problem is converting ideas into reality. Ms Aquarius' favourite position is man on

top, but Aquarius man likes this least of all males. She's also far more keen on manual sex than him. He likes three minutes more foreplay and six minutes more penetration. He's the man most likely to make the sex act last over an hour, but she's the woman least likely to. But one of the few results they do share is lack of orgasm—7% of men, and women, say they never climax. And both are above-average keen on finding out what it's like to wear rubber.

PISCES MAN AND SEX

*Tactile Mr Pisces is the man most turned on of all by a shared shower, shared romantic meal and caresses on his face, throat, stomach and feet! But he does prefer reality to fantasy to get in the mood, and is the one man in the zodiac who likes a sexy movie least.

*Asked to choose his sexiest setting, Pisces opts for a top-flight hotel room. But he's also the man who awards the highest score to a private apartment with black walls and candlelight—showing something of a darker side?

*Pisces is a water sign, and he certainly likes that setting for love. More Pisces than other male signs have had sex in the shower (64%), on the beach (42%) and in a swimming-pool (18%). And he's also the man most likely to have made love in a train (21%). "There's something about the rhythm that really gets me going," comments one Pisces. "In a sleeper compartment I could keep going all night. Everyone wonders why my wife and I always take the train instead of flying. Especially when we always arrive at our destination looking exhausted because we haven't actually had time to sleep." In general Pisces has above-average experience of most love-locations, except the park and aeroplanes.

*Oral sex is the position he finds most exciting (58%), then woman on top (56%) and woman on hands and knees (49%). He, along with Aquarius, is the man least keen on the missionary position (18%), but he does like sex when both partners are standing.

*Pisces is the man who most likes fast, firm and passionate caresses

(26%). "It adds a certain air of urgency to sex that I like," says Callum, 24. "It's great to feel a woman can't wait to feel you inside her."

*Ideally, he would prefer 31.7 minutes of foreplay, that's mid to upper range. 4% want instant sex (second highest figure), 9% seek five minutes of foreplay. For 26%, 15 minutes is perfect, while another 30% choose half an hour and 30% want love play to go on for hours.

*Penetration time is in middle range, at 22.4 minutes on average.

*Pisces is the zodiac man least likely to orgasm four times (1%), but he's also one of just three starsigns who say they never fail to climax. 47% climax once, 38% twice, 10% three times, and 4% in all manage more than four orgasms during a period of love-making.

*One in 10 Pisces men admit they sometimes fake orgasm. That's slightly below average.

*What varieties of sexual fun and games has Pisces tried? Well, he's had more paid-for sex than almost every other man (17%, joint highest score with Sagittarius), and also has above-average experience of oral sex, erotic videos, sensual massage, sex toys, eating food off bodies, threesomes, swapping partners and wearing rubber. But he is the least likely man of all to have tried talking sexy on the telephone. And he's less keen than most on spanking and bondage. "I do find it hard to balance a loving relationship with things like spanking, but that's just me," says Pisces Jake, 31. "I think I would feel happier doing them with a woman I didn't know well, rather than my wife or girlfriend. But I'm too faithful to do that either."

*His lack of experience of bondage is the one thing Pisces would like to remedy—29%, more than any other male sign, admit they'd like to try it. And he's also the man second keenest on sampling three-in-a-bed sex. But that's about as far as Pisces' fantasies stretch, for overall he is the man who lusts after least in the zodiac. Pisces is less interested in trying sensual massage, erotic videos, sexy undies and telephone sex than any other man, and shows below-average desire for every other variation on offer too.

*A middle range 93% like a partner to make sounds of pleasure while making love.

*Pisces is the man most likely to turn a partner into someone else during sex—almost exactly half, 49%, confess to doing so. "When I close my eyes, my girlfriend can by anyone from Princess Diana to my old high school teacher, the one I discovered by accident never wore any panties. My imagination is my best sex aid of all, and it isn't hurting anyone," says one Pisces man.

Familiarity may spell frustration for Pisces man, but his rich fantasies rarely escape from his head.

PISCES WOMAN AND SEX

*What gets Ms Pisces in the mood? A tender massage, and a sexy movie (both 78%), and then caresses on her breasts (76%). And the two things she is more aroused by than other zodiac females are a sexy movie and hot dancing (36% of Pisces women rate this a top turn-on).

"My boyfriend and I play this game where we watch a red-hot film together on the couch, but we have to sit apart and not touch each other at all while it lasts," says Raquel, 26. "When we see the words The End we make a dive for each other and rip each other's clothes off..."

*She's the lady second most keen on a gift of flowers (26%), but rates playing sport least (8%) of all women.

*A warm, deserted beach at sunset, half in and half out of the water, is Pisces idea of sexual bliss (42% vote for this).

*Pisces has had sex on more sofas than most women (93%), in more swimming-pools (12%) and on more planes. Places she's made love less than average are few, but include kitchens and trains.

*Women on top is her most exciting sexual position (42%), and of all the zodiac's women, she's the one who rates the missionary position least (37%). And although she shows a preference for woman face down, she's least excited overall by both-standing sex and sitting on laps.

*22% prefer fast, firm and passionate caresses—most of all women.

*She would prefer an average of 27.6 minutes foreplay, in the mid to lower range. 2% request none at all, 10% like just five minutes, 35% opt for 15 minutes, 30% opt for half an hour and 21% think foreplay should last for hours.

*Penetration time is in the lower range again, at 20.4 minutes. More Pisces women than any other sign say they keep their man inside them for 16-30 minutes.

*Orgasms may disappoint Pisces. 9% never climax at all, highest score of all women, while 7% manage over four orgasms (lowest female result for this section). Pisces is also the woman most likely to climax just once (45%). And her overall average of 1.8 per session is lowest in the female zodiac.

*Could that be why she's also the most likely to fake orgasm? 35%, more than one in three Pisces women, do so. "After a while I feel bad my partner is holding back for me, or sacrificing his own pleasure", says one. "So I fake it to let him orgasm too. I am trying to be more assertive and selfish in sex, but it's an uphill struggle."

*So it may be a surprise to learn Pisces is the zodiac's second most experienced woman in term of what she has already tried. She's watched more erotic videos than most, had more oral sex, telephone sex, threesomes, partner-swapping and rubber. And there's not one of the suggested variations than Pisces has tried less than average. "Mind you, just because I've tried bondage or licking champagne out of my lover's navel, it doesn't mean I've enjoyed it," is one Pisces comment.

*Her current breadth of experience may explain why Pisces seems less interested than many signs in trying new things. But she does show a preference for sensual massage, erotic videos, telephone sex and paid-for sex. And she wants to wear sexy undies less than almost every other female sign.

*Pisces is the woman who most likes a partner to produce appreciative sounds of pleasure. "How else can I know if what I'm doing feels good?" asks one.

*She's also most likely to imagine a partner is someone else—36% do so.

Pisces woman may let a lover's desire push her up paths she'd rather not go—and stop her reaching the big O.

HOW DO THE SEXES DIFFER?

Pisces men and women have more similarities than many starsigns. They've both made love more than usual in swimming-pools (18% men, 12% women) and cite woman on top as their most exciting position. But the scores differ somewhat— 72% of men, and 42% of women! Overall, Pisces men and women are the ones who most want hard, urgent caresses (26% men, 22% women), and the most likely to imagine a sex partner is someone else while making love (49% men, 36% women). But they do differ on choice of sexy setting—she likes a beach more than all other women, he likes it less than all other men. And while Pisces women are most likely never to orgasm at all (9%), Pisces men are least likely (not one says he can't climax). But both are bottom of the zodiac table for multiple orgasm—7% of women and just 1% of men climax over four times per bout of passion. And Pisces women fake it over three times as much.

3

MARRIAGE

*WHICH STARSIGNS HAVE MULTIPLE
MARRIAGES * WHO MARRIES ONCE, BUT WOULD
NEVER DO SO AGAIN * WHO MARRIES FOR LIFE
* WHO NEVER MARRIES AT ALL * WHICH
STARSIGNS MARRY THE LOVE OF THEIR LIFE *
IS SEX BETTER IN SECOND MARRIAGES * WHICH
STARSIGNS ARE VIRGIN BRIDES AND BRIDE-
GROOMS * DOES MARRIAGE HAVE A GOOD OR
BAD EFFECT ON SEXLIVES
* THE 12 STARSIGNS' MARRIAGE PROFILES*

Is marriage still popular? In the survey, almost half the starsigns
have been married for 10 years or more. And most of them say
that being married has made their sexlives better. But astrology's traditional views of who make the best marriage bets are given
a shake-up by the survey. Who, for instance, would have picked out
Cancer men as the one starsign that marries six times? There are
also significant differences in the answers from men and women in
the same starsign.

WHO GETS MARRIED MOST OFTEN?
Grouping all the starsigns together, roughly a third of all men, and
the same number of women, marry more than once. But when the
figures are broken down by starsigns, a clear pattern emerges.

MEN WHO FIND ONCE IS NOT ENOUGH

The men most likely to get burned by a first marriage and then try again (and again, and again, in some cases) are: Cancer (43%), Aquarius (41%), Leo (39%), and Pisces (39%). And sexy Scorpio lives up to his intense, love-for-life image by being least likely to try multiple marriage (just 24% of Scorpio men have wed more than once). "Things may not always be brilliant, and yes, temptation is all around. But I believe marriage is for life," says one Scorpio husband. "And it deserves the effort." But, extreme as always, when he does embark on a search for perfection he can prove hard to please, making him one of the most likely five times or more serial husbands.

STARWATCH

Finding Cancer at the head of this list conflicts with traditional astrology's view of Cancer as the sign of marriage and lasting loyalty. It seems the water sign's romantic and idealistic side can overrule an inborn need for security.

FIVE TIMES A LIFE — AND MORE

Who are the men who marry most? Two in every hundred Gemini, Virgo, and Scorpio men have married five times, but when it comes to multiple weddings, Cancer man takes the lead again. For 3% of men born under the sign of Cancer have married five times, and a further 2%, six times or more. Cancer is the only man to appear in the six plus list.

CASE HISTORY OF A CANCER MAN

Cancerian Matthew, 45, is now happily married to wife number six, Helen, 29, a Taurus.

"I'm a driving instructor and several of my wives started off as my pupils. But we always had a very intense, romantic relationship before we had sex — I love all that hearts and flowers and secret meetings stuff. The forbidden element of sex is a real turn-on for me. But then, once we had slept together, to be honest I'd feel I had to do the decent thing and marry my girlfriend. Twice I broke up with my then current wife because I'd got a lover pregnant. And almost as soon as the next wedding was over, things would start to go wrong. And then another pretty pupil would come along...

"I suppose I was in love with the idea of love, not with real women. I picked dependent, possessive sorts of women who'd want me to look after them. Then I'd feel trapped. It was a really destructive pattern.

"I wouldn't say any of my marriages, until now, were truly happy. Except perhaps the first one — Eileen was my first girlfriend and we married when we were both 18. That lasted nine years, longest of them all. The others ranged from a few months to four years."

"I've got five children now in three different homes and a tangled web of maintenance and child support. It's a constant worry, especially since I want to do my best for all my ex-wives and families, and really try to get on with them all.

"Helen's a steady Taurus, and she has helped me see marriage can survive rocky patches without sinking. This time I'm determined to stick at it. We've only been married a year, so it's early days. But she's totally different to the others, she has her own career and I don't feel the need to 'look after her.'

"My mates find my marriage career a bit of a joke, but to me it's all too serious. I've left a trail of broken homes and broken hearts, and it's not something I am proud of."

WOMEN WHO WED MORE THAN ONCE

Which female starsigns are most likely to have multiple marriages? Aries (37%), Virgo (37%) and Scorpio (36%). And Leo ladies, starsign of loyalty and pride, may need their independence but are least likely to give up on matrimony. Only just over a quarter of Leo women have taken the plunge more than once. And they are also by

far the most likely starsign to stick at one partnership through thick
and thin (74%).

STARWATCH
**Virgo women leave other earth signs Taurus and Capricorn
standing —they are more than twice as likely to marry three
times or more. Perhaps traditional astrology should revise its
view of Virgo as homeloving and conformist.**

CASE HISTORY OF A VIRGO WOMAN
*34-year-old Janine, starsign Virgo, has just divorced her third
husband who is a Scorpio.*
"I'm looking for respect, commitment, romance, and satisfying sex,
but I just can't seem to find them all in one man. Each of my
marriages has started off well but gradually I've got bored, frustrated, or both, and started picking holes in my husband and our life
together.

"I couldn't go for counselling, I'd find it too embarrassing. And
with no children, it's easier to walk away and start again. My last
husband said I was cold and wouldn't try to compromise. He could
be right. Or maybe I'm just too fussy, and expect too much of
marriage."

WHICH WOMEN MARRY MOST?
For sheer number of ceremonies, independent Aries is out in front,
with 31% married twice, 4% married three times, 1% with five
marriages and a further 1% having six or more trips down the aisle.
But there may be a reason — Aries women are second most likely
to say marriage has made them more interested in sex. One in every
hundred Libra and Pisces women have also got through over six
husbands.

"My family have nicknamed me Liz Taylor because I've had so

many husbands," reveals 51-year-old clerical worker Marie, who is a Pisces. "I always marry for love, of course I do. But love just doesn't seem to last. Now my daughters are urging me just to live in sin if I meet someone new, to save myself the trauma of divorce. But that just wouldn't be right, would it?"

WHO STAYS MARRIED LONGEST?

When it comes to lasting matches, perhaps surprisingly, Libra leads in both men and women. A total of 57% of Libra men and 51% of Libra women have been married for 10 years or more. The sign least likely to stay the course is commitment-challenged Sagittarius, here matching the starsign's traditional astrological profile with just 37% of husbands and 35% of wives reaching the 10-year mark.

LONG-TIME MARRIED MEN

A sign by sign breakdown of men shows Libra (57%), Capricorn (55%), Taurus (52%) and Gemini (51%) are the best bets for more than a decade of marriage.

Least likely to make anniversary number ten are Virgo (42%) and Sagittarius (just 37%) men.

WIVES WHO MAKE IT LAST

While among the women, it's Libra (51%), Cancer (48%), Scorpio (46%) and Leo (45%) who survive the seven year itch to keep a successful marriage going.

Sagittarius (35%) and Gemini (34%) women are the wives least likely to last!

CASE HISTORY OF A LIBRA COUPLE

Libra couple Graham, 33 and Sharon, 32, have been happily married for 12 years.

"What's the secret of our success? Talking about anything and everything and stopping problems or arguments before they get out of hand," says Graham. "And we believe in giving each other a lot of freedom to have different interests and friends. Too much togetherness is so artificial and can be totally stifling."

Sharon, meanwhile, says romance and a touch of mystery are essential marriage elements, too. "We still surprise each other and take nothing for granted. And however much we love our three kids, we make sure we get away from them for a weekend just the two of us. It's easy for sex to become another part of home routine, with the shopping and cleaning. Something so special is worth more than that. We certainly don't have the perfect marriage, but it's the best we can make it!"

SINGLE MINDED — OR UNHAPPILY UNMARRIED?
Over half the replies to the AstroSex survey came from people not married at the moment—but feelings about this turned out to be very mixed. Comparing men and women, men were in almost all cases far more determined to stay single. Notable exceptions are Aries, where both sexes score 11%, and Sagittarius, where both score 12%.

But this is by no means a fire sign pattern, as fellow fire sign Leo throws up the biggest difference of all starsigns. A massive 29% of Leo men are happy never to marry, but for Leo women the figure is just 9%.

BACHELOR BOYS
Starting with the men, getting on for one in three Leo men are determined to give matrimony the cold shoulder, followed by Gemini (25%), Virgo (20%) and Libra (19%).

"I think marriage is out of date. If you need a piece of paper to keep you with somebody you shouldn't be together," says 26-year-old Leo man, Erroll. "I have a good relationship going at the moment, but marriage would just spoil it, start putting restrictions on what I can do and who I can see. I like my own place and my own space. It's only natural ..."

LADIES GOING IT ALONE

Among the women, restless Gemini is the most likely to want to stay single, with 12% saying they have no intention of getting married, ever.

And Gemini also has the lowest number of women who say they're single, but hope to marry one day (43%) plus one of the highest response rates to the question Married Once and Never Again (20%). Add this to the single figures and it means 32%, or almost one in three, Gemini women say no to marriage.

Other determinedly single females are Sagittarius (also 12%), Cancer (11%) and Aries (11%). Least keen on hanging on to the single status is Miss Pisces, with just 6%.

STARWATCH

While it's no surprise to find fiery Aries and Sagittarius, or flirty Gemini, relishing single status, once again "clingy" Cancer challenges traditional astrological thought.

CASE HISTORY OF A GEMINI WOMAN

Katie, 21, is a Gemini. She has just given up her banking job to go travelling

"I can't see myself ever getting married and playing the dutiful wife bit — I love my freedom too much. And however open a marriage may be, it still puts restrictions on what you can do and who you can see.

"I've been saving up now for a year so I can go and travel around South America, I did the same round Europe a couple of years ago. Can you imagine me doing that if I had a husband? He would just be another burden I don't need.

"I have had boyfriends, and I like sex as much as anyone, but I'm just not interested in getting serious. One lover bought me a 'surprise' engagement ring for my 18th birthday. But I think he got the biggest surprise when I finished with him there and then! My mum says I'm young and I'll change my mind one day, but I just tell her, don't hold your breath..."

WHO ARE THE SINGLE MEN WHO HOPE TO MARRY?

Out in front here is Capricorn, with almost one in two (49%) of the steady earth sign hoping to swap single life for marriage. But once Capricorn does take the plunge it may not work out so well — divorced or widowed Capricorn men are least likely to want to give marriage another go (just 17%). Single Scorpio males are also very keen on marriage (48%), along with Aries (48%), Taurus and Cancer (both 47%). But cautious Pisces likes the idea least of all, with just a 36% score.

WHICH WOMEN WANT A WEDDING?

Over half (53%) of all single Sagittarius women hope to marry one day, more than any other starsign. Yet Sagittarius also tops the list for single women saying they'll never marry! Sagittarius is nothing if not the starsign of strong feelings!

Pisces (52%), Taurus (50%) and Libra, Scorpio and Aquarius (all 48%) are next keenest on tying the knot. But true to form, only 43% of change-loving Gemini women are hoping to marry for the first time.

CASE HISTORY OF A SAGITTARIUS WOMAN

Sagittarius-born Eleanor, 28, works in a department store and is between boyfriends at the moment.

"I spend at least one lunch break a week in the bridal department of the store where I work, looking at the latest dresses and head-dresses and planning what I'll wear when I walk down the aisle. I want the works — attendants, pageboys, masses of flowers, a horse-drawn carriage, and of course a wonderful long white dress. Unfortunately, I need a fiancé first!

"On the surface I'm quite a strong, independent person, but I do have a deeply traditional streak that makes me long for a special day to start a lifetime of romantic togetherness. Yes, it's idealistic, but what the hell?"

ONCE SMITTEN, TWICE SHY

Who has tried marriage, and now swears never again? Over one in five of all Sagittarius men, followed closely by Scorpio (19%), Pisces (17%) and Aries (17%). These starsigns all exhibit an element of perfectionism, which could explain this trend. And they may well also share a tendency to stay bitter over bad marriage experiences.

"I gave her everything, and she still left me," laments one Aries ex. "So now I'm happy to play the field. Why should I want to put myself through that again?"

But it's no surprise to discover the AstroSex king of multiple marriages, Cancer man, is least likely to say once is enough (only one in 10).

WOMEN UNWILLING TO WED AGAIN

Second, third, or more chances at matrimony are least likely to be attempted by Virgo women, an astounding one in four of whom admit, "Yes, I've been married before, but never again!"

That's a full 5% more than any other female starsign, and 9% more than Virgo males. Also unwilling to take the plunge more than once are Gemini (20%), Aries (19%) and Scorpio (19%) women.

HOPING FOR HAPPINESS SECOND TIME AROUND

It may have eluded them before, but Pisces and Aquarius men don't give up hope of happy, lasting marriage. A total of 32% of Pisces males, and 30% of Aquarians, say they've been married before and hope to wed again. And 29% of home, and security-loving, Taurus men feel the same way.

Capricorn brings up the rear in this category, with just 17% eager to take the plunge again. Leo scores a low 19% and Scorpio 21%. Perhaps the one thing these signs have in common is pride, which makes failure difficult to accept ...

CASE HISTORY OF A TAURUS MAN

High school teacher Leon, 39, is a Taurus. Last year he was widowed after 15 years of happy marriage to a Leo.

"I think it's a tribute, not an insult, to my late wife Gina that I am very keen to marry again. Although it may seem callous to some people that I have joined an introduction agency so soon after Gina's death, I've done it because I miss the happiness we shared so much. And I want to have that back in my life.

"Marriage is man's natural state, it provides a secure base and loving support on which to build a successful life. I really do believe that. And though of course no one could ever replace Gina, I hope to experience again the sort of marriage we shared for so long. I know I have her blessing, and her support."

DO WOMEN WANT WEDDING NUMBER TWO?

On the whole, women who have tried marriage are slightly more likely than men to want to have another go, with an average of 26% of women from all starsigns hoping to wed again, compared to just 24% of men.

And way out in front of other women is rock-solid Capricorn, with 33%, or one in three, hoping to marry again. "My marriage was far from perfect, but now, three years on, I wish we hadn't divorced," says one Capricorn lady. "If I had a second chance I'd be less stubborn and less cautious. I was always so afraid of showing how vulnerable I was."

Hopefully she can get together with one of the 49% Capricorn never-married men who also dream of saying "I do."...

Next in the queue for a second shot at wedded bliss are Libra, Leo and yes, Cancer again, all with 27%.

Bottom of the list is Virgo, with just one in every five reckoning matrimony is worth another chance.

STARWATCH
Most likely by far to say "never again", least likely to dream of a happy ending, Virgo women seem even more disillusioned by love than conventional astrology might expect. Or have they broken their star profile and been first to say no to the traditional restrictions of marriage?

WHO MARRIED THE LOVE OF THEIR LIFE?
"She was blonde, beautiful, bright—and lived next door. I worshipped and adored her and sent her an anonymous Valentine's card every February for years. Then one Christmas we kissed under the mistletoe and I plucked up courage to ask her to a movie.

"We went out for nine months and they were the happiest of my life. It's over 10 years ago now and I can still remember the way her skin smelt the first time we slept together. We were both virgins and sex wasn't wonderful straight away, but we were so in love it didn't matter.

"Then she went away to college and met someone else. She was the love of my life and there's still a part of my heart that aches for her. I'm happily enough married now, but what I have with my wife isn't the same. I wish it was ..."

Pete, a 27-year-old Aquarius man, admits he didn't marry the love of his life—and he is certainly not alone. The AstroSex survey revealed that, sadly for romance, the majority of people of all signs and both sexes (51% of men and 52% of women) say they did not marry their one true love.

And the reasons they gave were many, from one partner being already married, to being too young or love alone not being enough to base a future on. But their true love has certainly never been forgotten...

On the male side, Aquarius men like Pete are least likely to have married the love of their life. A staggering 59%, almost three out of five, answered no to this question. But Capricorn was not far behind with 58%, nor Libra men, who scored 55%. The starsigns who did manage to marry a dream lover are Pisces, way out in front with 58% answering Yes, and, a touch surprisingly, Aries men — 54% say they married the love of their life.

STARWATCH
More Aries men than average admitting they married their true love questions astrology's accepted passion profile of Aries as wild womanisers seeking excitement, not stable romance...

WHICH WOMEN WED THEIR ONE TRUE LOVE?
More women born under the starsign of Taurus claim to have married the love of their life than any other. This sensuous but faithful sign scores 54%...

CASE HISTORY OF A TAURUS WOMAN
Lorraine, 41, is Taurus and works as a barmaid.
"As soon as I met Billy-Joe, a Scorpio, I knew he was the only one for me. He came into the bar where I was working at the time, and pow! Before he'd even spoken to me I knew we had to be together.

"Our thoughts and emotions are so in tune I'm convinced we loved each other before in a past life. And although we were both involved with other people at the time, we went home together that night and haven't been apart since. We got married just two weeks after we met. And yes, 20 years on, he's still the love of my life!"

Fellow earth signs—who might be expected to be steadier and more romantic in love—also score above average Yes answers to this question, Capricorn (53%) and Virgo (50%). But fickle, demanding fire signs all come in below average, with Aries scoring 45% Yes and Leo and Sagittarius both 43% Yes.

But the woman most likely NOT to have made a match with the man of her dreams is poor Gemini. Almost six out of ten female Geminis admit no, they didn't marry the love of their life.

WHO WAS STILL A VIRGIN WHEN THEY MARRIED?

Staying pure until the honeymoon is undoubtedly not expected today. For over all the AstroSex subjects, with ages ranging from 16 to over 50, only an average of 13% of men and 14% of women were still a virgin when they got married. But there are still a few unexpected results in store looking at each sign, and each sex, in turn.

MEN WHO SAY NO

The man most likely to save himself for his wedding night is not among the romantic water signs Pisces or Cancer, although both score a high 19%.

No, most intent on preserving his virginity for his Mrs Right is Gemini man with a score of 21%, or more than one in five, virgins when they marry. Other air signs are more inquisitive, with just 7% of Libra men marrying with their virginity intact. And curious Aquarius is least likely of all starsign men to be prepared to wait. Just three in every hundred Aquarius men are virgins when they say "I will."

CASE HISTORY OF A GEMINI MAN

Gemini-born Dexter, 33, is getting married next year, to Sheila, another Gemini, and will be a virgin when he does so.

"I'm a committed Christian, but that's not the reason I believe in keeping sex for marriage. I just think something so special and sacred should be kept for the person you're going to spend your life with. Promiscuity cheapens it and would leave a lifelong blot on my conscience.

"But don't think I'm some sort of dull goody-goody! I'm quite a flirtatious person and I've had lots of girlfriends. And I certainly fool around now with my fiancée Sheila, who is also a virgin, but we both hold something back. It's not always easy, but it makes the promise of passion to come even more exciting.

"Of course I sometimes wonder what I'm missing — I wouldn't be human if I didn't. But I could say the same about drugs, and I don't go rushing off to try them, do I?"

STARWATCH
Cool, casual Gemini the keenest of all men to enter marriage a virgin? Traditional astrology might have problems explaining that away...

LADIES IN WAITING
Starsign Virgo tops the table of women willing to wait for sex until after their wedding, with 19%.

"I'm so glad I waited," says one Virgo newlywed of a few months. "Although my wedding night was a strange mixture of sheer shock — and, eventually, pleasure. I know I have a lot to learn about sex, but my husband is the best teacher I could wish for."

Among the women it's high-principled Leo and Aries that come next, with 18% and 17% respectively. But like the men, for the lowest number of virgin brides, look no further than experimental Aquarius. At eight in every hundred, the number of Aquarian virgins marrying is way below that of any other starsign.

"I saw my virginity as an unwanted encumbrance, I guess," says

Aquarian Patsy, 42. "And I was 16 when I set out to rid myself of it. It wasn't perhaps the most romantic of encounters, but it was such a relief afterwards that I'd 'done it' and joined the club! I had lots of lovers before I married my husband, and I think the experience has made me better in bed. I've certainly never had any complaints!"

Libra and Capricorn women both scored 11% Yes on this question. Like Aquarius, these starsigns are perhaps more practical than romantic in their approach to love, and life.

DOES BEING MARRIED IMPROVE SEXLIFE?

Yes, marriage makes sex better, is the resounding reply from the majority of men and women of all starsigns. Although a significant number also said it had made no difference to their love-making.

MEN RATE SEX AFTER MARRIAGE

Looking first at the men, Scorpio leads the way with over one in two singing the praises of the marriage bed (58%). Next comes security-loving Pisces (55%), Leo (52%) and Gemini (49%).

Yet Scorpio men are also second most likely to say marriage makes sex worse (21%), and least likely of all to say it has stayed the same (21%). So it seems love is all or nothing for this intense starsign.

By far the most dissatisfied husband of all, however, is Virgo — over one in four reveal being married has made their sexlife worse, just 38% say it has improved, and 36% opt for no change. The starsign of high standards may find them just too difficult to meet.

CASE HISTORY OF A VIRGO MAN

Virgo Robbie, 28, has been married to Francine, also 28 and a Capricorn, for three years.

"It's not that I love Francine any less now we're married, it's just sex has lost all the excitement and urgency it used to have when we were dating. We lived in different cities and snatched sex sessions anywhere, any time, we could. We just couldn't keep our hands off each other.

"I know it's unrealistic to expect that to continue after marriage, but without that excitement sex seems such a non-event. And I've found sharing the everyday aspects of life together—watching Francine shave her legs, or seeing her in a face-pack, for instance, a real turn-off. All the mystique has gone and with it most of the attraction."

WIVES REVEAL ALL

Happiest about sex within marriage are Taurus women, 55% say being wed has improved sexual relations. And just 16% say sex has got worse within a marriage. Surprisingly, next in line is cool Aquarius, scoring 52%, Scorpio (51%) and Leo (50%). Earthy Capricorn, however, likes the status quo — 43% of Capricorn wives say lovemaking has stayed the same, and they are least likely of all the starsigns to see an improvement (40%).

But when it comes to sex actually getting worse after the wedding, look no further than Gemini women—almost a quarter say marriage has made their sexlife worse. And 22% of Aquarius and 20% of Aries women say the same thing. But is this really a surprise from starsigns known for their love of variety, low boredom threshold, and tendency towards selfishness?

DOES REMARRYING MAKE SEX BETTER, OR WORSE?

All starsigns show the advantages of learning from experience, with the vast majority of both sexes saying sex gets better in a second or subsequent marriage. In fact the lowest Yes figure in the response to this question is 70%, given by Leo women, and Libra and Virgo men. In general, women are more likely than men to say remarriage makes for better sex, except for one noticeable exception. While Leo men are most likely to say sex is better second time around, (88%), Leo women are least likely to say it (70%)!

MEN AFTER REMARRIAGE

Most satisfied with second marriage sex are Leo men, closely followed by Capricorn (82%) and Pisces and Aries (both 81%). But even when they get a chance to try again, Virgo men are still most dissatisfied—30% said remarriage hadn't improved sex. And Libra figures were exactly the same.

WOMEN ON SECOND SEX

Nine out of ten Sagittarius women who have remarried say it has made sex better — a massive majority even for this positive sign. The most common reasons given are more experience, less inhibitions, and feeling more committed and secure.

And Taurus scores high too, with 88%, followed by Pisces with 87%. These are all starsigns who value loyalty highly and share a strong streak of romance.

CASE HISTORY OF A LEO WOMAN

Claudia, 35, is Leo and married for the second time last year to Cancer-born James, 40. They have five children between them.

"You know that rhyme, there were 10 in the bed and the little one said.... well, that could be our house some mornings, and some nights, too. James and I never seem to be alone together between the sheets, what with children, stepchildren, dogs, cats — you name it — wanting to snuggle up to us!

"So no, I wouldn't say sex has got better since our marriage — the second for both of us. In fact, it's all but disappeared! But we've been so busy building our new family together it hasn't mattered too much.

"We cling to the hope that things can only get better — once we buy a bolt for our bedroom door!"

THE 12 STARSIGNS' MARRIAGE PROFILES

ARIES MAN AND MARRIAGE

*66% marry once, 30% twice and 4% of Aries men have been wed three times. This puts them in the middle range. 44% have stayed wed 10 years or more. Just 11% are single and want to stay that way. The lowest response of all starsigns. "I like being looked after," admits one Aries man honestly. 48% are single and want to marry.

*17%, the third highest number, are determined never to wed again. As one Aries commented: "Marriage may be a national institution, but so is the prison system. Who wants a life sentence in either?"

*24% have been married and hope to marry again one day.

*54% of Aries men married the love of their life, in this they are the second luckiest starsign.

*16% were virgins when they got married, 45% say being married has improved their sex life. 16% say the opposite. 81% reckon being remarried makes for better sex.

ARIES MAN likes the idea of marriage but may like the reality less. If it works, wonderful. If it doesn't, he walks.

ARIES WOMEN AND MARRIAGE

Aries women have the second lowest number of first marriages (63%), and the highest of second marriages (31%). Plus 1% have been married five times, and another 1% six times. Aries is the most likely of all females starsigns to marry more than once (37%).

*40% have been married 10 years or more, slightly below average for all starsigns, 11% intend never to marry, exactly the same as Aries men.

*45% are single and hope to marry, 19% say they'll never marry again.

*26% have been married and want to repeat the experience.

*45% married the love of their life.

*17% were a virgin on their wedding night, "And I was so uptight I almost stayed a virgin that night, too," confesses one Aries virgin bride.

*48% reveal marriage has improved their sexlife. 20% say it's made sex worse. Their main reasons are boredom, lack of variety, husbands letting themselves go...

*Of those who have remarried, 79% reckon sex is better second time around.

Less inclined to marry at all, when ARIES WOMAN does take the plunge it can become a habit.

HOW DO THE SEXES COMPARE?

Aries women are more likely than Aries men to have multiple marriages, and less likely to stay married more than 10 years. Women are also less keen on second marriages. Aries men, meanwhile, are almost 10% more likely to marry the love of their life, but less likely to say sex gets better after marriage. Still, they're also less likely to say it gets worse. Numbers of Aries wedding day virgins are the same for both sexes.

TAURUS MAN AND MARRIAGE

*70% have had just one marriage, 23% two, and 4% three marriages. Overall, Taurus man's chance of marrying more than once is second lowest, at 29%. "I don't believe in giving up, things can always get better," says a Taurus hubby of seven years.

*An above-average 52% have been married over 10 years.

*12% are determined to stay single, 47%, the fourth highest result, are single but dream of marriage. Just 12% say marriage has put them off for life, one of the lowest results.

*And 24% have been married and hope to marry again one day. "But it would have to be to the right person, I'm in no rush," is a common Taurus comment.

*52% married the love of their life.

*17%, in the higher range, were virgins when they married.

*An average 47% say sexlife improved within marriage, while 17% reveal it got worse.

*71% in second or subsequent marriages say sex is better this time. That's at the lower end of the scale.

TAURUS MAN is loyal, faithful and more likely to weather any storms than cut and run. In love with love — and marriage.

TAURUS WOMAN AND MARRIAGE

*69% have taken the plunge once, 26% twice and 5% three times — Taurus women have a 31% chance of marrying more than once, fourth lowest of women overall. 42% have been married more than 10 years. "I'd like to leave, but habit has become more important than happiness," admits one Taurus long-term wife.

*A middle range 9% set their sights on staying single.

*A high 50% say marriage is their goal, 18% of Taurus women have tried marriage, and now say never again.

*22%, one of the lowest figures, say past matches have failed but they'll try again. "I'm amazed life alone can be so fulfilling and complete," says one. "I might want a man again, but I won't need one."

*54%, more than any other female starsign, married the love of their life. A below average 11% saved themselves for their husband and their honeymoon.

*Enthusiastically, the top score of 55% say sexlife has improved after marriage. And Taurus is second most likely to say remarriage has made sex better (88%).

Romantic yet realistic, TAURUS WOMAN will wed her true love first or second time around — but not as a virgin!

HOW DO THE SEXES COMPARE?

Taurus men are 10% more likely than Taurus women to pass their 10th wedding anniversary, and they're 6% more likely to be virgins when they marry. Both sexes believe in romance and blossom within marriage, but women are far more inclined to say sex improves within marriage (55% women to 47% men). And they're 17% happier in bed second time around, too.

159

GEMINI MAN AND MARRIAGE

*69% of Gemini men score one marriage, a low 23% marry twice, but 6% wed three times and a further 2% five times.

*Giving Gemini an overall chance of 32% of marrying more than once. Perhaps surprisingly for this famously flirty starsign, that's lower than average.

*An above average 51% of Gemini men have been married over 10 years.

*25%, second highest total of all men across the zodiac, vow to stay single for life.

*And 38%, one of the lowest figures, are single yet hope to marry.

*16% have been husbands before, but now swear "never again."

*And 22%, in the lower range, do want to give marriage another try.

*Only 45% of Gemini men married the love of their life. "I didn't realise she was, until it was too late," one admits. A much-mentioned reason is not feeling ready for commitment at the time.

*Of all the male starsigns, Gemini is most likely to stay a virgin until marriage—a surprising 21%. "There are far more important factors involved in choosing a life partner, like intelligence, humour, friendship," says one. "Sex is really irrelevant." But... 49% say marriage has improved sexlife, and just 11%, lowest number of all, say it's made it worse.

*But 78% reveal remarriage improves sex.

Against marriage in principle, GEMINI MAN finds it more satisfying than he expects, with sex well worth the wait!

GEMINI WOMAN AND MARRIAGE

The mirror image of Gemini men, 69% of women have also wed once, 26% twice and 5% three times. That gives them a 31% chance of marrying more than once. But just 34% have stayed married 10 years or more, lowest of all women. 12% are determined to stay single, more than any other woman in the zodiac.

*And Gemini brings up the rear, too, among women who are single but long to marry—for this starsign, just 43%.

"Why marry? It would only cramp my style and restrict my freedom," says one single Gemini.

*20%, or one in every five, Gemini women has been married but won't do it again! But another quarter (25%) hope to give wedded bliss another go.

*Just 41% married the love of their life, lowest number of all.

*A below average 12% were virgins on their wedding day.

49% say sex has improved within marriage. But a high 24% say it's got worse.

*Sex is better second marriage around for 79% of Gemini women.

Freedom loving GEMINI WOMAN wants to stay that way and can find traditional marriage stifling — and tedious.

HOW DO THE SEXES COMPARE?

Both cherish single status, and though roughly the same numbers of men and women marry, Gemini men (51%) have a much higher chance of staying married than Gemini women (34% last 10 years). And the women are far more likely to be put off marriage by a failed attempt. One area men score highly in is virginity — 21% are virgins on their wedding day compared to just 12% of women. And Gemini women are also more susceptible to boredom within marriage — 24% say sex has got worse since the wedding. But only 11% of Gemini men agree...

CANCER MAN AND MARRIAGE

Once just isn't enough for Cancer men. Only 57% have stopped at one wedding, 36% have married twice, and 2% three times. But Cancer man also scores 3% with five marriages and another 2% married six times or more. At 43%, his chance of multiple marriage is higher than that of any other starsign. "But I do make a brilliant bridegroom's speech," says one Cancer man on his third marriage. "I ought to, I've had enough practice!"

*An average 45% have made lasting marriages of over 10 years.

*19% are single and hope to stay that way.

*47% would like to marry one day.

*10% (lowest figure) have been put off marriage for life. "Each time a new relationship starts I think, this time I'll make a go of marriage," says one more hopeful Cancer man.

*24% are out of marriage now but hope to be in it again one day.

*An average 49% married their true love.

*19%, the second highest figure, were virgins when they married.

*44% say marriage has perked up their sexlife, but a high one in five (20%) say it's had the opposite effect.

*80% rate sex more highly after remarriage.

CANCER MAN finds variety is the spice of wife — and tends to go for quantity, not quality, in marriage.

CANCER WOMAN AND MARRIAGE

*67% marry once, 26% twice, 5% marry three times and 2% go for four weddings. That gives Cancer woman a one in three chance of marrying more than once.

*But Cancer wives have staying power — almost half (48%) have passed the 10-year mark. "I was born to look after people, I have to be married," say many.

*11% are singles, set on never marrying.

*47% are single but do hope to wed.

*16% have tried marriage, and been put off for life.

*But 27% still want to remarry, even though they've failed once. That's the second highest result of female signs.

*52% married the love of their life.

*15% were virgins when they got married. But although she's keen on marriage, it may not match up to Cancer women's expectations — a low 43% claim marriage improved sexlife. Although 38% do say the ceremony had made no difference.

*79% said sex was better for them in second or subsequent marriages.

Whatever marriage throws at her, CANCER WOMAN never stops believing it's worth the effort.

HOW DO THE SEXES COMPARE?

Both are the marrying kind — Cancer man perhaps too much so! And it's the women's marriages that are more likely to last, although they are less keen on marrying again. Cancer men are more likely to be virgins on their wedding night (19% men to 15% women). But Cancer women marry their true love more often (52% women compared to 49% men).

LEO MAN AND MARRIAGE

*First marriages number 61%, second 33%, third 5% and fourth 2%. At 40%, Leo man's chance of multiple marriage is third highest of all men in the zodiac.

*44% have stayed wed for over 10 years.

*29% are single and want to stay that way, thankyou. That's a full 4% higher than any other male starsign. "I can give love without giving my name, my apartment or my car," says a 27-year-old bachelor Leo. "I've seen too many women out to get what they can from marriage."

*Only 38% are single and hope to marry. That's the second lowest figure overall.

*13% have been put off marriage by past bad experiences.

*19%, second lowest again, have been burned before but would still wed again. "Marry again? I'd rather sail the Atlantic in a sieve," comments one Leo.

*An above average 52% did marry the love of their life.

*On the low side, just 9% were virgins on their marriage.

*But a high 52% reckon lovemaking is better within the bonds of matrimony.

*Leo is most likely (88%) to find sex improves following remarriage. "I think less of my own pleasure now, and more of my partner's."

Confirmed bachelor boy, LEO MAN still has a strong streak of respect, and is ready to learn from mistakes.

LEO WOMAN AND MARRIAGE

Way out in front in the once-only marriage stakes — Leo woman chalks up 74% married just once. Just 19% have been married twice, 5% three times, 1% four times and a further 1% five times.

This gives Leo women the lowest chance of all female starsigns of multiple marriage, at 26%. "I'm loyal, and I believe vows are for life. I'd let myself down if I broke them," says a 36-year-old Leo wife.

*But does it last? Yes, at least for the 45% who've been married over a decade.

*9% of Leo women vow to stay unmarried.

*46% are single but want to wed.

*18% promise themselves never again after past marriage mistakes.

*Yet 27% still hope to find happiness in remarriage, the second highest number.

*A low 43% claim to have married the love of their life.

*And 18%, second highest number, were still a virgin when they got married.

*Exactly half, 50%, rate marriage as an improver of their lovelife. And Leo women are among the least likely to say sex got worse in marriage — just 14%.

*Remarriage is a different story, however. 70% do say it makes sex better, but this is way below all other signs.

LEO LADY is a one man woman, willing to try anything once. Lion-hearted pride keeps the ring firmly on her finger.

HOW DO THE SEXES COMPARE?

Leo women are more likely to stick marriage out through thick and thin—and to see it as desirable in the first place. Just 9% of Leo women want to stay single, but 29%—a full 20% more —of Leo men cherish their bachelor status. But Leo men do marry the love of their life more often, and fare better sexually in second or subsequent matches.

VIRGO MAN AND MARRIAGE

It's first time lucky for 71% of Virgo men, while 25% marry twice, 2% three times and 2% five times. This adds up to a 29% chance of Virgo man marrying more than once, and puts him low on the marriage risk register.

*Yet only 42%, second lowest of the zodiac, have been married 10 years or more.

*20%, one in every five Virgo men hope to stay single.

*41% are unmarried now but don't want to stay that way.

*16% vow never again after past marriages and 23% still hold out hope for happiness through remarriage.

*49% married the love of their life.

*14% (slightly above average) were virgin bridegrooms.

*Only 38% of Virgo husbands have found marriage a sexlife-enhancer. That's the second-to-bottom result. And more Virgo men than any other male starsign say marriage has made loving worse—a total of 26%. "I plan a seduction scene, and we're just at the crucial moment when the kids wake up and ruin it. It's easier not to bother," grumbles one.

*Remarriage doesn't fare much better. 70% of Virgo men say it perks up sex, that's less than any other men's sign.

A steady marriage bet, but VIRGO MAN may end up just going through the motions.

VIRGO WOMAN AND MARRIAGE

*Just 63% marry once, second lowest figure, 25% marry twice — but Virgo women are most likely to marry three times, with 11% — and a further 1% go on to wedding number four. And overall, Virgo has the highest chance of all women of marrying more than once (37%).

*42%, in the middle range, have been married 10 years or more.

*10% are determined never to marry.

*44% are single but long to become Mrs.

*One in four, 25%, have been married and now say never again —

and that's a clear 5% higher than any other female starsign. "Now I know what I'm missing... I'm more than happy to miss it!" comments one bitter ex-wife. And just 20% think marriage deserves another chance — that's LOWER than any other female starsign.
*Exactly half, 50%, married their true love.
*19% were a virgin on their wedding day, again more than any other sign. "I wouldn't have settled for anything less," is the most common reason.
*Below average 47% of Virgo women reckon marriage has made sex better. But 78% do say lovemaking improved after second or subsequent matches.
VIRGO WOMAN has high ideals and high standards that may be hard for marriage to meet.

HOW DO THE SEXES COMPARE?
Marriage stands the same chance of long-term success for both Virgo men and women (42%), but in general the women are a much higher marriage risk than the men. Virgo woman's overall chance of multiple marriage is 37%, Virgo man's only 29%. Twice as many men as women want to stay single, but once they've tried marriage, many more women (25%) than men (16%) say, "Never again!" Yet ironically Virgo women have a greater chance of better sex if they remarry.

LIBRA MAN AND MARRIAGE
66%, two in every three, marry just once, 28% wed twice and 6% manage three marriages. That places Libra man in the middle range.
*He's tops for sticking power — 57% of Libra men have passed their 10-year anniversary, the number one score. "Each year that passes, I love her more," says one Libra-born romantic.
*19% are single and happy to stay that way.
*45% of unmarried Libra men hope to wed.
*A low 12% have been married and found it put them off for life.
*And 24% who've tried marriage still want to give it another go.

*Just 44% married the true love of their life, significantly below average.

*He doesn't believe in waiting — 7% went to their wedding a virgin, the third lowest score of all men.

*43% reckon marriage has improved their lovelife, and that's in the lower range.

*But roughly the same amount (42%) say sex has stayed the same within a match, and that's in the upper range. "We lived together before and it was great. Why should a piece of paper change anything?" one Libra asks.

*70% find sex sizzles more when they remarry — joint lowest score of all starsigns.

Strong and stable, LIBRA MAN has realistic expectations of marriage.

LIBRA WOMAN AND MARRIAGE

*A massive 71% have one marriage (second highest of all signs) while 22% have two (second lowest of all signs). And 4% of Libra women marry three times, and 1% four times. Still, Libra woman's overall chance of multiple marriage is also second lowest of all, at just 27%.

*Marriage is for keeps, they believe — 51% have been brides over 10 years. That's more than any other starsign.

*A low 9% are unmarried and don't intend to change that status.

*48% hope to swap Miss for Mrs one day.

*16% say marriage has put them off for life.

*A high 27% have tried marriage before and want a chance to try again.

*Above average 53% did marry the love of their life. "Although I waited 50 years to do it," comments a 71-year-old Libra lady who was separated from her childhood sweetheart when her family emigrated.

*A middle range 11% were virgin brides.

*47% say being married makes for better sex.

*And 73% vote lovemaking improved after marrying for the second, or more, time. That's the second lowest score.
LIBRA WOMAN marries for life, but she's looking for a soulmate, not a cell-mate.

HOW DO THE SEXES COMPARE?
Both Libra men and women are the zodiac's best bet for lasting marriage. They are secure inside and don't need a partner to provide that for them. Libra women marry their dream love more often than men—and are more prepared to wait for sex until after the ceremony. Women are also more likely to go for remarriage—and to find sex gets better in both first and subsequent matches.

SCORPIO MAN AND MARRIAGE
*Scorpio is more likely than any other sign to marry once, for life, at a massive 76%. That's a full 5% more than the nearest starsign.
*And just 19% marry twice, lowest of all starsigns. Add 3% marrying three times and 2% five times and it still gives Scorpio man an overall remarriage chance of just 24%—lowest in the zodiac.
*43% have passed their 10th anniversary.
*13% vow to stay single for life.
*48% are single but still want to marry, second highest result.
*19% have been put off marriage for life, again the next-to-top score.
*21% have been married and hope to marry again one day, the third lowest result.
*An average 46% married the love of their life.
*15% made their marriage vows a virgin.
*Security of marriage must suit Scorpio men, a massive 58%, more than any other men's starsign, say sex is better within a marriage. Like Harry, who comments, "Each time my wife and I make love, it increases the intensity of our feelings for each other. Sex is

meaningless without love. But if we stopped fancying each other, then that would be a problem, too. Because, to me, love is meaningless without sex."

*But Scorpio man is also second most likely to rate marriage a sex-wrecker. And least likely of all men to say lovelife is unchanged by marriage.

*Indifference is obviously not a Scorpio trait... 75% find remarriage makes sex better, too.

SCORPIO MAN is made for lasting marriage, as long as that sex spark doesn't go out!

SCORPIO WOMAN AND MARRIAGE

*64% marry once, 31% twice (more than any other woman), 4% three times and 1% four times. That adds up to a 36% chance of more than one marriage for Scorpio woman — second highest of all.

*46% have been married over 10 years, putting Scorpio woman in the upper range.

*9% are happy to stay single.

*48% are single but hoping to marry — exactly the same number as Scorpio men. "So what are we waiting for, let's introduce ourselves!" jokes Scorpio Pattie, 41.

*19% have been married but vow, never again! And that's also an identical figure to Scorpio men.

*24% have been married and would like to marry again some day.

*49% married the love of their life.

*15% were virgins when they took their marriage vows. Yes, same as men again!

*51%, in the upper range, reckon marriage gives a booster to sexlife.

*An average 82% say sex has grown better after a remarriage. "Sex in my first marriage was like fine wine, but second time around, it's vintage champagne!" says one satisfied remarried Scorpio.

SCORPIO WOMAN is well suited to marriage — as long as that marriage suits her!

HOW DO THE SEXES COMPARE?

Attitudes to getting married are astonishingly similar in Scorpio men and women. It's after the wedding bells that they change! For while Scorpio men stick to one wife no matter what (only 24% remarry), Scorpio women prefer to wipe the wedding slate clean and start again (36% remarry). Yet the women of this starsign are more keen on the perks of marriage like sex and security.

SAGITTARIUS MAN AND MARRIAGE

*64% marry once, 32% twice, 2% three times and another 2% four times. This gives Sagittarius, at 36%, an above average chance of remarriage.

*Just 37% of Sagittarius matches have lasted past 10 years, by far the lowest result, and a full 5% less than the next starsign. Paul speaks for many Sagittarius men when he says, "I don't think people are made for monogamy, it's just not natural. You wouldn't expect to stay in the same job for 10 years without a change, so why a marriage?"

*Yet... a below average 12% of Sagittarius men say they are single and want to stay that way.

*40% are single now but want to marry one day, that's in the lower range. But... Sagittarius men head the ranks of those disillusioned by married life—21% say they've tried marriage, and won't be trying it again!

*27% have wed once and hope to try again.

*45% married the love of their life.

*8% were virgin bridegrooms, well below average. "Life's too short to say no to sex! You're bound to regret it," says Rudi, 19.

*47% say sex has taken an upturn since their wedding day.

*77% rate remarriage as a sex improver.

SAGITTARIUS MAN likes the company of marriage but is less keen on the commitment.

SAGITTARIUS WOMAN AND MARRIAGE

*Two in three, 66%, of Sagittarius women marry just once, 27% go for two weddings, 6% for three and 1% wed four times. So the chances of remarriage are average.

*Only 35% of marriages make it past 10 years, one of the lowest figures of all.

*12% of restless Sagittarius women are single and out to stay that way, more than almost all other female signs.

*53%, again higher than any other starsign, are single but hope to marry.

*Yet positive Sagittarius also scores low on anti-marriage points. Just one in 10 (10%) has been put off enough by marriage to vow never again.

*24% have been married and hope to marry again. "Anyone can make a mistake — the trick is to learn from it!" they say.

*Only 43% married their dream lover.

*An average 13% were virgin brides.

*Exactly half, 50%, say yes, marriage has improved their sexlife. And they're least likely of all women to say marriage makes sex worse (12%).

*But it's remarriage that really scores with Sagittarius women. Nine out of 10, a stunning 90%, reckon getting married again does wonders for their lovelife. "This time I know it's for keeps, so we've been able to take it slow and really find out what gives each other pleasure. Sex is an all-over experience now, not a mad rush towards orgasm."

Romantic dreams that are dulled, but not doused, by bad experiences. SAGITTARIUS WOMAN may break up, but never breaks down...

HOW DO THE SEXES COMPARE?

Love on the run that is least likely of all starsigns to last a lifetime, that's true for both Sagittarius men and women. But while Sagittarius men are put off by failure (21% vow never

again), Sagittarius women learn from it (just 10% don't want to marry again). And the vast majority find things improve second time around. Single Sagittarius women are far keener on the idea of marriage (53%, to just 40% of men, want to try it) and are 5% more likely to be virgins on their wedding day.

CAPRICORN MAN AND MARRIAGE

*66% marry once, 29% marry twice, and a total of 5% wed three times.

*55% of Capricorn husbands have been happily married 10 years or more. That's the second highest number, placing them firmly in the upper range.

*19% are single and intend to stay single.

*A romantic 49% are unmarried now but hope to be a husband one day—more than any other starsign.

*A below average 15% have been put off marriage for life by previous experiences. Yet...

*17%, less than any other sign, have been married before and want to be so again. So what's gone wrong? "I gave that marriage everything I had, and I don't think I could give that much again, I'm too proud," says one divorcee.

*Just 42%, the second lowest result, of Capricorn men married their dream woman.

*And down-to-earth Capricorn husbands are second-least likely to marry as virgins, just six in every hundred.

*A below average 45% vote marriage as an improver of sex.

*But remarriage fares better. Of those who have married more than once, 82% say sex is better second, or more, time around. That's the second highest of all the men's starsigns.

CAPRICORN MAN believes marriage is forever, and may not allow himself to fail.

CAPRICORN WOMAN AND MARRIAGE

*Single marriages number 68%, doubles 27% and triple marriages

5%. At 32%, Capricorn woman's overall chance of more than one marriage is slightly below average.

*Just 42%, in the middle range, have stayed married for 10 years or more.

*Of those that are not married right now, 9% are single and want to keep it that way.

*45% of today's singles hope to marry.

*A low 13% have tried marriage before and now say Never Again!

*While more than any other sign, one in three (33%) Capricorn ex-wives want to get married again. They miss the company, the security, and the sex, they say.

*Second most likely of all starsigns to marry the love of their life, 53% say they did. "Or at least I TELL him I did!" jokes 53-year-old Sophia.

*11% were virgins on their wedding night, almost twice as many as Capricorn men!

*Marriage makes little difference to sex for Capricorn women — 43% say lovelife stayed the same after the ceremony. But Capricorn is least likely of the women's starsigns to vote marriage a lovelife boost, at just 40%. "It's comfortable, and satisfying—but as exciting as a pair of woolly socks," says one.

*84% rate sex better after remarriage.

CAPRICORN WOMAN marries for security, not excitement —but may be more easily bored than she thinks.

HOW DO THE SEXES COMPARE?

Capricorn women go easier on themselves and allow themselves to make mistakes—33% who've failed before are eager to marry again, compared to just 17% of Capricorn men. But perhaps they need to be! Since Capricorn women's marriages are much less likely to last than men's—just 42% pass the 10-year mark, while 55% of men's matches do so. But women are much more likely to marry the love of their life. Neither finds getting married the first time does much to perk up their

lovelife. **But remarriage does the trick for men—82% find sex improves when they marry again. Compared to just 72% of Capricorn women.**

AQUARIUS MAN AND MARRIAGE

*59% have just one marriage, second least of all starsigns. 29% wed twice, and Aquarius men are most likely of all to have three wives, at one in 10 (10%). Another 2% go on to wedding number four! Overall chance of marrying more than once is 41%, the zodiac's second highest.

*43% of marriages last over 10 years, in the middle range.

*13% are bachelors who don't want to wed.

*43% are single now but hope to marry.

*13% have been married before and now say once was more than enough. Yet...

*30%, second most of all male starsigns, have been married and hope to get another chance at wedded bliss. One Aquarius man admits, "I want to prove to myself I can make a go of marriage. It's a challenge."

*Aquarius men are least likely to marry the love of their life, just 41% have done so.

*And they're least likely to be a virgin when they do marry, by far the lowest result at just 3%, or three in every hundred.

*That may be why marriage makes little difference to satisfaction —a huge 44% say sexlife stayed the same after marriage, while the second lowest score of 38% report an improvement.

*72%, in the lower range, found sex was better in a new marriage. **Low on romance, high on risk, but deep down AQUARIUS MAN likes marriage more than he lets on.**

AQUARIUS WOMAN AND MARRIAGE

*67% have one marriage, 25% wed twice, 8% three times and 1% four times. That gives an overall remarriage chance of 34%, in the middle range.

*Just 39% of marriages pass the 10-year mark, firmly in the lower range.

*10% of Aquarius single women are happy to stay that way.

*48% hope to change their status to married.

*16% of those with previous marriages have vowed to give wedding bells a wide berth in future. But...

*26% have been married before and hope to marry again.

*A below average 44% of Aquarius women married the love of their life.

*They are least likely to be virgin brides, at just 8%. "I like to know what I'm letting myself in for!" is one reason given.

*52% vote sexlife better after marriage, second most of all star-signs. Yet this contrary sign also has 22% saying marriage made sex worse, and that's also second most for women across the zodiac! Aquarius women are least likely of anyone to say there was no change!

*Remarriage improves sex for 77%.

AQUARIUS WOMAN'S cool front hides hot loving that can either burst into bloom or wither away in marriage. A sign of extremes.

HOW DO THE SEXES COMPARE?

Neither Aquarius sex is likely to walk down the aisle a virgin— just 3% of men and 8% of women do so. And both prefer realism to romance, although Aquarius women are more likely to marry the love of their life, and to find sex improves after marriage—and remarriage. Both sexes are independent, but the women maintain it better—16% vow never to marry again, compared to 13% of men. And while 30% of Aquarius men would like to give marriage another chance, for women the figure is just 26%.

PISCES MAN AND MARRIAGE

*61% marry once, 29% marry twice, 9% marry three times and 2%

four times. This, perhaps surprisingly, places Pisces in the upper range when it comes to chances of marrying more than once.

*45% have been husbands for more than 10 years.

*15% are set on staying single.

*Less than any other men's starsign, just 36% are single and hope to marry. "I'm scared of what it might mean, how marriage would change my life. So I'd rather avoid it all together," says Pisces-born Ralph, 29.

*Once they try marriage though, they like it, as although 17% swear never again, the top score of 32% Pisces men hope to find themselves married again one day.

*A stunning 58%, way out in front of every other sign, married the love of their life. "I saw her face in a friend's wedding pictures and just had to meet her. When I did, I proposed after just 10 minutes," says one Pisces. And he may well have kept himself for that special woman, as 19% of Pisces men are virgin bridegrooms, second highest number.

*For 55%, sex improved after marriage — and Pisces man is least likely to say it got worse (just 12%).

*81% rated sex as better after marrying again.

Reluctant but romantic groom, PISCES MAN grows into mature marriage, and keeps his dreams intact.

PISCES WOMAN AND MARRIAGE

*66% have only one marriage, 30% have two, 3% have three, 1% four and another 1% marry six times or more. Pisces woman's total chance of marrying more than once comes to 35%, in the upper range.

*41% have been wives for more than a decade.

*Pisces isn't sold on the single life.

*She's least likely of all the women's starsign to be single and want to stay that way (6%), and second most likely to be single but hoping to marry (52%). "All my friends are married now and I'm starting to panic about being left on the shelf. And it shows —I found out the other day that the men at work call me The Husband Hunter!" says one Pisces.

*16% have tried marriage and prefer not to try it again.

*26% have been married and would like another chance.

*47%, in the middle range, married the love of their life.

*16% were virgin brides.

*An average 48% say marriage improves sexlife. "I've kicked a lot of my hang-ups in the last five years, but I still find it hard to initiate sex—my next goal," says Joan, 34.

*87%, the third highest score across the zodiac for women, reckon remarriage makes sex better.

PISCES WOMAN—wannabe bride who may not find that marriage is the miracle she hopes for...

HOW DO THE SEXES COMPARE?

Pisces men don't want to get married but like it when they do, Pisces women long for a wedding ring but may be disappointed by marital reality! Men are much more likely to want another chance at marriage (32%, to 26% women) and are 11% more likely to marry the love of their life. They also find sex improves more after marriage—55% of Pisces men say it does, compared to 48% of women. But Pisces women do lead the way in one category—losing their virginity! 16% marry as virgins, easily beaten by 19% of Pisces men. But women find more sexual satisfaction after marrying again.

4

INFIDELITY

* WHO HAVE THE MOST AND LEAST AFFAIRS
* UNDERSTANDING, REVENGE, OR GOODBYE—
  WHAT HAPPENS WHEN A PARTNER IS
  UNFAITHFUL * REAL REASONS FOR AFFAIRS
* THE 12 STARSIGNS' INFIDELITY PROFILES

Which starsigns slide into infidelity? Do more men or women stray from a relationship? The starsigns astrology has always tagged as faithful, and the ones with roving reputations, are shown to be very different players of the love game according to the AstroSex Survey ... flirty signs stay faithful, quiet homelovers have a half-a-dozen lovers. Once more the survey rewrites the rules of astrology.

WHO HAVE MOST AFFAIRS?

There is certainly a difference between the sexes when it comes to infidelity—and this means straying from a committed relationship, whether legally married or not.

More men than women are unfaithful. Looking at all the starsigns as a whole, almost half (47%) of all attached men stray. But for women, infidelity levels run at just over one in three (35%)— perhaps because they are more committed to a relationship, or simply too tired juggling job, home and children. Anyway, as we shall discover later, women's reasons for being unfaithful tend to be very different from men's...

And while male and female figures for one affair only are roughly similar (23% men, 20% women), men are over four times as likely as women to have been unfaithful more than five times (9% men, 2% women).

MEN MOST LIKELY TO WANDER

First surprise in this section are the two partners least likely to look for sexual gratification elsewhere. For supposedly hard-to-hook Sagittarius (63%) and Gemini (62%) lead the field of male starsigns who have never been unfaithful. While steady stay-at-home Capricorn husbands (according to traditional astrology) are the least likely of all to answer no when asked "Have you had an affair?"

One explanation could be that Gemini and Sagittarius men spend so long choosing exactly the right partner that they are less likely to need extra loving elsewhere. While conventional Capricorn may rush into commitment before he's really ready and regret it later.

"I'm a prime candidate for a mid-life crisis," confesses Adrian, a 42-year-old Capricorn accountant. "I've got it all—lovely wife and kids, money in the bank, successful business, holiday home. Yet increasingly I find myself thinking, is this IT? My life is so predictable now and I'm starting to wish it wasn't. A new girl has started in the office an she's made it obvious she's available. I'm more tempted than I've ever been in my life. No one need ever know..."

ONCE IS ENOUGH—OR IS IT?

Sex-hungry Scorpio men, who need to experience all life has to offer, are the most likely to stray once (26%). And many do admit they just had to taste forbidden fruit to know what it was like. However Scorpio's not overkeen to repeat this particular experience. It may well prove too hot to handle—and certainly clashes with this intense starsign's hopes for a lifelong marriage.

CASE HISTORY OF A SCORPIO MAN

Squash coach Andy, 31 and a Scorpio, still recalls the agony, and ecstasy of his wicked, once-only affair with another Scorpio.

"I've seen countless women in squash kit and none of them has ever had the effect on me Marilynne did. I remember handing her a racquet once and almost starting at the electrical charge that seemed to pass between us. It was lust, pure and simple, and although I could be objective about Marilynne when I was at home with my family, when I was with her I just couldn't seem to resist.

"One day after her lesson I followed her into the changing rooms and we made love in a shower cubicle. It was incredible and just made my situation worse. Because now I couldn't wait to repeat the experience.

"I hated myself for what I was doing but couldn't seem to stop myself. She was my drug and I was addicted, it was as simple as that. Yet nothing would take me away from my wife and children.

"I did take my guilt out on Marilynne and treated her very badly. But I believe our affair might still be going on today if she hadn't got fed up waiting for me to leave Kate, my wife who's a Libra and threw a brick through Kate's car windscreen, with a very detailed note wrapped round it.

"Faced with the reality of what I'd been doing, I realised what I'd risked. I couldn't go through that trauma again, no matter how wonderful the sex."

Cautious Capricorn and in-love-with-love Pisces (both 24%), as well as sensible but sensual Taurus and experimental Aquarius (both 22%) men are also likely to venture into one-time unfaithfulness.

At first glance lusty Leo seems to surprise us by being the male starsign least likely of all to stray once (15%). But two factors influence this. First, for all-or-nothing Leo that one lapse is highly likely to lead him to break-up with his old love and take up with his new.

But secondly, he may find he likes the drama of illicit love too much to stop at one. The survey shows Leo is the man most likely to have between two and five affairs—one in four Leos (25%) admit to having done this. And Taurus (24%), Libra (22%) and Aries (21%) are next in line in this section. These are all slightly selfish starsigns who may find one taste of danger is simply not enough.

MEN WHO HAVE MULTIPLE AFFAIRS

Which men just can't be trusted out of their partner's sight? So-romantic Libra, it seems, is top of this table, as a stunning 14% of the air sign confess to having five affairs or more.

Add this to the 22% who've had between two and five and it means a total of 36%, over a third, of attached Libra men have had multiple affairs.

13% of Cancer and 12% of Capricorn husbands have also had over five infidelities—a shock for partners of these supposedly loyal and caring signs.

While the man least likely to have strayed several times is, again, Sagittarius. It seems he is not such a bad marriage bet as the zodiac has always maintained.

CASE HISTORY OF A LIBRA MAN

Italian-born Libra Tony, 38, is a former singer who now runs a fast-food outlet.

"If I'm totally honest, I have always cared a lot about the way I look and the impression I make on the opposite sex.

"And I knew lots of women fancied me. I was in a glamorous job, away from home a lot, and picking up girls was unbelievably easy. I always enjoyed that great first rush you get when you start an affair, so saying no was never an option.

"My first wife, a Pisces, was one of those people who likes to pretend things aren't happening—and I hate rows too. She seemed quite happy, seeing me now and again. I always made a big fuss of her when I did get home.

"But my current wife is a Sagittarius and a lot sharper. I know I can't talk my way past her. Also I owe her a lot. I was very ill with a kidney complaint and couldn't work. So she became the breadwinner for quite a while.

"Yes, HIV and AIDS have made me think again too, also I'm not in showbiz any more so the opportunities just aren't there. Even if they were, I'd be able to resist them now, I reckon. I've grown up, it's as simple as that—and better late than never."

WOMEN WHO LOOK FOR OUTSIDE LOVE

Who are the committed women who say a firm no to illicit love? Once again, surprises are in store as Sagittarius females surge to the top of the most-faithful list. For 73% of Sagittarius women say they have never had an affair, reflecting the men's result.

Among female signs, however, it's Cancer who comes next, with 71% never having strayed at all, followed by Virgo (68%). "Marriage is for worse as well as better, so why bother starting if you're going to give up so easily," is a very common comment.

Least likely never to have been unfaithful at all is sexy Ms Scorpio (58%), with Libra a close second (59%). But again, just like her male counterpart, Scorpio is also the woman who is most likely to have had just one lover, on 29%. For female Geminis, the figure is almost as high, 28%. But for both starsigns, it's a case of once-bitten, twice shy—the chances of repeating their experience of infidelity fall firmly in the lower range.

CASE HISTORY OF A GEMINI WOMAN

Gemini Sally, 33, has boys of seven and five and has lived with Phil, a Virgo, for 8 years. She's been unfaithful with a Scorpio for six months.

"I knew Richard was pretty young, because he was one of a group of students who came into the winebar where I work nights. But it wasn't until we slept together that I found out there was a 10-year gap between us. He's 10 years younger—and 10 times more interested in me.

"I wouldn't do anything to hurt Phil, my partner, and I'd never leave him because the boys adore him so. I come from a broken home myself and it's the last thing I want for my kids. But Phil does take me for granted and what I love most about Rich is the attention he pays me. He really listens to what I have to say and takes me seriously. We have these lovely long phone calls during the day when we talk about everything from sex to the state of the nation.

"Sexually, too, Rich is so refreshing—and so energetic. But I'm realistic enough to know it won't last. Rich doesn't even know my real age, or that I have children. And when he finishes his exams, he wants to travel. The chances of me going with him are zero, so I'm just enjoying it while it lasts."

WOMEN WITH WANDERING EYES

When it comes to multiple affairs, once again the women's results mirror the men's, at least at the top. For again the starsign most likely to have more than one lover (though not necessarily at one time) is Leo.

16% of attached Leo women admit to between two and five affairs, while a further 2% have over five lovers. And Libra is not far behind, with 15% having been unfaithful up to five times, and 2% more than five.

Perhaps the main characteristic these two signs share is a lack of insight into others' feelings—both tend to focus on their own needs before those of a partner, and crave attention, at any price. They're creatures of impulse too, who may be embroiled in a steamy affair before they even notice.

Many who deceive their full-time partners, like 29-year-old Libra Emma, go on to marry their illicit lover. "I am about to wed number three," she laughs. "But I'm sure that this time, it's going to work

183

out because the others weren't as mentally compatible. It's not that I don't think marriage counts for much—I do. But I see no point sticking with someone you no longer fancy and who no longer treats you well."

When it comes to over five affairs, however, it isn't Libra or Leo who have the highest rating amongst the zodiac's women, but "homebody" Ms Taurus and ultra-feminine Ms Pisces. Four out of 100 of each of these unlikely starsigns have had half-a-dozen extra-marital flings, or more.

STARWATCH
According to her traditional star profile, Taurus woman should be too cautious and lazy to indulge in infidelity. And Pisces is, in theory, too wary of the dangers involved. It seems both signs are more sexy, and less willing to suffer frustration or boredom, than has always been believed. And the reverse is true for Sagittarius.

WHAT HAPPENS WHEN A PARTNER HAS AN AFFAIR?
Reactions to a partner's infidelity are markedly different between the sexes—but not in the way we might expect. For our survey reveals that women are more likely to ask for divorce (more than a third of all women—34%—would do so, compared to less than a quarter (24%) of men) or take a "revenge" lover of their own. While wronged men's instinct is to pretend infidelity never happened, or work together to deal with it and keep an existing relationship going.

MEN WHO CAN'T FORGIVE, OR FORGET
The male starsigns most inclined to see infidelity as the end of everything, and so ask for a divorce are Pisces, Gemini and Aquarius (all 28%).

But while Aquarius and Gemini can switch off and walk away from broken dreams, without looking back, Pisces' reaction is rather

184

different. Instead of cool contempt, many Pisces men suffer hasty get-the-hell-out-anger—then regret their rage. But by that time it may already be too late.

CASE HISTORY OF A PISCES MAN

Pisces Jason, 27, works as a chef. Last year his wife, Jenny, a Libra, confessed she had had a brief affair with a work colleague.

"I was so shocked, I was physically sick outside the restaurant when Jenny told me. It was the thought of someone else touching her, loving her... I couldn't bear it.

"I rushed home and started tearing all her clothes out of the wardrobes and flinging them out of the bedroom windows. All the time I was crying and screaming, 'Slut, you slut.'

"She'd followed me home and was trying to calm me down, but as I looked at her I had such violent feelings it terrified me. I could have killed her. Instead I gripped her shoulders and literally shoved her out of the front door into the street. It was the middle of the night but I didn't care. I couldn't stand to be in the same room as her. She sickened me so.

"After Jenny had gone I went through our wedding album and ripped up the pictures one by one. Then I drank a whole bottle of whisky and passed out.

"After a few days I had calmed down and realised I still loved Jenny and wanted her back. But nothing I could do would persuade her to come back—and I can't say I blame her."

Meanwhile, the man who is least likely to blow the whistle on a relationship after infidelity is Scorpio (15%). So although he's a firm favourite to be unfaithful himself, Scorpio can be understanding when a partner strays. That much is in keeping with his traditional star profile as an intense starsign who marries for life.

STARWATCH

This reaction of Aquarius men—refusing to work things through—sits oddly with the accepted astrological view of this starsign as non-conformists with open minds. Perhaps it's not embarrassment that makes them seek divorce, but that the serious Saturn side of this man can't bear anyone or anything to break through his private emotional defences. He figures if he's been let down badly once, then it can happen again. And that, to analytical Aquarius, is a risk not worth running.

WOMEN WHO DRAW THE LINE

41% of Aries, and 40% of Capricorn women don't accept excuses for infidelity and consider it the final straw in a relationship. Women born under these signs aren't necessarily angels themselves, which could explain why they have zero tolerance of their man's failings. But both are also proud, and practical to a degree—in that they realise once trust is broken it will never be the same again for them, no matter how well patched up.

CASE HISTORY OF AN ARIES WOMAN

Aries Angela, 30, is a home-based hairdresser with one son aged seven. Her ex-husband Dan is Aquarius

"I decided that if my husband—ex husband now—hadn't got the self-discipline to stay loyal to me and our son, then he was basically too weak a man for me.

"Funnily enough, I was extra furious with him because he'd burdened me with a long-drawn-out confession about his infidelity. I really didn't want to know all the gory details. It was stupid, really, because I think he expected me to understand and appreciate his honesty. Like he was switching the burden of guilt from himself to me. Well, I wasn't having that.

"He really thought things at home could carry on as normal. But

I insisted he found a place of his own and we separated almost immediately. I never muck about. And I don't like people who do, either."

Yet when it comes to the least inflexible female starsign, the one who will not automatically insist on divorce after an affair, it is the opposite result to the zodiac's men. For Aquarius scores lowest in this section—just over one in four, 26%, would insist on a clean break. And Gemini, one of the highest male scorers, is next lowest woman on just 28%.

"I was able to stand back, look at my life objectively and see I'd lose out more than anyone if we divorced," says Rhonda, 50. "It's not been easy, in fact it's been horrendous, but we're surviving, just. I'm no creature of impulse, at least not where my future—and my children's future—is concerned."

STARWATCH
As far as reactions to infidelity are concerned, the same starsigns seem to produce opposite reactions according to sex. Traditional Aquarius and Gemini cool heads lead men to call it quits, but women to stay put and fight. Another important discovery that rewrites accepted astrological rules.

WHO TAKES A REVENGE LOVER?
Overall, slightly more women (14%) than men (13%) reckon they would give an unfaithful partner a taste of their own medicine. Again, the survey reveals totally different starsign behaviour patterns between the sexes.

MEN WHO GET THEIR OWN BACK—FAST
Both Libra and Scorpio men—among the most unfaithful male signs themselves—top the list of those whose wounded male egos

can't wait to retaliate, in kind. Libra men are top of the hit-back list at 19%, with tail-lashing Scorpio hard on their heels at 18%.

Chances are, though, that these two already have a standby lover waiting in the wings anyway. And remember, this is just how men think they would react to infidelity, and speaks volumes about these two signs' own attitudes towards it.

CASE HISTORY OF A SCORPIO MAN

Shane, 36, and a Scorpio, was married for just 18 months when he discovered his wife Pip, a Capricorn, was seeing an old lover.

"I knew Pip had never really got over this man and had married me on the rebound, but somehow I thought my loving her so much would make everything all right. Of course, it didn't.

"I felt so hurt and humiliated, I wanted to hurt Pip the way she'd hurt me. I knew her little sister Anne-Marie had always had a soft spot for me, so I couldn't resist seducing her. Kicking my wife in the teeth, emotionally, mattered more to me than how much I fancied Anne-Marie.

"But the only person who got hurt was Anne-Marie. I hate myself now for using her like that. And when Pip found out she just despised me more for being so weak and childish. Neither of them has had anything to do with me since, and I don't blame them. It will be a long time before I feel ready to trust another woman, let alone marry her."

Least likely to play the revenge lover card are Taurus, Capricorn and Pisces men (all 10%)—all level-headed individuals who can see a retribution affair would be a hollow victory. "What would it solve? It would just make an already terrible situation even worse," says Taurus Jeremy, 42. "And it's the worst reason for an affair I've ever heard."

STARWATCH

Findings in this section may not reflect traditional astrological thought, but they do reinforce what the survey has already discovered—that Libra and Scorpio men are inclined to be unfaithful more than other men, for whatever reason.

WOMEN WHO WANT REVENGE

"I thought, if he can do it, I can too. So I put on a skimpy dressing-gown and rang our neighbour and friend, Alex.. 'My shower spray seems to be broken, Alex,' I told him. 'And Chris is out for the night. Can you come and help?'

"Yes, I took advantage of Alex's good nature, and the fact I knew he was secretly attracted to me. You can always tell these things, can't you? I didn't enjoy it when we had sex, but it was one in the eye for Chris, I gloated. We'd been living together nine years and I'd discovered he was having an affair with his boss at the hospital where he worked. Now I'd got my own back.

"Inevitably, however, Alex fell properly in love with me and wanted to leave his wife. I realised not only did I not love him, I didn't love Chris, either. So I walked out on both of them. I'm on my own now, and love it.

"But I wish I'd been strong enough to tackle our relationship problems without a 'cushion' to fall back on. It's not like me, really, dragging someone else in to help me fight my battles."

This story told by Aries Jo, 27, reflects the calculated way many Aries women set about exacting revenge on an unfaithful lover. The fiery sign is top of the list of women who believe in tit for tat (16%). And love-for-life Pisces scores the same. But her response to infidelity may well be more emotional and impulsive than Aries, and spurred on by a few drinks too many...

Overall, women's responses to this question are more consistent than men's. But the female sign least likely to err for revenge reasons is Cancer.

CASE HISTORY OF A CANCER WOMAN

Cancer woman Izzy, 31, was shattered when she discovered erotic love letters in her Libra husband Clive's briefcase.

"The worst thing was, the letters were written by my best friend. I felt like I was suffocating, a dark hole had swallowed me up and I couldn't get out again. And yes, the first thought that crossed my mind was to go out, get drunk, pick up some guy and screw him.

"But I soon dismissed it—that just wasn't my style, and would have hurt me more than it hurt Clive. Anyway I refused to bring myself down to his level.

"So what did I do? I took a deep breath and confronted him. And the whole story came flooding out, how he'd had sex with Debbie just once but she'd developed an obsession for him and started writing all these filthy letters. He'd been afraid and ashamed and didn't know how to tell me, in case I left him.

"I believed Clive—I had to, to save my sanity. But we worked it out together and we're still married. I hope we can stay that way."

WHO SAYS NOTHING AND HOPES THE AFFAIR WILL END?

The sit back and hope for the best school of marriage guidance does not score too highly with anyone in the zodiac—but it is popular with twice as many men as women.

8% of male starsigns, and a tiny 4% of female ones, say they would adopt the ostrich approach, sticking their head in the sand and hoping for the best.

MEN WHO CLOSE THEIR EYES

Trying to ignore the situation when a partner strays is the mark of both Cancer and Virgo men—12% of each choose this path of least resistance, and least rows... they hope.

Infidelity

Much-married but still terminally romantic Cancer has problems facing reality and prefers to pretend all is well. But Virgo, who can't bear others to see his marriage isn't perfect, will do it to save face—until he can't bear it a minute longer.

CASE HISTORY OF A VIRGO MAN
Virgo Dave, an ex-policeman, recalls the torture of knowing about his Scorpio wife Sylvia's affair, but saying nothing.
"I have three children from two marriages to support and was working a lot of overtime at the time. Yes, I know I was distant and cool with Sylvia, and I was often too tired for sex. In some ways I don't blame her for being unfaithful.

"I discovered the affair when I overheard a whispered conversation on the phone. Suddenly it all fell into place—her odd absences, distracted air. Suddenly I saw how much I loved Sylvia and didn't want to lose her.

"I though a confrontation might make her leave me, the last thing I wanted. So, although it was sheer torture, I decided to sit it out and hope she would choose me. I still remember long nights at work when I'd do anything to take my mind off what was happening at home. But when we were together I was extra attentive and loving—and sure enough, after about six months the affair fizzled out. It was absolute hell. I don't think I could ever go through that again."

The men who are least likely to play this relationship waiting game are impulsive Aries and practical Capricorn, who both score 4%. Neither is inclined to let lust run its course—and both want to know where they stand, as soon as possible. Also these two are extremely honest starsigns, who would have trouble concealing their secret knowledge without a partner noticing something.

STARWATCH
At first glance, Cancer and Virgo seem a strange pair to be

191

lumped together this way. But perhaps traditional astrology can explain it—Cancer does nothing because it is one of the most unrealistic starsigns, and Virgo does nothing because it is one of the most realistic.

WOMEN WHO IGNORE INFIDELITY

Among women, Aries, Libra and Sagittarius (all 3%) are the ones least likely to keep quiet and hope their partner's fling won't last. "I could never live with myself if I did nothing," admits one Sagittarius wife. "My pride would be damaged forever. Anyway that's not the way I operate—give me a blazing row and a whole dinner service to smash any day. I want him to know, and see, exactly how furious and hurt I am."

The women who are most inclined to look the other way are something of a surprise, however. For 6% of Pisces, and of Aquarius, women say they would do so. Could Aquarius' reaction show cool, analytical strength, while Pisces' reaction reflects fear of confrontation and what it might mean?

CASE HISTORY OF AN AQUARIUS WOMAN

Terri, 23, works in a shoe store and was born Aquarius. Last year she caught husband Tim, a Capricorn, in bed with another woman. "I closed the door softly and walked back downstairs. My heart was thumping loudly but my head was clear. I remember thinking, 'I'm above all this, I won't come down to his level'. So I said nothing, I did nothing, I just carried on as normal.

"I knew my indifference would drive Tim mad, and it did. It also forced him to admit what was really bugging him about our life together. Apparently he was angry with me because I didn't want to start a family yet and he thought I should, while we were both still young and had lots of energy.

"His fling was a way to make his point, if a rather immature one.

But it did work to a certain extent—it got us talking and we've reached a compromise on children now."

STARWATCH

Aquarius woman redesigns her usual star profile again—she is least likely in the zodiac to ask for a divorce after infidelity, most likely to ignore a partner's fling and first in the queue to try to understand and adapt. For Aquarius men, however, the opposite is true. Which is sticking to traditional astrological thought? Or is it neither?

WHO TRIES TO UNDERSTAND?

Time to put those sexist clichés back where they belong—for the survey reveals that men are more understanding and willing to adapt and change after a partner's affair than women are. 58% of the zodiac's men say they would ask why an affair had happened and try to adjust the relationship. For women, the figure is less, at 52%.

LET'S TALK—MEN WHO WANT TO MAKE UP

So-practical Taurus man hates to smash up the happy home for what might prove a passing fancy—so more than six out of 10 (65%) of men from this starsign favour talking things through and trying to find a solution together.

"I wasn't going to give up my wife or bust up our family business, or sell the house, just because some stupid, arrogant pig of a commercial manager had taken a shine to her on a course," says hotel-owner Will, 36.

"I was stupid enough not to suspect Sandie was anything more than flattered. And once we'd sat down and talked properly, I realised the truth—that Sandie was worn out and bored by us both working round the clock and never having any fun anymore. Even sex had to be specially scheduled, we were both so busy in the hotel.

"No way would either of us let our marriage go after so many good years. We took on a manager who deals with most of the hotel's day-to-day running, so now we have more time for each other. But I have made it clear to Sandie that I wouldn't be so understanding a second time."

Male starsigns who also favour clearing the air and trying to start over are Scorpio and Sagittarius (both 63%). But while straight-up Sagittarius can't deal with situations any way other than head on, Mr Scorpio's motives may be more mixed. For this starsign mixes passion with power, and could use the knowledge of his partner's affair against her long after he's "forgiven" her.

The man who's least inclined to kiss and make up is Aquarius. Just one in every two (50%) of this starsign would want to ask why an affair happened and be prepared to change. And Aquarius is also one of the men most likely to ask for divorce and just walk away.

WOMEN WHO ASK WHY

Again, the zodiac women's response is the reverse of the men's. For while Gemini and Aquarius men are the ones who split up at the first suggestion of unfaithfulness, these are just the female signs who are most inclined towards talking things through and finding out why a fling happened. 58% of Gemini women, and the same number of Aquarius, say they would be understanding.

CASE HISTORY OF A GEMINI WOMAN

Gemini Roberta, 39, is married to Joseph, also 39 and Sagittarius. They have five children.

"As far as I know, Joseph has never had an affair—but if he did I'd look for some reason for it. These things don't just happen out of the blue when you've been together 20 years like we have.

"I've never met a man who understood me as well as Joseph does, or was prepared to give me as much freedom. And that's not something I'd give up without a fight. Physically we are compatible, but mentally even more so. We are so in tune we are almost telepathic.

"That's why I say there are worse betrayals than sex. If all Joseph did was make love with another woman I could cope with that, just. It's just bodies doing what nature intended. But if he started to love someone else, share private jokes and nicknames with her the way he does with me, then that would be something else again.

"But I've never understood couples who just part without even trying to talk. There must have been something badly wrong in the first place, I guess."

At the opposite end of the female spectrum is all-or-nothing Aries, this time showing all the intolerance and stubborn pride traditional astrology ascribes to her. For only 43% of Aries women would be prepared to talk things over with a partner and mutually adjust. "Why should I change, I'm not the one who's done something wrong," is a common Aries comment. And may explain why she is also the zodiac woman most likely both to ask for divorce straight away, and to take a revenge lover of her own.

WHY DO AFFAIRS HAPPEN?

Pure physical attraction is the one overriding reason for illicit affairs, according to 45% of the zodiac's men and 35% of women. "It just happened and I was powerless to stop it," is how many starsigns describe the beginning of an affair, when physical chemistry cancels out conscience, and commitment.

But this is one of the few factors where men and women agree on their reasons for being unfaithful.

The next most common reason for men is not getting enough sex at home (35%), while this is justification for less than half that number of women (just 17%). But female starsigns select instead, "My lover made me feel attractive" (32%), showing once again what the survey has consistently found, that women across the zodiac look for emotional reassurance first and foremost before physical satisfaction. Feeling attractive rates just 13% with the men.

Women vote 30% each to the reasons "I just fell in love" and "I was bored with my partner," while for men overall these sections rate just 20% and 23% respectively.

Almost twice as many men as women say that a younger lover revitalised them, however—and 22% of male signs compared to 16% of female admit to revelling in the thrill of the chase.

"I do love my wife and still fancy her like hell. But I feel our lovemaking has a touch of 'been-there, done that' routine," says Martin, 32, boss of a clothing import company. "I know every inch of her body intimately, there are no surprises left. So that's why I adore chasing after young attractive women. I make love to them once, and that's enough. I'm notorious in our company and girls know what to expect. A brilliant one-night stand, but nothing more."

WHAT TEMPTS MEN TOWARDS TROUBLE?

Which starsign strays because he's not getting enough sex at home? Not Scorpio this time but supposedly loyal Virgo—almost one in every two Virgo men (48%) who've had affairs say it was because of insufficient sex.

"It's was my wife's fault entirely," says music producer Miles. "She only works part-time and we don't have a family, so I can't see how she can be so tired all the time. She goes to bed before me every night—to sleep—and isn't interested in trying new places or positions. I was sick of rejection and feeling frustrated. My wife says she loves me, but sometimes I really wonder..."

Libra (41%) men are next most inclined to blame lack of sex for their infidelity. But Cancer man (just 25%) rate this reason the lowest of the zodiac. He is, however, the starsign who declares boredom with his partner as a contributing factor most often. One in three (33%) of Cancers who've dabbled give this as the reason—

and it could also explain Cancer man's tendency towards multiple marriage.

Leo (31%) and Libra (28%) also have a low boredom threshold in love. But Capricorn (just 12%) is the partner who loses interest least.

CASE HISTORY OF A LEO MAN

Richard, 29, a Leo, recently split up with his wife, a Taurus, after a series of affairs.

"Sex to me is the lifeblood of a relationship, and ours was draining away fast. Billie lost interest after our two girls were born and never got it back. She just couldn't be bothered with me and lovemaking became mechanical. It was sex by numbers—pull this, tweak that.

"About as exciting as a plate of cold mashed potato. No, come to think of it, not that good.

"Billie let her looks go, too, and put on weight. She stopped reading the papers or following the news and talked about nothing but burps and baby rusks. So when a glamorous woman at work made it obvious she was interested, I didn't put up much of a fight. That was the first of many affairs and now I've separated from Billie. But, as I see it, she has only herself to blame."

Pure physical attraction is the biggest pull for Aries (55%) and Pisces (52%), while this matters least of all to Cancer men (31%). But surprisingly the man who rates the thrill of the chase highest is Capricorn (31%), while only 15% of supposedly sex-driven Scorpios, and the same amount of flirty Geminis, feature this as a factor in their affair.

Capricorn is also most susceptible to compliments—21% were unfaithful, most of the whole zodiac—because a lover made them feel more attractive. And least swayed by this is Aquarius man (just 5%).

Cancer man is nothing if not open to all comers. For he is the one starsign who has been unfaithful most because both a younger lover revitalised him (21%) and an older lover taught him so much (12%). And Capricorn, again, is the man who answers yes to these two sections least. Just 5% of Capricorn men have been revitalised by a younger lover—and not one has been taught anything at all by an older one.

Only a very small percentage of all male signs saw an affair as a way out of a marriage—but of those who did, again, Cancer scores top, with 6%. And not one Pisces man rates this as a reason.

"I just fell in love" , is given as an explanation for infidelity most by Sagittarius men (32%, almost one in three). Is this a reflection of their open, trusting character, or perhaps a way of justifying their fling to themselves? Fellow fire sign Aries is least likely to cite falling in love as an excuse, with just a 9% score.

STARWATCH
Virgo as sexual predator, caring Cancer bored with established love and dabbling with both older and younger lovers, level-headed Capricorn loving the thrill of the chase and revelling in compliments, casual Sagittarius falling in love at first sight... The survey shows men's true needs may not be being met within marriage. But do they only feel free to show their secret selves within the no-ties safety of an affair?

WOMEN'S MOTIVES UNMASKED
Like men, the first deciding factor for women contemplating infidelity is sheer sexual attraction—35% of the female signs of the zodiac agree. And it's certainly no surprise to discover the women who rates chemistry highest is Scorpio, on 41%. Sagittarius is least interested in mutual attraction, on 29%.

Next, women tumble into infidelity because a lover makes them feel more attractive, and less taken for granted. Top score here is awarded by vanity-conscious Libra (39%) followed by Capricorn (38%). These capable women could well need a break from wearing the trousers at home. Many are official or unofficial heads of their household and may welcome the chance to play the traditional role of lusted-after female when a new lover puts them on a pedestal.

"It seemed like such a long time since anyone had ever really looked at me and liked what he saw," says Capricorn Bonnie, 27. "By contrast, my long-term boyfriend used to criticise me constantly and make my confidence even lower.

"Then my lover started coming as a customer to the bank where I worked. He obviously couldn't take his eyes off me, and used to slip adoring notes and poems under the counter to me. Yes, I was flattered, and fascinated to make love with someone who worshipped me—rightly so. All he thought of was my pleasure and my satisfaction. It was incredible."

Aries women, who are already secure in their self-image, are least inclined to be influenced by compliments and attention (24%).

Being sex-starved at home is a factor for far less women than men—but top starsign in this section is sensual Ms Taurus (20%), who has a warm, giving sexuality that may be hard to match. And one in five intensely emotional Pisces partners have the same problem. But unlike the male starsign pattern, among the women Virgo rates this least (11%).

42% of fickle Libras slip into infidelity through boredom with their partner, but only 29% of supposedly fancy-free Sagittarius do so. Perhapsthe difference is that Sagittarius woman can't hide her feelings so well, so hastens a showdown rather than a fling. And sexy Scorpio woman gets the biggest zodiac kick from the thrill of the chase—23% give this as their main reason for straying.

More Virgo women than any other sign (12%) say a younger lover has revitalised them, but only a minuscule 1% of Sagittarius females agree. And Capricorn is first to claim both that an older lover gave her a sex education and an affair was a get-out clause from her marriage. (8%) and (14%) respectively.

THE 12 STARSIGNS' INFIDELITY PROFILES

ARIES MAN AND INFIDELITY

*Half (50%) of all attached Aries men have affairs.

*17% go astray just once. "Mind you, my one affair has lasted 15 years," comments one unfaithful Aries.

*Just over a fifth (21%) have between two and five illicit romances.

*11% are unfaithful more than five times.

*55%—top score for all male starsigns—throw up their hands and blame sheer physical attraction for their affair. "I just couldn't help myself," is a common Aries remark.

*31% blame infidelity on sexual short-changing at home, that's below average.

*A slightly above average 23% couldn't resist the thrill of the chase.

*21% got bored with their partner.

*Very few male Aries indeed—at 9%, theirs is the lowest score in the zodiac—say they had an affair because they fell in love. "Sex, lust, excitement, danger—I've felt all these for my mistresses, but only my wife deserves my love," says 42-year-old Kirk, veteran of many affairs.

*8% were revitalised by a younger lover, 5% taught so much by an older one.

*Just 5% saw an affair as a way out of an unsatisfactory marriage.

HOW HE HANDLES HER AFFAIR

*A middle range 24% of Aries men would ask for a split straight-away if their partner was unfaithful.

*16% would grab a get-back-at-her lover.

*Way over half, however (58%) opt for conciliation and show Aries is more understanding than traditional astrology has always believed.

*There's hardly an Aries male alive who can button his lip when deceived. Only 4%, joint lowest zodiac score of all, look the other way and hope for the best.

Believe it or not, Aries man is no more, no less, likely to have an

affair than average. When he does, it's an absorbing sport, not an obsession.

ARIES WOMAN AND INFIDELITY

*65% of Aries women have never had an affair. That puts them in joint fourth place, among the zodiac's most faithful.

*25%, exactly one in four, go off the rails just once.

*9% do it again, up to five times.

*2%—average overall for female signs—push the affairs total over five.

*Why do they do it? Because they fall in love, according to a staggering 39% of unfaithful Aries women. That's the joint top score for this category. "But I do wonder if I confuse love with that heady first rush of lust," admits Connie, 24, who's only been married two years but has had two lovers in that time. "I throw myself head over heels into an affair and I always get hurt."

*33%, exactly a third, strayed because they couldn't resist a lover's physical attraction.

*25% get bored with their partner.

*Almost a quarter (24%) say a lover made them feel more attractive. That's the lowest score of all women.

*A minority (15%) feel deprived of sex at home.

*Only 12% are turned on to infidelity by the thrill of the chase.

*Very few (8%) are revitalised by a younger lover, while even less (7%) fall for an older passion "teacher."

*Just 8% see infidelity as an easy marriage exit.

HOW SHE COPES WITH HIS AFFAIR

*41%—highest of our survey—want a divorce when their partner fools around. "When trust is broken what's left is just pretence and who can build a good relationship on that?" asks one wronged wife.

*Impulsive Aries is also the woman most likely to take a lover herself purely for spite—16% say they would do this.

*Only 43%—lowest figure in the survey—want to sit down and work things out.

*A tiny 3% can bear to pretend they don't know what's going on.

Aries woman is passionate and prone to follow her heart, but she can handle monogamy as long as it doesn't mean monotony. And she offers few second chances if deceived herself...

HOW DO THE SEXES DIFFER?

Men born under Aries are more unfaithful, and more often, than women. They're more than five times as likely to have six or more affairs (11% to 2%). And while male Aries admit they stray for purely physical reasons, it's emotions that lead Aries females to infidelity. 39% say they were unfaithful because they fell in love, compared to just 9% of men. But when a partner is unfaithful, Aries men are far and away the more understanding.

TAURUS MAN AND INFIDELITY

*Just under half (48%) of all Taurus men have had an affair.

*For 22%, above average, this means straying just once. "Once was enough—the guilt will stay with me for the rest of my life," confesses Eddie, 35.

*24%, second highest of all male scores, have allowed themselves to sin two to five times.

*Very few—just 6%—clock up more than five affairs. That's in the lower range for men.

*Asked why they were unfaithful, 42% fell for powerful physical attraction.

*Over a third, 35%, blame insufficient sex at home. For touchy-feely Taurus, that's tantamount to physical cruelty.

*One Taurus man in four, 25%, got bored with his partner.

*21%, slightly below average, were drawn by the thrill of the chase.

*17% reveal they fell in love.

*An average 13% did it because a lover made them feel more attractive.

*12% were rejuvenated by a younger lover, while far less (5%) were switched on by an older sex teacher.

*5% were looking for an excuse to end their marriage.

HOW HE HANDLES HER AFFAIR

*Taurus is the most understanding of all deceived men—65%, highest score in the zodiac, want to find out why their partner was unfaithful, and strive to give their relationship another chance.

*19%, in the upper range, turn a blind eye. "To start with it was because I couldn't decide what to do, and by the time I did decide, the affair was over," says one Taurus husband.

*Only 10%, lowest of all male signs, would react by taking a lover themselves.

*17%, second lowest of all, would seek divorce straight away. "If you can end a bond that easily, it can't have been too good in the first place," is an opinion expressed by several Taurus men.

Sensuality may lead Taurus man to temporary insanity, but in the long run he's a one-woman man, hitched for life to his home comforts. He'll go to great lengths to keep a relationship.

TAURUS WOMAN AND INFIDELITY

*Overall, 62% of Taurus women don't have affairs. So 38%, in the upper range for women, have been unfaithful at some time.

*24% make just the one slip.

*Only 10%, in the lower range, go in for two to five flings.

*But 4%, joint highest score for all women, do it over five times. "I've become addicted to picking men up when I'm away on business," confesses one Taurus wife of 20 years. "I suppose I just like to prove to myself I can—it gives me such a kick, especially when they're much younger. I tell them a false name, or no name at all, and there's no way they could ever track me down. I love my husband very much but my sex drive is, and always has been, much higher than his. I see these men as helping rather than damaging our marriage. It's just lust, after all, not love."

*And for 39% of Taurus women, pure physical attraction accounts for their infidelity.

*But the same number, 39%, put their affair down to falling in love. That's the joint highest score of all women.

*29% say their lover made them feel more attractive.

*26%, below average, were bored with their partner.

*20%, one in five, blame lack of sex at home. That's more than any other woman for this sensual, earthy sign.

*Just 13%, in the lower range, were simply tempted by the chase.

*8% fell for the energy and enthusiasm of a younger lover. Just half as many, 4%, went for someone older and sexually wiser.

*7% used an affair as a way of ending a failing marriage.

HOW SHE COPES WITH HIS AFFAIR

*55%—that's in the upper range—delve into the causes of a partner's affair, and want to put things right.

*But 31% reckon the answer is to take a lover themselves. "At least then I'd know what the attraction of infidelity was," says Geena, 29.

*An average 4% stay silent and hope it will end soon.

More lust-led than she looks, Taurus woman needs attention at home or she could develop a taste for playing away. But where her heart goes, her home often follows...

HOW DO THE SEXES DIFFER?

Both need lots of loving, and lusting, or they'll feel neglected— and Taurus men and women show similar levels of both boredom and physical attraction. But she's more than twice as likely to fall for flattery—29% of Taurus females, compared to 13% of men, had an affair because they were made to feel more attractive. And while he'll do all he possibly can to keep an old

marriage going, she may be more inclined to start afresh with a new one.

GEMINI MAN AND INFIDELITY

*Only a total of 38% of Gemini men have affairs—that's second lowest in the zodiac, unexpectedly for this "flirty" sign.

*Fewer than average, however, 18%, lapse just once.

*But Gemini's also the least likely of all men to have two to five episodes of infidelity, at 9%.

*A rather higher proportion (11%) make it a habit, with six or more lovers.

*For 38%, the driving factor in their affair was sheer physical chemistry.

*36% complain about not getting enough sex at home. "After my wife had refused me for two whole weeks because she said she was tired, I felt I had to prove I was still attractive, so I seduced a barmaid at the squash club," says one 32-year-old Gemini. "But I didn't take things from a one-night stand to an affair. You see my wife was pregnant at the time and my conscience wouldn't take it."

*For 26%, second highest score in the male zodiac, justification for the affair was falling in love.

*21%, in the lower range, really enjoyed the thrill of the chase.

*Just 18%, well below average, got bored with a partner.

*16%, above average, found a lover made them feel more attractive.

*13% declare that a younger lover gave them a new lease of love. But just 8% say the same about an older one.

*Just 2% used an affair as a means of quitting their marriage.

HOW HE HANDLES HER AFFAIR

*More Gemini men than most other male signs—28%, the joint top score—would immediately demand a divorce if they discovered a partner's cheating. Reasons given range from wanting a clean break to start again, to saving face. Geminis do tend to be influenced by what other people think.

*However, well over half Gemini men (56%) do adopt a reasonable approach and would be willing to re-adjust their relationship. That is in the lower range for men.

*An average number (13%) say they would stomp off and take a lover themselves. "It might not solve much long-term, but it would certainly make me feel better there and then." says one Gemini.

*A lower range 6% would find it best to make no comment at all and let the affair fizzle out.

His gift of the gab wins Gemini man extramarital offers—but, more talk than action, he has to fall in love before getting physical. He's first to speak up if he suspects a partner is sinning...

GEMINI WOMAN AND INFIDELITY

*Well over half, 62%, have never been unfaithful, and of those who have the second highest number in the zodiac, 24%, have cheated just once.

*Just 9%, in the lower range, have had two to five affairs.

*And only one in 100, least of all women, tots up more than five lovers.

*38%, second highest female score, say they were unfaithful because they were bored with their partner. "If we did it twice a month it was a miracle—and that's just have a conversation," grumbles Fran, a 41-year-old teacher. "Sex was even less frequent, and even more dull. After trying everything I could to perk my husband of 13 years up a bit, and failing miserably, I seduced my local librarian. He's a student and so stimulating in every way..."

*Exactly a third, 33%, were lured by physical attraction alone.

*An average 32% were drawn towards a lover because he made them feel more attractive.

*Just 23%, joint lowest of all women, had an affair because they fell in love.

*Almost as many, 20%, did it purely for the thrill of the chase. "Those delicious moments of flirting, of wondering will he, won't he, of almost dying with desire for him to touch me, but playing hard to get... there's nothing like it," says one Gemini.

*19% felt sex-starved at home—that's above average.

*8%, highest score of all women, were taught so much by an older lover—and 6% were invigorated by a younger one.

*An above average 12% treated an affair as a marriage emergency exit. "But I didn't realise consciously that's what I was doing until after it was all over," many admit.

HOW SHE COPES WITH HIS AFFAIR

*Most of all female signs (58%), Gemini likes to find out why infidelity happened and try to work something out together.

*Less than a third, 28%, seek a divorce. That's second lowest overall.

*Only an average 4% take a revenge lover themselves.

*An average 4% also play dumb and look the other way.

Whether deceiver or deceived, Gemini woman never allows hot emotions to cloud her cool head—but can use people to achieve her own ends. Still, chances are those "used" enjoy every minute.

HOW DO THE SEXES DIFFER?

Gemini men and women are at opposite ends of the forgiveness spectrum—when a partner errs, he's the man most likely to ask for divorce at once, and she's the woman most likely to look for reasons and try to start afresh. Yet the sexes actual scores are very similar, so they may have more in common than they think! Although identical percentages of male and female Geminis have been unfaithful, 10% more women than men have tried it once only, while 10% more men than women have gone for more than five. Yet she is the one with the low boredom threshold (38% blame affairs on boredom, compared to 18% of men). So it's no surprise that she enjoys the chase more than him, too.

CANCER MAN AND INFIDELITY

*Less than average, 45% of Cancer men have been less than faithful at some time.

*18% lapsed once only... so far.

*14%, in the lower range for men, admit to two to five affairs. "It's such a turn-on when women show they are interested in me, I simply can't resist it. I love having my ego—and other parts of me as well, of course—stroked," says 51-year-old company director Cy, a Cancer man.

*But second highest score overall, 13%, have had more than five flings.

*What led to the affair? For Cancer, more than any other man, it's boredom pure and simple. A massive one in three (33%) name this as the main reason for straying.

*31% responded to sheer physical attraction, that's by far the lowest score for men overall (average is 45%!). "I never want to sleep with someone until I've really got to know them," says one Cancer. "But then I always fall in love with them and it gets very messy. I wish I could just act on lust instead of insisting on feelings being involved."

*25%, lowest of all men, blame lack of sex at home for infidelity.

*23%, slightly above average, go for the thrill of the chase—but the same number, 23%, confess they simply fell in love and that was that.

*21%, highest male score overall, say they were revitalised by a younger lover, and Cancer is also the man most likely to blossom in the embrace of an older woman—12% say they've done so.

*He's susceptible to compliments, too, as 19% admit to falling for a lover who "made me feel more attractive."

*He's the man most likely to engineer an affair as an escape clause from a dodgy marriage—6% admit to this.

HOW HE HANDLES HER AFFAIR

*A middle range 57%, confronted with a partner's infidelity, would want to know what went wrong in a relationship, and how to put it right.

*He's not one to act in haste—a lower range 22% would ask for divorce there and then.

*14% would take a lover themselves.

*But Cancer is the man most likely to play the aching, waiting game—12% say they would look the other way and hope a partner would come back to them.

Cancer man has deep feelings and dreads break-ups, so he tries to ignore a partner's infidelity. His own affair is seriously love-led, and likely to end up as another marriage.

CANCER WOMAN AND INFIDELITY

*She's one of the most faithful women in the zodiac—71% of Cancer women have never had an affair.

*17% stray once—that's the lowest overall score for this category.

*One in 10, 10%, have between two and five lovers.

*And an average 2% have been through more than five affairs.

*Most common reason for being unfaithful is sheer physical attraction—for 35%, more than one in three.

*32% were wooed by the fact a lover "made me feel more attractive." No one should ever underestimate the importance of being told, and shown, you are loved, was the comment from several Cancer women.

*30% had an affair because they fell in love—that's in the upper range.

*26%, below average, blame boredom.

*16%, again below average, felt they weren't getting enough sex at home.

*13% were challenged by the thrill of the chase.

*9%, in the middle range, saw an affair as a way out of wedding vows.

*8% felt fresh again with a younger lover, and just 5% were encouraged by an older one.

HOW SHE COPES WITH HIS AFFAIR

*49% would talk things through and try to understand.

*Cancer woman is above-average inclined to demand divorce (38%).

*But she's least likely of all women to take a revenge lover herself (12%). "Well, chance would be a fine thing, left on my own with four kids, two dogs, a mortgage and a terminal mistrust of the male species," says Amanda, 38, whose husband has run off with her twin sister.

*4%, average for women of the zodiac, would opt to say nothing and hope and affair wouldn't last.

Anti-affairs in principle, Cancer woman finds them hard to handle in practice—either her own or a partner's. But she's no silent martyr, and may be so hurt she'll want out—no excuses.

HOW DO THE SEXES DIFFER?

Fidelity is important to both Cancer men and women—but she finds it easier to achieve than he does. Both have emotional, giving natures that can make affairs all-or-nothing, but although Cancer woman (30%) is even more prone to fall in love than Cancer man is (26%), she's also less forgiving when a partner makes a mistake. 38% of Cancer wives would ask for a divorce right away, compared to only 22% of husbands. Cancer man's thirst for love, however, can send him off the rails rather than keep him on them—he's the man most likely to have been tempted by illicit lovers who are much younger and much older.

LEO MAN AND INFIDELITY

*Almost one in two Leo men (47%) do have affairs.

*He's least likely in the zodiac to be unfaithful just once (15%)...

*... but a quarter of unfaithful Leos have had between two and five affairs, and that's the highest score overall for this category.

*A below average 7% repeat the pattern over five times.

211

*Asked to give a reason for infidelity, a high 47% cited pure physical attraction that was impossible to resist. "I'm only human after all, what am I supposed to do, walk around with a blindfold on?" asks one Leo.

*37% blamed not enough sex at home.

*31%, well above average for men, state they were bored with their partner. "I like my wife more than any other woman I've ever known, but to be honest I don't fancy her they way I used to—and I'm sure she feels the same way about me," reveals Lennie, 34. "We've been to counselling, but they just gave us all these touching games to play and neither of us could be bothered. It's natural to go off the boil a bit as you get older, isn't it?"

*Leo is the man second keenest on the thrill of the chase (27%).

*And one in five, 20%, have been revitalised by a younger lover—only 5% have been given a love education by an older woman. "I just don't go for older women, surely the best bit of having an affair is sampling something you can't have at home," says one Leo.

*Exactly average 20% say "I just fell in love."

*14% say a mistress made them feel more attractive.

*5% saw an affair as a way out of marriage.

HOW HE HANDLES HER AFFAIR

*Above average 27% of dramatic Leos would ask for a split straight away.

*58%, in the middle range, would be prepared to talk and try again.

*13% intend to take revenge by bedding a lover themselves.

*Only 7% stay silent and hope for a miracle.

Leo man has a weakness for younger women—but flourishes under any female attention. Illicit love's a game he's out to win, especially if he's neglected at home.

LEO WOMAN AND INFIDELITY

*The majority of Leo ladies don't fall by the wayside, but 39% do have affairs.

*Below average 21% have a single attempt at infidelity.

*But way above average 16% have between two and five forbidden affairs. "When you've done it once and broken your marriage vows, you may as well do it a dozen times, that's how I see it," says one Leo.

*An average 2% extend this to over five times.

*Reasons are many and varied. For 32%, pure physical attraction is the key.

*31% of flattery-loving Leos fell for a lover who "made me feel more attractive."

*30% admit to feeling bored with a current partner.

*For 25%, falling in love was the only excuse they needed.

*Just 18% were feeling short of sexual satisfaction at home.

*And 15%—less than might be expected of danger sign Leo, were drawn by the thrill of the chase.

*11%, above average for women, saw an affair as a convenient marriage exit.

*8%, in the middle range, were revitalised by a younger lover.

*7% say they've learned so much from a lover who's older.

HOW SHE COPES WITH HIS AFFAIR

*Exactly one in three see immediate divorce as the only answer (33%). A reflection of Leo's famous pride?

*But just over half (51%) would want to analyse the problem and revive their mortally wounded match.

*An upper range 15% would get their own back with a "revenge " lover.

*Only 5%, but still above the average result for women, would turn a blind eye and wait for the affair to end. "I couldn't do that, the stress of it all would kill me," comments Janie, 28.

Leo woman won't openly admit she likes pursuing other men, but she's a secretive and successful huntress. After her first attempt, infidelity can easily become a habit that's hard to beat.

HOW DO THE SEXES DIFFER?

Look no further than Leo for the sign of the multiple affairs— both men and women born under this starsign are most likely in the zodiac to have between two and five flings. And the sexes are alike, too, in a fondness for flattery and tendency to use infidelity as a lazy way out of a relationship that's not working. Leo men are lured by younger lovers more than women, and revel in the thrill of the chase. But Leo women are the more liable to lash out when their own pride is hurt—33% would react to a partner's infidelity by insisting on divorce, 15% by taking a revenge lover. For Leo men the figures are just 27% and 13%.

VIRGO MAN AND INFIDELITY

*47%, exactly average, of Virgo men have affairs. So 53% don't.

*Only 17%, in the lower range for men, are unfaithful just once.

*19% take the total up to between two and five affairs.

*A higher-than-average 11% make it more than five times.

*More than any other man, Virgo is unfaithful because his partner isn't giving him enough sex. Almost one in two, 48%, blame this for their infidelity. "Sex is a vital part of a happy, healthy life and if I can't get enough satisfaction at home I think I'm entitled to look elsewhere for it," comments one Virgo husband of nine years.

*Another 40%, below average for a male sign, say sheer chemistry was the reason an infidelity started.

*25% were bored with their other half.

*For 19% the reason pure and simple is "I just fell in love."

*17% were seduced by the thrill of the love-chase. "All the time I was pursuing my mistress in ever more outrageous ways I was thinking, if only those people who think I'm so dull and boring could see me now." says Virgo Brad, 39.

*13% found a younger lover made them feel livelier and more adventurous, and 8% gained maturity and experience from being with an older woman.

*A low 8% fell for someone who made them feel more attractive, reflecting Virgo's pragmatic, honest approach to love.

*4% saw an affair as a way out of a marriage. That's middle range.

HOW HE HANDLES HER AFFAIR

*He's not very keen to ask for divorce right out when a partner cheats on him. Just one in five, 20%, of Virgo men choose this reaction.

*Only 12% would consider taking a revenge lover—that's on the lower side of middle range.

*More than most men, Virgo prefers to ignore the rift in his relationship and hope the affair will end on its own. 12% choose this reply, proof perhaps of the difficulty Virgo has with confronting both his partner and his own hurt.

*More than half (61%) want to talk things through and try to heal a marriage.

Virgo man is a cautious creature, who'll carry on pretending nothing's wrong while his wife is unfaithful. He can't be goaded or flattered into an affair himself, but beware sexual starvation.

VIRGO WOMAN AND INFIDELITY

*She's usually well-behaved and loyal—32% of Virgo women have affairs, that's slightly below the norm. Quite often Virgo women find it hard to admit everything in their life isn't perfect, so this figure may not be absolutely accurate.

*Only 18% admit to just a single affair.

*12% have been unfaithful more than twice but less than five times.

*Only an average 2% go for over five lovers.

*What are Ms Virgo's reasons for infidelity? 37% have succumbed to sheer physical attraction.

*36%, third highest of all women, liked being made to feel more attractive. "After a lifetime of thinking of myself as a plain Jane, suddenly here was someone who almost worshipped me, and my body," says 40-year-old Elizabeth. "It made me so much more confident, both in bed and out of it."

*32% confess to boredom with their current partner.

*Surprisingly few (23%) let their hearts take the lead and fell in love. Virgo is ever the practical starsign.

*The thrill of the chase was a deciding factor for 22%.

*12%, most of all women, reveal they were revitalised by a younger man.

*But only 11%, lowest score of the female zodiac, blame infidelity on lack of sex at home.

*7% treated infidelity as a way out of a marriage.

*Just 4% learned about love and life from an older lover.

HOW SHE COPES WITH HIS AFFAIR

*38%, in the upper range for women, head for the divorce court without delay. "If it's over, it's over, and a clean break is best," says one Virgo. "Some women might humiliate themselves by 'fighting' for their man, but I'm not one of them. She'd be welcome to him."

*Below average 13% would take a lover themselves.

*5% would say nothing and wait for the affair to blow over.

*49%, in the lower range, would be understanding and try to find out why an affair happened.

With a passion for younger men, and a need for intellectual stimulation, Virgo woman is a challenging package who easily separates body and soul when it comes to infidelity. But betrayed, she finds it hard to forgive or forget.

HOW DO THE SEXES DIFFER?

Virgo men look the other way when wronged—while Virgo women walk the other way. The only person betrayed Ms Virgo wants to talk things through with is her lawyer. Women born under this starsign have a soft spot for younger lovers that's lacking among their male counterparts—but Virgo men set far more store by their own sexual satisfaction.

They're the men most likely to stray because of insufficient sex at home (48%). But Virgo women, at just 11% in this category, are the women least likely to start an affair for this reason.

LIBRA MAN AND INFIDELITY

*Libra is one of the least faithful men—just 47% say they haven't had an affair. So 53% of the air sign have.

*Just 16% say they strayed once only, second lowest male score for this category.

*22% treat their marriage or other commitment promises lightly enough to take between two and five lovers.

*But more Libras than any other man, 14%, have been unfaithful more than five times. "I'm very sociable and friendly and in my job I meet a lot of women—somehow it seems so natural to take it a stage further and have relationships with them. They all know I'm married, it's not a secret," says Bill, 29, a health club manager. "I do like the idea of marriage, but sometimes I think I'm one of those men who could never be faithful. It's not in my nature."

*Almost half of those who strayed, 48%, just couldn't say no to a spark of physical attraction.

*41% blamed lack of sex at home, second highest score for this section.

*28% admit to boredom with a partner that led to looking elsewhere for love.

*26%, in the upper range for this mind-ruled starsign, enjoyed the excitement of the chase.

*Just 17%, in the lower range, attribute an affair to falling in love.

*11%, less than might be expected for this starsign prone to vanity, fell for a lover who made them feel more attractive. Perhaps because Libra is already so sure of his own attractiveness.

*9% were lured by a younger lover—4% instructed by an older one.

*Average 4% used an affair to lever themselves out of an uncomfortable match.

HOW HE HANDLES HER AFFAIR

*Libra is by far the most likely zodiac man to get himself a revenge lover instantly! 19%—compared to an average of 13%—play unfaithful tit for tat. "I'm a firm believer in an eye for an eye—and also in showing a partner just what they've put you through," says one Libra man. "How can they possibly appreciate the hurt, pain and jealousy you've suffered unless they feel it too. Yes, it's tough on the third person, and a terrible reason to sleep with someone, but life's tough, isn't it?"

*23%, slightly below the male average, however, would instantly file for separation.

*Barely half (52%) can face a sit-down discussion and repair job.

*Only 9% stay silent on the sidelines and hope the crisis will pass.

Heart's desire or irresistible hobby? Libra man can think of no overriding reason to stray, yet often he's unfaithful time and time again—even in response to a partner's infidelity.

LIBRA WOMAN AND INFIDELITY

*Libra woman is also at the top end of the infidelity scale, with 40%, or two in every five, admitting to having affairs.

*Only an average 23% are unfaithful once.

*15%, second highest of all women, have between two and five affairs.

*But just an average 2% clock up over five lovers.

*She's most likely to look elsewhere if she's bored with her partner—42%, highest female score overall—do so. Main complaints seem to be lack of attention and proper communication. Libra will only talk so long if she feels she isn't being heard. Somewhere, she knows, is a more receptive head, and heart.

*She scores top of all women in the vanity stakes, too—39% of Libras say they stray because a lover makes them feel more attractive.

*38% are influenced by the sheer power of inter-personal attraction, that's in the upper range.

*For 30%, the passion pull is falling in love.

*A high 22% were turned on by the thrill of the chase.

*Just 16%, in the lower range, revealed they hadn't been bedded enough at home. "Anyone who thinks affairs are just about sex needs to think again," is one wry Libra comment.

*9% got hooked on toyboy temptation.

*Only 5% were taught by an older lover.

*A lower than average 7% wanted the affair to kill their marriage.

HOW SHE COPES WITH HIS AFFAIR

*52%, exactly average, would want to sit down, talk it out and make changes together.

*34% would opt for immediate parting, followed by divorce.

*15%, above average, reckon they would snatch their own lover just for spite.

*A tiny 3% shut their eyes, cross their fingers and hold on till things improve. Reluctance to face facts is not one of straight-talking Libra's faults.

Libra woman needs a man as fan, feedback and foil—if she loses interest, there's no holding her. She adores playing the love predator, but it's for attention more than affection. When she's the hurt party she'll either hit back, talk back, or both.

HOW DO THE SEXES DIFFER?

He's twice as unfaithful as her—36% of Libra men have had multiple affairs, compared to just 17% of women. But she's more prone to err just once (23%) than he is (16%). Exactly the same percentage (52%) of both sexes want to talk things over when a partner is unfaithful, but Libra women are keener on a clean break while men prefer to get their own back with a retaliation affair. Brain-linked boredom and a boost to confidence are her prime reasons for infidelity—while his are body-linked lack of sex at home and pure physical attraction.

SCORPIO MAN AND INFIDELITY

*Just over half of all Scorpio men are unfaithful (52%).

*He's the man most likely to just try a single round of illicit loving. 26% have only strayed once. But given Scorpio's innate commitment to relationships, this may be because he leaves his wife to move in with, even marry, his lover.

*20%, one in five, stray two to five times.

*Only 6% get into a pattern of more than five affairs. That's the second lowest male score overall. "I give so much of myself and my energy to just one relationship, I can't imagine spreading that between more people," says one aghast Scorpio.

*46% are tempted by physical attraction.

*34% say they had insufficient sex at home.

*24% blame their wandering on boredom with a permanent partner.

*19%, second highest male score, liked the fact a lover made them feel more attractive and desired.

*15% fell in love...

*15%, joint lowest of all men's signs, attributed an affair to the thrill of the chase. "Since the one affair I have had didn't start till over a year after I'd met the woman involved, that must be the longest-lasting chase ever," says Scorpio Christopher, 39.

*12% fell for the energy and enthusiasm of a younger woman. but the same amount, 12%, appreciated the charms of an older lover. That's almost double the male average of 7%.

*Scorpio is the man second most likely to use an affair to engineer the end of his marriage.

HOW HE HANDLES HER AFFAIR

*Only 15%—less than any other male sign—seek to divorce without trying any other things first. "It would be madness to throw away all we've worked to build together just like that," says one Scorpio. "My home means so much to me, I'll do anything to keep it together."

* 63% want to sit down and thrash the problem out with a partner—even if it means changes on both sides.

* But a high 18%—second only to Libra—want revenge, too, and may take their own lover to get it.

* 9%, slightly above average, keep quiet.

Ever-open to amorous adventures, Scorpio man is at risk of at least one affair—and tempted by experienced older women. He may strke back when cheated but sees divorce as a last resort.

SCORPIO WOMAN AND INFIDELITY

*Scorpio is the woman who is least faithful—42% have had affairs.

*29% have tried infidelity once, that's the most of any female starsign.

*12% have been part of two to five extra-marital relationships.

*But only one in 100, 1% of female Scorpios have had over five affairs. She may be the sexpot of the zodiac, but Ms Scorpio is usually far from promiscuous.

*What led her to look outside her relationship? Top reason is that a lover was so physically attractive. So say 41% of Scorpios. "I stood behind Tom in the bank queue and I could feel myself prickling all over with desire just being near him," confesses Scorpio Lucy, 28. "I couldn't take my eyes off the black hairs curling on the backs of his hands—I adore hairy men. And his deep blue eyes seemed to hypnotise me. We went straight from the bank to a motel and started an affair that lasted two years."

*31% were hooked because a lover boosted their confidence in their own looks.

*27% were bored with their partner, sexually and emotionally.

*26%, in the lower range, blame infidelity on falling in love. "I'd probably feel less guilty if I could honestly say it was love—but who am I trying to kid?" says one Scorpio mistress.

*23% of Scorpios, more than any other woman, admit one attraction was the thrill of the chase.

*Just 15% found sex was lacking at home. That's quite a surprise for the sign considered the zodiac's sexiest.

*A younger lover was the draw for just 9%, an older one for 7%.

*Below average 7% saw infidelity as a welcome marriage-breaker.

HOW SHE COPES WITH HIS AFFAIR
*Over half (53%) opt to talk and readjust.

*34% ask for divorce, right now.

*14%, exactly average for women, go out in search of their own lover.

*An above-average 5% say nothing at all and play the waiting game...

Scorpio woman loves the hot excitement of chasing, and catching, a fresh affair—but she's so naturally secretive, her spouse may never suspect. Chemistry is the key to her attraction, but she's surprisingly keen to cling to marriage.

HOW DO THE SEXES DIFFER?
Both Scorpio men, and Scorpio women, are the zodiac leaders in one-time illicit love (26% of men and 29% of women have been unfaithful just once). But physical attraction and danger are more vital to her than to him. Scorpio males, and females, show above-average interest in older lovers, but she's more inclined to fall in love in an affair than he is (26% women to 15% men). As for a partner being unfaithful, where Scorpio men will resist forcing a split (only 15% would do so), Scorpio woment are less squeamish (34%).

SAGITTARIUS MAN AND INFIDELITY
*Sagittarius, the most faithful of the zodiac's men? That's what Astrosex found—63% of Sagittarius men have never had an affair, only 37% have been unfaithful at any time.

*Below average 19% stray once only.

*14% have between two and five lovers.

*Lowest result of all men, 4% of Sagittarius, have had more than five affairs.

*Chances are Sagittarius will only waver if he falls in love first—32%, most of any male sign, give this as the main reason for infidelity. "Does it make a love bond any less precious just because one of you is already involved? Less easy, perhaps—but not less special," states Sagittarius Grant.

*46%, however, are also driven by sexual attraction.

*And 36% land up with illicit love because of a lack of sex at home.

*27%, well into the upper range, succumb to the thrill of the chase.

*A low 18% got bored with a partner.

*Firmly less than the norm, 9% were drawn towards someone who made tham feel more attractive themselves.

*9% were revitalised by a younger lover, and the same number enjoyed the experience of an older one.

*4%, exactly average, treated an affair as a way out of maarriage.

HOW HE HANDLES HER AFFAIR

*63%, joint second highest score for men, want to talk together and rebuild bridges.

*25% would ask for a split.

*11%, less than average, would be tempted to take their own lover.

*Only 6% bite their tongues and look the other way.

Sagittarius man makes a very faithful partner indeed—until he falls deeply in love with someone else, anyway. He's highly practical and set on staying friends, whoever is to blame for a break-up.

SAGITTARIUS WOMAN AND INFIDELITY

*Sagittarius woman is the zodiac's most faithful, too. A stunning 73% don't have affairs, that's almost three out of four. "I'm perfectly happy with my boyfriend, why would I want anyone else?" asks Chloe, 27. "It just complicates life and makes people I love unhappy. And all for what—a quick roll in the hay?"

*20%, just one in five, admit to a single indiscretion.

*Just 5%, lowest score in the female zodiac, have clocked up two to five affairs.

*And an average 2% have featured in over five flings.

*For 35%, motivation for an infidelity was that a "lover made me feel more attractive."

*And just 29%, lowest of all women, reckon pure physical attraction was the cause.

*30% fell in love, that's bang in the middle range.

*23%, again the zodiac's lowest, were bored with a partner.

*19% say there wasn't enough sex at home.

*15% liked the thrill of the chase.

*Only 8% were looking for a handy marriage exit.

*An average 6% were eager to learn new love lessons from an older man.

*But Sagittarius is left cold by toyboys! Just a minuscule 1% put an affair down to the attractions of a younger lover. "I like my men to be men, and that means knowing their way around sex without my having to show them," says one Sagittarius. "I've enough trouble with my own energy levels getting too high without trying to control some man's, too."

HOW SHE COPES WITH HIS AFFAIR

*Sagittarius manages reasonably well when a partner cheats, it seems. An above-average 57% want to talk and start afresh together.

*31%, less than most women, ask for an immediate split.

*13%, below average, take a revenge lover themselves.

*And just 3% believe in turning a blind eye in the hope the affair will fizzle out.

Sagittarius woman has her heart set on storybook marriage and resists a senseless affair—she has enough fun, and sexy frolics, for two. If life does get stale she may size up her next husband— but he won't be someone younger.

HOW DO THE SEXES DIFFER?

One of the survey's biggest shocks is that both Sagittarius sexes are by far the most faithful in the zodiac. 63% of men and 73% of women are born under this starsign have never had an affair. And Sagittarius is surprisingly tolerant when a partner slips off the rails, too. Main differences crop up in reasons for being unfaithful—he does it for external reasons, because he falls in love or gets carried away by the chase. For her, disenchantment starts at home when she gets too little sex, or compliments, and starts to notice other men. But they won't be toyboys, she's far less enthusiastic than Sagittarius men about a younger lover.

CAPRICORN MAN AND INFIDELITY

*Supposedly steady Capricorn is the most unfaithful man of all— 54% admit to having had an affair...

*Almost one in four (24%) stray just once. That's the second-highest male score for this section.

*17% have more than one and less than five affairs.

*But an incorrigible 12% go on to have more than five, putting Capricorn in joint third place across the zodiac.

*The thrill of the chase is a key factor in infidelity for 31% of Capricorns, the top male score. "Targeting a girl who seems so unobtainable, then working on her slowly bit by bit, day by day— there's nothing like it," says Capricorn Michael, 32.

*And more Capricorns than any other men's sign also fall for a lover who makes them feel more attractive—21%.

*48%, or almost one in two is affected by physical attraction.

*38% tumble into an affair because there's too little sex on offer at home.

*Just 19% reveal they were unfaithful because "I fell in love," that's below average.

*But boredom with a current partner isn't a noticeable factor—this reason is given by only 12% of male Capricorns, lowest in the zodiac. "I think it's a cop-out when men blame infidelity on their partner—it usually happens because you fancy someone else, whatever the situation at home. Anything else is little more than a lie," proclaims one Capricorn who's recently been unfaithful for the first time after six years of marriage.

*Younger and older lovers both have little appeal for Mr Capricorn. Just 5%, well below average, and less than any other man, have been "revitalised" by a younger woman. But not one Capricorn man has got involved with an older woman!

*And he doesn't believe in using someone else to fight his battles— just 2%, half the average number, see an affair as a way out of a sinking marriage.

HOW HE HANDLES HER AFFAIR

*He's above-average likely to ask for a divorce (27%).

*But 60% of Capricorns would want to ask why and stop it happening again. That's also above average.

*He's the least likely man of all to say nothing and hope his wife's carry-on won't carry on—this is an option for just 4%.

*And taking his own tit for tat lover isn't popular either. Just one in 10 would consider this, that's least of all male starsigns.

Capricorn man is the kind of charismatic, powerful figure women will always fling themselves at. He's pretty good in catching them, yet if his wife has an affair, she can expect the cold shoulder but no underhand tricks.

CAPRICORN WOMAN AND INFIDELITY

*Capricorn woman is below average in her chances of being unfaithful—just 36% are.

*26% have had just one affair. That's in the upper range of the zodiac. 8% have two to five lovers.

*2% stretch to over five.

*14% of female Capricorns have affairs as a way out of marriage— that's way above the overall average of 9%. "I knew Keith, my husband, would never accept the shame of me having an affair with his rugby team-mate, so I set out to seduce him on purpose," reveals Fiona, a 29-year-old secretary. "I can't say it wasn't extremely enjoyable, mind you! It was easy to let Keith 'accidentally' find out, and next thing I knew he was filing for divorce. It was the best outcome all round if you ask me."

*38% were also influenced by the way a lover boosted confidence in their looks.

*And the same number, 38%, acted on sheer physical chemistry between a couple.

*28% admit boredom with a partner played a part.

*24% fell in love.

*An average 17% weren't getting enough sex in their current set up.

*Only 12%, joint lowest of all female signs, relished the thrill of the chase.

"I like to know where I stand—if we're going to have an affair, let's well get on with it." says one practical Capricorn.

*Just 5% warmed to a younger lover. But Capricorn appreciates maturity more than any other woman—8% admit they learned a lot from an older lover.

HOW SHE COPES WITH HIS AFFAIR

*48% are prepared to make do, and mend their marriages, or try to. But that's the second-lowest total of all female signs.

*Almost as many, 40%, or two in five, ask for divorce and that's that.

*Above average 15% go straight out seeking a lover of their own.

*5%, also in the upper range, say nothing and simply hope for the best.

If Capricorn woman's man messes about, it may be curtains for the match, yet she's likely to have tried illicit love herself, at least once. Perhaps as a sneaky way of winning her own freedom.

HOW DO THE SEXES DIFFER?

Capricorn woman is one of the more faithful starsigns, Capricorn man is one of the least. 36% of females born under this

starsign admit to infidelity—but 54% of males. Both relish a chance to feel fancied, but less up-front Capricorn woman is seven times as likely to use an affair as an exit route from a shaky relationship (14% women, to just 2% men). She's also more inclined to take a revenge lover (15% do, compared to 10% men) when a partner strays, and much less interested in his excuses.

AQUARIUS MAN AND INFIDELITY

*Slightly less Aquarius men than average have had affairs—just 48%.

*He's high on the list of one-affair men, at 22%. "I just had to know what it was like," is a common comment.

*14% have up to five affairs, that's in the lower range,

*But 12%, joint third highest number, manage more than five lovers.

*For 43%, the reason for having an affair was irresistible chemistry.

*A below average 30% blame not getting enough sex within a relationship.

*23% had fallen in love with the other woman—perhaps surprisingly for cool Aquarius, that's above average.

*22% were bored with their partner, and the same number enjoyed the thrill of the chase.

*One in 10, 10%, reveal they were revitalised by a younger lover.

*7% learned a lot from someone older.

*3% used an affair as a means of escape from marriage.

*And just 5%, lowest of all men and way below average, yielded to temptation because a lover made them feel more attractive. "I know who I am and what I am, I don't need to have that backed up by someone else," says one indignant Aquarius. "If I'm going to have an affair it's for more positive reasons than having my ego flattered."

HOW HE HANDLES HER AFFAIR

*Divorce is high on Aquarius man's agenda—28%, joint top males' score, go for this.

*Above average 15% take a lover themselves out of spite.

*8% play dumb and keep jealousy, and anxiety, hidden in the hope the affair fizzles out.

*But Aquarius is the man least likely to talk things through and make compromises—let alone accept any blame himself. Just one in two (50%) wants to ask why infidelity happened.

He doesn't need the flattery, so why would Aquarius man have an affair? Curiosity, being chased, or simply an escape from being conventional. But on the receiving end of infidelity, he's less new man, more Mr Angry...

AQUARIUS WOMAN AND INFIDELITY

*Just 36% are unfaithful, that's in the middle range for zodiac women.

*22%, just over one in five, have just one affair.

*13%, above average, dabble from two to five times.

*But just one in 100 Aquarius women make it a five-plus pastime. "I'm so fussy, I haven't had more than five lovers in my lifetime, let alone during my marriage," says one Aquarius wife.

*Why does she do it? No one reason really stands out for Aquarius woman. For 33%, pure physical attraction was a prime driving force towards infidelity.

*30% blame the onset of boredom with a current partner.

*28% say they fell in love.

*28% again, second lowest of all women, responded to being made to feel more attractive by a lover.

*17% couldn't resist the thrill of the chase.

*15% say there wasn't enough sex, or satisfaction on offer at home.

*9%, second highest of all women, were fired with sexy enthusiasm by a younger lover.

*But just 2%, lowest of all women, felt in awe of an older man. "To

me, love and sex is about youth and beauty," says Paulette, 25. "Wrinkled old men with beer guts and saggy skin have no place in that picture. I certainly don't fancy anyone over 35."
*A below average 7% were prepared to use an affair as a way-out of a marriage they didn't want any more.

HOW SHE COPES WITH HIS AFFAIR
*Aquarius is the woman most likely to work at reconciliation, and put her own hurt aside to try again (58%). "Nobody said it has to be easy, but I cope by distancing myself from Doug's affair, and always keeping it in perspective—it lasted six weeks, our marriage has been going 16 years," says one cheated-upon wife. "I used to torture myself with images of them making love together, but why bother? It happened, it's over—now let's get on with the rest of our lives."
*Just 26% of Aquarius females would ask for a divorce straight off after a partner's infidelity. That makes this the most tolerant starsign of all women.
*15%, above average, would consider taking a lover themselves to get back at an errant husband.
*6%, most of all women, would say nothing at all. Because they don't care—or don't want to be seen to care?
Aquarius woman makes her own marriage rules—and that includes how she reacts to infidelity. She might play games, but isn't keen to let adultery, hers or her partner's, sour her life...

HOW DO THE SEXES DIFFER?
Aquarius men and women are less free with their love than might be expected—but men are 12 times more likely to indulge in multiple affairs than women (12% to 1%). The opposite of most starsign couples, if a partner has an affair, Aquarius woman is keenest to understand, while Aquarius man is the zodiac's most inflexible. Compared to other signs, neither needs a lover to back up their own self-image, but men of this

starsign are **twice as likely as women to stray** because of insufficient loving at home (30% to 15%).

PISCES MAN AND INFIDELITY

*46% go astray at some time, just on the lower side of average for the zodiac's men.

*24%, second highest male score, sin just once.

*14% have between two and five affairs.

*7%, less than the male average of 9% have over five lovers.

*Pure physical attraction is emotional Pisces' weak spot—a whopping 52% attribute infidelity to this.

*30% weren't getting enough sex at home. "Sex is a way of expressing love, and if the sex goes, then so does the love," one Pisces speaks for many with this comment.

*24%, almost a quarter, relished the thrill of the chase.

*20% or one in five, second highest male score, were revitalised by a younger lover's energy and ideas. "My skin looks better, I'm fitter, and even my clothes have been updated. I can thoroughly recommend a fling with someone 25 years younger for any man facing middle age. The only problem is when your wife wonders why you've changed..." so says Roger, a 45-year-old dentist with a 20-year-old nurse.

*Below average 19% blame boredom with a partner for their infidelity.

*Just 17%, on the low side for romantic Pisces, fell in love.

*13% reveal their lover made them feel more desired and attractive.

*9% melted into the arms, and charms, of an older lover.

*Virtually none of honest Pisces men stooped to using an affair to end a marriage.

HOW HE HANDLES HER AFFAIR

*Badly. Getting on for a third of Pisces men (28%) are so hurt they ask for a permanent split straight away.

*53%, in the lower range, are willing to ask why it happened and try to work out a future together.

*10%, lowest of male starsigns, would try to take a lover of their own.

*Another 10%, above average this time, would say nothing and hope things work out in their favour.

He can play the philanderer, and when he does Pisces man may well choose a younger woman. But however he revels in passionate storms, marriage is his emotional anchor. If he can't ignore a partner's affair, he'll abandon ship.

PISCES WOMAN AND INFIDELITY

*Pisces is the tops for multiple love affairs! 4%, double the female average, have had more than five lovers.

*Yet her overall infidelity rate is lower than average—61% of Pisces women have never looked at another man.

*24% have been unfaithful, but only the once.

*11%, exactly average for women, have entered into affairs between two and five times.

*More Pisces women than any other female sign blame lack of sex at home for their fling (20%). "Not even sex itself, but cuddling and kissing are what suddenly dried up in my long-term relationship," says Sandra, 37. "There just wasn't any romance around any more."

*But top Pisces reason for infidelity is pure physical attraction, which earns the zodiac's second highest score of 40%.

*35% fell in love (third highest score for all women).

*35% felt more attractive in the light of a lover's attention.

*Just 16% enjoyed the thrills of the chase.

*9%, second most of all women, were revitalised by a younger lover.

*8%, joint top female result, relaxed into the mature experience of an older man. "It's so nice just to lie back and be adored by a man who knows exactly what he's doing," admits one Pisces.

*Pisces is least likely of all women to use an affair as an emergency marriage exit. Just 6% do so.

HOW SHE COPES WITH HIS AFFAIR

*She's the woman most inclined to go straight out and wreak revenge via her own lover (16%). But all too often this act hurts tender Pisces more than her hate object.

*6%, also highest score of the female signs, choose to lie low and look the other way.

*31% demand divorce, with no messing.

*A below average one in two (50%) opt for trying to understand and revamp the relationship.

Pisces woman often deceives herself as well as her husband—falling in love, and lust, too easily and acting on instinct, but she never intends an affair to affect her marriage, whoever has it.

HOW DO THE SEXES DIFFER?

Although they're generally more faithful than the starsign's men, Pisces are the women who have most multiple affairs—and taking a lover is their first reaction to a partner's cheating too, while Pisces men are least likely to do so. Chemistry plays a large part in Pisces affairs for both sexes—but women in particular may feel sex-starved at home (20%). Male members of this starsign have had over twice as many younger lovers as women (20% to 9%), but women are twice as likely to fall head over heels in love (35% to 17%). Whatever the situation, neither Pisces sex sees infidelity as a way out of marriage.

5
Sexuality Profiles

*WHICH STARSIGNS MAKE LOVE MOST, AND LEAST, OFTEN * WHO WANTS MORE SEX * STARSIGNS WHO GET TOO MUCH SEX *WHO HAS THE MOST SEXUAL PARTNERS *COUPLES WITH DIFFERENT SEX DRIVES *WHO DOES ALL THEY WANT TO IN BED * WHICH STARSIGNS LOVE THE SAME SEX *WHO THINKS WHAT ABOUT SEX *RAISING THE SATISFACTION LEVELS * THE 12 STARSIGNS' SEXUALITY PROFILES*

Who are the real sheet-scorchers of the zodiac? Will Scorpio be the sexual champion-and is the female of the starsign more daring than the male? Which starsign believes sex is pure magic? Many starsign secrets, shrouded in mystery until now, are revealed by the AstroSex survey. Some results match traditional astrological ideas—but many do quite the opposite.

WHICH MEN MAKE LOVE EVERY DAY?
Looking at the zodiac men's responses overall, an average of 12% make love every day, 23% four or more times a week and 34% one to three times weekly. 14% opt for one to three sex bouts per month, 10% make love rarely, and 6% are completely celibate at the moment.

But when results are looked at individually, it is love champion Leo who roars into first place for frequency of lovemaking. For almost one in four, 24%, of Leo men make love every day. That's double the male average of just 12%. But Leo's fellow fire sign Sagittarius lives up to his rather lazy reputation in this section—only 5%, or one in 20, make love every day! That's the lowest score for all men.

CASE HISTORY OF A LEO MAN

David, 42 and a Leo, has made love every day, for 20 years.

"Most people see sowing their wild oats as a youthful adventure that tails off as they settle down. Especially when they marry. Not for me—sex has been my lifelong love affair, despite starting relatively late.

"Believe it or not, I was a virgin when I left home at 20. But once I hit London and moved into a shared flat, there was no stopping me. My first real affair was with a beautiful girl who showed me what I'd been missing. If anything, her sex drive was greater than mine. We'd leave parties early so we could rush home to make love. At weekends we'd wear the sheets out. But perhaps inevitably, our passion burned itself out. Somehow we never got around to finding out more about each other than where our erogenous zones were.

"After she left me I eased a broken heart with a succession of one-night stands. I was, and still am, an outrageous flirt. It still gets results. Sex has been a priority in my life ever since. I physically hurt if I go a day without sex. And I have to make up the next. That leads me into trouble. I've been married twice and had too many affairs to count during them. Yet I'd still say quantity can't replace quality. Both my wives were crackers in bed, that's what attracted me.

"One thing I'm not is a dirty old man. My marriages didn't fail because I was always off with a younger model—in fact both my wives and most of my memorable girlfriends have been older than me. There's something about an experienced woman I find more of a turn on. I love women and I love sex. So I try my best to be a good lover. But I draw the line at paying for it. I couldn't enjoy making love to someone who didn't want me as much as I did her."

STARWATCH
That fiery Leo should enjoy a larger share of loving than men of any other sign is no surprise. But the starsign who comes second to him for sexual frequency is Virgo, on 17%. So behind that cool exterior, this sign is smouldering, ready to explode with desire in the right company...

Looking at the average number of sexual experiences per week, Leo again comes tops among the men, with 3.3 times, way above the overall male average of 2.7. Next comes Pisces at 3.2 and adventure-loving Aquarius at 2.9. "I've been married two years," says Jamie. "And I'm delighted to say sex has not become a must-do-it-to-prove-love chore. We treat every night as a romantic experience. Often that doesn't mean full sex. We both love massaging each other which, after a long day at work, can send us into a blissful sleep. But spontaneous lovemaking in the kitchen, living-room, even on the stairs, thrills me more than anything."

The male starsign who makes love least often is Sagittarius, on just 1.9 times per week. And Gemini is second least frequent on 2.5 times a week.

STARWATCH
To find deep, dark Pisces hot on the heels of loveking Leo for frequency of sex defies traditional belief that Pisces, although in love with love, is somewhat slow and cautious. The 40% of this sign who make love one to three times a week—putting him in the lead in this section—must have found their soulmates.

Libra and Scorpio men lead the field in making love more than four times a week—27% of each claim this pattern. But only 13% of

Virgos manage four plus, the lowest score overall for this category.

Favourite frequency for the majority of men is one to three times per week, with 34% of men overall saying this is their usual sex pattern—and here Pisces soars to the top with 40%. Taurus, Leo and Cancer trail behind other men with 29% each. But only because all three signs prefer to have sex even more often than that.

MEN WHO HOLD BACK

Only 5% of Sagittarius men make love every day, that's by far the lowest score overall. Just 15% have sex four or more times a week (second lowest overall), but Sagittarius is the man most likely to opt for one to three times a month (21%), to admit he has sex rarely (13%) or is completely celibate at the moment (10%, or one in 10). Next lowest participants in love every day are Gemini men, with just 8%, followed by another fire sign, Aries, on 9%. And Gemini men are also second most likely in the zodiac to be celibate at the moment (8%).

STARWATCH

Sagittarius is a high-energy lover who sees sex as an adventure—or so we thought. Now we see him holding back from non-stop loving. Is he fussy, lazy, low in libido—or is there a come-tempt-me lover lurking behind that worldly-wise exterior?

CASE HISTORY OF A SAGITTARIUS MAN

Sagittarius Paul, 25, is a computer programmer, single at the moment.

"My friends think I'm pretty cool, I know, because I always have a gorgeous girl on my arm when I turn up at parties and discos. But it's a bit of a front. Because although I know a lot of women, and feel comfortable in female company, once the chat-up is over, it's rare for me to want to take things much further. A girl has to be very special for me to want to start up much of a relationship. And I don't think it's fair to lead someone on, then drop them the next day.

"When I do have a steady girlfriend, I like her to be my friend as well. Sex is only part of the fun. If I can't talk to someone the morning after, I'd rather not bother with the night before. Then, when I am in a physical relationship, I've got everything.

"I never feel deprived of sex, even if I go months without it. Probably because I'm arrogant enough to think I could get it whenever I want it. But I want more than that, and I believe I have more to offer. Friendship is an essential part of loving for me."

WHAT THE WOMEN SAY

How often do the women of the zodiac make love? 2.6 times per week, on average, that's just a fraction behind the men's weekly average of 2.7. But only 9% of women claim to make love every day, compared to 12% of men. 41% work out at one to two times a week, by far the most common sexual pattern. 16% make love one to three times a month, 7% rarely and 5% are celibate right now. In both cases, these are less than the men's figures of 10% "rarely" and 6% celibacy.

Scorpio woman streaks ahead in the making love every day stakes—14% do so, well above the female average of 9%. Yet again, as so often in the survey, she lives up to her image as the sexiest sign. Next comes lusty Ms Leo (12%) and, perhaps more unexpectedly, Gemini (10%)—the sign often considered all talk and no action.

And the female starsigns least likely to make love every day are Taurus and Virgo, who both tend to prefer quality rather than quantity. "It takes me so long to get fully aroused and relaxed, I'd never find the time to make love every day." comments 29-year-old Virgo Dawn.

CASE HISTORY OF A SCORPIO WOMAN

Ella, a single 25-year-old Scorpio window dresser, knows how vital sex is to her.

"Making love has always been a crucial ingredient in a relationship as far as I'm concerned. In fact, the last long-term affair I had, which finished a couple of months ago after 18 months, only kept going because every time I thought of ending it, I'd remember the great time we'd had the night before.

"On the other hand, I've known lovely men who would have made loyal, hard-working husbands—but I couldn't go on seeing them because they did nothing for me when it came to the tingle factor. That's the term I use for grading men. Do I only have to think of their name to feel a tingling sensation down my spine? If the answer's no, I end it, regardless of other factors.

"This hasn't always made for a smooth life. For some reason sexual attraction and that slight element of danger go hand in hand for me. Consequently, I've been involved with hopeless layabouts and even someone whose business dealings wouldn't have impressed my father, a policeman. But I can't help myself."

One in every four Aries, and Aquarius women (25%) has sex four or more times a week, joint top female score for this section. And the least keen on this frequency are Ms Cancer and Ms Sagittarius (19% each). Almost one in every two Sagittarian women, however, do make love one to three times a week—with 46%, she's far out in front here.

Virgo woman, with a rating of 21%, is the woman in the zodiac most inclined towards passion once or twice a month—hot on her heels is Leo, with 20%.

And in a result exactly the opposite of the men's, Sagittarius is the woman least likely to rate her frequency of sex as "rarely"—just 6% of women do so, compared to 13% of men. This reflects a general trend, since overall 7% of women on average make love rarely—for men the figure is 10%. And if men, on the whole, are making love more, some are also making love less—6% of male starsigns describe themselves as celibate at the moment, compared to 5% of women. And twice as many men as women have given up sex for life. That includes 2% of Leo men, who are the most highly-sexed sign.

Looking now at general frequency of sex, Ms Scorpio's 2.8 times a week puts her out in front yet again. But hot on her heels are Aquarius, Aries and Leo, all boasting 2.7 times. The female signs who average least often are Aquarius and Cancer, both 2.4 times a week.

STARWATCH

Demanding Aries is in a surprising position, coming second of the sexiest female signs. Her need to control usually places her in the slow-to-get-going category.

WHO CAN'T GET SATISFACTION?

A staggering 94% of men, and 89% of women, who responded to the survey say they would like more sex in their lives. "Not to mention more life in my sex," jokes Aries George, 41. For Aries and Libra are the two male signs who give out the loudest cry for some extra loving, on 97% each. Put another way, only three in every hundred men born under these signs wouldn't like more sex.

The reasons for this may become apparent, looking back at the sexual frequency results. For only 9% of Aries, and 11% of Libra, men make love every day, both below average, so perhaps they feel they are getting less than their fair share. Sagittarius, the man who makes love least often of all, would also like to do something about this state of affairs—96% would like more frequent sex. But as ever with Sagittarius, ideas rarely catch up with reality.

Some men, however, would happily make do with less lovemaking—notably Scorpio, Taurus, Virgo and Aquarius (9% each). "Sex is one of life's great pleasures," says Mark, a married 30-year-old Scorpio, "But there are no prizes for performance. I'd rather have fabulous sex once a month than boring sex every night." So though only 10% of Scorpio men are having sex daily, compared to an overall average of 12%, this doesn't seem to be a problem to them.

Taurus and Virgo are already getting all the sex they can handle—or so it seems. 14% of Taurus men, and 17% of Virgo males, already make love at least once a day. "If I didn't seduce my wife every night she'd be suspicious," says Joe, a Taurus. "And she does very much rely on her power to arouse me for reassurance. I'm not saying sex is a duty, but I'd have to find an easier job if she decided she wanted even more."

STARWATCH
Who would have believed that sensuous Scorpio or sexdynamo Aquarius man would be first in the queue to complain about too much sex? Yet undisputedly, AstroSex proves this is the case.

WOMEN WHO WANT MORE, MORE, MORE
Gemini, Leo and Scorpio (all 92%) are the female starsigns who would most relish some extra loving. That's despite these same three signs also being the women most likely to make love at least once a day already. In this respect the women differ from the men completely—since it's the male starsigns who are already getting less sex than average who want more, and among female signs it's those women who already get most sex who want even more.

CASE HISTORY OF A GEMINI WOMAN
Maria, 31, and a Gemini, is a caterer who's now on her third marriage, to a Virgo.

"All my life, I dreamed of being swept off my feet by a man. No one is more shocked than I am that two marriages have failed and my third one isn't going well.

"Each time it's followed the same pattern. A glorious honeymoon period that's vanished into thin air. I try to tempt my husband into making love more often—we used to do it three or four times a week. But he says these days I always leave him feeling that he's disappointed me. And that puts him off.

"The trouble is, when I say our sexlife isn't what it was, my husband interprets that as needing to do it twice a night instead of once. What I mean is, I wish we could do it in the afternoons, or on a blanket on the lawn. Instead it's become a nightly ritual as exciting as flossing my teeth."

STARWATCH

Gemini is the flirt and flit sign—but rarely seen as sexually insatiable. That she leads the cry for more loving could be due to a need for the partner who will fulfil her cherished fantasies.

Topping the list of women who would like less sex in their lives is Ms Cancer, on 15%, followed by Capricorn and Aries (both 14%).

But since quiet, home loving Ms Cancer is already having more sex than average, it may be a question of being satisfied with life as it is rather than shying away from sexual demands.

"Friday night is the time we set aside for lovemaking," says Rachel, a Cancer-born secretary who's been married three years. "We probably have sex a couple of times a week as well, but that really depends on how busy we are, and how tired.

"But by making a regular Friday date with each other, even though we're married, we make sure other aspects of our lives don't swamp the romantic side. It might sound a bit formal to other people but it works well for us. We do nothing else on Friday nights except please each other. That wouldn't work if it was more times a week. Then I'd feel it was some sort of endurance test."

But the bad news for the boys is, in general almost twice as many women (11%) as men (6%) would be happy to have less sex.

WHO HAS THE MOST PARTNERS?

Once again men lead the way—24% of the male starsigns who responded to the survey claim to have bedded down with more than 20 lovers. Whereas among the women of the zodiac, the corresponding figure is only 9%.

Way, way out in front in the male stakes is Mr Libra—more than one in three (34%) have scored with over a score of partners. Yet his female opposite number is the least likely woman to have done so (just 7%). And while Scorpio woman is joint leader in the most lovers section for women (11%), among the men this is the sign that rates lowest. Once again, AstroSex shows up huge differences between each gender within the same starsign.

STARWATCH

The Scorpio male totally smashes the love-em and leave-em sexual rogue image by being the least likely of all men to have had a harem of lovers. And Libra proves traditional astrology wrong in casting him as the sign most devoted to commitment— love hungry Libra is the man most likely (34%) to have had over 20 partners, way above the 24% average.

CASE HISTORY OF A LIBRA MAN

Elliot, aged 28, works in PR and is a Libra. He is currently "in the throes" of leaving a girlfriend of a year, a Cancer

"Since I was 18 I have been in one long-term relationship after another, each lasting between one and two years. Whenever an affair has started to go wrong—and I can always spot the warning signs—I go on a bit of a spree with my mates.

"I love that sudden rush of freedom, the novelty of going to a party and not knowing who you'll leave with. But what I can't stand is the forced conversation next morning. Or, worse, the obligatory date just to make it seem you were interested in more than sex. A girl may look irresistible in her disco gear, but that doesn't mean she's going to be sparkling company over dinner.

"My love life is a bit of a yo-yo. I'm either bogged down with one woman, or fielding phonecalls from so many different ones I can't put the face to the name.

"One ex-girlfriend I had stayed friends with me. It isn't often that that happens. I don't have the free time. She thought I should give myself a complete break from women for a while until I could decide just what I really want from a relationship. But I couldn't do that. I'd miss the sex too much."

The men who have had more than 11 sexual partners are Libra (49%), Aquarius (46%), Capricorn (45%) and Leo (43%). Two of these starsigns, Leo and Capricorn, appear for the female side, too. 26% of Leo ladies have enjoyed a wide range of partners, 25% of Capricorns claim a minimum of 11 sexual partners and 24% of Scorpios say the same.

"Actually, I was rather shocked when I came to add up the number of partners I've had," says Capricorn-born Louise, 39. "It makes me sound promiscuous, which I certainly don't feel I am. Normally I go out with someone for quite a while before actually sleeping with them. But I suppose I did go a bit wild in my twenties—curiosity, I suppose.

"I'm married now, but even if I wasn't, I wouldn't be jumping into bed with different men every Saturday night."

The most common number of partners for both men and women is between two and five—30% of men and 44% of women opt for this answer. Among the men, Sagittarius (38%) says yes to this group more than any other male sign, and Libra (18%) says it less. While the woman most likely to have had two to five lovers is Aquarius (47%)—a surprise for the sign normally thought of as experimental. Ms Leo, at 34% a full 10% lower than the female average, is the woman who scores lowest in this section.

But loyal Leo ladies are also by far the starsign most satisfied with a single partner. 16% of Leo women have had only one lover, compared with 8% of Geminis. While 15% of Gemini men boast only one sexual partner, compared to just 3% of Sagittarius men. That makes Gemini men five times more likely than Sagittarius to be one-woman men.

CASE HISTORY OF A GEMINI MAN

Gemini Len, 18, is a trainee accountant, with a Libra girlfriend, Jayne.

"Why have I had only one lover? Because I haven't had time for more—yet! Not that I am consciously thinking of cheating on my girlfriend. At the moment we are very happy, and being each other's first sexual partner does give us a special sort of bond. It does seem inevitable, though, that we won't be together for life.

"Sex was a bit of a disaster at first, but with practice, it's got better. We are still at the experimental stage, if you like, so don't need the novelty of other people. What I can't deny is that I've got a wandering eye even if, so far, the rest of me hasn't followed, and only ever having made love to one woman, I do wonder what the rest of them are like.

"I'd be furious if I found out my girlfriend was seeing somebody else. I suppose I'm still pretty nervous about whether I'm any good at sex, and would immediately think she'd gone elsewhere because I'm useless."

STARWATCH

Gemini is a fickle sign. The survey shows the Gemini male most likely by far to have only one lover in a lifetime, but the female from this same starsign is least likely of all women to stay true to only one partner.

HOW DO PARTNERS' SEX DRIVES COMPARE?

More than half of the zodiac's men (53%) rate their own sex drive as higher than their partner's—but less than a third (31%) of the female starsigns say the same thing. But while just one in 10 (10%) of males replying to the survey say they are overwhelmed by a lover's lusty needs, for women the figure is 27%.

Though the zodiac's women take the lead in judging their relationship perfectly matched sexually (42%), men are not far behind with an average score of 37% in this category.

LUSTFUL MEN

The men who claim to have the most highly revved sex drive are Aries (63%), Capricorn (60%) and Pisces (57%). "In 15 years of being sexually active, I've yet to meet the woman who wants it as often as I do," says Aries Rob, 32.

Aquarius is the man most ready to admit his sex drive is lower than a partner's—15% in total. "When a relationship is right, I know because our sexual alarm clocks are perfectly in tune," says Aquarius Mike, aged 42. "A rhythm develops that keeps both partners happy. As soon as this balance starts to go, the relationship hits the rocks."

CASE HISTORY OF A TAURUS MAN

Taurus Tony, 45, has been married to Claire, a Capricorn, for 15 years and has three children. He's gone back to college to train as a chef.

"My wife and I struggle to make our marriage work for the sake of the kids, and because we like living together. But sex is a major hurdle. I know I have a high sex drive, and always have had. A lot of my girlfriends were flattered by it, they said it made them feel irresistible when I couldn't keep my hands off them.

"Sadly my wife, Claire, doesn't see it that way. She says she's too tired, we're too old for all that sort of thing. But my sex drive hasn't diminished with age, and I don't feel I'm an old man.

"We have sex once a month and it's always as though she's doing me a favour. Sometimes it's worse than that, I hate myself afterwards because I know she's just lying there letting me get on with it. I've tried talking to her but she always changes the subject. She wouldn't dream of watching a sexy movie or something to get in the mood, she thinks they're perverted.

"Flattery is supposed to get a woman going. But believe me, the old flowers and champagne routine doesn't work when a woman's set her mind against it. I've tried all that too.

"I'm starting to feel like some sort of pervert in my own bedroom. The obvious thing to do would be to have an affair. But I would feel crippled with guilt, although maybe Claire would feel relieved that at least I wasn't nagging at her for it any more.

"The other day I even toyed with the idea of phoning up an escort agency. Then I thought how sleazy I'd feel if anyone, especially one of the kids, found out. I long for things to change between us. We used to have a loving, if not wildly exciting, sex life."

LUSTFUL LADIES

Among the women, the starsign who feels most sexually charged compared to a partner is Sagittarius—35% rate their sex drive as higher. Next come Pisces and Leo, both with 34%. Virgo (30%) and Capricorn (30%) are the women who judge their desire potential as lower than a partner's most often.

Ms Leo is least likely to rate her own sex drive below a lover's, and Ms Aries, totally the opposite of her male counterpart, is the female starsign who is best matched within a relationship—48% say their sex drive and a partner's are the same. But only 32% of Aries men do so, lowest figure overall.

CASE HISTORY OF AN ARIES WOMAN

Marianne, 28, is an Aries legal advisor. She has been married for five years, to Ian, A Leo.

"We row about everything else from the washing up to where we'll go on holiday, but once we're in bed, no one is more compatible than me and my husband. Both of us seem to feel like doing it often, what we have learned is to pace ourselves to please each other.

"I'm naturally fairly shy, but my husband has brought me out of myself, he loves me to take the lead. I can seduce him away from everything, and the more unlikely the time of day the better as far as he's concerned. Luckily he's a taxi-driver, so being late for work isn't a problem. I don't know how many times he'd have been fired for not getting in until lunchtime otherwise.

"We make sexy calls to each other during the day, too, to hint that we want something special when we get home. I've had boyfriends who could never be bothered with all that and, really, it does make a big difference.

"More often than not in the past, I've felt partners had a higher sex drive than me. But now I realise that was because it was for sex their way, without really being bothered about how it was for me. Of course you get fed up with that sort of treatment. Just like you would if someone kept feeding you meals you didn't really like.

"My husband says I'm the first girl who has kept up with him in bed. I suppose that just goes to show, when you're right for each other the magic makes things click."

STARWATCH

Aries men have a higher sex drive than a partner most often—and perfectly-matched lust levels least often. But for Aries women the opposite is true. Perhaps the aggressive, energetic starsign traits that leave Aries men more unsatisfied than other men just work to more positive effect in women.

How important is it for sex drives to match anyway? The survey's responses seem to say that if everything is fine in a relationship, a couple can cope with different levels of desire, but it takes compromise on both sides. Not something Aries and Capricorn men, or Sagittarius and Leo women (the most highly sexed signs of both sexes) are famous for.

But Leos are the male signs who find lust best matched within a relationship (41%), so perhaps they are just very choosy who they settle down with in the first place.

MEN WHO LOVE MEN

"Although I started sleeping with girls from my early teens, I didn't have a sexual experience with a man until I was 25—and suddenly it explained vague feelings of dissatisfaction I'd been having," says Leo Chas, who's 32. "Now I have a regular girlfriend, but I still need the excitement that comes from picking up a man every now and again. I'm always very careful and my girlfriend is understanding. Recently, though, we've started talking about starting a family and I feel I will have some major decisions to make."

Chas is one of the 5% of Leo men who revealed to the survey that they are sexually attracted to both men and women. Leo emerges as the most strongly bisexual of the zodiac's men, equalled by fellow fire sign Aries (also 5%). But least turned on by bisexuality is starsign Libra—not one Libra male who replied reported being interested in both men and women.

Sexmaster Scorpio takes the lead among men who love men, with 8%, compared to an overall male average of 5%. While Capricorn is least sexually attracted to other men, scoring just 1% in this already small category. Capricorn men, living up to their slightly conventional reputation, are in fact the most solidly heterosexual of the zodiac—97% reported interest in women only when it comes to sex. While Aries, Taurus, Leo and Scorpio are least likely to be solely heterosexual, although at 90% they are only 2% below average.

WOMEN WHO LOVE WOMEN

Only 5% of all men who replied to the AstroSex survey loved the same gender—but that's still five time as many as the female side. for just 1% of women prefer to have sex with other women, while 2% overall are sexually attracted to either sex.

The women out ahead are Leo, 6% in total, and Aquarius, 5%, both starsigns that have shown an adventurous and uninhibited attitude to sex in general.

CASE HISTORY OF AN AQUARIUS WOMAN

Glenda, 19, is a student born under the sign of Aquarius.

"To be honest, I have to say that I am sometimes attracted to other women. And I once had an affair with a girl at college. The loving was so different than with a man—gentle and caring, and we both knew exactly what to do to give the most pleasure.

"At the moment I have a boyfriend—well, man friend really as he's 20 years older than me, but I wasn't just experimenting with sexuality. I did feel the same attraction to the girl as I would have done if it was a man I'd met at a party and wanted to sleep with. There's no way I see sleeping with women as second best until a man comes along, as my sister suggested when I told her about it.

"But I do feel confused—sex with women feels right, but so does sex with men. It certainly doesn't make life simple."

The least likely woman to be attracted to her own sex is Ms Capricorn—not one in the survey said they were. The levels for Libra women were almost as low—and virtually no Libra women said they were bisexual either. This makes Libra and Capricorn women, like Libra and Capricorn men, the most solidly hetero-sexual starsigns across the zodiac.

STARWATCH
Perhaps it's expected of play-by-the-rules Capricorn to come first in the heterosexual stakes. But supposedly free-thinking, inquisitive Libra? Traditional astrological thought may need to revise its view of this air sign...

WHO IS DOING EVERYTHING THEY WANT WITH A PARTNER?
The women of the zodiac are far more satisfied in bed than the men—62% report that they are doing all the sexual things they want to with a partner. But 54% of the men aren't.

Among the male signs, it's Libra, 63% No, and Aries, 60% No, who are the least satisfied. So the most sexually- motivated sign, Leo, has obviously found a partner to go along with, and revel in , his desires.

On the plus side, however, the male sign with the least to complain about between the sheets is Cancer, with 53%, way above the male average of 46%, saying yes, they do everything they want to in bed. Also reasonably happy are realistic signs Aquarius (51%) and Virgo (50%).

"There are things I long to try, but I don't know how to suggest them to my lover," says Geoff who, being Capricorn, is one of the least sexually contented signs. 58% said no, they are not doing everything they want to in bed.

"It's not that I want to get into anything kinky," Geoff insists. "It's

251

more a matter of where I'd like her to touch me to make me feel more aroused. I read that guiding her hand during foreplay is a good way of putting the point across, and I'm going to try that.

"Sex isn't a subject I feel comfortable about talking over. And if you say how you would have liked it afterwards, it sounds like criticism. What I'd like is more guidance from her. We always do the same things, and although that's nice enough, I wouldn't be surprised if she had a few needs of her own that I'm not doing anything about. It would be a great compliment if she would share her fantasies with me. And that could lead to some fabulous times together."

ARE WOMEN GETTING WHAT THEY WANT?

Gemini, Sagittarius and Pisces women (all 43%) voice the most dissatisfaction with the variety in their sex lives. It could be argued that these are all signs big on ideas, but less good at translating them into reality. So sexual fantasies and variations could stay locked up inside their heads...

But two very different starsigns, Aries and Cancer, both come tops in the sexual satisfaction league, with 67% saying they are doing everything they want to in bed. Perhaps because up-front Aries is not afraid to ask for what she wants—and gentle Cancer tends to put a partner's pleasure first anyway? Two out of three Scorpio and Taurus women are also having all their sexual needs met, they say. That's above the female average of 62%.

CASE HISTORY OF AN ARIES WOMAN

Aries-born Gemma, 24, has had a live-in relationship for two years with James, a Libra.

"I only have to hint at a change in our lovemaking and my boyfriend can't wait to give it a try. Which is just as well, because I have had some very boring lovers in my time and that has been a real problem in the relationship.

"Guiding a man to just what, and where, feels good has never embarrassed me. But if he ignores my hints, I take it that he isn't really all that interested. And if he can't be bothered to make it great for me, why should I put myself out for him?

"Sex is not the only thing in a relationship, for me it isn't even one of the most important things. What matters is taking trouble over each other. If someone doesn't even have enough interest to take on board what you're saying, then it's never going to work."

PUTTING LOVEMAKING INTO WORDS

When the survey asked men and women to put their view of sex into words, the two sexes came up with very different answers. For while the largest female vote (38%) describes passion as merely "pleasurable", the top sex description for men is "pure magic" with 43%. And more than twice as many women as men say lovemaking is "overrated", with 7% of female votes and just 3% of male.

We would perhaps expect women to invest more emotion in sex—and they do. For 28% of female starsigns reckon sex is "an expression of love that keeps us together." Among male signs in general the corresponding vote is less, 23%. But men are more likely to see sex as a normal, everyday part of life—20% do, compared to 17% of women.

LOVE MAGICIANS

Who is entranced by the sheer magic of sex? Leading the men are love-fan Leo, 47%, and charmers Libra and Aries, both 46%. "Making love is one of the best things in life," says Libra Martin, 24. "From an early age I've been hooked on it. I wouldn't give it up for the world. And if I can make my partner feel as thrilled by it as I am, I really think I've achieved something."

The women who are most under the spell of sex are, yes Scorpio again, with 38%, Leo, 34%, and sensual Taurus, 34%.

CASE HISTORY OF A TAURUS WOMAN

Taurus-born Lauren, 29, is a radiographer, recently divorced from a Scorpio.

"Probably because I'm a very tactile person, I yearn for a lover's touch when I'm not in a relationship. When I have got a special partner, trying out everything new we can think of is part of the fun.

"Once a lover and I went away for the weekend and we worked our way through one of those sex guides. That really was what I call pure magic. But you have to make sure you are with the right man. It's incredible how many men waste all their energy trying to get you into bed, then aren't interested in doing anything special with you once you are there.

"I particularly like candlelight and the subtle smells of burning aromatherapy oils. I'm a mood person. Massage is great, as long as you don't get so relaxed you fall asleep. It's vital to keep to the erogenous zones, otherwise all the sexual tension slides away. I have had a lot of fun with ice-cubes too, great for awakening the senses once the body has warmed up.

"Sex isn't always pure magic, of course. Sometimes it's less exciting. But never dull."

The man least likely to rate sex pure magic is, unexpectedly, Scorpio, at 37% way below all other male signs. And an above-average 4% of this supposedly steamy sign also vote lovemaking as "overrated." Among the women, it's Sagittarius who comes in last—just one in four, 25%, of this starsign say sex is pure magic.

STARWATCH

Scorpio man's live-for-sex image is seriously dented by his lack of enthusiasm in this section. Do the women of this starsign have enough energy and interest for two?

LOVERS LEFT OUT IN THE COLD

Twice as many Gemini men as average (6%) judge sex overrated, and male Virgo and Aquarius (5% each) aren't overly impressed either. These are mostly brain, not body-ruled starsigns, and perhaps expect too much of physical passion in the first place. But on the plus side, only one in every 100 sensitive Pisces men say sex is overrated.

CASE HISTORY OF A VIRGO MAN

Dental technician Tariq, 24, was born under starsign Virgo. He has been with his current girlfriend Tasmin, a Gemini, for three years.

"There is an awful lot of pressure on us to see everything in terms of sex. Every time you switch on the TV, open a magazine, or look at street hoardings, there's an image supposed to make you think of bonking, and buy the product to make you better at it—whether that product is a new pair of shoes or a car.

"Everyone talks about sex all the time. And there's such kudos to be got from claiming more than your fair share of it. But why?

"To my mind, a girl's who's good in bed means nothing compared to someone who'll stand by you when things go wrong. Or just cheer you up when you've had a bad day. Yes, we spend a lot of time in bed—but most of it's asleep.

"I used to pick up and seduce a different girl every Saturday night. Now I do have a steady girlfriend and I like making love with her. I'm not going to lie and pretend it raises the roof, though. Why should it?

"Lots of nights we curl up together and that feels lovely, warm and secure. That's what love's about."

Which starsign women reckon sex is overrated? Capricorn, most of all, with 9%, then Gemini, Cancer, Libra and Aquarius, all 8%.

"On balance, I would rather read a good book or eat a bar of chocolate," reveals May, a 37-year-old Gemini. "I've tried almost every position and technique known to man, and woman, and they've all done absolutely nothing for me. I really can't see what all the fuss is about. Maybe I just haven't met the right man."

STARWATCH
Cool, controlled air signs may focus on the mental rather than physical expression of love. But how can traditional astrology explain Capricorn's negative view? Perhaps as a defense mechanism, writing sex off through fear of failure?

PASSION AS A NORMAL PART OF LIFE
For 28% of Virgo, 27% of Aries and 22% of Sagittarius men, sex is no more, no less, than a normal part of life. "I get up in the morning, I brush my teeth, I have sex, I have a shower, I go to work," says Johnny, a 25-year-old Sagittarius gas fitter, who's been married six months.

"As far as I'm concerned, sex is as natural as eating, sleeping or breathing. Though it can be a lot more fun, of course. I do think people can place too much importance on physical passion and create problems for themselves where none really exist. And I'm certainly no fan of gadgets and gismos in bed. Give me clean sheets, clean skin, and Nature does the rest. That's the way it's been since time began, and that's the way I like it.

"My wife may not be the sexiest woman I've ever been with. But she's the one I want to build a home and have babies with. That's what it's all about for me—and a lot of other people too, if they are honest about it."

Down-to-earth Sagittarius women are also among those most likely to view sex as a normal part of life, with 21%, same score as Leo ladies. But out in front among the female signs is Cancer—a sign traditional astrology might expect to harbour far more romantic ideals about love-making. Ms Cancer also scores well below average in rating sexual love as either pure magic, or even merely pleasurable. Could it be a case of the martyr sign putting everyone else's needs, and demands, before her own? Or is usual astrological thought wide of the mark again?

Aquarius women, and Leo men, are the ones who want sex to be special, not a normal part of life at all. Both these signs could run into trouble when the novelty of a new sexual relationship wears off.

PLEASURE SEEKERS

Sagittarius men are the ones who most describe sex as pleasurable (38%), followed by Capricorn (36%) and Leo (35%). But only 21%, by far the lowest male score, of Aries men settle for this definition. Aries is the sign of extremes and pleasure alone may not be enough for him—he needs excitement.

Ironically, though, when we turn to the women, we find Aries women describe sex as pleasurable more than twice as often as the starsign's men—44% in total. But the roles do reverse when it comes to passion being pure magic—46%, second highest score, for Aries man, but 28%, second lowest score, for Aries woman.

Taurus (42%), Gemini and Sagittarius (both 41%) women also opt for the pleasurable description.

CASE HISTORY OF AN ARIES WOMAN
Anne-Marie, 37, is an Aries and works as a hotel receptionist. She has lived with a steady girlfriend Cancer-born Sue for 10 years.
"Sex is the greatest pleasure because it takes over all the senses. Alcohol doesn't intoxicate me like sex does. But earth-shattering? That's not the description I'd use. It's more a warm, comfortable feeling, like being enveloped from head to foot in softest wool on a cool day.

"Sex can make a good relationship better, but it can't make a bad one good. After the passion has to come reality. Never mind could I wake up with this person—could I spend a wet Saturday with her in a power cut?"

SEX AS AN EXPRESSION OF LOVE

Leo is the man who most rates sex as an expression of love that keeps a couple together—31% do so. And it's significant that Leo is also the male sign first to rate sex as pure magic. Nothing mundane about this starsign's loving.

Next most romantic signs in this section are Cancer man (29%) and Scorpio (28%). But the man least likely to see sex as a way of showing love is often introspective and detached Aquarius (16%).

CASE HISTORY OF AN AQUARIUS MAN

30-year-old Russ in an Aquarius. He has had an "open marriage" for 20 years, with Karen, a Sagittarius.

"What is sex to me? Physical sensation, release of tension, erotic imagination—anything but a time of real intimacy. Getting too close, even to my wife, makes me panic, so I deliberately switch off when I am making love. I make sure she gets her share of pleasure, but even if she calls out 'Russ, I love you' as she orgasms, I never reciprocate. I just can't seem to find the words. And afterwards, when she wants to cuddle up, I rush to the bathroom to wash myself.

"I was brought up to think of sex as dirty and I suppose that could explain my behaviour. It was my idea to have an open marriage, I know my wife doesn't like it, she puts up with it to please me. But I certainly don't see sex as a way of proving I love her—I do that by supporting her and our children and always coming home to them every night."

Scorpio is the woman least likely to see sex as an expression of love, but at the top of the list it's Capricorn, 35%, Aries, 34%, and Libra, 30%, who reckon passion binds a couple together.

"Not only do I think sex is a way of expressing the love I feel for my partner Stephen, but I find making love is different with him," says Margaret, a 28-year-old Capricorn. "It's far more special than with any other man—and because of that I could never be unfaithful. Sex now is only for Stephen.

"If I found out he'd had an affair, or even a one-night-stand, I'd be devastated. It would be like letting someone else into our bedroom, sharing what I thought was just between us. I want to think that this is the best of him, as it is for me, and purely ours."

WHAT COULD MAKE SEXLIFE MORE EXCITING?

In this section, the differences between the sexes were more evident than those between the starsigns. For instance, being the right weight themselves would be a definite love-improver for 62% of all women—but only 37% of men. For both sexes, slightly vain Sagittarius is the starsign most concerned about their size, scoring 68% of women and 45% of men. Male and female Leos, meanwhile, are among the least bothered.

But if the men go easier on themselves, they are far harder on their partners—one in four, 25%, reckon sexlife would be better if their lady was the right weight. Only 16% of women say the same about their man.

In both sexes, Taurus was the supercritical partner, 35% for men and 20% for women. And, unexpectedly by traditional astrology's rules, image conscious Libra is the kindest, with only 18% men and 12% women saying size affects desire.

STARWATCH
Let's not be too quick to assume Libra is less influenced by appearances than this sign's usual star CV suggests. Perhaps Libra men or women would simply never dream of settling for a partner who was overweight in the first place.

Body image, in general, is a big influence on how the zodiac views sexual performance, that much is undisputedly proven by the AstroSex results. 23% of men reckon they'd have a better sex life if they had bigger muscles—39% of women feel the same way about a bigger bust. Biggest muscle-fixation is found in Mr Scorpio—

36%, more than a third, think they could pump up passion along with their biceps. Leo men, just 16%, are the least obsessed.

And they could be right—since when the zodiac's women are asked if sex would be better if a partner had bigger muscles, only 7% overall say yes. Virgo women are keenest, scoring 10%, one in 10. But only 5% of Sagittarius women agreed.

The same rules apply to the bigger bust debate, however. For 29% of women in total reckon bigger breasts would mean better sex—led by Ms Leo on 34%. But male starsigns only give this a 23% vote overall. Libra, 31%, is the man who'd most like his partner to have larger breasts, and at just 9%, Mr Gemini is by far least inclined to want a partner to go for bust.

"In fact, when I do notice breasts on a woman, I prefer then to be small—it's long, long legs that are my weakness," laughs Sean, an 18-year-old Gemini.

Predictably, perhaps, it's penis size that shows the greatest division of the sexes. For while 30% of men (and 36% of self-conscious Pisceans) think bigger means better, only 11% of women reckon a bigger penis makes the earth move more. Most up-front about it are Cancer, Libra and Capricorn women (all scoring 13%).

CASE HISTORY OF A PISCES MAN

Timothy, 32, is a Pisces. He works as a gym instructor and is currently half-way through a trial three months of celibacy.

"Because I'm a big, and fit, guy, girls automatically assume that will be proportional in every aspect of my physique. My penis isn't small, probably average. But that comes as a disappointment to women who are expecting to be wowed by its sheer size.

"I've tried everything to build up size, length, width, anything to impress the ladies. Not that it bothers me as such, it's just that I can't stand the look of let-down when I take my clothes off.

"Naturally I do all I can to make up for being Mr Standard Fixture And Fitting with my technique. But if there's one myth in this world it's that size doesn't matter to women. The number of girls who've been dead keen, coming on all strong until we get back to my place... then barely speaking to me when they leave. Women are entranced by big members, and if they don't get what they've bargained for, they take it out on you."

CAN MONEY BUY YOU LOVE?

Over a third of the zodiac's men—but under a quarter of the women—think more money would boost their sexlife. And out in front is Scorpio on 42%—a male starsign who takes his responsibilities very seriously, and also tends to let worries affect his libido.

"Nothing kills my desire off faster than worrying about cash," says Scorpio Colin, 40. "It's impossible to relax when you're waking up in the night wondering what you're going to do about the garage bill, and how you're going to get the refrigerator replaced without taking out another loan.

"My wife tries to take my mind off our financial problems by enticing me to make love. That makes things worse. Where her hands usually set me alight, I become intensely irritated by her touch. I suppose it's all down to the nervous system. And lack of cash puts mine on edge."

Which man is least likely to let money worries affect his sex drive? It's laid-back Leo again. But although he gives cash the lowest vote overall as a sex-enhancer, Mr Leo still rates it higher than having a better job, a bigger penis, bigger muscles or even his partner having bigger breasts.

"For as long as we've been married, we've had just enough to get by," says Leo Tim, 49. "Never any serious worries, but nothing to spare, either. Because we couldn't even afford a proper honeymoon, we had a long weekend in my brother's camper van. The one thing I long to buy Helen is a luxury exotic holiday. Proper hotel with everything done for you, disco at night, pool in the day and nice new clothes to take with us. Would that improve our sex life? You bet. As long as we didn't get sunburn in the wrong places."

Far less women, only 23% overall, reckon money would buy better loving. But although Ms Leo's score, 28%, is the same as her male counterpart, among the less-materialistic women this puts her in first, rather than last, position. Notoriously fond of luxury, is she perhaps just being more realistic, or more honest, than the rest?

For when the figures are looked at relatively, even the lowest female score in this section, Ms Virgo's 17%, rates money higher than a better job, partner's bigger penis and/or muscles, or a partner being the right weight. So cash comes out as pretty important to most people. Although no woman rates a bigger bank balance higher than a bigger bust.

CASE HISTORY OF AN AQUARIUS WOMAN

Colleen, 27, is an Aquarius, and a single parent to two small children. Her husband, who walked out, was a Libra.

"Don't tell me love conquers all until you've tried living with no job, no money and no hope. My husband tried everything after he was made redundant to pay to keep us. In the end, I managed to get some bar work. It helped bring a bit of cash in, but destroyed his confidence as a man. He became depressed, irritable, and impotent.

"One day I came home and he'd just left, not even a note. I heard from his mother that he was travelling around looking for building work and couldn't face me until he had found something. I was so hurt that he thought I wouldn't stand by him.

"The weeks went by, then the months. After a year, I accepted that he was never coming back. Ironically, by putting all my energies into my job, I was promoted. I got a good job managing a chain of bars, and met another man.

"Was everything great then? No way. My new man discovered I earned more than him and that soon became a bone of contention. Money does make a difference to your sexlife. Particularly when you haven't got any."

THE 12 STARSIGNS' SEXUAL PROFILES

ARIES MAN AND SEXUALITY

*Nearly half, 46%, of Aries men describe sex as pure magic, but only two out of five, 40%, are doing all the things they really want to in bed—that's below the 46% male average.

*9% make love daily, 24% more than four times a week, 34% one to three times per week, 15% one to three times per month, 11% rarely, 5% are celibate and 1% intend to stay that way. Frequency averages out at 2.7 times per week, in the lower range for men.

*But Aries is one of the two male signs who would most like to make love more often—a stunning 97% say they would. "Any man who says he wouldn't like to have sex more often is either living in a harem or lying," says Dennis, 42.

*And indeed there may be a reason for Aries' dissatisfaction. He tops the list for saying his sex drive is higher than his partner's, with 63% compared to a male average of just 53%. "Although my girlfriend just had a baby two months ago, so it's not hard to have a sex drive higher than hers, which is nil!" says one Aries in his mid-20s.

*Unexpectedly, Aries is not one of the most promiscuous of signs. 12% have had only one lover, well above the average of 9%. Most have had six to 10, 28%—and although a quarter, 25%, can boast of over 20 conquests, that's just a fraction over the male average.

*Where Aries does dare to be different, compared to other signs, is in who he's attracted to. Only 90%, joint lowest score, say they are attracted only to women. A middle range 5% admit to feeling drawn to men, and 5%, highest score of all male signs, are sexually aroused by both sexes.

*To make himself a better lover, in common with most men, Aries wants to be the right weight (42%). But he is above the average of 37% in choosing it, so falls in the upper range.

*He doesn't set as much store as other men by job or money as sex-enhancers, but Mr Aries does fret about the size of his penis—an above-average 32% think sex would be better if it was bigger.

ARIES MAN may not be getting enough sex—but he still rates it higher than almost anything else.

ARIES WOMAN AND SEXUALITY

*25% of Aries women make love more than four times a week, the highest female score overall for this category. 9% partake of passion on a daily basis, 38% (lowest female result here) have sex one to three times per week, 18% one to three times per month, 5% rarely and 4% are celibate right now. Not one of these, however, intend to make it a permanent arrangement. "Since my husband died, I haven't been able to look at another man," says Amy, 44. "But I do miss the cuddles we shared and, as time passes, I realise there will be a stage when I feel I can share that intimacy with someone else without feeling disloyal." Ms Aries has sex 2.7 times a week, in mid to upper range for women.

*An upper range 14%, however, would like to make love less often. "My boyfriend got used to sex every night when we moved in together," says Elaine, 26. "So it's now become a bit of a routine to make love before we go to sleep. I'd rather spend all Sunday afternoon trying something special and not bother so much during the week."

*26% of Aries women have had between six to 10 sexual partners, highest female score for this category. 10% have had just one lover, 46% two to five partners, and a total of 17% over 11.

*Of all women's signs she's the most confident that her sex drive is in tune with her partner's—48% say it's the same. And 67%, again the highest female score, of Aries women reckon they are doing everything they could possibly fancy between the sheets.

*Unlike Aries men, just an average of 1% are sexually attracted to other women—and 2% are sexually aroused by both.

*She is the woman who's least likely (5%) to say sex is overrated, but also least inclined to describe it as pure magic! 44%, more than any other sign, describe love-making as pleasurable.

*Apart from being the right weight (60% vote for this, below average for women), the two things Ms Aries thinks would best boost her love life are bigger breasts, 31%, and more money, 26%. Partner's penis size, muscles (or lack of them) and weight do not matter much.

She puts so much of herself into sex, ARIES WOMAN would appreciate it less often...

HOW DO THE SEXES COMPARE?

Both are body conscious—but far more concerned with their own attributes than their partner's. In fact, female Aries rate a partner's penis size as the least important of all sexual assets. More men than women make love rarely or not at all—and more intend to stay celibate, too. So could that be why Aries women seem perfectly happy with their passion lot—and Aries men don't? He wants more sex, she wants less, she's doing all she dreams of with a partner, and he isn't. Yet he still insists sex is pure magic.

TAURUS MAN AND SEXUALITY

*Along with Virgo, Scorpio and Aquarius, Taurus man is most likely to complain about having too much sex—9% against the male average of 6%.

*He's also the least likely man to have sex one to three times a week (29%). An upper range 14% have sex daily, 24% over four times a week, 16% one to three times a month, 8% rarely, 7% are celibate now and 1% intend to carry on being that way. "I've got a major research project going on in the hospital where I work," says Jim, 43. " And I've found just forgetting about sex has focused my mind wonderfully well. I'm getting through the work far quicker than I would have done normally." Overall Taurus average is 2.8 times a week, in the upper range.

*5% have had just one sexual partner, well below average. 34% have known two to five partners, 22% had sex with between six and 10, and 39%, in total, have slept with over 11 people.

*Sex drive is higher than partner's for an average 53% of Taurus males. And 46%, again average, reckon they are doing everything they want to in bed.

*5% are sexually attracted to other men, 90% to women and 4% to both sexes.

*Taurus man's favourite description of sex is "pure magic." "Now I realise my body was only half alive until I learned the secret of great loving," says Michael, 18.

*Sex would be better for 59% of Taurus men if they were the right weight—here reflecting everyone's main complaint. But Taurus is also the man most critical of his partner's weight—20%, well above average, said loving could be better if a partner was slimmer! And 32%, above average, wanted bigger muscles themselves to boost sexual satisfaction. But at 23%, he's the man least concerned with penis size in the whole zodiac...

TAURUS MAN—highly sexed, but can be highly critical, too.

TAURUS WOMAN AND SEXUALITY

*Although 45% of Taurus women make love one to three times a week, and 7% do so every day, she, along with Cancer and Libra, is the female starsign most likely to be celibate, with a 7% score. It seems this is through necessity not choice, however, as only one in every 250 wants to remain that way. "I'm happy to have a break of a few months, but a lifetime without sex? That's like trying to give up food," says Gabby, 31. 21% of Taurus women have sex over four times a week, 11% one to three times per month, and 8% rarely.

*An average 11% would like to make love less often.

*31%, again exactly average for the zodiac's women, reckon their sex drive is higher than their partner's. "But it's selective, "says one Taurus wife of nine years. "When we're on holiday or the kids are at their grandparents, my sex drive suddenly soars ahead of his. But why is his always highest when the baby's waking up all night and I've got a stinking cold and my period?"

*Two thirds of Taurus female partners, 66%, are happy to say they are doing everything they want to sexually. That's in the upper range.

*An above-average 13% have had only one sexual partner. 45% have had between two and five, 23% from six to 10 and a total of 19%, in the lower range, over 11 lovers. Steady Taurus will always prefer a relationship to a one-night stand, and it shows in these figures.

*Although only 2% of Taurus women prefer to make love to other women, that's still double the average for all female starsigns. And 2% have strong sexual feelings for both sexes.

*How would Ms Taurus best describe her view of sex? She's among the women most likely to say it is pure magic (34%) and pleasurable (42%). And joint least inclined to describe the pleasures of the flesh as overrated, with just 5%. 14%, in the lower range, say sex is a normal part of life. "Once it becomes normal, why bother? It should be a romantic, unforgettable experience at least some of the time," is a comment from several Taurus respondents. 26%, again below average, define sex as an expression of love that keeps a couple together.

*She worries less about being the right weight (60%, lower range) than about having big enough breasts (32%, upper range), when it comes to improving her sex life. But Ms Taurus is also the woman who most wants to improve her man—20%, well above the average of 16% say sex would be more exciting if a partner was the right weight. 9%, again above average, would expect improvement if he had bigger muscles. But penis size is less of a concern and just 8%, that's well below average, reckon that would make any difference. **Appearances matter to TAURUS WOMAN— but not as much as feelings and friendship.**

HOW DO THE SEXES COMPARE?
Down-to-earth Taurus men and women get on with doing what they like most—and with who they like. They are among the most likely starsigns to admit to attraction to the same sex. And

they're the most critical of their partner's physique, although neither sex cares much about penis size. Twice as many Taurus men as women make love every day, but she's far more likely to favour one to three times a week (45% to 29% men). 7% of each gender are celibate for now, but more men want to stay that way than women. Male Taureans are also more likely than female to say they want less sex. When it comes to number of partners, men lead again—39% have had over 11 lovers, compared to 19% women.

GEMINI MAN AND SEXUALITY

*Believe it or not, Gemini is the man most likely to stay true to his first, and only lover—15%, top of all male signs, have had just a single sexual partner. And 8%, lowest of all male signs, boast of 11 to 20 lovers. But it could be feast or famine for Mr Gemini, as a massive 25%, one in every four, says he has had over 20 sexual partners.

*94%, exactly average for men overall, would like more sex. Perhaps because at an average of 2.5 times per week, Gemini's frequency falls in the lower range.

*8%, well below average, have sex daily. 23%, four or more times per week, 36%, one to three times weekly, and 15%, one to three times a month. For 8%, sex is a rare occurence, that's below average, while another 8%, second highest of the male zodiac, are celibate at the moment. Do they want to stay that way? Not likely.

*Compared to other men, Gemini quite often reports a lower sex drive than his partner's—12% in total. But he's also above-average in claiming lust levels in perfect harmony, with 39% score in this section. "Living with someone whose sexual urges don't synchronise with yours is my idea of hell," says Ted, 40. "Someone is always pestering, or rejecting, and that can't make for happiness, can it?"

*More Gemini men than any other starsign say sex is overrated (6%). But by far the majority, 38%, still opt for pure magic as the best description, although this is still lower than average for men.

*Perhaps because more than one in two Gemini males, 55% are not doing everything they want to sexually. That's in the upper range.

*An above-average 6% prefer to have sex with other men, below-average 90% are strictly heterosexual and the remaining 3% will have sex with either men or women. That's in the middle range.

*Like all signs, Gemini thinks being the right weight would improve his sex life (41%). And he's more likely to want a partner to lose weight (27%) than the male norm. But he's by far the least interested male starsign in bigger breasts (just 9%, compared to male average of 23%). A third (33%) would like a bigger penis, and even more (37%, in the upper range) would like more money. "When I want to impress a girl and make myself feel sexually charged, I take her out for a great night on the town," says Gerard, 26. "No expense spared. It gives me a real buzz."

GEMINI MAN may expect too much of sex, his partner—and himself.

GEMINI WOMAN AND SEXUALITY

*Gemini's the woman least likely to stick to one lover—just 8% have done so. Most—45%—have had between two and five sexual partners. And further 25% number six to 10 partners, one in 10 (10%) have had 11 to 20 lovers, But Gemini takes the lead among women when it comes to having sex with over 20 different people—11% claim they have done so. "I wouldn't dream of deciding which food I liked best until I'd tried lots of different varieties—what makes sex any different?" asks Leila, a 24-year-old Gemini.

*She prefers to have sex one to three times a week—40% opt for this choice. 10% make love every day, 22% (exactly average for women) four or more times a week. One to three times a month is the frequency for 15%, 8% (joint highest female score) have sex rarely. 5% are celibate just now, but only one in 100 wants to stay that way. Overall, Gemini makes love 2.6 times a week, the average.

*Gemini is one of the women most likely to judge her sex drive as lower than a partner's—30% do so. And only 39%, below average, have the same level of desire as the other half of their couple. "It's only natural that men should want sex more than women—that's the way men are built, isn't it?" says Gail, 37. "But I don't believe in doing it just because my husband wants to—surely it's worth waiting until you're both in the mood together?"

*To most, 41%, sex can be described as pleasurable, although Gemini is also the woman second most likely to say passion is overrated (8%). "Give me a good game of Scrabble or a heated argument about politics any day. Sex has its place in life, but you have to keep it in its place," says Christine, 28. "In fact, many times I've thought of giving it up altogether. I can see the attraction of doing that."

*Yet here the notorious two sides of Gemini show themselves again—for she is also the woman least satisfied with what she's doing in bed with her partner. 43%, highest female score, say their love life is just not adventurous enough.

*And 92%, highest again of the women, want more sex.

*Gemini is one of the female signs most likely to be attracted to her own sex—2% say they are. But she falls in the middle range for fancying both men and women, 2% again.

*What would improve Ms Gemini's sex life? 65%, in the upper range, reckon losing weight herself would increase enjoyment—but she's less critical than other women of her partner's size, as only 14% say a lover losing weight would make any difference. 30% would like to have bigger breasts, 5% want a partner to have larger muscles. 11% would like a lover to have a larger penis, 13% think a better job would improve sex, and 21% believe the same about more money.

Too much, yet not enough—that's GEMINI WOMAN'S view of her sexlife...

HOW DO THE SEXES COMPARE?

Both Gemini men, and women, long to do more in bed—yet many of both sexes have so far found sex overrated. Ms Gemini

appreciates money as an aphrodisiac, but the starsign's males do not. Both dream of a perfect world, where they and partners have perfect bodies and achieve effortless ecstasy—it's the everyday reality of sex they may find hard to handle. But male Geminis are almost twice as likely to stay true to their first love as women.

CANCER MAN AND SEXUALITY

* Although the bulk of Cancer-born men go for the usual one-to-three episodes of love-making per week, 29%, this is still the lowest score in this category. Nearly as many, 26%, have sex more than four times a week. 13% schedule passion on a daily basis, 15% one to three times a month, 12% (second highest male score) have sex rarely and 4% are currently celibate. But not one Cancer man plans to make this a permanent arrangement! At 2.8 times per week, the Cancer average rate of love-making is in the upper range for men.

*Cancer is the most sexually fulfilled man in the zodiac—according to the AstroSex results. For 53%, more than any other male sign, say they are doing everything they want to sexually.

*And loving it too. For an above-average 45% of Cancer men describe love-making as pure magic. Just 4% would say sex is overrated, for 17% it's a normal part of life, 27% rate lovemaking as pleasurable, and 29%—second highest male score for this romantic sign—as an expression of love. "My best relationships are the ones that have been given time to develop," says Stuart, 29. "When I trust someone, and encourage them to trust me, we are free to explore our fantasies together."

*13% of this starsign's men have had just one sexual partner, well above average. Exactly a third, 33%, have had sex with two to five people, 19% with between six and 10 partners, and 11%—in the lower range—with 11 to 20. But almost a quarter (24%) have had over 20 lovers, that's exactly average for men.

*How does his sex drive compare to his partner's? A lower-range 51% rate theirs as higher, 9% say their desire is less. But for 40%, second highest rating amongst the zodiac's men, sex drives within a couple are exactly equal. "To begin with, I wanted to make love more often than my wife. But whereas I've settled down to being happy with three times a week, she's wanting it more and more," says Brian, 33. "But surely that's what a relationship is all about, negotiating and being flexible according to changing needs?"

*Cancer men are among the least critical of their partners. Only 18%, lowest score in this bracket, said love-making would be more exciting if a lover was the right weight. and although 35% reckon a change in their own physique would perk thing up, this is still below average for a male sign. 22% think having more impressive muscles would help arousal levels, 24% would like a lover to have bigger breasts. 28%, again below the male norm, opt for a bigger penis themselves, and just 14%, in lower range too, for a better job.

But one attribute Cancer men do rate higher than other males is money—36% reckon more cash would lead to better sex. "I hate being in debt," says Gordon, 50. "And when my books won't balance I can't think of anything else. Some men say sex is a great stress buster, but I can't even get an erection when I'm weighed down with worries."

*An above-average 7% of Cancer men prefer to have sex with other men. 91% are strictly heterosexual, and 2%, in the lower range, will make love to either gender.

Appearance doesn't affect CANCER MAN's sexual potential—but affluence does.

CANCER WOMAN AND SEXUALITY

*Less would be more for Ms Cancer—as 15%, more than any other female starsign, say they are getting too much sex.

*Yet she's already getting a less-than-average amount of loving. At 2.4 times a week she falls in the lower frequency range. Although an average 9% of Cancer women make love daily, just 19%—lowest score of all women—have sex four or more times per week. For 40%, love-making takes place one to three times a week, while an upper-range 18% schedule it just one to three times per month. 8% have sex rarely, and 7% are celibate for the moment, although they hope to change that situation soon.

*Two to five lovers is the usual quota for Cancer—with 44% opting for this selection. But an upper range 15% have had just one sexual partner. 23% can count between six and 10 lovers, and just 18% in total have had 11 or more.

*31% say their sex drive is higher compared to a partner's, 29% rate it lower and for a lower range 39% it's the same. "But my desire varies enormously according to how I feel about my boyfriend," says one engaged Cancer. "If he's been off-hand or critical, or done something that makes me fume, I turn right off. But if he's attentive and paying me compliments, I can't get enough of him. But, typical male that he is, he hasn't quite cottoned on to this yet."

*Whatever other figures might suggest, the survey results show Cancer woman is generally happy with her lovelife. 67%, joint highest female score, are content they are doing everything they want to sexually. But could that be because she wants to do less than other women anyway?

*Asked what would best describe their view of sex, 29% of Cancer females said pure magic, 8% (second highest among women) overrated, and she is the woman most likely to judge it as a normal part of life, with 22%. Just 28%, well below average, rate sex as pleasurable, while 29%, in the middle range, opt for an "expression of love that bonds a couple."

*Although response to the bisexual section was very small, it does show that Cancer women are more-than-average attracted to the same sex (2%).

*She's more inclined than most women to look to a partner to improve love life. For while a below average (61%) of Cancer women thought being the right weight themselves would spice sex up, an above average 9% voted for a partner having bigger muscles, and 13% for a partner having a bigger penis, to achieve the same results. And while a better job might make a difference to 14%, money was less important to Cancer than other female signs. 22% said having more cash would mean more, and better, sex.

CANCER WOMAN sees sex as a daily ration rather than a rare treat.

HOW DO THE SEXES COMPARE?

Cancer man is twice as likely to have had over 20 lovers than just one, while Cancer woman rarely moves out of the two to five partners bracket. She may be getting less sex than her starsign sisters, but she isn't complaining—quantity isn't something she sets much store by. But she does long to do more in bed and improve on quality!

Meanwhile, Cancer man helps himself to a higher-than-average passion ration, yet still wants more. And while he's among the male signs least critical of a partner's body, Cancer woman is just the opposite...

LEO MAN AND SEXUALITY

*Leo is the sex champ. 24% (more than any other male sign) make love every day, and a further 21% have sex more than four times a week. 29%, joint lowest male score for this section, choose a frequency of one to three times a week, 9%, also well into the lower range, opt for one to three times per month. For 8%, lovemaking is something they do rarely, and a further 7% are celibate at the moment. Astonishingly, Leo is the sign who most wants to stay celibate, with 2% saying yes to this.

*Even though Leo's weekly average is by far the highest of all men, at 3.3 times, and an above-average 47% reckon they're doing all they could want in bed, 94% of this lusty sign still want more sex. "When I stop wanting more, I'll stop wanting it at all, I think," is a common Leo comment.

*Hardly surprising then that 47% of Leo males describe sex as pure magic—that's more than any other man. Just 2% say passion is overrated, and 14% (lowest score overall) that it's a normal part of life. 35% vote for pleasurable as the best description but 31% say sex is an expression of love that binds a couple together, highest male response again.

*Variation pleases Mr Leo. He ties with Capricorn as the male sign most likely to have had over 11 partners (23%). And a further 20% have had over 20 lovers. 9%, the average, have had a single sexual partner, and 26% have had more than two and less than five.

*Nearly one in two Leo men rate their sex drive as higher than their partner's. "But I do so fantasise about meeting a woman who makes bigger demands on me than I do on her," says James, 29. But shared happiness does matter to Leo—he's the male sign most inclined to judge sex drives equal within a couple (41%).

*When it comes to attraction, 5%, the average, fancy other men— and 5% again, the joint highest male result, feel a passion pull towards both sexes.

*What would increase excitement levels in lovemaking for Leo? He's the man least likely to look to his own weight as a fun factor, with 31%. But above-average critical of his partner's weight, on 28%. and while just 16% think having bigger muscles himself would help, 23% would expect more excitement if a lover had bigger breasts. "Muscles don't matter too much to women—but believe me, breasts certainly do matter to men, whatever they might say." remarks Dan, 31. 27% would like a bigger penis, just 12% a better job—and Leo is the male sign least turned on by money— lowest overall score of 28% said more cash would be sure to make sex better.

Raunch meets romance in LEO MAN, the zodiac's biggest and boldest sex fan.

LEO WOMAN AND SEXUALITY

*At 12%, Leo woman is only half as likely as Leo man to make love daily—but she still scores the second-highest female result in this section. 20% have sex over four times per week, 40% one to three times weekly, and 20% one to three times monthly. She's least likely of all woman to have sex "rarely" (just 4%), and also in the lower range for being celibate now (4% again). Not one Leo woman plans on living without sex for life. Her overall average frequency for sex is 2.7 times per week.

*64%, just above average, are doing all they want to sexually.

*But just 22% of Ms Leos report that their sex drive is lower than their partner's—that's least of all female signs. 34% rate their own desire levels as higher, 44% say they're the same.

*So it's no surprise that Leo tops the list of women wanting more sex—with 92% yes to this question. "I think my boyfriend is scared of me and my demands," admits Chloe, 20. "It takes me a while to trust a man, but when I do, I'll do anything, and expect him to do the same."

*When Leo's needs are met, however, she is fiercely loyal—16%, more than any other female sign, have had only one lover. But once she does start experimenting, it may be difficult to stop. For just 34% of Leo ladies have had between two and five partners, a full 10% below average and lowest result of all women. But 26% have had more than 10 lovers, well ahead of the other women of the zodiac. "Am I addicted to sex? I certainly hope so." says one very experienced Leo.

*More female Leos than any other sign are bisexual—5%, compared to an average of 2%—are attracted to both men and women.

*How does she see sex? Pure magic is the answer for 35%, second highest female score in this section. 6%, below average, say sex is overrated, for 21% it's a normal part of life. 34% describe it as pleasurable and 25% as an expression of love. "When a marriage goes wrong," says Stella, 35, "the first place to look for trouble is in the bedroom. You can forgive your partner anything if that sexy spark is still there."

*More than any other sign, Leo reckons a bigger bust would make for better sex (34%). "I want to be a mysterious, voluptuous woman, and that just doesn't work with a 32-inch bust," comments 25-year-old Faith. "I've got about as much mystery as a plank of wood." 58%

opt for being the right weight as a prime attraction factor, 12% for a partner reaching the right weight. 6% would like a partner to have bigger muscles, 11% a bigger penis, 15% a better job—and at 28%, Leo is the woman who sets most store by cash as a love life enhancer. "When we finally got out of debt, we celebrated in bed, went to a night-club, then came back and made love again," says one Leo. "That's more than we'd done it in the month previously, so our sexlife was already much improved."

Vanity, variety and verve all play a part in LEO WOMAN's loving, but she stays practical about passion, too.

HOW DO THE SEXES COMPARE?

Leo is the sign that roars into bedroom action and has a voracious appetite for sex. And that's true for both sexes. Leo men, and women, take a pride in good loving, and neither see sex as a laughing matter. They like it often, they like it varied. They expect both partners to be in peak condition to enjoy it, and they are rarely disappointed—or disappointing.

Unusually, 5% of each sex are bisexual, but Leo men are more likely to say their sex drive is higher than a partner's. Men from this sign are also more inclined to choose celibacy as a way of life—2% of men have done so, but not a single woman. 28% of each sex say more money would make sex better—lowest male score, but highest female score.

VIRGO MAN AND SEXUALITY

*His high standards make Virgo man the least likely to have sex more than four times a week—his 13% was the lowest score recorded on this option .Yet he is also the man second most likely to have sex every day (17%). 36% make love between one and three times a week, 19% between one and three times a month. A below average 9% describe sexual frequency as "rarely", while 5% are celibate. Not one Virgo man wants to stay celibate. His average of 2.6 times a week is in the lower range.

*Virgo is among the men who would most like to make love less, with 9% score here. "It's just another pressure in my life, trying to match up to averages of so many times a week," says Roly, 32. "If it was just mating twice a year, like dogs or something, that would suit me just fine."

*Between two and five lovers is the norm for Mr Virgo (37%). Just 5%, second lowest score, have had one sexual partner only, while 18% boast of six to 10 and a total of 40% have 11 or over.

*Virgo is the man least likely to say his sex drive is higher than his partner's—just 46% do so (male average is 53%). 14% say it's lower, and 39% opt for sex drives being the same.

*Ask Virgo males if they're doing all they want to sexually and the answer is split 50-50. That puts them in the upper range for satisfaction.

*An upper range 6% of Virgo men prefer to have sex with other men, and a lower range 1% are bisexual.

*How do they see sex? They're the male sign who plump most for sex as a normal part of life (28%). But the majority, 44%, do describe love-making as pure magic. 5%, in the upper range, say it's overrated, 32% opt for pleasurable and 24% as an expression of love keeping a couple together.

*A bigger penis (33%), a better job (19%) and a partner the right weight (28%) with bigger breasts (25%) are all things Virgo man rates higher than the average man for giving his sexlife a boost. but he's below-average interested in more money (32%). "Splashing cash about may be a good way to attract a woman," says Gary, 41. "But being well-endowed is a better way to keep her."

When sex becomes routine, that suits VIRGO MAN best of all.

VIRGO WOMAN AND SEXUALITY

*Virgo woman lives up to her shy image by being joint least likely female sign to make love every day (7%). But a mid-to-upper range

23% do manage more than four times weekly. Virgo also comes last in the one to three times a week sector (38%), but she turns in the top score for one to three times a month (21%). A below average 5% make love rarely, while 5% are currently celibate. Her average of 2.5 times per week is slightly below average.

*12%, above average for women, would like to make love less often.

*Perhaps because Virgo is one of the women who finds her sex drive lower than her partner's—30%, almost one in three, say this is the case. 32% rate their desire levels as higher, 39% as the same, compared to a lover.

*Yet an above-average number of Virgos, 64%, state they are doing all they could want sexually.

*How many partners does Ms Virgo have? Two to five is the top scorer with 46%, but Virgo is also the woman joint most likely to have had sex with six to 10 different partners. "Each time I don't make love with a man until I decide this is the real thing," says Eunice, 34. "But then a few weeks later the "thing" turns out to be not so real after all." 9% have had just one lover in their life, and 19% altogether have had over 10.

*Virgo hits the highest score, 2%, for being attracted to her own sex. but she comes in below average in the bisexuality stakes.

*Top description of sex is "pleasurable", this is the case for 37% of Virgo women. 30% say it is pure magic, 28% an expression of love, 16% a normal part of life and just a lower range 6% overrated.

*Ms Virgo, more than any other female sign, equates bigger muscles on her partner with better sex (10%). "It's something to do with being swept into strong arms and knowing you're at his mercy," says Charmaine, 27. "Sex with a seven-stone weakling just doesn't have that element now, does it?" But relax, men, for Virgo also places joint least emphasis of all women on a bigger penis, with 8%. 59% would expect better sex if they were the right weight, 13% if a partner shaped up weight-wise. 33%, one in three, long for bigger breasts themselves, 12% for a better job for either partner, and a well-below-average 17%—lowest of all women—rate more money as a route to better sex.

VIRGO WOMAN dreams of a big strong lover to keep her safe—with or without sex.

HOW DO THE SEXES COMPARE?

Virgo men and women both live up to this sign's reputation as the most selective, and secretive, of the zodiac. Behind that cool facade lies a body waiting to be warmed up to a fire of passion. Ms Virgo longs for protection and metes out loving sparingly only to those who prove they deserve it. And she doesn't find herself sexually frustrated while she waits for the right man. Virgo man, however, will play the field to find his princess. Both sexes are lower-sexed than other signs but happy about it—in fact they're inclined to want even less sex. Men rate a bigger penis as more than four times as important as women—and they're almost twice as keen on more money, too.

LIBRA MAN AND SEXUALITY

*More Libras than any other men make love four times or more a week—27%, top male score, answered yes to this question. And with just 8% response, Libra man comes last in the one to three times a month category, too. 11% don't let a day go by without having sex at least once, 37% prefer one to three times a week, and 11% are making love "rarely." And although an upper range 7% of Libra males are currently celibate, not one envisages staying that way. All in all, Libra man averages out at 2.8 sexual experiences a week.

*But he still wants more. At 97% seeking to have sex more often, Libra is the zodiac male joint least satisfied with his quota.

*34% of Libra men have had over 20 sexual partners—that's way above average and by far the highest score of all male starsigns. Is it because of Libra indecision, flattery, the thrill of conquest, or just good old romance? Something of all these, if the AstroSex answers are anything to go by... 9% have had just one lover, 18% claim between two and five, 24% have slept with six to 10, and 15% with more than 11 but less than 20 different partners.

*No matter how many partners Libra has had, he still isn't satisfied—for 63%, highest score in the zodiac, say they are not doing everything they want to sexually with a lover. "Sex fascinates me, I'm always reading about it in books," says Tim, 24. "But when it comes to real life, I can never find the right partner to share an exploration into different positions."

*Surprisingly, a lower range 51% rate their sex drive higher than a partner's. 14%, second highest score, say it is lower, 35% judge it the same.

*A below average 4% are most attracted to other men. 96% prefer women and not a single Libra owns up to bisexual tendencies.

*46% describe sex as pure magic, that's in the upper range. "It's the greatest feeling in the world," says Gerry, 34. "And I do like to experiment a bit. Luckily my girlfriend, Jane, is as keen as I am. Nothing can be good if only one partner wants, or likes it, can it?" Just 3% of Libra men say sex is overrated, 21% describe it as a normal part of life, 28% as pleasurable, and 17% as an expression of love.

*Although Libra, like all men, said sex would be improved by being the right weight, just 29% did so, that's lowest across the male zodiac and a shock result for supposedly so-vain Libra. And he's lowest again in wanting a partner to lose weight (18%). But 31% of Libra would like a partner to have bigger breasts, and that's the top male score. "Perhaps I'm very influenced by what I see in magazines," says Vince, 22, "but a really voluptuous woman does it all for me." Exactly one in three, 33%, would appreciate a bigger penis themselves, but only 10%, well below average would rate a better job as a sex bonus. 31% go for more money, that's in the lower range again.

LIBRA MAN makes love most often with most people, yet is least satisfied...

LIBRA WOMAN AND SEXUALITY

*When it comes to timing, top choice for Libra woman is sex one to three times a week, with 40% selecting this option. A below average 8% make love every day and an above average 8%, rarely. 22%, in the middle range, get passionate four or more times a week, and 14% one to three times per month. 7% are celibate at the moment, joint highest female response. But none seeks to be celibate forever. At 2.5 times per week, their frequency of love-making falls just below average for women.

*90% would like to make love more often, that's in the upper range.

*A lower range 58% say they are doing all they could dream of sexually.

*10% have had just one sexual partner so far, 46% record two to five, and 21% between six and 10 lovers. But more Libras than any other woman have had over 11 passion partners, with a 16% score here. Although only 7% claim more than 20, and that's lowest female score overall. "I don't like the idea of women putting themselves around," says Nancy, 24. "Especially with all the diseases about at the moment. I'm not saying I'll be a virgin when I marry, but I take time to get to know a man before diving under the duvet."

*46% rate their sex drive identical to a partner's, 31% put their own higher, while 23%, well below average, say their drive is lower.

*Libra women are resoundingly heterosexual. 99% are only interested in sex with men, the highest proportion of all signs. And too few Libra women to even register on the survey results are attracted to women, or to both sexes.

*Yet Libra woman is among the female signs most likely to dismiss sex as overrated, 8% do so. 29% prefer the description pure magic, 20% see sex as a normal part of life, 34% as pleasurable and 30% as an expression of love.

*Exactly two thirds, 66%, reckon sex would improve if they were the right weight. That's above average for women. But only 12%, joint lowest score, say the same about their mate. Second top priority was having bigger breasts (27%), then more money (23%). 8%

would like larger muscles on a partner, 13% a bigger penis, both above average. But only 11% would rate a better job.

LIBRA WOMAN—conventionally feminine, but could end up frustrated.

HOW DO THE SEXES COMPARE?

He goes for quantity of sex more than her—and quantity of partners, too. For while Libra is the male sign most likely to have had over 20 lovers (34%), Libra woman scores least in this section (just 7%). Yet in the 11-20 lovers category, it's female Libras who take the lead (16% women to 15% men). Both are by far the zodiac's least bisexually inclined, and both also feel their sexual needs aren't being completely met. Criticism of partners runs high—Libra's the man most likely to wish a lover had bigger breasts, Libra's the woman who would most like her man to have a bigger penis.

SCORPIO MAN AND SEXUALITY

*Scorpio's passionate, yes—27% score puts him out in front in the four-times-a-week-plus sex sessions. However most Scorpios, 34%, still say one to three times a week is their usual pattern. So he's not the non-stop love machine traditional astrology would have us believe! Only 10%, below average, make love on a daily basis. "Why do people think frequency means potency?" asks Colin, 35. 13% of Scorpios have sex one to three times a month, 11% opt for "rarely", and the sign has a standard number of celibates, at 6%. But no one who sees celibacy as a lifelong option.

*9% of Scorpio men would like to make love less often, that's joint highest score for all male signs. "I never thought I'd say no to sex," says Timothy, 32, "but since I got divorced, women are throwing themselves at me. At first I was like a kid in a candy store. Now I'm realising that emotional blackmail can go with a one-night stand. And it isn't really healthy to put it about too much, is it?"

*Scorpio is the man most likely to have had between six and 10 lovers (32%), and least likely to have numbered over 20 lovers (18%). An upper range 12% have had only one sexual partner, 25% claim two to five and 14%, 11 to 20.

*55%, in the upper range, reckon sex drive is higher than their partner's, just 6% rate it lower. 39% say levels of desire work out roughly the same..

*More than any other male sign, Scorpio is attracted to his own sex (8%). 90% prefer women and 3% are drawn to either sex.

*48%, above average, are satisfied they are doing everything they want to sexually.

*How would Scorpio man describe sex? He gives pure magic the lowest thumbs up of the male zodiac, with 37%. It's a normal part of life for 21%, pleasurable for 31% and an expression of love to another 28%. An above-average 4% say sex is overrated, another big surprise for sex sign Scorpio.

*More than any other sign, Scorpio thinks more money (42%) and having bigger muscles (36%) would make sex better. But being the right weight, every starsign's priority, narrowly made the top of Scorpio's list with 43%. 26% would like a lover to be the right weight, 24% dream of bigger breasts. An upper range 32% say sex would be better if they had a bigger penis. 19%, though the smallest group of Scorpio men, is still an above-average response to the positive sex power of a good job. "Since I became a sales rep, my sex life has revved out of control," says Clive, 33. "Women really respond to the smart suit and charm. Plus I get to meet masses of gorgeous girls."

Material things matter to SCORPIO MAN, who's less raunchy than his reputation.

SCORPIO WOMAN AND SEXUALITY

*Ms Scorpio lives up to her sex siren image by beating all other women to top spot when it comes to frequency of lovemaking. 14% claim to have sex every day, way above the 9% female average. "If I don't make love within 24 hours of the last time, I'm edgy and tense—it's a physical need, like food or water," says Carole, 40. 20% of Scorpio women have sex four or more times per week, 40% opt for one to three times a week, while for 11% (lowest female score in this section) one to three times a month suffices. Although Scorpio woman is still above-average inclined to have sex rarely (8%) or not at all (6%), her overall score of 2.8 times a week is highest of all women.

*And she wants even more. Only 8%, joint lowest female score, would like less loving in their lives.

*Scorpio is, along with Gemini, the woman most likely to have had over 20 lovers—11% say they have. The same number have had only one sexual partner, 44% have had between two and five, while for 21%, six to 10 is the total. Finally 13% claim to have got physical with 11 to 20 different people.

*Unexpectedly, only 29%, below average, say their sex drive is higher than their partner's. 42% say it is the same, and 28% have men who like sex even more often and more varied than they do!

*An above average 2% of Scorpio women are attracted to the same sex, while 2% claim to be turned on by either gender.

*A lower range 34% are less than happy about what they do sexually. "I'll try anything," says Sara, 25. "And always want more. What I need is a man with an even more fertile imagination as I'm stuck for ideas at the moment, yet bored with routine."

*Pure magic sums up Scorpio's view of sex more often than any other female sign, with 38%. Plus 40% say it is pleasurable, 16% a normal part of life and just 6% overrated. But Scorpio, with 24%, scores lowest in saying sex is an expression of love that keeps a couple together. Can it be because her interest is more physical than emotional?

*As with all signs, being the right weight would be the best recipe for more exciting sex—63% agree with this. 21% would want a partner to be the right weight, 25% to have bigger breasts themselves and 9%, a partner to have bigger muscles. For below average 10%, enjoyment would increase with the dimensions of a lover's penis, while 10% would get more aroused as a result of a better job, and 23% with more money.

Vamp, tramp or scamp—SCORPIO WOMAN's sexuality has many sides, but is always central to her life.

HOW DO THE SEXES COMPARE?

While the male of the sign is surprisingly staid in his sexual attitudes, Ms Scorpio reinforces all the qualities the sex superstarsign is associated with. Her lust is almost without limits. She wants more sex, with more partners, in more ways— and the body every man adores to do it with. Mr Scorpio keeps a tighter hold on his erotic self, and is more swayed by material than physical assets. Yet he's far more likely than Scorpio woman to have a higher sex drive than his lover.

SAGITTARIUS MAN AND SEXUALITY

*Frequency isn't the first priority for Sagittarius men—only 5%, lowest result of all male starsigns, make love daily. But Sagittarius does come top in the one to three times per month group with 21%. 15% manage to make love four or more times per week, 36% one to three times a week, and Sagittarius is the male sign most likely to make love rarely, with 13%, and to be celibate (10%). So it's no surprise this starsign averages out at the lowest number of sex sessions per week, with 1.9.

*96%, however, do admit they'd like to have sex more often...

*A little bit of experience goes a long way. Only 3% of Sagittarius men have had just one sexual partner, that's lowest of all male signs. But 38%, highest of all men, have made love with two to five people. 26% have had six to 10 partners, 14% 11 to 20, and 19% claim over 20 lovers.

*53% of Sagittarius men say their sex drive is higher than a partner's. 8% describe it as lower, 39% the same.

*Only 2% report sexual attraction towards other men. 3% fancy both sexes, that's in the middle range.

*47%, just above the male average, say they are satisfied they're doing all they want to in a sexual relationship.

*Sagittarius may opt for quality over quantity, as 40% describe sex as pure magic. Another 38% rate it pleasurable, top score in this section for men. 22% would describe sex as a normal part of life, 19% as an expression of love, and just 2%, below average, as overrated. "Ask me when I'm with a different partner, and I could give a different reply," says Robin, 27. "My attitude to sex varies according to my current experience of it."

*Sagittarius is the most self-critical of male signs—45% reckon sex would be more scorching if they were the right weight. And an above-average 30% say the same about their partner. One in five, 20%, say having bigger muscles would perk things up, 26% would be more turned on if their lover had a bigger bust. Sagittarius is below-average interested in having a bigger penis (24%), but more aroused than any other man by good career prospects (24%). "Sitting in my designer office all day giving orders to a beautiful secretary, striking a multi-million dollar deal, then driving home in a gleaming new car, taking calls from all over my business empire. Would I find that a turn-on? Are you kidding?" says one middle management Sagittarius. One in three would also expect an improvement between the sheets due to extra cash (33%).

SAGITTARIUS MAN appreciates quality but might rather be at his job than on the job!

SAGITTARIUS WOMAN AND SEXUALITY

*Although an average 9% of Sagittarius women have sex daily, she's the sign joint least likely to make love more than four times in seven days (19%). By far the majority, 46%, choose a frequency of one to three times per week, opting for this more than any other woman. 15% make love on one to three occasions a month, 6% rarely and an average 5% are celibate right now. But only one out of every 250 would fancy making that permanent. Her overall total of 2.6 sexual episodes a week is exactly average for women.

*90% would like to make love more often.

*Sagittarius is the woman who most often rates her sexual appetites as higher than her partner's (35%). 23% say their sex drive is lower, and 43% that it's the same.

*An above-average 14% have had just one sexual partner. 44% have had between two and five, 25%, between six and ten. Sagittarius scores lowest of the female signs on over 11 partners, with 9%. And a further 9% can claim over 20 lovers.

*98% only fancy men, and only 1%, in the lower range, are attracted to both sexes. "I can't imagine going to bed with another woman," says Cherry, 27. "I've nothing against people who do, of course, but the very thought is a turn-off for me."

*43% say no, they're not doing everything they would like to sexually. "I can't stand lying there thinking next he'll tweak this, then he'll twiddle that, it's sex by numbers," complains one Sagittarius wife of 10 years. "What I really want is more oral sex and different love locations. But every time I try to introduce change, my husband gets all hurt and sulks."

*She's least likely overall to describe sex as pure magic (25%), but also least inclined to put it down as "overrated." 21%, the second highest female score, say sex is a normal part of life, while 41% opt for pleasurable. For 29%, making love is an expression of affection that binds a couple together.

*More than any other woman, Sagittarius expects sex would sizzle more if she was the right weight, (68%). Having bigger breasts comes next, at 29%, then having more cash, on 22%. A slightly above average 17% would like a partner to be the correct weight, and 10% would appreciate a bigger penis. But just 5%, lowest of all women, think a lover with bigger muscles would have any effect. 11% would be more easily aroused with a better job, and 22% with more money.

SAGITTARIUS WOMAN adopts a quite practical approach to pleasure, but hides a secret erotic imagination.

HOW DO THE SEXES COMPARE?

Both men and women take the midway in sex, keeping to an average of two to five partners in total and having sex one to three times a week. But women, on 2.6 times weekly, make love more than men, on 1.9. They all yearn to do more, yet aren't quite sure what would set their passion fuse burning. Probably not experimenting with their own gender. Both are the most self-critical of signs when it comes to their own weight, but set gentler standards for lovers. Ms Sagittarius is slightly less inhibited than the male of the sign, but the difference is less marked than in signs such as Scorpio.

CAPRICORN MAN AND SEXUALITY

*Capricorn's claim to fame is he is the man least likely to be celibate—just 3% of this starsign's males admit they are. That's exactly half the overall male average of 6%. And not one Capricorn wants to stay celibate, either! 11% make love on a daily basis. 24% have sex more than four times in a week, 35% one to three times per week, and 17% one to three times a month. 11%, in the upper male range, say they have sex rarely. In any one week the Capricorn's sexual average is 2.7 times, falling exactly in the middle range.

*93%, below average, want sex more often.

*8% have had just one lover, 38% lay claim to two to five sexual partners, and 18% to between six and 10. 23%, highest male score, have had 11-20 different partners, and 22% over 20.

*60%, that's well above average and second highest result for men, rate their desire levels as higher than a partner's. 7% say their sex drive is lower, and 33% that it's exactly the same. "I've yet to meet a woman who can keep up with my libido. I like it five times a night and, if I can, every night," says Terry, 22. "Sometimes I meet a woman who is great the first night, she just doesn't want to stop. But the next time, it's once and then go to sleep. I don't know if women are naturally more easily satisfied, or just lose interest after the first burst of passion."

*Only 1%, least of all male signs, of Capricorns are attracted to other men. Another 1% prefer either sex, but he's overwhelmingly heterosexual, on 97%.

*42%, in the lower range, are fulfilling their every desire sexually.

*Yet a high 45% would still describe love-making as "pure magic." 36% opt for sex as pleasurable, 22% as an expression of love, 17% a normal part of life, and just 3% say it is overrated. "After the first time, I wondered why everyone went on about sex," says Jimmy, 22. "And put it down to my lack of experience. I've tried it three times with two other partners, but still would rather play a good game of football."

*32% think sex would sizzle more if they were the right weight, but that's below average. And a lower range 20% think the same about their lover's weight. 22% would like bigger biceps, 24% would like a lover to have bigger breasts. A low scoring 26% think having a bigger penis would make a difference, 20% would like a better job. But 38%, well into the upper range, rate more money as a sex-life tonic. Capricorn is the only male sign to make this his number one choice...

Money can't buy CAPRICORN MAN love? Try telling him that...

CAPRICORN WOMAN AND SEXUALITY

*For 8% of Capricorn women, sex is a daily event. 24%, in the upper range, make love over four times a week, and 38% (lowest score of all women) one to three times per week. 17% opt for one to three times a month, and 8% have sex rarely. 4% are celibate now, and 1% want to stay that way.

*She's most likely among women to want less sex—14% say they'd like to make love less often.

*Most, 44%, say they have had two to five lovers. But Capricorn rates lowest among women in the six to 10 lovers category, even though this is their second most popular choice. 12%, just above average, have only had one lover, and a total of 25%, or one in four, have had over 11. "It might be unusual in some circles to marry the man you made love to first," says Bernadette, 22. "But where I live, it's still normal."

*Only 27%, lowest across the female zodiac, report a sex drive higher than a partner's. And 30%, top female score along with Gemini and Virgo, rate their own desire level as lower. 44% reckon sex drives within a couple are roughly similar.

*Not one Capricorn is attracted solely to her own sex, although 2% would describe themselves as bisexual. The remainder, 98%, like sex just with men.

*More than the average, 64%, are having all their sexual needs, and ideas, answered within a relationship.

*Yet Capricorn is first to say sex is overrated, with a 9% vote, or almost one in 10. "As a teenager you're led to expect so much, fireworks, passion, heat and lust. Yet the reality is so often messy, unsavoury, with as much desire as a cold cup of coffee," says one Capricorn. 29%, in the lower range, would describe sex as pure magic, while 19% opt for a normal part of life. 36%, again below average, find it pleasurable, and Capricorn is the woman most likely to describe it as an expression of love that binds a couple together. So even if she is less than impressed physically, she sees the place for sex emotionally.

*Yes, like everyone else, being the right weight would make Capricorn's sex life more thrilling, she thinks (63%). And 16% say the same about a partner's shape, or lack of it. Interest in her own chest is lower range (24%), but interest in her partner's scores average marks (7%)! 13% would get more excitement from a bigger penis, highest female score for this. "Size doesn't make a difference? Rubbish. Bigger is definitely better," says Collette, 29. While 16%, again highest among female signs, rate a better job, and 24%, more money, as passion enhancers.

CAPRICORN WOMAN's a cool customer who expects her man to measure up—physically and financially.

HOW DO THE SEXES COMPARE?

His sex drive is double hers—60% of the time Capricorn man's lust levels are higher than a partner's, while 30% of the time Capricorn woman's are lower. Yet far more women (64%) than men (42%) report they are doing everything they want to when it comes to sex. Both are the signs least interested in their own gender sexually, and while Capricorn man sees sex in term of pleasure, Capricorn woman tends more towards duty, love and loyalty. Yet she still exhibits an earthy interest in a man with plenty to offer in bed. Cash and career are bigger turn-ons to these two than any other sign.

AQUARIUS MAN AND SEXUALITY

*In his attitudes towards sex, as in everything else, Aquarius ploughs his own path. But this adventurer sign does manage to make love an above-average number of times per week, with 2.9. 14% have sex every day, 24% four or more times in an average week, and 36% anything from once to three times. 11% opt for one to three times per month, 8% make love rarely and an upper range 7% are celibate right now. But that's a situation they all hope will change. "I wouldn't mind if I chose to go without sex, but as it's a situation forced on me, I intend to get out of it as quickly as possible," is one typical Aquarius remark.

*Just 7% have had one lover only, 34% lay claim to two to five sexual partners, while 13%, lowest male score by far, boast of between six and 10. Aquarius makes up for it, though, by being well into the upper range for men with multiple partners. 20% have had over 11, and a further 26% over 20, lovers.

*Aquarius is among the four male signs who would most like to have less sex (9%).

*Yet 51%, second highest male result and well above average, report they couldn't be happier with their sex lives.

*That's despite the fact Aquarius is the man most likely to rate his own sex drive as lower than a partner's—15% do so. "If I'm honest,

I enjoy the fact my girlfriend comes on strong to me and tries everything to get me interested," admits Trent, 37. "It's nice to just lie there and not have to make all the effort." But a further 38%, above average, do reckon desire levels work out about the same.

*He's the male sign second most likely to describe sex as overrated (5%), and least inclined to see it as an expression of love (16%). But 41% still say passion is pure magic, and for 35% it's pleasurable. 19% state their view of sex is as a normal part of life.

*He's above-average heterosexual, with 95% attracted to women only. Something of an unexpected finding for the sign supposedly the zodiac's most experimental. "If you can spend a lifetime loving and exploring one person's body, who needs anyone else?" says Blake, 49. A lower-range 2% are attracted to both men and women, 2% fancy other men most.

*What would make sex more exciting for Aquarius man? Like everyone else, he'd most like to be the right weight (35%), have a bigger penis (32%) and more money (31%). But the only one of these he's more interested in than the average man is the penis size! 28% would expect an improvement if their partner was the right weight, but a lower range 18% think bigger breasts would make any difference. 22%, second highest score in the zodiac, would feel sexier if they or their lover had a better job.

For slow-to-boil AQUARIUS MAN, less is more in sex, except when it comes to penis size.

AQUARIUS WOMAN AND SEXUALITY

*Aquarius tops all other female signs when it comes to having sex four or more times a week—one in four, 25%, of the air sign claim this frequency. 9% make love every day, 41% one to three times a week, 13% one to three times a month. 7% say they have sex rarely, while 5% would describe themselves as celibate at the moment. Although none of them wants to stay that way... Aquarius' overall average is a middle to upper range 2.7 times per week.

*9% would like to make love less often. That's exactly the same percentage as for male Aquarius, but among the women has the opposite effect—by making Aquarius the female sign second most keen on more sex. "It's like everything I do, I want to make sure I've tried every option on offer," say several Aquarius women.

*She's the woman most likely to have had two to five sexual partners (47%). 9% have had only one lover, 22% between six and 10, 13%, 11-20 and 9%, over 20.

*62%, exactly average for the zodiac's women, are doing all the sexual things they want to with a partner.

*And she's second luckiest in finding a mate with the same level of lust—46% rate their sex drive as on a par with a partner's. A lower range 30% say theirs is higher, 24% rate their own lower.

*A middle range 62% are doing all they want to sexually.

*4%, twice the female average, are attracted to both men and women equally. "It's got me into some terrible situations, I can tell you," says Shantelle, 25, "especially when I fancy both the man and woman in a couple." 95% are turned on only by men, and 1% only by women.

*How does Aquarius woman see sex? She's second most likely to describe it as overrated (8%), and least likely of all to treat it as a normal part of life (12%). "Not one of the five men I've slept with has made lovemaking come up to my expectations," says Delia, 25. Pleasurable is her favourite choice with 35%, an expression of love scores above average 31%, while a lower range 30% opt for the description "pure magic."

*Give her a change for the better in her own weight (62%), bigger breasts (29%), and partner with a bigger penis (11%) and better job (12%) and Ms Aquarius would expect sex to be more thrilling. But the only thing she's above-average interested in is more money (26%). Her partner's weight, or muscle size, do little for her.

AQUARIUS WOMAN is hard to shock, but hard to satisfy, too.

HOW DO THE SEXES COMPARE?
Two complex, demanding lovers who want adventure and

earth-moving ecstasy every time. And they'll soon lose interest if love moves become too lazy or routine. Compared to other men and women, she'd like more sex and he'd like less, and she is also twice as experimental in her choice of lover. Both accept a partner for what they are physically, but focus on material things as a means to sexual satisfaction. For Aquarius woman it's cash, for Aquarius man, it's career. They may dismiss sex as overrated because of impossible expectations.

PISCES MAN AND SEXUALITY

* How often does Mr Pisces make love? More often than almost every other male starsign, with a high 3.2 times-per-week average. 15% manage to make love daily, 25% four or more times per week, and 40% (highest male score for this section) one to three times a week. 9% limit themselves to one to three times a month, and just 6% have sex rarely, lowest score here for the male zodiac. Fewer than average, 4%, are celibate—and all are actively planning to change this state of affairs. "When I'm not getting regular sex I can't sleep or concentrate on anything else," admits Lenny, 23.

*The 57% of Pisces men who say their sex drive is higher than their partner's are above average for all signs, and so are the 57% who want to do more in bed than they are doing right now. And, yes, so are the 95% who'd just like more sex!

*A lower range 7% have stayed with just one sexual partner. Two to five lovers is the most popular choice, with 35% subscribing to this. 21% estimate their sexual partners at between six and 10, 11% at 11 to 20 and an upper range 25% at over 20.

*For a high 45%, sex is pure magic. 25% each describe it as pleasurable and an expression of love keeping a couple together. For 20%, it's a normal part of life. But just 1% of all Pisces males, lowest score in the whole zodiac, reckon sex is overrated. "That's like saying breathing, touching or loving is overrated. They, like sex, are an integral part of being human, being alive," says Keith, 31.

*A lower range 3% of Pisces men are attracted mainly to other men, another 3% enjoy both sexes. And 94% are strictly women-only.

*Ask Pisces what would make sex more exciting and he has no doubt—for Pisces, read penis. For more than any other male, 36%, he reckons bigger would make for better in bed. Even the top favourite for almost every other sign, being the right weight, is beaten into second place by Pisces obsession with penis size! He's also above average, 27%, in fantasising about his partner having bigger breasts and in wanting bigger muscles for himself, too (27%). "Every night I'm in the gym pumping iron," says Adrian, 24. "Women love my muscles, and although my dad keeps going on about it all going to fat if I stop training, I know that isn't going to happen. And I promise you it's improved the size of my love muscles, too..." Pisces man is also more turned on than Mr Average Starsign by more money and a better job, for either partner.

High performance love machine who still sees sex as a special treat, that's PISCES MAN.

PISCES WOMAN AND SEXUALITY

*A below average 8% have daily sex, while Pisces is the least likely of all women to make love more than four times per week (19%). 41% choose one to three times a week, 16% one to three times a month, and 7% would estimate sex as "rare" in their lives. 6% are celibate now, slightly above the female average, but they don't intend it to last. Overall, Pisces' sex pattern of 2.4 times per week falls below the female 2.6 average. "I would have sex 10 times a day if I could," says Terri, 25. "The problem is finding the right partner. I seem to wear most men out. And if they haven't got the stamina to keep up with me, my interest goes."

*Pisces is the most frustrated of women—43% are not doing everything they would like to sexually with a partner. "Yet I can't seem to ask for what I want, I was brought up to think any interest in sexuality was dirty," says Nell, 30. "I worry my husband might go off me if I became an active instead of a passive lover."

*Only 37%, lowest score for the zodiac's women, rate their sex drive and a partner's as equal. 34% say their own desire is stronger, that's in the upper range. And 28% rate a partner's higher.

*This could explain why 91% want more sex, placing Pisces woman second from the top in this category.

*When it comes to number of partners, Ms Pisces falls firmly in the middle range, but she is below-average disposed to stick to just a single sexual partner (9%). 43% have had between two and five lovers, 24% six to 10, 13% 11 to 20 and another 10%, over 20.

*A high 4% of Pisces women are sexually attracted to both men and women. 1% prefer their own sex, 95% prefer men.

*The description of sex she opts for most often is pleasurable, with 40%. 29% say lovemaking is pure magic, 25% that it's an expression of love, 18% a normal part of life, and an average 7% judge sex completely overrated.

*67%, way above average, are sure sex would be more exciting if they were the right weight, and for 18%, above average again, the same would be true about a partner's weight. A lower range 25% would appreciate bigger breasts, while 8% want a partner to sport bigger muscles—and 11% would like him to be better endowed everywhere! 11% rate a better job, and 19% more cash, as turn-on potential—both less than the average starsign female.

Unfulfilled dreams and desires haunt PISCES WOMEN—but she's working on it!

HOW DO THE SEXES COMPARE?

Pisces is a very physical sign. Both men and women want to have the best body for themselves, plus a well-equipped partner, both physically and emotionally. But Pisces men seem luckier in getting this than Pisces women. The females of this sign yearn for more sex and more adventure, yet are generally short-changed. Perhaps that's why they're seven times as likely to say sex is overrated... Men, meanwhile, are already getting over

their fair share, yet still want more. As usual it's the male of the sign who passes through most beds, and his self-image seems the shakier of the two. Both sexes are desperate to reach full sexual potential, they just choose different ways of doing it...

Part Two:

Lovematch
The 288 Zodiac
Partnerships

THE ARIES MAN'S LOVE MATCHES

ARIES MAN—TAURUS WOMAN

He-man meets earth mother—a strong, traditional partnership and one that she's likely to make. Even though, she says, she doesn't instantly find his bouts of in-your-face aggression or his disengaged approach to sex much of a turn-on. He reckons she's the woman he's least likely to end up with and he hardly fancies her at all! But he's missing out if he doesn't warm to her sultry smile and caring, passion-brimming eyes, or take time out to enjoy her kind-heartedness and loyalty. After all, these are the qualities he usually appreciates in a partner. She could teach him to slow down and savour more sensual loving, and if he wants someone to look after him (and he doesn't do too good a job on his own), he need look no further. Comfort-craving Taurus was born to create the cosy homestead he always says he's looking for.

But here's the hitch. He's the man who most rates sexual attraction—she's the woman who values it least! Sexwise, he's into adventurous romps (the more the merrier) with lots of experimentation. She's seriously romantic and can't really let herself go with a man she doesn't trust. And while she blooms when making love within her marriage, he can't say he notices any difference in its quality. Still, both are in a dash to get hitched and both may well hit the jackpot when it comes to marrying the love of their life.

Surprisingly, for such an upfront sexy sign, he's more likely than her to save himself until he meets the partner of his dreams.

ARIES MAN—GEMINI WOMAN

She'll hate it when he tells her what to do, but he's still one of her favourite partners. Sometimes, she names him as a sexy beast—other times, she reckons he's not fanciable at all. All part of her mercurial charm. But he doesn't often go for her as a lifelong mate nor does he fancy her. Her ideal man needs to look well turned-out, and out-to-impress Aries often manages that rather well.

His clued-up talk amuses her—and she's far too much of a jabberer herself to ever worry that he might hog the conversation! He says he needs a competent homemaker who'll pamper him, though, and out-having-fun Gemini isn't the lady to iron her way through a pile of shirts if she can help it! She'll expect him to tune in to her mindset—vital to such a communicative on-air sign.

He'll appreciate her adventurous lovemaking style and hope she never changes. He reckons that lasting sexual appeal holds the key to long-term relationship contentment. Yet while her sexlife improves with time and partner familiarity, established loving can lose its spark for him though he is the male sign most likely to report that post-marriage sex stays just the same. He's got more chance of making a lasting match than her—she's on the fickle side. In fact, she is the zodiac woman who's least likely to notch up long wedding anniversaries. He is keener on marriage all round. She may well opt to stay single—unless she changes her mind again, that is.

ARIES MAN—CANCER WOMAN

She strikes him as shy and tongue-tied at first impression—and not nearly raunchy or experimental enough in bed! Yet he can also find her very sexy. He votes her his most popular partner. Why? Because he knows he can coax out her siren side, in time. Meanwhile, she's the ideal homemaker he's been looking for—even though he may find himself taking on more of her family than he bargained for.

On her side of the deal, she wants her partner to show great kindness and loyalty and to be able to run with her deep, often almost uncontrollable, emotional swings. So selfish and bossy Aries will have to do a home tuition course on sensitivity, fast!

He rates sexual magnetism far more highly than she does. He's also the man who, glumly, reports that he rarely finds his sexlife moving into a higher gear after he's got married. She is the woman, though, who most often sees a noticeable improvement (probably because she loses many of her inhibitions once she feels emotionally secure). She has more chance than him of striking up a lasting match—nearly half of all Cancer women hang on to their husbands. And she's also more likely than him to want to remarry if things go wrong in the first set-up. She likes being a Mrs. She's not so keen on being a mistress, however, and is one of the female starsigns who's least likely to have an extra-marital affair. If he cheats though, she's more likely than most women to ask for a divorce.

ARIES MAN—LEO WOMAN

Both value the magic of sexual chemistry and are lucky enough to find that, for them, it stays strong as their loving relationship deepens. Both vote each other as very hot stuff—but watch out. Without careful nurturing, this partnership could end up a vivid snapshot, not an album. To take it from intoxicating fling to interesting marriage of minds and bodies, it's vital that he curbs that inbuilt tendency to wander. Her own sexy eyes and megawatt smile probably lured him from someone else's address book in the first place. But she demands more lover loyalty than any other female sign—even though she's no saint herself! Her brow's bound to furrow once she finds out that he has an above-average weakness for infidelity. Some pretty binding promises will have to be made before she commits herself.

Once she does, though, it'll probably be set in granite. She's the female sign most likely to marry for life. He remarries more often, but is still only in the middling bracket. Naturally, she's more likely to be there for her tenth wedding anniversary. He's got the winning ticket, though, when it comes to marrying the love of his life—he's often luckier than her. It's quite probable that both will wed as virgins. But being married is more likely to give her sexlife a big buzz than it is his, and if things do go wrong, she'll be in much more of a hurry to get out and start afresh with spouse number two.

ARIES MAN—VIRGO WOMAN

He's probably not the tidiest of men and hasn't the patience to make his pad particularly comfortable, so he's on the lookout for a well-organised homemaker to settle down with. He probably thinks that helpful Virgo is perfect for the job. But she's less interested in clear-cut domestic roles than he imagines—she's one of the female signs least likely to get herself hitched to a good provider. Still, she is one of his favourite partners and he finds her fanciable. Pity that she plays so hard to get! She doesn't single his sign out for preferential treatment in the marriage stakes very often and says he's not for her in the passion stakes, either.

Once together, she values loyalty, humour and fun—more than he does—while he believes that physical attraction is more of a must for long-term satisfaction with a partner. Marriage won't change either's interest in sex significantly. But having children can either make or break his libido. She stays on a more even course, finding little difference. Virgo is one of the female signs who's likely to marry more than once. He's only in the middle remarriage category, but he's luckier than her at marrying the love of his life and making his relationship last.

ARIES MAN—LIBRA WOMAN

Finding a faithful relationship she can treasure really sets her sexuality free. Bad news for Aries men who can't, or won't, ditch those bachelor-days' phone books. These two have a near-average chance of being partners, nevertheless, and that's even after voting each other among the least sexually appetising signs. She does like a man with a gift for vocabulary, but could go off him if he interrupts her (an Aries fault) or repeatedly dominates a conversation. And she'll only be the excellent homemaker he wants—and knows she can be—if she's allowed to combine it with her live-and-kicking social scene.

Libra is the female starsign who least rates a good provider, so Aries can put away his spears, or designer briefcase, because they won't impress her. In fact, she may not feel at ease with the olden days Mr and Mrs roles he's mapped out for them both.

For long-term success, she values loyalty and kindness, while he puts sexual attraction high on his list. She usually marries for life and has more chance than any other sign of keeping at it. He makes a lasting bond less often, and has an average chance of marrying more than once, but they are both eager to get married and both are often rather lucky at finding the great romance that goes the distance. She's less likely to be a virgin at the altar, though, and more positive than him about the beneficial effects that marriage has on her sexlife.

ARIES MAN—SCORPIO WOMAN

This isn't the most obvious of pairings. But though she votes Aries the least sexy male starsign, sensual Scorpio fancies muscular men. So, if he's got a sporty enough physique, he could easily seduce her! They're set to make a good match, too, when it comes to the kind of roles each wants to take around the home. He wants a good homemaker, she's seeking someone successful who can bring home good money. Both agree that sexual attraction is absolutely vital to continuing happiness, and both demand total loyalty, with a fair sprinkling of kindness, from their partner.

Hers is one of the female signs most likely to marry several times. He's in the middle range and more often settles down with the great love of his life. To make things fair, she's got more chance of enjoying a tenth wedding anniversary. Both will probably be sexually inexperienced when they wed. But she'll go on to get a bigger charge out of her sexlife as it improves from there on—he doesn't get nearly as much fillip from marriage. Having children can either improve this couple's lovelife, or wreck it. If their dream crumbled and one of them had an affair, it's quite likely that both of them would say never again to marriage!

ARIES MAN—SAGITTARIUS WOMAN

You'd expect these two outgoing, sporty firesigns to get on like a house ablaze—but not necessarily so. Surprisingly, they can't make up their minds if they fancy each other or not. They can either rate one another as sexy—or not attractive at all! Knockout smiles and gorgeous eyes are prime pulls for both. He also appreciates a curvy feminine shape (she automatically expects him to be as fit as she is). She's smitten by any man who can weave a web of fascinating words around her—though pushy Aries must take care not to build the subject matter exclusively around himself if she's to stay interested! For lasting romance, both expect warmheartedness and loving loyalty. She's the female sign who, despite her many opportunities and easygoing nature, is the least likely to have an affair. She thinks having a sense of humour matters more than he does, while he believes sexual attraction is a must.

In practice, neither are especially good at building marriages to last. They're far better at striking up new acquaintances! Both come into the middle range when it comes to marrying more than once, but he's more easily put off remarriage than she is. He has more chance of netting the love of his life, though. She is the female starsign who's least likely to say that marriage makes her sexlife worse—both often report that it stays the same. But she's got far and away more chance than him of finding that remarriage shoots her lovelife into the pleasure stratosphere!

ARIES MAN—CAPRICORN WOMAN

She's a very powerful woman who knows what she wants in life, and his first reaction to her may well be to run a mile! Especially if she looks like undermining some of his cherished chauvinistic prejudices. But, in fact, she rates him very highly as a life partner and admits that she finds him moderately sexy. He wouldn't want to pick her name out of the hat, though, and goes on to report that he find this female sign unsexy. But that's probably before she turned her charming special smile on to him—both signs give this feature the thumbs up (and it gets absolute top female vote from her). Loyalty and kindness are joint quests as well, but he goes on to name sexual attraction as a vital marital happiness ingredient, while she'd rather have humour and understanding.

They've both mapped out clear-cut roles for their partners and, despite her superbly successful working life, she is the female sign keenest to find a good provider while he's the male sign who most appreciates a good homemaker. They're traditionalists at heart. Neither finds that long-term love recharges their sexual batteries very much, and she's the star woman most likely to see the libido decrease.

Both are keen to marry, however, and they're also both lucky when it comes to nabbing the love of their lives. But if things go awry, he's not as willing as she is to give wedlock another break. She's less likely to have an affair, but if he did so, she may well want to call the marriage quits and get a divorce.

ARIES MAN—AQUARIUS WOMAN

There's a good chance he'll pick her out as a suitable partner, but he doesn't find her cool brand of sexuality especially appealing. She finds him one of the least fanciable signs, but both may easily find themselves switched on to their new love if their eyes and smiles are their best features. Quirky Aquarius goes on to give kindness in a mate the lowest possible female vote. Instead, she's the woman who most craves a man who can unlock her mysterious mind, being a sign who just loves to share ideas as well as bodies. Self-centred Aries will have to consider his lover's feelings and needs, instead of always putting his own first if he wants to win her trust.

Naturally, traditional roles don't come easy to this unconventional woman. Already, he's twice as keen to find himself a good home-maker as she is to land a reasonable breadwinner. Instead, she's keener to get a partner who really is an equal partner, someone who's loyal and overflowing with a sense of humour. Sexual attraction heads his list. She's only half as likely as him to be a virgin when she marries, and she can find that wedlock booms or busts her sex drive, while he's more likely than most to report no noticeable change. He is luckier than her at making a lasting marital match— and he marries the love of a lifetime more frequently, too.

ARIES MAN—PISCES WOMAN

Sensitive soul, he's not, but he'll have to dredge up much kindness of heart, understanding and good-natured humour if his relationship with this highly emotional woman is to thrive. Even though he doesn't find her especially sexy and she votes him the least fanciable male sign of the lot, this pair are still popular partners with each other. Their smouldering glances and irresistible smiles make them notice each other—but he'll have to back them up with the giving qualities she needs.

He gives sexual attraction the top male vote—something she thinks is only of moderate importance in a long-term coupling. And while he wants a competent, imaginative homemaker to take good care of him, she's not really searching for a meal-ticket and probably won't be particularly comfortable with the traditional slot he's prepared for her!

They're both very keen to marry—but it could turn out to be tougher work all round for her! He sees himself as the partner with his feet up, while she can fall into the trap of trying to be the perfect housewife. He has a slightly greater chance of making a lasting match, while she's more likely to tie the knot at least twice. He's luckier than her at settling with his great love. But while she reckons marriage puts a sheen on her love life, he says it stays the same. Having kids can make sex better—or worse—for both, however. An affair can see either offended party trying to settle the score by taking a lover of their own.

ARIES MAN—ARIES WOMAN

She lusts after him all right—and he finds her a generous 10% sexier than any other sign! So why don't they name their fellow Aries as their favourite partner? He's only slightly keener for them to pair off than she is, and that's not saying much. Well, she might not be much kinder than he is, deep down, but she certainly expects this kind of emotional warmth from her man, and he's more used to taking than to giving! He, on the other hand, firmly believes that sexual attraction holds the key to marital happiness. They can't ignore that first sexy glance, though, nor that unforgettable smile—both are vulnerable to these attractions. He goes for a curvaceous figure and splendid legs, too, while she likes him to be tall, confident and to look smart.

Aries is the female sign who's at highest risk of remarriage. He makes his wedded bliss last better than she does—and is also luckier at getting the love of his life to say I Do. Both have an average chance of being wedding-day virgins, but she's more likely than him to find that wedlock lifts her sexlife (though she admits that it can worsen, too). If he were to stray, she's liable to ask for a divorce. He might simply take a lover of his own, to equal the score.

THE ARIES WOMAN'S LOVEMATCHES

ARIES WOMAN—TAURUS MAN

If he's not got an inner core of self-confidence that's as tough as steel, he needn't bother to apply to be her spouse! He's one of her least probable partner selections, in the cold light of day, and she says she doesn't find his sign very sexy. But he's hard to deter once he's made up his mind and she's popular with him, anyway. This is the male who most rallies to an unambiguous smile and who loves a fit, yet curvy, body. She goes for men with crinkles at the corners of noticeably attractive eyes, men without an ounce of hesitation or shyness in them. They both think kindness is vital in any properly balanced relationship.

Comfort-loving Taurus is out to find a cosy domesticated nest-builder, though, and Aries isn't especially shopping for a dependable provider. There'll need to be room for manoeuvre over household tasks and roles. Above all, this female wants to have fun (and there's more than a hint of outrageous recklessness about her enjoyment tastes). He rates this quality far lower than other men.

Once he's settled, he's a low remarriage risk—while she runs the highest risk of all women. His chances are greater, too, of making a long-lived match and of setting up home with the love of his life, lucky fellow. He isn't as easily put off remarriage as she is and he is more likely to find that the sex side of his relationship takes on a whole new meaning once he's married. Pity—she can report that it gets worse! Once they've had children, he's more likely than her to find his partner more sexually attractive.

ARIES WOMAN—GEMINI MAN

He names her as one of the highest on his lovelist and finds her oh-so-fanciable. She doesn't quite return his enthusiasm but, if she has marvellous legs and a loud, sexy roar of a laugh, he'll turn all his unstoppable flirtatious charm on to her. If these two then find they've got interests in common, they'll be well away! She normally likes her men to be tall, muscular and to have a good voice—she's a great admirer of self-confident, fluent talkers like Gemini, but she does give kindness a stronger vote than he does. In fact, hers is the top women's vote of the lot for kindness.

He places sex skills, sexual attraction and having fun higher up on the list than she does. It is likely that she'll marry more than once—she's the female sign most likely to go in for serial monogamy. He's far more attuned to long-haul love. Despite his flighty image, he remarries less.

Yet this Mr Contradiction is also much more prone than her to want to stay single for life. Neither are likely to get the love of their life to marry them—his problem is that he leaves it too long to commit himself. Often, his bird has flown by then. He is the man most likely to be a virgin when he marries and she's got an above-average chance of being a virgin bride.

Sex, for both, often improves after marriage, but she can also report it taking a turn for the worse. He's an unlikely candidate for an away-match affair, but may favour divorce if she strayed. She would take a lover of her own if he was unfaithful.

ARIES WOMAN—CANCER MAN

Watch out that this relationship doesn't smooth down into too much cosiness. Certainly, they name each other without hesitation as favourite partners, but they also think each is their least sexy match, too. So there's plenty of domestic contentment here—but not much in the way of thrills. More than other women, she likes a man's eyes, and she also sets enormous store by kindness in her mate. He loves a mellow smile and gives loyalty the top male vote.

She'll probably want him to be more confident (and stand by like a puppetmaster to supply any deficit herself, if needs be).He'd prefer it if she had a gentler, more conventionally feminine manner. Sensitive Cancer, who seems to be missing at least one layer of protective skin, needs her to understand the way he thinks, too. So self-centred Aries will have to learn to see things his way.

Both agree, however, that you don't just need sexual attraction to tango for years on end. This pair are both at considerable risk of embarking on more than one marriage. He has more chance than his spouse, though, of making his relationship last and he's also keener to remarry. He has more hope, too, of going down the aisle with the love of his life.

Long-term loving can really perk up his sexlife—or have quite the opposite effect. For her, things thankfully only get better by and large. He's one of the signs who's least likely to have his head turned, but he may want a divorce if she's unfaithful. She'd settle scores by taking her own secret lover.

ARIES WOMAN—LEO MAN

She sees him first as a sexual challenge, but doesn't really consider him seriously in the long-term partnership category. He has an average chance of singling her out as a lifetime's mate, but says he doesn't find her very sexy. He may secretly resent her ability to take the spotlight away from him! More than other men, though, he adores looking deeply into his partner's eyes and he's also drawn by a sultry smouldering half-smile and curvy, though sporty, body.

Aries woman knows how to make the most of these assets. She is bound to love him if he has eyes and smile that shoot out unmistakable signals to her through a crowd.

She's extremely aroused by his attention-grabbing confidence. He likes the excitement that surrounds fiery, hyperactive Aries—gentler, less spontaneous women and good little homemakers win less votes from him, than from almost any other male sign.

Kindness is vital to both for long-term love success—especially to her. Loyalty and understanding matter a lot, too. She gets the biggest sex boost in our survey from an established relationship. He reports that loving either gets better, or at the very least, stays the same. She's far less likely than him to be a virgin on her wedding day. And he has more chance than her of making a long-lasting bond. Both could find themselves with new partners at some point in their lives. But she's keener on marriage than he is. In fact, he's the zodiac man who's most likely to want to stay single!

ARIES WOMAN—VIRGO MAN

His usual type is like a Victorian lady with gentle manners—so he may find forceful Aries too hot-tempered (and tactless) to handle! She appreciates his kindness more than other women do, but she's bound to want him to be bolder, brasher and more self-confident—more of a knight in shining armour, and reserved Virgo could find all this imposed aggression a bit hard going. There's a near-average chance they could end up partners, though.

Neither finds the other sexy, but closer acquaintance could change all that. More than other men, he will appreciate a slender, yet shapely, figure and attractive voice (provided it's not giving him orders!). Both are in total agreement that loyalty, and a sense of humour, are what it takes to make a long-term relationship really tick.

Unexpectedly, the male perfectionist of the zodiac isn't looking for a good homemaker after all (he's so efficient himself). This will please active Aries no end, for she feels she's far too busy to keep a perfect, dust-free house. He likes the single life more than she does, though, and is less eager to remarry. They're both in the below-average bracket for staying married for more than 10 years. He's more likely to wed the love of a lifetime than she is, but on the down side, he's the man who most often says that marriage has harmed his sexlife—she reports more mixed results!

ARIES WOMAN—LIBRA MAN

She's more likely to pick him out of the pack than he is to choose her as his partner, and they either get the hots for one another straight away or don't fancy each other one bit! She likes the confidence and charm of a smoothychops Libra man and adores his sexy eyes and quick smile (provided she doesn't notice how widely it's aimed). He isn't at all fazed by her strong personality—he goes far less than other men for the gentle-manner woman (though he likes curves). He puts good looks, sex skills and physical attraction higher up his list than she does. But with her super energy and enthusiasm for lovemaking, it won't take her long to match up to his adventurous ways in bed!

Even so, he's more likely than her to report that wedlock brings a sexual boost. She does find that loving can get better—but it can also get worse. Libra is the male sign most likely to make a truly long-lasting lovematch and yet has most affairs! But she has far fewer successes and actually remarries more frequently than any other female starsign. Neither are very lucky when it comes to getting hitched to the love of their life. But one thing's almost 100% certain—he won't have saved himself for that special person, while she just might!

ARIES WOMAN—SCORPIO MAN

With her voracious sexual appetite, it's no wonder she finds this hypnotically sensual man so attractive. Not only does she find him powerfully appealing in the short term, but she says that he's one of her most successful partners. However, he may be initially dumbfounded by her too-direct approaches and list her as one of the least sexy signs around! He prefers his females to play harder to get, so Aries is one of his less likely long-term choices.

But, drawn inexorably by his mesmerising eyes and bold self-confidence—and amazing insight into how women think—she soon learns to play more helpless! For starters, though, he's bound to notice her if she has smashing legs, hotlips glances and a disconcertingly open, warm smile. Once together, both will want loyalty from their partner—and she goes on to value kindness, too, even more than he does. He believes that consummate bedroom technique, sexual attraction and a big element of fun matter more than she does, and while she's the female starsign who most often goes in for more than one husband, he's the male sign who is most likely to get hitched just once, for life. They both find that getting married can nurture or knacker their sexlife! But he's more likely than her to think a partner's sexier after having children.

ARIES WOMAN—SAGITTARIUS MAN

She's such a creature of impulse! She's his best-loved partner and he finds her raw sexuality more than a match for his own. Yet, capriciously, she says she's unlikely to settle with him and either finds him fanciable or a real turn-off! Magnets for both include brazenly encouraging smiles and sexy eyes—and both have energy and decisiveness to share and spare. She's mightily impressed by his totally carefree confidence, delighted to discover the kind-hearted nature that lies behind it.

He's attracted to faithfulness—and will be relieved to hear that she's got a slightly below-average chance of having affairs! In turn, her self assurance will get a boost from the knowledge that—although he's very sociable, he's the sign least likely to stray. Both put kindness at the top of their requirements for long-term bliss. Loyalty, understanding and humour are highly rated by both, too.

And neither think sexual attraction is vital to wedded happiness—though they do find that established love improves their sexlives. He is more likely that she is to find a partner less sexy after having children, and both do have a high chance of marrying more than once (her in particular). Neither hits the jackpot when it comes to getting hitched to the love of their life or making long-lasting matches. But if one marriage fails, he's more likely than her to want to try marriage again.

ARIES WOMAN—CAPRICORN MAN

She's good at drawing out the streak of sexual abandon in this seemingly buttoned-up, high-powered man. And he's not in the least afraid of her bossiness! In fact, he's drawn to her blunt, outgoing nature in no small measure. He says that she's a popular long-term partner, and he can find her either very sexy indeed—or, if she's a shade too dominating—unsexy. But she may find him too reserved for the long haul of a live-in-partnership. He's not one of her favourite mates and she has no strong feelings about him sexwise, either. But once she's distracted him sufficiently from his work fixation, she could be startled by the throbbing physical dynamo she finds before her!

He is, for one so career-conscious, in quite a hurry to get married. In more of a rush than she is, in fact. He picks his spouse carefully and logically and also has more chance than the Aries woman of making his lovelinks last a lifetime. He has less chance of wedding the love of his life, though (his decision is too calculating for that) and he's not likely to have saved himself for marriage, either. She has more chance of being a wedding day virgin. She often finds that sex improves in a long-term relationship—he reports that it either stays the same or gets worse. Divorce would be an option if either were deceived by their partner's affair, but he's more likely than most men to want to sit down with his erring spouse and work things out.

315

ARIES WOMAN—AQUARIUS MAN

Each strikes lucky with this redhot match! These two signs often pick each other as partners and they have warm smiles, kind-hearted personalities and attractive eyes that say Go—so find one another mutually appealing. Both lap up the loyalty and understanding they get from each other, too. He wants her exciting, athletic and curvy body—and finds her home-making skills (lavished on only the chosen few) a bonus. But he wants her to be a bundle of fun, as well, and lively Aries won't disappoint him here. She is captivated by his quirky, brilliant ideas and his go-it-alone individualism and self-confidence.

Both are, however, on the highly at-risk register for remarriage. They fall in the middle range for reaching a tenth wedding anniversary, which is slightly better news. But neither are lucky at settling with the love of their lives. And she's almost a staggering six times more likely to be a wedding day virgin than experimental, impatient Aquarius. Perhaps that's why sex tends to carry on unchanged for him afterwards, while for her, it either gets better or worse, compared with past performance yardsticks! Neither are at great risk of having affairs. But if someone does dare to come between them, either injured party may well opt for divorce.

ARIES WOMAN—PISCES MAN

He's a highly imaginative lover and she's lucky that there's an average chance they'll get together—even though she says she can find him unfanciable at first bite. She can either strike him as very sexy to start with, or he can find her starsign generally unsexy (it rather depends how obvious her aggression is). If she does decide to attract him, she should work on that knockout smile, which he loves. He could also grow addicted to her eyes, her supple legs and lovely shapely figure. She loves his sensual smile and sexy eyes but may wonder how to handle emotional, disorganised Pisces—so very different to the sporty, supremely confident men she's normally

316

attracted to. Yet she does rate his kindness more highly than other female signs do. And her loyalty earns her the top male vote from him. Both truly appreciate the other's understanding and warm humour.

Each may tie the knot with more than one partner, but he has more chance than her, on balance, of forming a lasting bond. He's much more wary of marriage than she is, but once he tries it, he likes it and scores top for men who'd be willing to marry again. She's less enthusiastic. This is the male zodiac sign who is luckiest at settling down with the woman of his dreams and consummating his greatest rc.nance—she's less likely to do so. He has more chance, too, of seeing sex soar to fresh heights of enjoyment within marriage. She finds that it either gets better or takes a downhill plunge!

ARIES WOMAN—ARIES MAN

They might hesitate to sign on the dotted line and wonder whether a joint mortgage is wise, but one thing's sure in the short-term. He finds her the sexiest thing on the planet, casting a huge chunk of male votes her way! She names him as a highly fanciable playmate, too, though with slightly less abandonment. What does he love about his woman? Warm smile, those eyes and long legs—not forgetting her curvy torso, of course. She goes for great eyes and gymnast's build, including a slim, well-shaped rear. Most of all, she can't help admiring his mega-large helping of self-confidence. Maybe he's a touch self-centred and doesn't always pause to show her the consideration or kindness she looks for in a partner. And she can find it hard to meet her own ambitions while trying to be the good homemaker he wants. But being an Aries, she finds no problem hauling him up when necessary and spelling out her needs.

She's far more likely than him to notice a lift in her sexlife once she's in a long-term relationship. And, luckily, she usually finds loving hasn't changed even after children appear on the scene. New arrivals can ruin his sexlife—or improve it. Both are keen to wed and may well choose to remain virgins until they say I Do. She runs a greater risk than him of having more than one marriage, while he gets lucky more often than her in getting the love of his life. He's also more likely to take his relationship up to the tenth anniversary and beyond.

THE TAURUS MAN'S LOVEMATCHES

TAURUS MAN—GEMINI WOMAN

They certainly find one another highly sexy. They can hardly stop touching—and there's a chance they'll end up together, too. He falls for her smile and smooth-skinned, curvy body while she melts at one glance from his gorgeous eyes! But he'll have to pull his socks up—literally—because she likes a smart dresser. She also wants someone who's a good, emotionally open talker. In turn, super-sociable Gemini might have to stay in more to be the perfect homemaker he's seeking.

Both say kindness is vital for long-term loving. And she's the highly communicative sort who wants someone who understands how she thinks—and knows she's a girl who wants to have fun. He's the steady type, though, not so hell-bent on pleasure. He's keener to get married, too, and probably a sounder marriage bet! But if either strays, it won't be the end of the world. They'll both want to work things out.

TAURUS MAN—CANCER WOMAN

The whisper is—they don't really find each other very sexy! But don't worry, because supercharged physicality isn't what this couple are really about. Being loyal and warm and truly kind-hearted is what each is looking for in their ideal partner. This family-minded female could easily fit his bill and she's unlikely to wander off and have an affair, so his possessive, jealous panic button is unlikely ever to get pressed. He'll offer her all the security she needs, and then some more!

First, though, he'd probably have to change his image—she likes her men to look smart. Although a third of women in her starsign remarry, and he's far more likely to make a lasting match, she'll show her staying power if she's really found the love of her life.

Perhaps she won't want sex quite as often as he will once they're married—but she's subtly sensual and he could win her round. She won't forgive him if he tries to make up any lovemaking shortfall elsewhere, though. If he's unfaithful, she's prone to seek divorce.

TAURUS MAN—LEO WOMAN

She's sure he ranks top on her list of favourite partner. Sad to say, he doesn't feel quite as steamed up over her. But he does admire her luscious shape and megawatt smile—who wouldn't? It might not be a bad idea for him to go on a diet before an early, important date with her because her glance is bound to wander eventually from his own super eyes to a less delightful feature. His stomach. No use him denying his food addiction—but he'll need to curb it because her metabolism is higher than his and it just doesn't show so much on her!

She's naughty, demanding full-blown loyalty from him while being as bad—according to the survey—as he is when it comes to having affairs. She'll certainly reach for another lover if he does stray, while he'll want to talk problems through. So they'll have to live with their differing outlooks there. Both may find the understanding and warmth they want and both share a desire for marriage that lasts a lifetime. Luckily, both are highly sexed and their drive doesn't flag long after the post-wedding high jinks have faded to fond memories.

Both might be virgins when they get hitched. For him, this is likely to be the big love of his life.

TAURUS MAN—VIRGO WOMAN

It's official. He can be faithful—with a bit of effort. But there's no copperbottomed guarantee, so it's no use her asking for one. And her constant chipping away in search of reassurance will drive him crazy long-term. That said, both like a partner who's first and foremost a hard-worker, a funster companion next. Both go for warm, welcoming smiles—so plenty of mutual satisfaction on that score—and he does rate her body shape.

They have different views on marriage, though. He often wants to wed for life, and does—she's likely to marry several times (she can't live with faults once she's spotted them). Yet she's more nervous of remarriage than he is. Neither may bring much sexual experience to their partnership and her lust levels may be lower than his. But happily, they won't lose interest as time goes on.

Divorce is likely to be her option if she ever does catch him out. But he'll feel mentally soothed by the fact she's not the type to try anything behind his back.

TAURUS MAN—LIBRA WOMAN

He's not naturally much of a talker. In fact, he probably despises idle chitchat. He'll have to give that part of his mind that controls speech a good workout, though, if he's to make a hit with her. It may take her a bit of time before she values the goldcard security he can offer, too. He, at least at first, rates as one of her least favourite partners (she doesn't find him overtly sexy) and they could take a while to warm up to one another. He knows he wants her, though. Yet he's soon caught in a double bind. For while he drools over her warm eyes, ready smile and giving nature, he does worry that she'll be giving it all away to the rest of the world, not concentrating sufficiently on him!

They could both strike oil, though, meeting the love of a lifetime and both want their marriage to last. Their sexlife never dims. While she may well take a revenge lover if he does let her down, he would handle her infidelity differently. He would want to know the whys and wherefores and remodel their relationship. Both put a high premium on loyalty and trust, though, so the worst may never happen.

TAURUS MAN—SCORPIO WOMAN

They start a bit unevenly. She says he's one of her favourite partners, sexy, too! But, though he's never ungallant enough to say it outright, she's not his foremost fancy. His trump card with her is his workaholic power and she adores his super eyes and muscular build, too. What she wants is an ace provider. He's mightily moved by her girly curves and potent seductive smiles. But she'll have to partially hide her ambitions if she's to go partway to being the homemaker he wants so much.

Truthfully, she thinks sexual attraction is more vital to happiness than he does. She wants humour and fun, too, while he puts them on the back burner. Having children can make or break her sex drive—at least temporarily—but both will tend to stay keen throughout their marriage. Maybe she is far more likely to remarry than he is, but both stand a fair chance of making their relationship stay the course. They both have high expectations when it comes to being loyal and kind. Neither should disappoint the other.

TAURUS MAN—SAGITTARIUS WOMAN

Stranger things have happened! On the face of it, she's his least popular partner of all the starsigns. He's unlikely to pick her first time round, too. This pairing doesn't ring any bells in the sex ratings, either. But on the plus side, both value honesty, loyalty and kindness, and are likely to get more than their fair share from one another. She'll want him to get more chatty and to open up his heart more often—and she'll succeed in helping him enjoy the lighter side of life, too. He can't resist her outgoing nature and agile, sexy body—but she'll have to curb some of her up-and-at-them adventurousness if she's to settle down with him and give him the homelife he wants.

Like him, she can be keen to marry. Yet, if things get stormy, she's more likely than him to want out. Sometimes, she may falter at the altar, before their marriage even gets off the ground, because she does value her freedom so strongly. Both find matrimony boosts their sexlife, though. And if it's second time around for her, her erotic charge is likely to be even more boosted. She's the sign least likely to have an affair—which certainly pleases jealous Taurus.

TAURUS MAN—CAPRICORN WOMAN

Woosh—they're away! From the moment they first meet, each knows the other is right for them. He's tops with her and she votes him sexiest sign in the universe. He often picks her to settle down with and never stops fancying her! She's got such flair for home-making, too, seamlessly combining her considerable work skills and fierce ambition with family life. She worships him because he works so hard and makes her feel so secure.

Perhaps, initially, her sex drive is slightly lower than his—and there's a risk she might go off lovemaking more in the long-term. But both often marry the love of their life—each other—and are well prepared to work at keeping their sexlife alive. He does have a marginally better record for making marriage work, according to our survey. But there's no room for smugness. If she ever finds out that she's been cheated on, she's proud and tough enough to seek a divorce straightaway so that she's free to look around—and marry—again.

TAURUS MAN—AQUARIUS WOMAN

She's far and away his flavour of the month—every month. And he may well find her very sexy indeed. But to her, he's Mr Average! She has no strong feelings either way. True, she rather likes his eyes but wonders—rightly—if he really understands her. After all, she does view the world from rather an odd angle! Straightforward Taurus does find her puzzling, yet endlessly intriguing.

They look at relationships, in general, differently. He likes a big heart. She wants a load of laughs. But he can get hooked on her wacky humour and end up being more fun than he looked at first.

He has more chance than her of making a lasting love match in his life. But both agree that their partner is sexier after having children. When it comes to remarriage, she's got a better chance of doing so than him. But she's less likely to end up with the big love of her life. In a first marriage, impatient Aquarius is unlikely to be a virgin—but there's a good chance he will be.

TAURUS MAN—PISCES WOMAN

She gives the thumbs down to his serious approach—his nose-to-the-grindstone ability to work around the clock. He certainly wishes she'd show more of this quality! But she ranks him her best partner and she does appreciate his super-sensual lovemaking techniques. She needs his rock-steady stability, too. Each loves the way the other can be so kind and giving. But while she thinks a sense of humour is vital in a partner, he won't always agree.

They either vote each other as highly fanciable or, at the other extreme, as one of their least sexy sign choices.

Both want to wed, but he'll have to work hard to fan her waning interest in sex. He's more likely to make a marriage last, not surprisingly. And he's luckier than her when it comes to marrying the love of his life. Usually, both are very loyal indeed. But she may well take a revenge lover if he strays. He'll be keener to try to work towards a better mutual understanding if cracks begin to appear.

TAURUS MAN—ARIES WOMAN

Their relationship can get off to a scratchy start—until they decide to swop one or two roles. After all, she'll never be the cosy homebody of his dreams, but why not let her loose on the DIY and learn to live with her intense work ambitions? She's more than happy to hand over household management to him because she knows he'll do it so much better.

He says he's likely to settle with her, although he doesn't find her, first and foremost, that sexy. But he's statistically her least popular choice and that goes for the sexual attraction, too. She does go for his supreme confidence, though, and reckons he's the best provider she'll ever meet.

Both might stay virgins until their wedding day and she could put off tying the knot for ages. And she's the female starsign more likely to marry more than once, while he likes to make one partner last the course—ten years plus. But she is more faithful than average. If their marriage is challenged by adultery, though, she'll preempt his moves towards reconciliation by seeking a speedy divorce. Or taking a lover pretty quickly.

TAURUS MAN—TAURUS WOMAN

Put up the please don't disturb signs. Yes, it's rare that same-sign matches work. But this one does. Both name each other as their favourite partner choice—and the sexiest one, too. With her, it's his eyes that have it. He can't wait to get his arms around her soft, generous form—though he loves her smile, too. She's his ideal homemaker, he can give her the material and emotional security she needs.

He does rate sexual attraction as more important than she does. And while she wants a partner who's fun, he doesn't bother much about this quality. Both want to wed. But if things do go wrong, she's in far less of a rush to remarry. She does find sex better second time around, though (he's not so sure).

Marriage improves her sexlife even more than it does his—and that's saying something! Both stand a good chance of landing the love match of their life. But he has a slightly better record of taking it past the ten-year finishing post.

THE TAURUS WOMAN'S LOVEMATCHES

TAURUS WOMAN—GEMINI MAN

She's looking (though not desperately) for a mate who's kind as well as sensual. He wants great legs, a sexy laugh and a come-on smile. So, though neither is the other's favourite first choice, this pairing can work unexpectedly well. He does name her as his least sexy starsign and reckons, at first glance, he'd be unlikely to choose her. But he's more than willing to be proved wrong.

He soon knows he's hit gold with her loyalty, understanding—and finds ways to coax out her sense of fun later. She feels less strongly about his potential—though she'd never pick him out as a winner first, either. She prefers kindness to verbal wit. He values sexual attraction more.

She is keener to get married, too. But both say marriage improves their sexlife and do stand a good chance of finding lasting happiness together. For her, it's more likely to be the love of a lifetime. He's more than twice as likely to stay a virgin until marriage. Both tend to be faithful, but he may well ask for a divorce if she strays, while she's far more forgiving.

TAURUS WOMAN—CANCER MAN

He certainly finds her a turn-on, even if she isn't his first partner choice. She, though, can either take him or leave him—in the early days. She can be rocked by his mood swings and has to grit her teeth through his sulks. Yet both can really thrive inside a rich web of emotional security.

They're both keen to wed, but, statistically, he's far more likely to marry several times than she is. Yet, once he has found the right woman, the odds are on their partnership lasting. One warning—he could go off sex at times, after marriage. A little delving will usually unearth the jealousy that's bugging him.

He rates loyalty even more than she does. He's more likely than her to be faithful. More likely to a virgin on the wedding night, too. But there are a few of both their signs who have five or more affairs! Interestingly, neither will opt for a big bust-up if the other is untrue. They both want to shelve their differences and concentrate on understanding one another. They agree that sexual attraction isn't the be all and end all.

TAURUS WOMAN—LEO MAN

He can think she's his perfect partner. But he won't necessarily find her super-sexy. She's unlikely to single him out as the tastiest hunk in the world, or the most suitable spouse. Which is guaranteed to get him keen—he can't stand being overlooked. But while she may be on the lookout for a man who's a good provider—and he usually attracts wealth—he isn't in the market for a good homemaker. He might not appreciate her skill.

They both rate gorgeous eyes and warm smiles in a partner, though, and both need kindness and understanding within a relationship. But, quite unlike her, he's in no dash to get hitched. Yet he may end up marrying more than once, while she thinks it should be for life. But, provided this is the Big One for him, he's able to make marriage last. Both agree, too, that sex gets better and better once they've tied the knot. If he catches her out in an affair though, he's faster than most in asking for a divorce!

TAURUS WOMAN—VIRGO MAN

She really fancies him, so the good news for her is that they've a fair chance of ending up together. But he finds her easily the least overtly sexy of all the signs! What he does like is a curvy, yet slim, body so she'll have to watch that Taurus tendency to put on weight. He also goes for an attractive voice and gentle manner—so he may not warm to her stubborn moods!

But, surprisingly for the perfectionist in the zodiac pack, he doesn't believe that being an ace homemaker (which she often is) would be a great asset in a partner. She drools over his mental prowess as much as she rates his body. While he loves her undentable loyalty, she values his kindness above diamonds. And they both appreciate each other's humour.

She likes the fact that once he weds, it's usually once and for all— just like it often is with her. He may tend to lose interest in lovemaking once wed, though overwork is likely to be to blame. If either ever has an affair, it won't necessarily be the kiss of death. Both prefer working things out to breaking up their happy home.

TAURUS WOMAN—LIBRA MAN

They probably first touched hands when reaching for the same cake—and he doesn't actually mind if she's more cuddly than him!

327

They both feature highly among each other's favourite list of partners. She certainly often finds him extra sexy—though she can also find some men of this sign a real turn-off. It's the same for him.

But he admires strength, rather than gentleness, and so he appreciates her sure-minded attitudes. If she's good-looking, then that's even more of a bonus. Libra comes out on top for making marriage last (though she might have to keep an eye on him!) and Taurus has a good record for staying power, too. But for her, the marriage is more likely to be the love of her life.

He expects lovemaking to be adventurous while she prefers an aura of gentle romance. But both agree that marriage improves their loving.

TAURUS WOMAN—SCORPIO MAN

He says he doesn't find her more than averagely sexy. But he does admit that she's quite a popular partner—it's because she's so subtly sensual. Together, they can make an emperor's orgy out of their secret time together. And although, for her, his sign doesn't buzz and fizz, she soon gets mesmerised by his penetrating, smouldering gaze.

He likes her eyes, too—they're so warm and come-on-ish—like her smile. but her awkward, stubborn streak could make her less of a gentle woman than he'd really like! And her flair for creating a super-cosy home out of a packing crate isn't a quality he's especially seeking. Like her, he puts kindness, loyalty and a sense of fun high up on his shopping list. But he thinks sexual attraction is more vital for long-term loving than she does.

Both want to marry and know that marriage can improve their sexlife—and he reckons that it gets even hotter after children have filled the nest. He is more likely than any other sign to marry only once—for life—and that suits her down to the ground. If she keeps on reassuring him about how sexy he is (yes, he does need telling) he won't wander. Both want to mend marriage rifts.

TAURUS WOMAN—SAGITTARIUS MAN

No good her trying to lug him along on shopping sprees. The only kind of trip he'll be interested in is halfway up the Amazon—probably travelling solo! Yet he names her as one of his top matches, even though he doesn't find her very sexy! She reckons he's the man she's least likely to end up with. Perhaps she didn't calculate on how thoroughly her woman-of-the-world manner and dazzling smile would win his heart. Or how easily she could succeed at keeping him by her side where other women had failed.

They complement each other. He can cajole her into slimming and stop her being a dull homebody when he makes her share his interests. She injects a sense of realism and responsibility into his life. Like her, he doesn't think that sexual attraction holds the only key to long-term happiness, either.

Both agree that sex often improves after marriage, yet he's almost twice as likely as she is to find a lessening in a partner's attraction after children arrive. And while she's highly likely to make a lasting bond, he could well wed more than once. He'll need coaxing into marriage second-time-around. For her, he's probably the love of her life. She'll be greatly reassured by the fact that he's the male sign least likely to have an affair.

TAURUS WOMAN—CAPRICORN MAN

She votes him one of her all-time favourite partners (the man who makes her earth move!) Yet, he says she's his least likely love-match, and hers is the sign he finds least sexy, as well! But he does concede that she fits the bill when it comes to the other vital things he's looking for; lovely eyes, an attractive voice and a welcoming warm smile.

What she wants first and foremost is a good provider and ambitious Capricorn is certainly that. Both put loyalty high on their agendas and expect plenty of it. But she thinks kindness is more important in a relationship than he does, while he's the man who most values a sense of humour.

Theirs is a match that starts out OK and ends up great. He's less likely than her to marry the great love of his life, but they often do make their partnership last. Both are very keen indeed to marry—and neither are likely to be virgins. But, though she reckons marriage improves her sexlife, his interest may start to flag. And once children come on the scene, he admits that he finds her less sexy. She should avoid letting herself become mumsy at all costs if she doesn't want him to look elsewhere. She can't rely on his overpacked work schedule to keep her marriage intact.

TAURUS WOMAN—AQUARIUS MAN

Despite the fact that their relationship often has to take a backseat to his wild and whirling schemes, she is definitely his favourite partner choice. She's also one of the signs he most fancies. She's in two minds about him, though—often finding his sign sexy, but more often not! He's drawn to her promising lips, often poised to smile. He loves her curvaceous body. She adores his eyes and thinks they're gorgeous. No one could value understanding more than he—and she agrees it's vital.

They both believe a sense of fun is important, too, and that sexual attraction alone isn't the most vital ingredient for long-term togetherness. He's far more likely to marry more than once. Yet both may well make a lasting bond. But while she may easily marry the love of her life, he's not always so lucky. It's quite rare for either to be virgins on their wedding night—in his case, only 3% of his sign will be.

Happily, getting hitched does nothing to stem their sex drives. Perhaps she's slightly more likely to have affairs than he is, but both are normally loyal. She is forgiving, but he may well want a divorce if she does the wandering.

TAURUS WOMAN—PISCES MAN

He's often a bit of a cold fish toward her to start with. But Pisces never did know what was good for him. These two are among each other's least popular partner, funnily enough. And he says he finds her unsexy. Deep down, he's very keen to pair up with a capable homemaker, though. And if she's also got great legs, a slim body and a sexy laugh, this fish should be home and dry. For their love to last, however, she must try to stay loyal at all cost. He rates this quality higher than any other male starsign. She wants kindness in return.

For him, it's probably going to be a lightning strike, the legendary love of a lifetime. He may well have stayed a virgin, waiting for that special person. She's often just as lucky emotionally—but less likely to have put her sexual experience on hold while waiting! He's less hurried than she is to wed—far keener second time around. Both say that marriage improves their sex, but his lovemaking style might be a touch too adventurous, too full of unusual fantasies, for her tastes. It's unlikely that he will stray. But watch out—if she does, he could ask for a divorce and it's likely to be messy, not amicable.

TAURUS WOMAN—ARIES MAN

He claims she's not sexy—because of her extreme unadventurousness in bed. But we all know how boastful Aries men are! Still, he does rank her his most unlikely mate. And although she finds him a favourite partner, she says he's a turn-off, physically. Love can still win through, though. Especially if she's got the kind of girlish grin, nice eyes and shapely body that means his type, after all. He's also after someone who can make him a comfy, homely nest, despite all his he-man bragging and thirst for adventure.

Both want a person who's loyal and kind. Back to square one on the sex front, though. He rates sexual attraction more highly than she does, for long-term happiness. Yet he's even keener than her on marrying—and they may both end up with the love of their life! It's odds on them making it last, too.

He's more likely than she to be a virgin, pre-wedding. Unlike her, he's not so sure that marriage has improved sex for them. And even though remarriage proves a love-booster for both members of this team, neither are in any rush to tie the knot again.

TAURUS WOMAN—TAURUS MAN

They break all the rules in the book by showing how same signs can, and do, make fantastic love partners. Naturally, each names the other as their hot favourite and as the sign they fancy most, too! Eat your heart out because it's the love of a lifetime for both, too, and they've a wonderful chance of making it last.

He's first drawn to her smile and inviting, softly curvy body. She loves his super eyes and feels safe because she knows he's bound to be a good provider. With that menu, what's a little surplus weight between friends? It gets better, too.

Sex improves within marriage for both but it may niggle him that she's less likely to have walked down the aisle a virgin than he was. Both seek, and find, a kind nature and loyalty. And even if, despite such blessings at the start, their marriage does go badly wrong, they'll both rush to fix it through counselling. If one has an affair, they'll want to know why—so they can do all in their power to stop a repeat performance.

THE GEMINI MAN'S LOVEMATCHES

GEMINI MAN—CANCER WOMAN

Her warm, giving heart reaches parts of him that others can't—no wonder she's very popular with him. He doesn't quite get the same vote from her as a partner, though. He'll first sit up and take notice, if she has endless legs and so-sexy laugh; she'll swoon when swept by a flirtatious gaze. She likes the stylish way he dresses when he's off on his social rounds, too.

Neither of them rates the other tops in the sexual attraction stakes—on paper! Loyalty, depth of understanding and tender loving care are what both crave in a long-term relationship, but he thinks having fun together is pretty important, too, while she is less fussy than him about the importance of shared interests.

He may wed more often than she does—though neither are high-risk, multi-marriage people. She's probably keener to say I Do in the first place, yet he's got the marital staying power—and is slightly more likely to make the tenth anniversary. A bit more likely not to marry at all, too! He may well be a virgin when he marries—though it may not be to the love of his life. He's more likely than her to find marriage a sex-booster. Both are unlikely to stray—but he'll be more forgiving than her.

GEMINI MAN—LEO WOMAN

Each is the other's favourite audience—he's just a little more likely to choose her as his perfect playmate than she is him. There's not much in it. But neither finds the other very sexy, even though they agree that this is a necessary ingredient for happy coupledom. On the sly, she ogles a man with a slim body and likes a great smile. His mischievous eyes score a big hit, too. She's never less than a bundle of fun and they effortlessly find things in common. For her part, she's so glad he's one of the signs least likely to stray—she values loyalty a lot. He tends to want to find a partner who really fathoms his mind—she concentrates more on kindness.

Hers is the sign most likely to marry once, for life. He, in his turn, tends not to remarry. But he stands more chance of making a long-term marriage—though he's also one of the signs who likes the single life. She's usually keen to get married—once. They've both a good chance of never bedding before wedding, and report that sex either stays the same after marriage—or gets even better. Neither reckon their partner is the love of their life—but in their case, this seems to be a mere blip.

GEMINI MAN—VIRGO WOMAN

This match strikes lucky for both—she's his best girl partner pick and he's just as popular with her. Each votes the other among the most fanciable starsigns. Her attractions for him are her lovely legs and sexy laugh—and he likes the way they can share common interests. She rates his faithfulness and great self-confidence. They're the two signs who best appreciate a fun-loving partner, too. But he thinks good looks, sexual attraction and understanding are more important than she does. And she puts a higher price than he does on loyalty and kindness.

Here's the big surprise. Flirty Gemini is less likely than most to remarry—while Virgo is a sign very likely to wed more than once. He'll need coaxing down the aisle in the first place—and might well prefer to stay single—yet he has a higher chance than her of staying married for a decade or more. He's also more likely than her to find sex improves after marriage. Both are the signs who most often say that having children doesn't affect their lovelife. Like her, his chances of having an affair are less than average—but both may want a divorce if the other dares to stray.

GEMINI MAN—LIBRA WOMAN

By neat coincidence, each votes the other as both fanciable and among their partnership hotshots. He quickly tunes into sociable Libra's interests and can't get enough of her sexy laugh—what a pair of flirts they are. His brilliant chat-up lines really hit home. Both value loyalty, but she rates kindness higher than he does, while he puts more emphasis on finding a partner who can plug into his thoughtwave patterns. Fun is top of his list, too—but hers is the female sign least likely to be looking for that in a mate. She values humour generally more than he does, but perhaps she looks to her platonic friends for this. He reckons sexual attraction is twice as vital as she does.

Neither runs much risk of marrying time and time again—and she's the sign most likely to make it last. He's a good long-haul marriage bet, too—but when it comes to leaping in the first place, she's far keener than him. Her luck in settling with the love of her life is greater than his, and he's more than twice as likely to resist premarital sex than her. Both reckon marriage greatly improves the physical side of their partnership, though. She's a higher affair-risk than him. And he's more likely to want a divorce through infidelity—she's open-minded.

GEMINI MAN—SCORPIO WOMAN

This isn't a likely partnership. In fact, he's one of the signs she finds the least sexy! He rates sexual attraction just as much as she does—along with great legs and a sexy laugh—but he thinks that being able to have fun together is more important. She goes for men with gorgeous eyes (well, his may have a certain come-hither look) and adores a great smile and he can certainly supply that. Normally, she lists a muscular build among her top priorities, too, but she may be drawn by Gemini's spare super-fitness. He loves great legs and a sexy laugh and needs a woman who'll share his interests. Both put a high premium on loyalty, kindness and understanding. But on the domestic front, they differ. She's keen to find a good provider (he's full of ideas, not so hot on following through) and he's only averagely keen about a good homemaker.

He has a better chance than her of making a marriage last and she's more likely to remarry. Yet she's keener to get hitched in the first place than he is—in fact, he's one of the most likely men in the zodiac to want to stay single! She's more likely to end up with the love of her life and he's more likely to be virgin when they wed. But she does find marriage a great sex-enhancer—and reports that remarriage, too, does wonders for lovemaking pleasure! If either had an affair, they'd both want to work things out—but Scorpio might take her own revenge lover!

GEMINI MAN—SAGITTARIUS WOMAN

This pairing has a lot going for it. She votes him one of the sexiest of signs—and he reckons she's pretty fanciable, too. But neither actually name one another as long-term favourites, perhaps because neither is used to thinking far into the future, anyway. She does adore talkative Gemini's excellent chatline and goes for his kindness and his superb eyes. He's highly appreciative if she has long, shapely legs and he likes a warm, sexy laugh. He's twice as keen as her to find a fun-loving partner although she does rate humour highly, too. Both want someone who will understand how their minds work. But he gives sexual attraction and good looks a rather higher rating than she does.

She isn't a marriage risk—though she is more likely than him to remarry—and he's the one with the best chance of taking the coupling past the 10-year mark. It's quite true that both would be quite happy to stay bachelors, but she can drum up more enthusiasm for naming the day than he can. He's more likely than her to be a wedding-day virgin. He's also got more chance than her of finding a partner sexier after marriage—though she reckons that remarriage can really boost her sexlife.

Neither are likely to deceive their partners with an affair—she's the least likely female starsign to do so. If the worst did happen, she'd ask why, while he might well opt for divorce.

GEMINI MAN—CAPRICORN WOMAN

He's one of her favourite partner choices—but he's not so gallant about her! He names her as unsexy because, he claims, she doesn't use her imagination enough in bed! Well, she says, he's not particularly sexy either, come to that. Of all the zodiac women, she gives a great smile her highest voting score and she's keenest on finding a good provider, too. He might strike her as a tad flighty to begin with, although he is lucky with money. He gives only an average weighting to good homemaking skills and he may well prefer shared roles to traditional ones—which suits her. He is attracted by friendly eyes, lovely legs and a contagious, sexy laugh. He does value a partner who has the same interests, too.

Both are low-risk when it comes to marrying time and time again, though he stands more chance than her of making a match last. She's keener in the first place to get married—or remarried—and he's keener than most men to stay fancy-free and single. He's almost twice as likely as her to be a virgin when they marry, she has a higher chance of pairing up with the love of her life. After marriage, their sexlife can prove as satisfactory as before—or it could get worse for her, better for him. Yet, for her, remarriage is a sex-booster. Both are unlikely to stray, yet faster than most to seek a divorce.

GEMINI MAN—AQUARIUS WOMAN

Unusually, neither of this duo put much value on kindness in their partner—perhaps they get enough of that from their joint legions of friends. On the face of it, this airy pair should meet up on cloud nine, yet—statistically—she's not one of his all-time favourites and he doesn't often find her sign fanciable. He is very popular with her, though, and she'll either vote him very sexy—or not sexy at all (no halfway measures!). She's the female starsign who most wants her partner to look inside her complex mind. He, on the other hand, only attaches average importance to this thought-reading skill. Instead, he's the starman who gets the biggest kick out of wonderful legs, a hot, turn-on laugh, shared interests and a love of fun.

She's in the middle range of those likely to marry more than once—so she's slightly more chance of doing so than he has. He makes a lasting match more often and, here's the big surprise considering he's the zodiac's Big Flirt, he's less likely to have affairs. She's much keener to marry, and remarry, while he may well want to stay single. Impatient Aquarius is the least likely female sign to stay a pre-nuptial virgin, while he's the man most likely to wait! Neither have particular luck in marrying their true loves. Sex stays pretty much the same for him after the big day but she reports a different story; marriage can make or break her sexlife!

GEMINI MAN—PISCES WOMAN

To make him sit up and really take notice, she'll need to have endless legs and a wall-to-wall smile. Chances are only average that he'll choose her from the whole zodiac range, and he often says he finds her sign not particularly fanciable. She, on the other hand, names him one of her best partner choices and she thinks he's rather sexy, too. He thinks fun matters much more than she does (and she'll need to share his other interests, too, if this is going to last). He also rates loyalty and understanding more highly than she does, while she believes that kindness is vital to long-term love and successful partnering.

Second marriage is more likely for her than for him. Pisces is very keen on the idea of marriage while we all know that run-around Gemini men put a very high premium on staying free. Her chances of going down the aisle arm-in-arm with the love of her life are slightly higher than his, but he's more likely to be a wedding-day virgin. For both, there's an average chance of sex getting better after marriage. But with remarriage, she's the one who'll get the biggest sex recharge. He is less likely than most men to have an affair— she's got an above-average coding! If he did wander, she'd either say nothing or take a lover of her own. Still waters do run deep with her. But if she was the unfaithful one, he may well seek a divorce.

GEMINI MAN—ARIES WOMAN

He loves her tough-tender qualities and names her as one of his all-time favourite partners—one of the sexiest, too! He is even keener if she has an inviting smile. But she's not half as likely to single him out, or even find him particularly sexy. His naughty eyes do appeal, though, and she is highly attracted to his talkative confidence. Both expect loyalty from their partner and he especially appreciates it if they have lots of interests in common. For long-term love, though, she rates kindness and humour higher up the scale than he does—while he's more likely to ask for fun, sexual attraction and more understanding. Loving after marriage hardly ever declines for him, though she's more likely than him to find it actually improves. Both find that having children makes no difference either way to their sexlife.

He's better able to make a truly lasting bond and she's far more likely than him to marry more than once. While one in four Gemini men vow to stay single for life, she's quite keen to be a Mrs. Neither are particularly likely to wed their life's love, but are more likely than most to be virgins when they marry. But while both partners are good, faithful bets, they are also among the speediest to ask for a divorce if either wanders.

GEMINI MAN—TAURUS WOMAN

These are the two signs who put the highest value on having fun in their relationships. Yet, he's one of her least likely choices—despite his famously fun-loving nature. She's not a particularly popular partner of his, either. She lacks bedroom fantasy and imagination, he reckons! But perhaps he can teach her to be more sexually exotic...

His eyes are her prime attraction feature—though she sets less store by them than other women do—while he gives the top male vote to shared interests, a wild sexy laugh and super legs. While she wants a man who'll provide well for her, he's not that cosy a domestic bet and doesn't particularly seek a good homemaker—which is her most famous strong point.

And though he reckons sexual attraction is pretty vital, hers is the female sign that awards it lowest score in the zodiac. For both, there's a high risk of marrying more than once. She's keener on the whole marriage business than he is (he's most likely to want to stay unhitched and unhindered). Having said that, he's more chance than her of celebrating 10 happy years together with his partner. She's much more likely to have married the love of her life, he's nearly twice as likely to be a virgin when he weds. She's surer, too, that sex improves on marriage, though he, happily, won't find it getting any worse! He's a below-average affairs risk, she's just above the norm. And though he's keener on divorce if she strays, she'd rather work things through if he's the one who's unfaithful.

GEMINI MAN—GEMINI WOMAN

Mirror images in some ways, each is looking for something slightly different in a permanent relationship. He certainly finds her the sexiest of all signs—but he's among her least popular partners! Warm, giggly smiles and heart-stoppingly gorgeous eyes attract them both and she, of all signs, really appreciates his wonderful line(s) in chat. She rates his smart clothes, too. He gives more votes than any other man to her well-turned, long legs and that slightly dirty laugh! They both expect great loyalty. But she is more on the lookout for kindness and understanding than he is, while his chief priorities are finding a partner who's going to stay faithful—yet sexy and fun. She doesn't think those factors matter quite so much.

They're both at low risk of multiple marriage. Yet while he's a fighting chance of celebrating a 10th wedding anniversary, she is the woman least likely to make it that far. Both truly like the single life and aren't in any hurry to give up their freedom. And neither are particularly likely to find themselves face to face with the love of their lives when they do tie the knot. He's more likely than her to stay a virgin until marriage, but both usually find sex improves after that. Sometimes, though, she reports that it can sadly deteriorate! He's more faithful than most, while she's at above-average risk of having an affair. She'd want to work things out if he wandered off, but if she was the one who was untrue, he may well ask her for a divorce.

THE GEMINI WOMAN'S LOVEMATCHES

GEMINI WOMAN—CANCER MAN

He's a good long-term love bet for her because he's loyal, and tenderly, lovingly faithful. No wonder she says he's her favourite partner. He may well choose to stay with her forever, too. But sexwise, they start off on different wavelengths. For while she names him as possibly sexy or unsexy, he definitely doesn't find her a fanciable sign. Heart-touching smiles and soulful eyes attract them both—but she'll have to show her softer, kinder side to keep him interested. She likes his smart clothes and imaginative way with words—and can't resist the way he's able to tune into her deepest thoughts.

While she's in the middling range for having affairs, he is more faithful than most men and values loyalty very much. That said, he is also far more likely than her to remarry. Yet if all goes smoothly, he also stands a better chance of making a lasting tie. He's keener to wed and less easily put off marrying again—she's the female sign most likely to stay solo. He's more likely to marry the love of his life and more likely than her to save himself for that special person, that special day. Cancer is the male sign who most often claims that a long-term relationship has either made him keener on sex—or far less interested! She, more level-headedly, reports finding marriage has either boosted her sex-life or left it the same.

GEMINI WOMAN—LEO MAN

He's entranced by her sparkling, flirty eyes and gives them more votes than any other male sign. He says she's very sexy, too—and has an average chance of choosing her as his partner. He, though, is less of a hit with her. She says she doesn't fancy him, really. But she is smitten by his attention-grabbing confidence, his patter and his eye-catchingly stylish clothes. He goes for livewire brain power, curvaceous figure and great legs. He appreciates her social butterfly nature, too—not for him the gentle-mannered, home-loving type.

The only hiccup in their relationship will be if he shoves her out of the limelight!

She values kindness a whole lot more than he does, though. And she's keener to find a partner who understands her thought processes. For his part, he puts a higher rating on sexual attraction. He's also at greater risk of saying I Do several times over. But he also has more hope than her of making a lasting match, once he's made that initial commitment. On the topic of commitment, we all know that she's the woman who most wants to stay single. But he is in even less of a rush to get married! He's luckier than she is at marrying a true love and he finds marriage more of a sex-enhancer than she does. Both agree that having children certainly doesn't put a damper on lovemaking!

GEMINI WOMAN—VIRGO MAN

Usually, he votes her sexiest female sign—unless she tries to rush things in bed. In which case, she gets a big thumbs down from him! Nevertheless, she's up there among his all-time favourite partners. She often goes for him, too, and finds him at least averagely sexy. To really appeal to him, she'll need a shapely, pert body—with no spare fat—good legs, plus a nice voice and a soothing manner. Definitely no manic party-party outbursts and not too much attention-paying to other men, either! She'll fall for him if his patter can match the glibness of her own and if he is well dressed. Good news for ever-so-sociable Gemini is that supposedly super-domesticated Virgo doesn't, in fact, set much store by finding a homelover after all. So she can carry on going out.

Long-term, though, she rates mental compatibility and understanding more highly than he does, while he gives more votes than her to laughs. He's a low remarriage risk—she's got slightly more chance. Both are among the ranks of those least likely to stay wed for 10-plus years. And both quite like the single lifestyle. He's more amenable to giving marriage a second try, has better luck settling with a true love and is more likely to have saved himself, sexually, for someone special. But both are the most likely signs to find that sex interest can plunge after marriage!

GEMINI WOMAN—LIBRA MAN

No denying that sexual pull they each feel for one another—but making a lasting linkup is another matter. It's a wonder these two ever manage to cram a second date into their packed diaries, let alone get married. And his notoriously wandering eyes go down like a lead balloon with surprisingly censorious Gemini. Still, she does say that he's a favourite partner choice and that she fancies him— a lot. And he finds her one of sexiest signs—though not necessarily a likely choice as someone to walk through life alongside. He loves her neat, curvy figure and outgoing, chatterbox nature. Not to mention those athletic, shapely legs. He wants a woman who's as sociable as him and he's the male sign who gives a gentle manner the wooden spoon. So at least she won't have to tone down her high spirits.

She likes a nifty dresser who's never at a loss for words—and Libra could carry on talking from inside a deep-sea diving suit. She doesn't go much on unfaithfulness, however—but his appalling track record might be abruptly terminated through her adventurous love-style.

There's a good chance he's going to have more than one wife— she's a lower remarriage risk. But he does better than her at passing the 10-year anniversary—he's the sign most likely to reach this benchmark. He's keener to wed, less easily put off remarriage and more likely to get the love of his life, too. But don't bank on him being a virgin on his wedding night. She just might be. She's the sign who most often reports that sex gets worse after marriage—he usually finds it stays the same.

GEMINI WOMAN—SCORPIO MAN

She can let her tongue run away with her. While he likes a woman with a gentle manner who, most importantly, lets him be in charge.

Tricky. He can give her the unfanciable vote, too, though she says he's one of the sexiest signs. Neither choose each other as lifelong partners very often. He's seeking someone who's physically appealing and fun and who's—let's be honest—good in bed. Gemini certainly isn't sexually shy, but she's not going to let anyone dominate her, either! Thankfully, he won't be looking to this busy gadabout for a spot of stay-at-home nestbuilding, though.

She likes his confidence and eloquence and, above all, can't resist his almost supernatural insights into her mental processes. But she can find him infuriatingly secretive and go from intrigued to thoroughly exasperated.

His is the male sign that most often marries once, for life, while she's a higher chance of saying I Do lots of times. He's far more likely to reach his 10th wedding anniversary—she's the sign who does this the least often. He's also hotter on getting married altogether than she is, more likely to stay a virgin and to find the love of a lifetime. And while he's the zodiac male most likely to discover that sex just goes from strength to strength within a committed, marital relationship, she's the female sign most likely to watch it take a turn for the worse!

GEMINI WOMAN—SAGITTARIUS MAN

If anyone can poke a pin into his sexual bragging when he gets carried away, she can—and she'll do it without leaving any wounded feelings. Although they don't, according to our records, often end up as a pair of old Darby and Joans and say they don't find one another particularly sexy, they've more in common than either will dare to openly admit. She confesses that she adores men who are confident, smartly dressed and full of entertaining spiel—doesn't that sound rather like chirpy Mr Sagittarius? And, more than other men, he appreciates a warm smile and values faithfulness. But while he's the male least prone to having affairs, flirty Gemini women have an above-average straying record. She also puts a lower price on faithfulness than other women...

She'll breathe a sigh of relief to learn he doesn't want a homelover, though. And they agree that while kindness is crucial to happiness, knock-'em-between-the-eyes sexual attraction is not.

They share one sad statistic: both are the least likely signs to reach a 10th wedding anniversary. Neither are in the remotest rush to wed, either—though he's happier about remarrying. He's luckier than her in settling with a life-love, but less likely to keep himself chaste. After marriage, she's more likely than him to lose interest in sex— though both have average scores for finding wedlock a sexual boost. If others ever come between them, they'd both want to know why their partner had a damaging affair. And they'd want to set their domestic world to rights again.

GEMINI WOMAN—CAPRICORN MAN

She finds so much to admire in him—if only he'd speak up for himself more often. The odd witty anecdote wouldn't go amiss, either. Still, he gives her his sexier-than-the-rest vote and they do have an average chance of ending up partners. She says, however, that at first take, he's one of the signs she finds least fanciable. She likes a man who's a good talker, who dresses smartly and bristles with confidence—more of a successful self-salesman, in fact. And though few men come more ambitious, powerful and successful than Capricorn, his style will always be subtly understated. He certainly believes in himself, but he could be too reserved for her extrovert nature. He finds his eye drawn to her super body and shapely legs and discovers that her sultry voice and sparky sense of humour give him quite a charge. But, in her search for a partner who understands how she thinks, she might mistakenly believe he's on a different wavelength.

He has more chance than her of marrying more than once—of keeping with the same woman for 10 years plus, too—and is the male sign who most wants to wed. She, would you believe, is the woman who most wants to stay unmarried. Whoops. Neither usually trips down the aisle as a virgin—at 6%, he's exactly half as likely to as she is. Neither hits the jackpot when it comes to marrying the big love of their lives. But she's more likely than him to report an upsurge in sexual interest after marriage. Instead, he finds remarriage refreshes those parts of him that other women couldn't reach. He is more of an affairs risk—though both will select divorce as a final solution.

GEMINI WOMAN—AQUARIUS MAN

They've so much to talk about—but is he too mentally tough, too sexually adventurous for her? Both are keen to unearth a lifelong partner who can read them like a book and who never grows tired of a good chinwag. So perhaps it doesn't matter too much that he names her as both sexiest, and unsexiest, sign and that their chances of matching are only average. Her feelings about him are none too clearly defined, either, but that leaves plenty of room for persuasion. He likes a lithe body which goes in and out in all the right places without being plump, a kind nature and—like her—is less attracted to the quality of faithfulness than most. And she reckons that if he's confident, dresses well and expresses himself well, he's practically home and dry.

He's a lot more chance than her of marrying more than once. But he's more chance of making a long-term match, too. Neither are in a mad dash to marry, but second-time-around, he's keener to give marriage a go again. These are the signs least likely to marry the love of their life. He's four times less likely than her to be a virgin when he gets hitched. And while she can find that marriage will either build or bust her love life, he's more likely to report back that the sex side carries on much the same.

GEMINI WOMAN—PISCES MAN

Can he be for real? Is a man ever that sensitive? She doesn't quite know how to take him—and often misjudges the depth of his feelings. But then she gets the urge to smarten him up, build his confidence, develop his vocabulary, generally take him in hand. At first, though, she reckons he's one of the least sexy signs (his signals are probably drowned out by her chatter) and he doesn't find her particularly alluring, either. But there's a near-average chance that they'll finish up partners. She does wish he wasn't so over-emotional and disorganised, though.

Happiness for him is a good homemaker (wish again, Pisces) but he can also be won over by a pair of good legs, a slim body and a turn-on laugh. Of course, she's far too busy to waste much time hemming the curtains and steam-cleaning the carpets, but perhaps he'll get to like being included in her great social life.

Only other snag is: while he rates loyalty more than any other starsign, she's an above-average extra-marital affairs risk! He'd best get along to her evening class. He's more likely than her to marry more than once, but he has much more chance of making it last. Both are the signs least keen to marry, fearing a loss of freedom. But once he tries marriage, he develops a taste for it and, unlike her, is in more of a hurry to give it another go, if needs be. He's also the luckiest sign when it comes to marrying the love of a lifetime, while she can be less fortunate. He's more likely than her to be a wedding day virgin, too. He's the man least likely to report a postmarital waning of sexual interest—she's the woman who most often finds this a problem.

GEMINI WOMAN—ARIES MAN

They're hot stuff together and she's mentally tough enough to handle his supercharged macho moods which can spill over into aggression. He's without a doubt one of her favourite partners and she loves his powerful brand of self-confidence, his entertaining patter and the snazzy way he dresses. She can either pick him out as her most fanciable sign—or the least fanciable one! But he chooses her as a partner less frequently and doesn't find her especially sexy—probably because he's always in too much of a tearing hurry to get a proper look at her! And while he likes her cheerful manner, welcoming smile and super eyes, he is keener than most men on finding a woman who'll make a nice, comfortable home.

This couple could argue whenever bossy Aries reckons sociable Gemini is gadding about, not allowing enough time to look after him. They'll just have to negotiate. He also rates sexual attraction more highly than she does. She's keener than him to find a partner who understands how she thinks. And he remarries more often than her sign does—though he has a better chance of making a superglued bond.

He's the second luckiest male sign when it comes to marrying the love of his life—while, sadly, she's the least fortunate female starsign in this respect! He's more likely, despite his formidable impatience, to be a virgin when he weds. He's also more likely to find marriage a sex-improver. Both run the risk of affairs. She'd want to talk problems through, he'd take a revenge lover.

GEMINI WOMAN—TAURUS MAN

She'll love to unearth his secret, soppy sentimental streak, adore tuning in to his deeply sensual sexuality, and he'll be endlessly fascinated by her curves and flip approach to life. She finds him one of the sexiest signs around—though he's less often attracted to her. They aren't the most common pairing in the zodiac, in fact. She's particularly drawn to him, though, if—apart from his obvious qualities as a lover—he's also a good communicator, confident and well-dressed. He's the man who most rates a kind nature and giving smile, too. Remember, though, that his other request is usually for a fine homemaker. And fungirl Gemini has never been happy staying in! Neither does she particularly appreciate Taurus man's skills as a good provider. Both think kindness is vital. He values fun less—and he'd be hard pushed to keep up with her partying, anyway. What he'd like is a hard worker and she can be—in spurts. For her part, she's keener on getting a partner who's on exactly the same brainwave frequency.

She's more chance of remarrying (he's the second least likely sign) and he's far more hope of staying married more than 10 years. She's the woman who's in the least rush to wed, while he's one of the males who can't wait. He's more often a wedding day virgin and is luckier than her at getting his life-love. But she gets more of a sex boost out of marriage—or she could find it taking quite a turn for the worse. If either went astray, they're level pegging on the likelihood of going for conciliation. Both are more likely than other signs to want to ask one another why it went wrong and then try to put things right between them.

GEMINI WOMAN—GEMINI MAN

This will never be a restful coupling—partly because he's even more of an outrageous flirt than she is—but she's one of the few women ever to get him to take loves games seriously. She's top sexpot as far as he's concerned and there's an average chance he'd choose her as a partner through life, too. The honour isn't two-way, though—she doesn't find him especially sexy and reckons he's one of the men least likely to match up with her long-term. He's every inch a fan, though, giving the top male vote to her marvellous lower limbs and infectious sexy laugh. But while he's the sign who rates fun most highly, she only gives that an average score. What she wants from her man is loads of confidence, head-turningly smart attire and an ability to sell ice to the Eskimos. Sound like anyone you know? They seem slightly at odds when he nominates his need for a partner who shares his interests and she says she wants someone who understands the way she thinks. But maybe these aren't incompatible aims.

Geminis of both sexes flirt—yet both are more likely than most to wed just once. He does even better than her at making it last and he's more faithful, too. She's the female sign who's least keen on getting married—but he can be more than twice as eager to stay free. Both are less lucky than most at getting their life-love. He's more likely to be a virgin when they marry and they have an even chance of finding that sex gets better and better within their union. She, though, has more than double his chance of finding it gets worse.

THE CANCER MAN'S LOVEMATCHES

CANCER MAN—LEO WOMAN

As someone to get all serious with, she's head-and-shoulders above the rest. But although she might be his far-and-away partner favourite, he admits that he doesn't find her especially sexy! She says he's the sign she's least likely of all to fancy. Yet she's still got an average chance of singling him out. He can't get enough of her come-play-with-me laugh—and just hopes she'll be the supergentle, understanding and kindly homemaker he seeks—probably a version of his mum!

Fiery Leo wants to get more physical and his initial appeal for her lies in his slim, yet well-muscled physique. Both want a partner who's loyal, above all other qualities. But while she gives top marks to sexual attraction, he's the male sign least likely to stress this in his vote. And though she's a zodiac goodtime girl, neither reckons having fun together is vital.

He's the male sign most likely to wed more than once—despite his faithful-unto-death ideals. She, on the other hand, is the woman least at risk of this. It's evens for both of them when it comes to making a marriage last. He's less easily put off wedlock than other signs, she's much more wary about trying again. He's naturally luckier, too, at finding the love of his life and both are likelier than most people to stay virgins until they marry. Long-term loving can make or break his desire quota, but she's the sign who most often find her sex drive continues, unchanged. Proud Leo may take a revenge lover if he strayed, cautious Cancer would say nothing and hope for the best!

CANCER MAN—VIRGO WOMAN

If caring Cancer's tall, well-muscled—and the faithful type—she'll go for that. She certainly finds him sexiest of all the signs and votes him her favourite partner. Trouble is, she's not top of his list and he doesn't usually fancy her very much to begin with! He might well fall for her surprisingly sexy laugh—which can so go against her appearance that it seems shocking. He's looking for someone who's lovingly gentle and kind-hearted (and she's more likely to be so as a pal than as a lover). But he could get stung by her critical tongue and quickly put up some emotional barriers

Both say loyalty in a partner is absolutely vital. But he's seeking a good homemaker, while she wants a tricky combination—a man who plays hard and works harder. She may resist a traditional set-up because she's too independent to want to ride in the wake of a successful, good provider.

These are the two starsigns who most often marry over and over. He stands a slightly better chance of taking a marriage past 10 years and is less easily put off marrying again than other signs. She, though, is the woman most likely to say Never Again to wedlock! Each has a near-even chance of settling with their life-love and both may well be virgins when they do. Both tend to be more than normally faithful, although neither finds marriage much of a sex-booster. If she was untrue, he's the male sign most likely to keep silent and hope her fling didn't last. But she's faster than most to ask for a divorce if he should choose to wander.

CANCER MAN—LIBRA WOMAN

Despite her social flair, good looks and charm, she's his least likely partner choice—he says he doesn't fancy her much. Probably because he realises, deep down, that partying Libra could never put on a pinny and transform herself into the homemaker of his dreams. With a less conventional approach on his part, though, this could be a stunner of a relationship. She certainly has faith in it—he's a popular choice with her and she votes him rather sexy. Smart clothes and a lean, fit body with well-defined muscles just visible make her take notice of him. And if he's got a beautiful speaking voice and a winning line in chat, she's hooked.

She gives finding a good provider the lowest vote of all, but both believe strongly in the need for loyalty and neither puts fun or sexual attraction top of their list.

She does tend to marry for life—but he's the man most likely to go in for serial monogamy. And while she's the most successful sign at making that match last and last, he scores only average marks. He fancies staying single more than she does, too, and at the wedding, there's much more chance he'll be the virgin. But she's luckier at picking a partner who's the love of a lifetime. She finds marriage a sex-booster—he reports this perk only on remarriage. But he is far less likely than most men to be unfaithful. She's at above-average risk for a female starsign. If—or when—she strays, he's likely to say nothing and hope it won't last, but if it happened to her, she'd find a lover herself.

CANCER MAN—SCORPIO WOMAN

She finds him one of the biggest sensual turn-ons in the zodiac—but doesn't necessarily want him as a permanent mate. She's mighty popular with him, though, and he also finds her sexually attractive. She's highly attracted to his soulful eyes and well-tuned torso, while he can't wait to let her take control of his heart. He likes her throaty, promising laugh and just hopes he can bring out the tender, softer side of her. In many ways, their ideals dovetail.

He's the man who most values an excellent homemaker—and she can create an intensely private, hideaway lovenest for them both to rest up in—and she gives top marks to a good, responsible provider. Lustwise, they can be out of sync—in theory—for while she's the female sign who gives most marks to sexual attraction, he gives lust one of the lowest male scores. She also expects more humour in a relationship than he does, while he pins his hopes on finding great loyalty and understanding. He should find it with her.

He has maximum chance of marrying more than once, though, and she's the second most likely female sign to follow suit. She's slightly better than him at making lasting bonds. But while he might be happier than her to stay single, he's also readier than her to try a second time. Both stand an average chance of settling with their life-love, but he's more likely to stay a virgin until then. And while she reports getting hitched can work miracles on her sexlife, he may even find loving takes a turn for the worse! Despite her sexual satisfaction, she's also the female sign most likely to stray while he's the most faithful male.

CANCER MAN—SAGITTARIUS WOMAN

Friendship, not passion, is probably first on the menu for this couple—but it could change overnight. They admit that they find each other unlikely long-term partners and there's not much initial sexual chemistry here, either. He's attracted by a sexy laugh (hers is more hearty) and he does value kindness and gentleness in a mate. She's got feelers out for a slim, tall man with wonderful, soul-searching eyes. She also wants a partner who's easy to talk to and has a warm heart. Cancer may be shyly tongue-tied to start with, but he sure is kind. Long-term, he puts higher value on loyalty and understanding, while playful Sagittarius gives humour more votes—more, in fact, than any other woman.

Neither set much score by sexual attraction and both avoid postmarital temptation—they're more faithful than most and she's the female sign who strays least often. He has a higher chance than her of marrying more than once. Yet he's also likelier to stay married longer—she's least likely to pass the 10-year watershed. Both are happier than most to stay on their own, but she's in a bit more of a hurry than him to wed.

Marriage seems to suit them both, though. So does remarriage. He's likelier to be a virgin before the wedding and has more chance of finding the love of his life. She finds marriage more of a sex aid, while he admits lovemaking can turn duller afterwards. Both find remarriage a much sexier prospect—she finds the greatest improvement in her sex drive, after remarriage, out of all the female starsigns.

CANCER MAN—CAPRICORN WOMAN

Both hide soft centres under brittle shells—and it's only when each drops their guard that they'll find how much they have in common. She says he's a popular partner choice for her—though she also nominates him least-sexy sign! And he doesn't fancy her particularly, either, or list her as a favourite mate. But both set greater store by kindness in a partner than others do. She's the zodiac woman who's most magnetised by a blowtorch smile, while he loves a gentle manner coupled with a sexy laugh. They both expect clearcut roles in their relationship; he wants a good homemaker, she gives a good provider the highest score.

He does expect rather more loyalty and understanding than she does, though, while humour is higher up her list than his. She has more marital staying power than him—he's definitely more at risk of remarriage while she excels at staying by her man for life.

Both have an average chance of notching up 10 years together. But —surprisingly—he's not as keen to wed as she is, whether first or subsequent time-around. She has more luck in settling with the love of a lifetime, he's more likely to be a virgin on marriage. She often finds that lovemaking carries on the same, but a long-term partnership can make—or break—his sex drive. They're usually a loyal, devoted couple. But if he strays, she could well want a divorce, whereas he would try to ignore it and hope her affair didn't last.

CANCER MAN—AQUARIUS WOMAN

Her cool, scientific mind can sometimes offend his sensitive soul, and they certainly don't see eye to eye on the vital qualities of a long-term relationship! For starters, she's more popular with him than the other way around and neither finds the other an instant turn-on. And they don't name each other as favourite spouse-material. She's attracted by eyes that promise deep, mysterious emotions and a great smile, while he goes for her understated, sophisticated manner and provocative laugh.

She's not a natural homemaker—which is what he's looking out for—but she knows where to get help and appreciates his efforts in that quarter, too. She's not too bothered about nailing a good provider, either—so she won't put him under pressure workwise. But while he's the man who rates a kind nature highest, she gives this the lowest female vote. She wants understanding from her partner, he craves loyalty. Neither rate fun or sexiness.

Cancer's the man who says I Do over and over, her risk of remarriage is lower. Yet he's likelier to pass his 10th anniversary. He's also keener than her to stay single—but less easily put off giving marriage a second go. He's more likely to settle with his true love, far more likely to be a virgin—and both signs score highly at finding marriage a sex-dampener. She, though, can also find marriage quite a sex-booster, too. And she's likelier than him to find a partner more attractive after having children.

CANCER MAN—PISCES WOMAN

There's only an average chance that they'll end up with one another—but when they do, it's a telepathic, tender shared dream. She rates him rather tasty—while he finds her either very sexy indeed or not sexy at all. This is probably because her sex appeal is largely mental and her outward appearance is subtly provocative. He does love her kind and gentle nature, though. If she's got a laugh that's full of innuendo and proves herself a good nestbuilder, he'll be hooked. She'll fancy him if he curbs his foodlust and stays slim and if he has a film star smile.

Long-term, he hopes for loyalty from her, she rates kindness more than most. She also awards more Brownie points to sexual attraction than he does—he says he needs plenty of understanding and a good rapport. Luckily, neither wants a workaholic. They'd far prefer to spend time pampering one another!

He's far likelier than other signs to remarry and she's at some risk, too. Yet he more frequently makes a match last and has more chance of marrying the love of his life. She's in more of a rush to wed— she'd die rather than pass her sell-by date. He's more likely to be a virgin on the big day, but she finds marriage much more of a sex tonic—remarriage improves her love life even more! But while he's more likely than other male signs to stay true, she's got an above-average chance of wandering. But both might well keep their lips sealed and pray affairs peter out.

CANCER MAN—ARIES WOMAN

He's one of the most intuitive males of the zodiac and he can laser through her brazen facade and spot the little-girl-lost inside. He certainly finds her the sexiest sign by far—and they often choose one another as long-term partners. She, though, doesn't say he's very sexy. He loves her wicked laugh—yet his hopes that she'll turn out to be the kind, cosy homemaker of his dreams are a bit over-optimistic. He definitely finds her fierce temper outbursts hard to stomach. Conversely, there's a chance that he's not as outgoing and self-confident as she would like. She is bound to fall for him, though, if he has gorgeous eyes and a tall, well-muscled frame, plus a honeyed voice. When the chips are down, he puts loyalty at the top of his Christmas list, while she gives her top marks to kindness.

This pair are the male and female starsigns who most often marry more than once. He does have a bit more chance of making a long-lasting match, but both are in the middle range. The single life holds more appeal for him and he's in less of a rush to remarry, too. But he's luckier at settling with a true love and there's more chance he'll have put off gaining sexual experience until meeting her. She's likelier to find marriage improves sex for her—but both report that, heaven forbid, lovemaking can get lodged in the doldrums. Both tend to be very faithful. But if his attentions do wander, she may well ask for a divorce, while if she's untrue, he may simply button his lip, cross his fingers and wait for it to fizzle out.

CANCER MAN—TAURUS WOMAN

Feeling secure before they can let themselves go in a relationship is a need they both share. He finds her one of the sexiest signs around—though she doesn't reciprocate! He appreciates her sensual loving, her warm and giving nature. He can find her too stubborn at times, but her homemaking skills create a comfy cave for them both to hide in. In turn, she values him as a wonderful provider—both may be content to follow old-fashioned conventional partnership roles.

She likes her fella to be smartly turned out, to sound good and to look coolly confident—even though Cancer may be putting on a show of kidology on that last count. Long-term, she wants kindness and loads of fun from him, he rates understanding and loyalty. Both agree that sexual attraction isn't everything.

He runs a strong risk of multiple marriages, while her risk is low. He's slower off the starting blocks than she is at getting hitched in the first place, but once he does commit, he stands a greater chance of making it last. She's the luckiest female sign of all at marrying the love of a lifetime—he's only got an average crack at that. But he's more likely to be a wedding night virgin. Sadly, while she's the woman who most often reports how her sexlife has blossomed after marriage, he admits it can really slacken off. If he wanders, she'll want to sit down and thrash out a solution—he'd try to ignore her infidelity.

CANCER MAN—GEMINI WOMAN

They're opposites in so many ways, and too-sociable Gemini might be too busy to give him the tender, one-to-one emotional massage he craves—but she could certainly lure him out of his shell and into an irresistible romance. He's actually her favourite partner. And there's a pretty good chance he'll pick her, too, though neither reckon much to the other's fanciability. Her outrageous laugh is what he notices first and he'll be putting her character under a microscope to try to spot minute signs of those other qualities he likes—such as kindness and gentleness with a fair sprinkling of homemaking talent. For her, it's vital that he understands her complex, formidable mind. He also rates this ability. She likes his clothing style and smooth-talking ways.

While he expects maximum loyalty, she prefers kindness. Neither believe sexual attraction is the linch-pin of a relationship. He's more likely than her to wed more than once and is in the middle range of those who make it past the 10 year mark. She's the woman least likely to reach this anniversary—and is also the female sign who most wants to hang onto her single freedom. He quite likes staying on his own, too. But once he's tried marriage, he takes to it like a duck to water and is the keenest male sign to remarry. She's far more wary. He's the likelier virgin and is more likely to settle with the love of his life. She finds married life boosts sex—but is also more likely than him to report that it has the opposite effect!.

CANCER MAN—CANCER WOMAN

They cling so close, it's hard to tell where one person ends and the other begins. It's rare that same sign couplings really work—but this one does. They vote each other most popular partner and he finds her far and away the sexiest female starsign of the lot. She thinks he's quite gorgeous, too. He's attracted to her intimate laughter and appreciates more than most her gentle, generous-hearted nature. She's his perfect wife and homemaker, while she's perfectly content to let him handle the serious stuff—he's her ideal provider. She can lose herself in his eyes and compliments his superb colour sense and clothing flair. Only difference is; he wants loyalty from her, she needs kindness from him.

He's the sign who's statistically most likely to remarry, yet only a third of Cancer women follow suit. She has more marital staying-power—nearly half make it to 10 years—while his score's only average. And he's more likely to want to stay single. But both can be pretty keen to wed—especially again. She settles more often with a life-love, but he's more likely to be a virgin when he goes down the aisle first time. Neither finds marriage much of a sex-booster (his score's higher than hers), but this pair are very anti-affairs. She would probably opt for divorce if he did the straying, while he might well prefer to say nothing if he stumbled upon any guilty secrets of hers!

THE CANCER WOMAN'S LOVEMATCHES

CANCER WOMAN—LEO MAN

He finds her easily his least sexy sign. Yet there's a fair old chance that they'll end up as a couple. Why? Because he secretly can't get enough of all the tender loving care she doles out. And while he makes out that he likes a socialite on his arm to laugh at his jokes at parties, he also wants his own place to look like a palace—and home-loving Cancer is more than willing to put in the necessary housework hours.

She reckons he's Mr Average—both sexually and as a life partner. But she is definitely drawn to his eyes and really fancies him when he puts on his best gear. And, more than other male signs, he's got a weak spot for eyes he can lose himself in—like Cancer's. He loves her warm, curvy body, her shy smile that's just for him—he can't resist flattery, remember—well-turned legs and passion-promising laugh. Long-term, both seek someone who understands how they think. Though he rates sexual attraction and humour more highly than her, and she wants kindness overall.

He's at greater risk of remarriage—and he's the male sign who most wants to stay single. She yearns to marry and more often makes it past the 10-year post. Luck on both their sides in that both often marry the love of their lives. He's less likely to be a wedding day virgin, has more chance than her of finding marriage a sex-improver. And he's also the man who gets the biggest sex boost from remarriage. On the affairs front, she's less likely than him to stray—but both are mighty quick off the mark (faster than most signs) to ask for a divorce if either one should stray.

CANCER WOMAN—VIRGO MAN

Because so much of him is kept in check by the cool front of a self-imposed emotional straitjacket, he often doesn't spot her partner potential as a passion-releaser. So he rarely settles with her. And she names him one of her least favourite partners, too. Neither finds the other particularly sexy—though he does rate an attractive voice and gentle manner more than other men do. He's usually drawn to a slim, yet shapely body (Cancer on a good day when she keeps her eye on her calorie-counter). She sits up and takes notice of soulful eyes that mirror her own and neat clothes-sense.

Long-term, she says she's looking for understanding and kindness, and Virgo men are full of insight into feminine psychology. He values loyalty, humour and sexual attraction in a partner. But though she's quite keen on getting a good provider, perfectionist Virgo gives her homemaking talents a surprisingly lukewarm vote.

He's less of a remarriage risk than she is, yet he's also the second least likely male sign to pass 10 years of matrimony. She does rather better. He's keener to stay single, in less of a hurry to remarry. She's more likely to wed her life-love—and both have an average chance of being virgins when they marry. She actually finds marriage less of a sex-tonic than most—and he's the male sign most prone to finding a nuptial no-go area developing after settling down. These blips apart, neither tends to make a hash of their relationship with affairs, though she'd more likely want a divorce while if it did happen, he'd ask why and try to make up.

CANCER WOMAN—LIBRA MAN

He's the most sexually adventurous man in the whole galaxy and he finds her well worth his attentions. Her sexual passions, though, need coaxing out and she finds it hard to let herself go without a partner's deep commitment. At present, neither gives the other their vote as best long-term bet and she doesn't think he's especially sexy. Nevertheless, she has a weakness for come-hither eyes and good clothes, while he notices female curves and an attractive voice. A nurturing personality and faithfulness attract him, too, but he also likes strong-mindedness, not gentleness, in a woman. In the long run, both need loads of understanding. But while he nominates loyalty, good looks and sex-appeal, she goes for humour and kindness.

Both have an average chance of marrying more than once, but he's the top sign for sticking power. And she has a good 10-year-plus marriage track record, too. At first, he's happier than her to stay single—and she's keener to give wedlock a second go, too. She more often finds the love of her life. He's less than half as likely as her to be a virgin when he gets hitched! Both are in the lower bracket for finding that marriage improves their sexlives and they're likelier than most to find that lovemaking stays pretty much on an even keel. He's notoriously high-risk when it comes to affairs, though, while she's the complete opposite, the model faithful wife. If he wanders, she could opt for divorce. But in the less likely event of her straying, he may decide to take a lover of his own in revenge.

CANCER WOMAN—SCORPIO MAN

Just try ungluing this couple once they've paired up. At first sight, she finds him the sex-machine of the zodiac and he votes her a hot number, too. He also names her one of his most popular partners— though her statistical chances of choosing him to share her life long-term are only average. Not surprisingly, she's hooked on his hypnotic eyes and finds him extra-fanciable in smart clothes. He longs to come in for some of her nurturing and finds her gentle manner and faithfulness so appealing (so soothing for his endemic jealousy). He also likes her legs. Long-term, she wants kindness and understanding (he's such a good listener), while he rates sex skills, physical attraction—and fun. He's more sensual than most and, with patience, can bring out her strong lovestyle, too.

He's the male sign most likely to marry just once, for life. She only has an average score for that. Yet she passes the 10-year mark more often than him. Both are keener than most to remarry, but he's also more easily put off doing it second-time-around. She has more hope of getting the big love of her life. Both stand a fair chance of staying virgins until the wedding. He finds marriage a bigger sex highlighter than her—and he's also more likely to report that it's a sex-wrecker, too! He has more chance of straying than she does and, if that happens, she may well want a divorce from him. But if she were ever untrue, despite his explosive, dangerous temper, he's likely to want to sit down and work things out afresh with her.

CANCER WOMAN—SAGITTARIUS MAN

A woman's strongest card, in his eyes, is superb faithfulness. For, despite being the most restless male zodiac sign, he sets enormous store by having someone who's always waiting for him at home. There is only an average chance that she'll choose him as a partner and she doesn't single him out in our survey as being ultra-sexy. He's slightly less keen to choose her and finds her one of the least fanciable signs. Still, she does have a soft spot for eyes that she can gaze into endlessly and if he dresses well, he's going to zoom up in her estimation. He can't resist a loving smile and a slim, well-defined body. He's also hot on shared interests and this pair might well meet initially through a mutual hobby. Long-term, both want kind-heartedness and deep understanding and neither think that sexual attraction is vital. But he does want more humour in a relationship than she does.

He's likelier than her to wed more than once—and is the man least likely to make an enduring lovebond. But he is the most faithful starsign and can usually rely on her to be true, too. She's luckier than him at finding a major love in her lifetime to marry and nearly twice as likely to stay a virgin until then. And she tops the list of those reporting that sex is better within marriage—though he's above average, too. He, though, more often finds a partner less of a turn-on after having children. If he ever did stray from her side, she might well want to ditch him via divorce. Other way round, he'd be keener to work things through.

CANCER WOMAN—CAPRICORN MAN

Conventional they may be but, as a couple, there's no doubt that they really work. He is one of her topmost favourite partners and he's quite keen on her, too. Each admits they find the other fairly fanciable—but neither are prone to advertise their tastes to all and sundry, so maybe they're more attracted than they're letting on. He's pulled to her side by her smile and stays to admire her great legs. Then he can't resist her lovely melodious voice. Her great faithfulness appeals mightily to him, too, and he's pleased that they have interests in common. She takes a shine to his so-intelligent eyes and expensive-looking clothes that make him look like a business big wheel.

In the long-term, she wants kindness from a man, plus understanding and a fair dash of fun. He's after sexual attraction, good looks and humour—the conventional package. He's also status-conscious—the male sign who most rates a partner with money! Caring Cancer isn't the gold-digger type at all—though she could inherit a family fortune, so Capricorn might be in luck.

Both have a one-in-three chance of marrying more than once. He's more likely than her to make a long-lasting match, but she's far keener to remarry. He's often too proud to try again! She does better than him at settling with a dream lover—and far more likely to be a virgin when she does. Marriage doesn't improve either's sexlife much, but he reports more often than her that remarriage can perk up his lovelife. He is also the male sign who's most likely to have an affair. She's at low risk. Neither delays in calling time on the marriage if the other is untrue—though he might just want to work things out instead.

CANCER WOMAN—AQUARIUS MAN

He's all head, while she's all heart. He needs a very long leash, she wants love ties and commitments. But they can work as a couple. He names her as a favourite partner, in fact, and he finds her sexy, too. She reckons he's fairish in the fanciability stakes. And she has an average chance of settling—if that's ever the right word to use for an Aquarius—with him. She'll certainly settle for his handsome eyes and loves it when he picks smart outfits that really suit his colouring. He may be cerebral, but he gets all physical at the sight of her well-placed curves. And he appreciates her soothing manner and acknowledged homemaking skills.

In the long run, both are after understanding—and fun. But while he rates loyalty very highly, she wants kindness most of all. She also values a homeloving man—and glad-handing Aquarius is usually keen to go out! But both reckon there are more important qualities than mere sexual attraction.

He's far more likely than her to marry several times and she has much more chance of bonding long-term. She's keener, too, to get married in the first place, though both are in more than a hurry than normal to remarry. He's the male sign who least often gets the love of his life and she's luckier than him in this respect. And sexually impatient Aquarius is five times less likely than her to be a virgin come the wedding. They both usually find that loving carries on much as before after their marriage. Neither are into affairs. If she strayed, he'd want to analyse the problems and work through them, but if the boot were on the other foot, she might well go for the divorce option.

CANCER WOMAN—PISCES MAN

Money doesn't interest this pair at all—neither wants to sacrifice valuable loving time in order to get out and get rich! They're both engulfed in their own sensual and richly imaginative little kingdom. From the word go, he's her favourite partner, in fact, and she also votes him one of the supersexiest signs. She's a bit less of a hit with him to begin with, and he doesn't find her especially fanciable. Cancer's sexuality is often waiting to be discovered. She soon falls for his sensitive, moviestar eyes, and likes his dress-style—it looks so effortlessly stylish. He's smitten by her sexy laugh, beautiful legs and the body she wisely works so hard to keep slim. He also thinks those homemaking talents are a major plus. Both feel that fun in a partner is vital.

While she puts a high premium on understanding and kindness—and wants her man to stay cosily at home with her—he heads his list of priorities with loyalty, sex skills and humour. In no particular order! Neither think money is that important.

He does slightly better than her at making a lasting match, but is also more likely to remarry. And he's also happier than her to stay single. But he likes the married state once he does try it and is keener than her to wed again. He is actually the man most likely to wed the love of his life! She's not quite that lucky. And he saves himself for that person more often, too. Marriage gives lovemaking a real shot in the arm and, unlike her, he rarely reports that sex gets worse. He is also likelier to fancy his partner more after children come along. Both have a below-average affairs rating. But if one does wander, both are quicker off the mark at seeking divorce than most other signs.

CANCER WOMAN—ARIES MAN

She's his most popular partner but he'll have to keep a grip on his runaway impatience if their sexlife is going to prove a lasting joy. He say he finds her very sexy—unless shy Cancer is unwilling to experiment in bed. In which case, he finds her unsexy, according to our survey! She, though, votes him far and away her least sexy male sign—which should give him pause for thought. And he's not a favourite partner in other respects, either. Still, his hot glances could change her mind and she may well be impressed by the power-image clothes that ambitious Aries wears. He's pulled by her melting smile, curvy figure—provided it's not too full; she must look fit—and her nice eyes.

He also gives homemaking skills the top male vote, which shows he knows where he's well off! For loving longer-term, she expects understanding (an Aries possibility once he stops to listen) kindness and fun. Sexual attraction and good looks are what count with him. But both share a liking for homelovers.

These two run only an average risk of remarriage, although she's the more likely to stick with a marriage for 10-plus years. Both are keen to marry—for different, yet thoroughly compatible reasons. She wants someone to look after, he just loves being pampered! Yet both can easily get put off trying second-time marriage. He has more luck than most men at marrying the love of a lifetime (she does quite well, too). And both stand a fair chance of being a virgin when they wed. Neither, alas, finds marriage does that much for their sexlife! He is more likely than her to stray. And she may well want a divorce if he did her wrong. If she was unfaithful, though, he is likely to take a lover of his own!

CANCER WOMAN—TAURUS MAN

They've a megadose of stubbornness to share, but few couples ever attain their sensual heights. She's actually more of a popular choice with him than he is with her. And neither finds the other initially very sexy. But he gives her brand of kindness the top male vote and then promptly falls for those other attributes he spots in her, like her easy-on-the-ear voice, subtle naughty laugh, her warm smile and great body shape. He really appreciates her low-key manner and good homemaking skills. She is drawn by his bedroom eyes and smart, but practical clothes. They both yearn for kindness and the kind of understanding that needs no words.

But while she values having fun and settling down with a fellow

367

home-lover, he rates sex skills highly. He's also one of the few signs who appreciate a partner who's a hard worker—perhaps because he needs someone to jog him back into action whenever he succumbs to natural indolence. Money—and this is a surprising finding for hard-nosed Taurus—doesn't particularly matter to either of them.

He's less likely than her to remarry, has slightly more chance of making his marriage last more than 10 years and is likelier to be a wedding-day virgin. Both are keen to get married, though she's quicker to remarry. There is a fair chance that both will settle with a lifelove. Wedlock tends to boost his sexlife more than it does hers, but neither score highly here. She tends to be more faithful than him. But if she did go off with another, he is the keenest of all the male starsigns to try and work things out, if possible. She, on the other hand, would probably want a divorce if he let her down.

CANCER WOMAN—GEMINI MAN

Provided she learns to take his outrageous and incurable flirting—he'll even make eyes at the dog—as lightly as it deserves, they could end up joining the bowls club together. In fact, Gemini man is a proven better long-term marriage bet than she is! From the outset, she's one of his most popular mates. But he does give her the unsexy vote—largely because, he reckons, she lacks bedroom imagination. She, though, has an average chance of picking him out as her partner, despite not finding him particularly sexy. The things that turn her on are knockout eyes and good clothes, while he goes all weak at the knees when faced with super legs, a slim body and a sexy laugh. Shared interests, faithfulness and a gentle manner also appeal to him.

Both this pair want understanding from their partner. But she has a deeper yearning for kindness while he rates sexual attraction nearly twice as highly as she does. He also reckons that being good looking and sexually skilled is also important. They share a liking for finding a homelover.

These two are less at risk than most signs of marrying more than once. But while she's always keen to marry in the first place, he is the male sign who's happiest staying in his bachelor pad. He is also less likely than her to wed the love of a lifetime—often missing out, incidentally, because of his reluctance to commit himself. He is a lot likelier than her to be a virgin when he marries (perhaps bearing out the allegation that he's hotter on the verbals than on the performance in his early years!). He finds marriage more of a sex-tonic. These are the second least likely signs to have affairs—but both are faster than most to ask for divorce if a partner went off the rails.

CANCER WOMAN—CANCER MAN

Same-sign sex pairings don't always spell harmony. But this is the star-blessed exception. Both name the other as popular partners, so they must have some moon-led instinctive premonition of success. He votes her by far the sexiest female sign, too. She finds him fairly physically stimulating—his love-me eyes and excellent clothes style are distinct plusses, too. He is attracted by her kind nature and gentle, if rather motherly manner. Her homemaking skills are another big hit, while her pretty, limpid eyes and unforgettable laugh get him going.

Long-term, they both need lots of kindness and understanding, but he gives a rather higher vote to loyalty, while she rates finding a homelover and getting a partner who's fun, more. But neither believe sexual attraction is the be-all-and-end-all in a relationship.

He is the man most at risk of marrying over and over—she reweds less often, and often makes a better long-lasting job of it. He is also keener than her on single life. Yet he's less easily put off trying again than other signs, while she can be more-than-usually wary. She is likelier to get her true love (though she's less often a virgin than he is) and neither find their marriage gives their sexlife a charge. She often reports that lovemaking remains the same. Both are usually the faithful types—but if he should wander, then she's more likely than most women to see her solicitor to start divorce proceedings. If she took a shine to someone else, he's the man for saying nothing and hoping that her affair just wasn't going to last.

THE LEO MAN'S LOVEMATCHES

LEO MAN—VIRGO WOMAN

Both fancy each other like crazy from the moment they meet. They name one another as so-popular partners—and she finds him even more of a turn-on than he finds her! She really gets the hots for this firesign showman if he's tall, muscular yet slim. And if he's true to her alone, then that's the best bonus of all. He loves gazing into her eyes and trying to guess the moods she so fastidiously hides! He also appreciates her quizzical smile, her sexy laugh, well-shaped legs and luscious, fit body.

He would like her to share his interests, ideally, and to cotton on to the way he thinks—though this last facility doesn't strike much of a chord with Virgo. Instead, she goes for loyalty—and he unfortunately gives that the lowest male vote of the lot! He reckons he needs someone who's nice-looking, funny, sexy—of course—and a wow in bed. She wants a rich, hard-working fun-lover—Leo to a T.

Demanding Virgo, with her ultra-high standards, is the woman most likely to wed more than once—or to say never again! Leo's at high risk of remarriage, but passes the 10-year test period better, though both are in the middle range. He's almost three times keener to stay single and stands out as the male sign who's wariest of wedlock! Both have good luck on their side in marrying the love of their life. He's only half as likely as her, though, to save himself for that special someone. Long-term, he has more chance than his wife of finding that lovemaking improves within the heartsafe confines of happy matrimony.

LEO MAN—LIBRA WOMAN

They won't take the normal, conventional route to anywhere. And as she isn't set on finding a good provider, and he's not remotely interested in having a good homemaker, they'll either share and share about the roles—or spend their lives arguing about whose turn it is for the washing-up! He's one of her favourite partner choices, though, and she does find him a very sexy number.

But he says she's an unlikely choice to pair up with (and he doesn't fancy her that much!). Still, he's the man who's most susceptible to a large dose of charm and a beautiful pair of eyes. Add to the package super legs, a shapely form, hello-there smile and sexy laugh, and Libra's buttonholed his attention well and truly. She can't take her eyes off him when he's wearing a smart outfit and she adores his commanding voice, dazzling smile and friendly chat.

What she wants in life is a partner who's kind and loyal while he wants a mate who understands him (she'll make out she does, anyway) and is amusing, attractive—and good in bed. She usually marries once, for life, while he's a higher remarriage risk. And she has far more chance of keeping her man by her side for 10-plus years. He's the sign, meanwhile, who is happiest to stay single—she's far keener to marry, or remarry. Both are quite fortunate when it comes to settling with The Real Thing—but she's a more likely wedding day virgin. He finds marriage more of a sex-improver—and gets an even bigger loving boost from remarriage. But if he ever strays, she opts to take a lover herself. He may well want a divorce if she's untrue.

LEO MAN—SCORPIO WOMAN

Strangely—given that she's so ultra-sensual and he's a dynamic, strongly physical lover—these two don't cotton on at first to their joint sexual potential. Neither rates the other as particularly fanciable, according to our figures. But she does name him as a favourite partner, nevertheless, and he's quite keen to team up with her, long-term, too. Both find gorgeous eyes quite irresistible—and he takes notice of a sexy laugh, warm smile, and great legs topped with a curvy body. Her man should be muscular, with a strong, well-modulated voice.

She gives the top female vote to his being a good provider, too, which shows her streak of pragmatism below her cauldron of inner passion. He, though, doesn't much value a good homemaker and may well prefer having equal, shared roles at home (though it's hard to picture Leo man dusting the furniture, isn't it?).

Both think sexual attraction's vital to long-term love and highly rate sex skills and humour. But he's keener to find a partner who understands him.

He's likelier to marry more than once—but both are high risk! She has marginally more success at making a long-lasting match and is keener to marry. He's the man who most wants the bachelor life. She's much more likely to be a virgin bride than he is a chaste groom. Both report a sex-boost after marriage—and he finds remarriage even sexier than she does. He's an average affairs-risk. She's the woman most likely to stray! If she does give in to temptation, he may well seek a divorce. She would probably ask why he did it and try to put things right in their marriage.

LEO MAN—SAGITTARIUS WOMAN

Perpetual playmates first, passionate lovers second—without a shared sense of humour, this relationship could never get started. In her book, he is always one of her sexiest signs—but she's firm that she could easily go off him if he got too bossy in bed! And while she rates him as a partner, he's not quite so smitten by her at the onset (and says she's only averagely sexy). They both find attractive eyes more appealing than most other signs, though. Her dreamboat is tall, slim, kind and a good talker. He likes a world-mellowed smile, curvaceous figure, good legs and a sexy laugh as well as shared interests. Both want understanding—and humour—in the long-term (she gives that top female starsign marks). But physical Leo gives higher ratings than her to sexual attraction, above-average looks and skilled sex technique.

There's a far greater chance that he'll marry more than once, though she is less likely than him to notch up 10 marital years. Both could be happy as singles (especially him!). She's keener to wed—and wed again—and more likely to be a virgin for her first marriage. But

373

he has better luck at marrying true love and marriage lights up his sexlife. She is actually the zodiac's most faithful woman—he's an average affairs risk. If he does wander, she'd want to work things out. He, on the other hand, would be speedier than most to ask for divorce if she was untrue.

LEO MAN—CAPRICORN WOMAN

These two power-dressed high-fliers may eye one another from across a crowded gathering, but it probably won't be love-and-live-together at first sight. While he nominates her as one of his partnership favourites, she's unlikely to choose him. Neither finds the other particularly fanciable. Her dream partner would be tall—and muscular—with a broadcaster's voice and dazzling smile. She expects him to be totally faithful and to provide well materially for her. She also wants self-confidence and kindness from him. His first port of call is bound to be her eyes followed by her smile, curvy body, smooth long legs. He also likes women to laugh flirtatiously. Both reckon a sense of humour's vital for their relationship to last, but she demands more of a measure of loyalty than he does. He, meanwhile, wants a mate who's understanding, nice-looking in a sexy way—and good in bed!

His chances of marrying more than once are higher than hers, though he also has more success at taking his relationship through the 10-year barrier. He's more than three times happier than her to stay single—she's also in more of a hurry than him to remarry, let alone marry. Both are luckier than the bulk of the population at marrying the love of their life. But she's more likely to have saved herself for that special someone. He also gets more of a sexlife boost from marriage, while she's the female zodiac sign who reports the least improvement! On the affairs front, she's less likely than most to go in for extramarital dalliance; his affairs risk is average. Both are quick to order up divorce papers when marriage goes wrong.

LEO MAN—AQUARIUS WOMAN

He doesn't quite know what to make of her cool, mysterious, manipulation of his emotions. This will be a slow-burn affair that takes time to erupt. He is, at first flush, more popular with her than the other way around. But both find each other fairly sexy. She is, admittedly, tough to please when it comes to attraction points in a partner—but she does like smart clothes and a distinctive, easy-on-the-ear voice. Leo likes his woman to have large, clear eyes, a shapely figure, sexy laugh and good legs—and if they share interests, so much the better.

Both want a partner who understands them (not so easy, fathoming an Aquarius woman) and who likes a joke. Being nice-looking and exciting in bed is another mutual draw. But while she rates a rather harder worker than Leo's likely to be, he wants a mate who single-mindedly pampers him—and she's always got her huge circle to cater for, too. He is also more certain than her that sexual attraction's vital to lingering romance.

He is at high risk of marrying more than once. She's mid-range, yet he stands more chance of making a lasting match. He's also happier not to bother with marriage at all—she's in more of a dash both to marry and to remarry. His chances of picking a lifetime love are greater, but both are less likely than most to be virgins when they wed. There's a strong chance they'll both find sex better within their marriage bond—but having said that, both are at average risk of turning to other lovers. If she did so, he'd probably want a divorce. She would be keener than most to work through it.

LEO MAN—PISCES WOMAN

This looks like a no-no—they're looking for quite different qualities from a partner—but it can work against all the odds. They are, in fact, each other's least popular partnership choice and neither gets high sex-ratings here, either. But both can have their minds changed by a look-again smile. And if he has a slim body and is full of promises of faithfulness, there's a chance she might fall for him.

She'll have no joy at playing out her hobby with him, though—reforming a man's character. Leo likes himself just the way he is. He, in turn, might be drawn to her eyes with their faraway look, her rounded body, shapely legs and sexy laugh.

But while she's keener than him on getting a kind-hearted partner, he's the zodiac sign who gives this the lowest marks. Both want a mate who understands them, though (she's pretty intuitive) and likes a sense of humour. He's more obsessed by sex-skills and physical attraction than she is—she fancies someone rich! They're both at high risk of marrying more than once, him especially.

He's slightly more likely than her to celebrate a 10-year anniversary. But while he's the happiest man to remain single, she's the exact opposite—the woman who most hates being unattached. She is likelier than him to save herself for marriage, but he is more prone to find the love of his life to settle down with. He also finds wedlock more of a sexual bonanza—though both get a physical boost from remarriage.

Highly emotional and open to many influences, she's more likely than most women in the zodiac to stray—he's only an average affairs risk. He would probably ask for a divorce if she wandered, while she is the type to take a revenge lover of her own if he was untrue to her.

LEO MAN—ARIES WOMAN

This could well be a second—or even third—time lucky try at marriage for both parties. No worries on the initial physical compatibility front; she votes him Sexiest Sign and he also finds her pretty fanciable, too. There's a fair to moderate chance they could end up partners. The eyes have it for both of them—a key pullability point—and she'll be extra drawn to him if he's a good head and shoulders above her (literally), muscular and full of confidence (Leo's chief attribute). It'll help if his voice sounds good, too. He won't be able to turn away if she has a sunny smile, hourglass figure, marvellous legs and a great, sexy laugh. An added bonus, of course, would be shared interests.

For long-haul lavish loving, she's the female starsign who's keenest on the kindness factor—and she values a homelover, too. He's tracking down a female who really understands him and is funny, lovely to look at, sexy and above all, good in bed! No beating about the bush with Leo!

She is the zodiac woman who most often marries over and over—and he's at high risk of remarriage, too. However, he's more likely to last the 10-years-plus course, and he's far happier on his ownsome, too, while she's usually keen to get hitched. His luck holds better than hers in marrying the love of his life. She's nearly twice as likely as him to be a virgin when she marries, but he does get more of a sexual kick-start from being married. Each has only a near-average chance of being unfaithful—but these two are keener than most couples on divorce if affairs should ever come between them to spoil their happiness.

LEO MAN—TAURUS WOMAN

They hit it off in bed alright—but is he kind enough for her? Both members of this team have a weakness for warm smiles. But while she's the female starsign who most needs a kind nature to underlie that smile, Leo man rates discovering this quality in a woman rather low on his agenda. On paper, he names her as a popular partner and says he either finds her sign very sexy indeed—or not at all fanciable! She gives him a middling rating as a partner choice and doesn't find him sexually irresistible. Her ideal man is someone she can look up to—he'd be tall, a good provider, muscular, confident and well-dressed. He'd also sound good, with a winning line in chat. Leo rates beautiful eyes more than other men and his other female favourite points are a sinuous body, shapely long legs and a girlish yet sexy giggle.

In a long-term partner, he'd look for good looks, sexual attractiveness, wit and stylish bedroom technique. What she wants most in the world is a homelover who isn't stodgy, a man who's always fun to be with. He runs far more risk than her of marrying more than once. Yet he's slightly more prone to making a bond last. She's far keener to wed, while he's the happiest male single of all the signs, but both can draw back from giving marriage a second go—she from insecurity, he from pride.

Taurus woman's the most likely female to get the love of her life—he often does so, too. Both are less likely than most to walk down the aisle or enter the registry office as virgins. Both reckon happy matrimony brings a glow to their sexlife—and she reports the biggest improvement of any sign.

LEO MAN—GEMINI WOMAN

If he acts the Sugar Daddy, she'll make a beeline for him and never leave his side! Otherwise, he's usually among her least likely life partners and she doesn't find him very sexy, says our survey. Smitten by her tinkling laugh, impressed by her social grace (and lured by a promise of more private love skills to be discovered), Leo says she's one of the sexiest signs around. There's an average chance he'll stay with her. While her fancy will be taken by his entertaining banter and clothes that look as if they've been hand-tailored for him, he soon falls for her delicate calves and smooth thighs, her curvy body and that warm smile that quickly turns to sexy laughter.

Shared interests? Then he's on to a winner. Long-term, both ask for understanding from their lover or spouse—and she gives this the highest female marks of all. He needs a woman to be funny, sexy, nice-looking and a smooth operator behind closed bedroom doors (provided she glosses over how she became so skilled). She wants a man to be kind and ever-so-rich!

These are the male and female signs happiest to stay single. But he's a lot likelier than her to marry more than once and more likely to stay wed more than 10 years. She's the least likely female long-termer and least likely woman to get the love of her life (his luck's better). He's also keener than her to give wedded bliss a second go. She's the more likely wedding day virgin and she finds sex can get worse after marriage! He finds it usually improves. If he wanders, she'll want to know the whys and wherefores and be keen to work things out afresh. If she meanders, stiff-necked Leo is likelier than most to opt for divorce.

LEO MAN—CANCER WOMAN

He may find her spasmodic carping a dampener, yet he secretly yearns for her intense possessiveness. Overall, he's more popular with her than she is with him, though. But physically, she reckons he's an OK proposition, while he finds her the unsexiest sign of all. His chief assets for her are his wide-awake eyes and dazzling charm, plus his flamboyant clothes flair. He gives the top male vote to lovely eyes, closely followed in popular attractions by a shapely body, super legs and sexy laugh.

Having interests in common matters more to him than most, too, but he doesn't grade Cancer's concerned kindly nature very highly. In the long run, both treasure a partner who understands them. But while he wants a real looker and sexbomb—with a sense of humour—on his arm, she's looking for something more subtle; a homelover who's kind and fun to be with.

He is likelier than her to have more than one marriage in his lifetime, while she does better at steering her ship past the 10-year rocks. He's also far happier than her to stay single—she's keener to marry, and remarry, too. They're both more fortunate than the mainstream at finding their true love to marry, but she's more prone to being a virgin when that time comes. He finds marriage shines up his sexlife more than it does hers—and says remarriage is sexier still. His chances of having an affair are average. She's one of the least likely female signs to stray. But neither would hang around if the other were untrue—they'd go for a hasty divorce.

LEO MAN—LEO WOMAN

They're both really into super bodies and soon notice one another's physical plusses. But each could spend a lifetime trying to shoulder their own way to star-rating and stop their other half hogging the limelight! Each names the other as a popular partner—with sexual attraction mutual! She is keener than other female starsigns on his slim body, particularly if its muscles are noticeable. He's marginally more attracted by her eyes, though he soon notices her tautly sinuous body, excellent legs, friendly smile and sexy laugh. He says shared interests will bring them even closer together.

Both believe sexual attraction to be a key element to the success of their relationship long-term. But, while she is the zodiac woman who most rates loyalty, he is the man who puts the lowest price tag on it! Instead, he asks for a pretty woman who understands him—well, there's no harm in asking—who has a sense of humour and who knows what she's doing in bed!

She is the female starsign most likely to marry for life. He's the man who most often weds more than once. He is also much more prone than her to stay on his own, but both have a near-even chance of making a bond last 10 years or more. He is luckier at marrying a true love, but half-as-likely as her to be a virgin on his wedding night. Happily, both report finding marriage a sex-improver—he reports slightly better results than her. But their responses to infidelity differ. If she were untrue, he would probably want a divorce right away. But if he played away, she would be faster than most women at finding a revenge lover of her own.

THE LEO WOMAN'S LOVEMATCHES

LEO WOMAN—VIRGO MAN

She'll have to woo him away from work and back to bed, time and time again—but could find the effort worthwhile. That's because few men have as good an insight into the feminine psyche as Virgo.

He fancies her a lot, too, even though she doesn't think his sign's very sexy and theirs is not the most likely pairing in the zodiac galaxy. He'll have to ignore the way she laps up flattery from admirers, too, if this is to work long-term. Like them, he's soon smitten by a supreme sense of style and attractive voice. He likes a woman who turns every head when she enters a room—effortlessly. She wants him to be trim, muscular—and she gives loyalty the top female vote. Both say sexual attraction is a must if their love's to stay on track. She needs a man who understands the way she thinks. He reckons sharing the same kind of jokes is more important.

Leo women most often marry once, for life; and he's also at low risk of remarriage. But she's slightly more likely to make a long-lasting liaison. She is also keener both to marry and to remarry, while he's more than doubly likely to want to stay single. When it comes to getting hitched to the love of a lifetime, punters should put their money on him, not her. She's more likely to be a nuptial virgin and she finds marriage a better sexlife sureshot than him—though these two are the signs who both report the lowest loving boost from remarriage. If he was untrue, she's so proud, she'd keep the problem to herself and wait for his affair to peter out. Or she might take a lover herself. He's more analytical and upfront and he'd be keen to pinpoint what had gone wrong.

LEO WOMAN—LIBRA MAN

He's smooth enough to catch her attention in a crowd, and enough of a flatterer to pretend she's always the one in charge. No wonder she says he's her favourite partner. He gives her only an average score in the long-term coupling stakes—and neither goes overboard when it comes to fancying the other sign. She's on the lookout for a slim, muscular male body, while he's drawn to her if she's faithful (though he isn't always!) kind and curvy. He also likes a clear, melodious voice.

They both need loyalty from their other half—she gives this the top female vote. Both set some store by appearances; he needs a good-looking woman (who understands him) and she says sexual attraction is a vital ingredient long-term. Neither think fun or humour is particularly important.

Hers is the female sign that's most prone to mating for life. He's at average risk of remarriage—although he's also the man who most often stays married for 10 years or more. He does better than her in this category. He's more than twice as happy to stay a bachelor—although both say they're keen to wed. Neither does especially well at marrying the love of their life; she's more likely to be a virgin on the big day. Both usually reckon that lovemaking stays on an even keel after they've got married (although he has more chance than her of finding that it gets even better). He's the most romantic zodiac male of the whole lot—and the one most likely to have affairs! These two get the lowest-of-all sexual boost from exchanging vows with fresh marriage partners.

LEO WOMAN—SCORPIO MAN

Maybe because he's such a capped volcano himself, he needs a calm, soothing, gentle manner from the woman in his life. There's a chance he may find a Leo lady too forceful for him! But she's already set her sights on him—she finds him one of the sexiest starmen—but often she has naughty weekends, not wedding bells, in mind! She doesn't often pick him as a long-term partner. She is, in fact, a bit more of a hit with him (though he doesn't rate her highly for fanciability).

But her legs (often tanned or shown off in soft, sheer stockings), basically warm-hearted nature and faithfulness could easily win him over. And if he's got a fit, slim, well-muscled body, he's got what it takes to turn her head. Both reckon continued sexual attraction's vital long-term—but while she gives loyalty the most marks of all female starsigns, he gives this the lowest male vote. All he asks for is a homelover who's a hot lover in bed, and a load of fun out of it, too.

This pair are the signs who most frequently marry only once in their lives. She has slightly more chance of notching up 10 or more years as a Mrs. And, while he's even keener than her to get fixed up, she's in more of a hurry to marry again. He is luckier than her at ending up with the love of his life; she's slightly more likely to be a virgin when she weds. Scorpio males most often report a gearing-up in their lovelives once they've found a wife—sex for her gets a boost from marriage, too. He, though, can also find that being married wrecks his sexlife (it certainly removes much of the mystery and secrecy he adores). Happily, she's the woman who is least likely to find this happening to her. But he's tops for finding his mate sexier after they've had offspring.

LEO WOMAN—SAGITTARIUS MAN

They wouldn't mind if they saw less of each other—both halves of this couple agree that slimness is really sexy. But, despite a shared taste for the daring and flamboyant—and a flair for self-advertisement—this duo don't automatically make a beeline for one another. She is, indeed, one of his least likely matches and he's not that popular with her, either. They don't find each other terribly fanciable. And although they agree that slenderness is hot, her dream date must be muscular, as well, while he's the man most drawn by faithfulness and a warm smile (provided it's just for him).

She'll be delighted to learn that he's the male sign least likely to stray, though, because long-term she wants more loyalty than most. But she thinks sexual attraction matters more than he does—he's looking for an understanding, kind partner who's also a bit of a gas.

He is the sign with the least flair for making a lasting match—and he's a lot likelier than her to marry more than once. Yet he's also the man most easily disillusioned by the whole institution of marriage, and she's much keener than him both to wed and to remarry. She's more than twice as likely as him to be a virgin for that first stride down the aisle, but he's luckier at getting the love of a lifetime. Not only does she find marriage helps her sexlife, but she also notes a big uplift from remarriage, too. He's the type who'd want to stay calm

383

and work out a solution if their relationship went wrong. But if he strayed, she'd probably take a lover herself—or stay silent and hope it didn't last.

LEO WOMAN—CAPRICORN MAN

She can't help noticing him—usually because he holds a position of some power in the workplace or just has a very coolly commanding manner. Yet he's one of her least popular partnership choices. She is more popular with him—though neither finds the other anything special as regards fanciability. An attractive voice will hold his initial attention, and so will her radiant smile and lovely legs. He is keener than most men on finding a faithful partner. But if these two do make an item, she'll need to extract some strong promises—for he's the man most likely to have affairs!

She fancies slim, muscularly powerful men. She's also the female starsign who most expects loyalty from a mate—in everything, not just sex. Sheer electric physical attraction matters more to her within a relationship. And while he's the man who most values a sense of humour in a partner, she rates having one less than other women.

She's the female sign who usually marries once and for life, and he's likelier than her to go in for a repeat performance. Yet he also has a higher chance than her of staying together as a couple for more than 10 years. First time round, Capricorn's keener than others to get married—but he's also the male sign who's wariest of remarrying. That easily wounded Capricorn pride, again! Neither are especially lucky at netting the love of their life, but she's far likelier than him to wed as a virgin. She finds marriage more of a sex tonic, though he gets more of a thrill from remarriage. If she strayed, he'd want to solve their problems—or go straight for divorce. She might opt to take a lover herself if he was untrue.

LEO WOMAN—AQUARIUS MAN

They'll need to chip away at their diametrically opposite attitudes to life and expand their minds, if their loving relationship is ever to be more than a brief and glorious affair. She names him as her least likely match, but he's keener on her and they find each other at least moderately sexy. She likes her men to look as if they used the gym—trim and strong without being muscle-bound. He, however, fancies something a bit more old-fashioned and less active, a woman who's curvy but not overweight, a good homemaker with a gentle manner. She's only averagely keen on getting herself a good provider.

As a partner, she expects him to be particularly loyal—but, like her, he's fractionally above average for having affairs! He wants more fun out of their life together than she does and gives understanding a higher vote. And while she reckons they'll get nowhere fast without sexual attraction—it's vital to her—he's the male starsign who rates this lowest.

One in 10 Aquarius men still manage to notch up three wives, making him a high remarriage risk. She, on the other hand, is the female sign least likely to wed more than once. But she's keener to marry than him that first time and has slightly more chance of staying in that partnership for a decade or more. She's also likelier, though, to say never again if her marriage fails. He's the man keenest to give it another whirl. She more often gets the love of her life, but neither are very lucky here. And while she's a probable wedding day virgin, he rarely waits! She reckons being married gets her sexlife going better, while he usually reports no change. But both get less of a boost than most from remarriage.

LEO WOMAN—PISCES MAN

It's not exactly lust at first sight but they can find it impossible to forget one another—or to break away, even if they should! He's one of her top-choice partners and she's one of his favourites, too. Yet he reckons she's unsexy and she thinks much the same about him, too, though she's not quite so undiplomatic. Certainly, she likes her men to be slim, yet strong, so there's no scope for Pisces overindulgence here. He wants a superb homemaker—a mixture of his mum, an expensive interior designer and a professional cleaner—who tempts him with her luscious thighs. He also wants a slim body and a sexy laugh.

These two are the zodiac man and woman who rate loyalty in a mate most highly. But while there's a below-average chance he'll have affairs, she's at higher risk than most women! Perhaps because she puts a higher premium than him on sexual attraction in the first place. But he does say he'd like to settle with a woman who's good in bed and who enjoys other kinds of fun, too. She's the star woman who usually weds for life—he's in great danger of remarriage.

There's an even chance for both of staying married for 10 years or more. But, while she's keen on marriage, he needs coaxing. Once bitten, twice as keen, though—he's the man who most wants to remarry. And he's the luckiest sign in marrying the love of his life— far more fortunate than her. Both are likelier than most to stay virgins until the honeymoon. He finds marriage, and its repeat, invigorates his sexlife more than she does. And both are the signs least likely to say that it's actually got worse.

LEO WOMAN—ARIES MAN

He's definitely her type if he is youthfully slim and athletically muscular, sporty and fit-looking. Indeed, they find one another quite sexy—especially if she's curvy, has unusually good eyes and gives him a smiling come-hither. There's a close-to-average chance they'll end up partners. But while she has only an average interest in hooking herself a good provider, he's the zodiac man who's keenest to find a good homemaker to look after him. She might want less traditional roles with more sharing. She's the sign who most expects partner loyalty, while he values this a bit less and is in the middle of the affairs-risk range. But both are united in believing that sexual attraction really matters—he gives it the top male vote. He also rates a home-lover who's good-looking enough to eat, by the way.

He's at average risk of multiple marriage, while she's the female sign who most often weds only once. Neither are keen to stay single, but she has slightly more chance than him of clocking up 10 happy years or more. He's luckier than most—certainly luckier than her—at wedding the love of his life, but she's a little more likely to stay a virgin until her wedding day. She reports a bigger boost to loving from marriage; remarriage does the trick for him. If either were to wander, the injured party might well take a lover in both cases. But there's also a chance that she might say nothing if he were untrue and just wait for his fling to founder.

LEO WOMAN—TAURUS MAN

Luxury turns them both on, though he has more idea of how to make the money to fund the lifestyle they both love. Little wonder that he's one of her favourite partners (even though she won't admit to setting much store in landing a good provider). She finds him very sexy, too. There's a middling chance he might pick her to live with, happily ever after, though he says he doesn't find her particularly sexy. He'll have to watch his weight if he's to fit her fantasy of a slim, well-tuned man and he'll need to brush up on his loyalty factor—she's the female sign who values this most. Meantime, he gives the biggest male vote to her glittering smile and really appreciates her generous, cosseting nature. He also rates a good homemaker more than most men and is the male sign who's keenest on kindness. Sexual attraction matters more to her, while he's one of the few male signs who rates a hard-working woman.

Both are among those who marry least often—but he's likelier than her to wed more than once, and she has more chance of making it past the magic 10-year-stint. He's both happier than her to remain unattached and also keener to remarry. And he's far more likely to get the love of a lifetime. Both may well be virgins when they wed. She finds marriage gives her more of a new sexual lease of life—he's likelier to report a decline in performance standards! If he wanders, she'll either simply turn a blind eye—or take a lover herself. If she strays he'd be keener than most men to thrash out problems.

LEO WOMAN—GEMINI MAN

She says loyalty's vital—he reckons it matters not at all. She rates kindness and he's the man who appreciates this least of all the male starsigns. They might be speaking different languages when each draws up their "I-Want" list, but there's no reason to call the whole thing off. On the plus side, she finds him moderately fanciable. She's a more popular choice with him—but he still doesn't vote her awfully sexy. But apart from his sparkling, dangerously adept flirtiness, he'll get her vote if he's slender, yet strongly built. And he won't be able to turn his back on her if she has good legs, a slim body and a sexy laugh. A gentle manner and interests in common would please him even more. Both believe that sexual attraction really matters. And while he wants his woman to shine in the dark when she displays all her sexual skills, he'd also like her to look nice, enjoy homemaking and be fun to have around.

While her sign's the one that most often marries for life, he chops and changes more often. But he has more chance than her of making a live-in relationship last over 10 years. One in four Gemini men say they're happier staying single—she's much keener to wed (and to marry again). Would you believe it—he's the male starsign who's most likely to be a virgin when he marries. She may be, too. But neither are lucky when it comes to settling down with the love of their life. Marriage improves both their sexlives—and they are among those least likely to report that it's got worse.

LEO WOMAN—CANCER MAN

He's often shy. She can be rather brash. But once she's winkled him out of his shell, there's a fair chance that she'll choose him to escort her on life's journey. She is his most popular partner and he finds her fairly sexy, too. She says he's unexciting in bed—but patience was never her strong point. She fancies men who don't have a spare ounce of body fat and who look powerful enough to effortlessly whisk her off her feet. He'll fulfil all her loyalty demands. He's attracted primarily by unforgettable eyes and sexy laughter, and he gives top male ratings to a good homemaker. But while he may want a little wifey, she's not fussed about finding a club-wielding hunter/gatherer type and may prefer less traditional, shared domestic roles.

He rates a kind nature and gentle manner more than most, too, and she's not particularly attracted by kindness. But both agree on the importance of loyalty. Sexual attraction matters to her—and isn't vital to him.

She's unlikely to marry more than once—and he's the highest remarriage risk in the zodiac. Yet they both have an even chance of making lasting matches. He's more enthusiastic than her about being single, though he's also less easily put off marrying again than other signs. Both are more likely than average to be virgins on marrying. She reports a sexlife lift from being a Mrs; he reckons it often gets worse (unless it's a remarriage, in which case it's better for him than for her). He's more faithful than most partners, while she's at average risk of going off the marital rails. They would both react to the other's affair with the same tactics. They'd either say nothing and hope it fizzled, or take a revenge lover of their own!

LEO WOMAN—LEO MAN

They probably first met when they accidentally cracked heads while darting to grab the microphone on talent night, but from the first, they vote each other among the sexiest signs. And it's on the cards that their relationship will be a long-term goer. She can't keep her hands off his taut, athletically strong body, while he's the man who gets the biggest kick from looking deeply into her eyes. Her smile—the one that's designed to reach the back of the stadium—can't help but make him take notice, either. He's turned on by a curvy body, wicked laugh and hosiery ad legs. But while she's the female who gives strongest backing to loyalty in a partner, he appreciates understanding far more and gives loyalty the lowest male vote. He also has a stronger need than she has for a sense of humour in a love relationship—she values this less than other women, in fact. Both set great store by powerful sexual attraction, though looks and Kama Sutra skills matter quite a bit to him, hardly at all to her.

They have widely differing experiences of marriage. He's among the men likeliest to wed more than once, she often makes a lifelong commitment. Despite this, she only does slightly better than him at nurturing her partnership for 10 years or more. He is three times keener than her to stay single—yet he's more blessed when it comes to getting the love of his life. He finds wedlock an even bigger sexual star prize than she does—and reckons remarriage is even sexier, getting the top male score for this. She's more than twice as likely to be a virgin on the wedding day. Each favours a different tactic for a marriage soured by infidelity. He would probably ask for a divorce if she strayed, she might say nothing or take a lover of her own if he was at fault.

THE VIRGO MAN'S LOVEMATCHES

VIRGO MAN—LIBRA WOMAN

She's full of admiration at the way he organises his life, and loves the way he can get inside her head. But secretly, she wishes he was more exciting, more spontaneous. She votes him the least sexy sign—and for his part, he doesn't think she's all that fanciable, either. Yet there is a running chance they will be star partners and their shared sense of humour goes a long way to smoothing the rough edges of their relationship. He's bound to be smitten by her slender, yet shapely figure (always so instinctively well-dressed).

He tends to like women like her, with attractive voices and gentle manners too, though Libra's maverick attitude to time-keeping will madden him. She goes for his knowing smile and intelligent conversation and both value, and expect, loyalty and kindness. But he's the more physical of the two (even though he may suppress it), giving higher marks to good looks, sex skills and physical attraction.

He's the sign most likely to complain that sex is less exciting after marriage (though it could be the fault of his near-obsession with work) while she finds more of a sex upsurge. Both are low-risk remarriers—and both get less of a sex boost from it, too. She's more likely to notch up 10 years of wedded bliss. He's more than doubly happy staying single, while she's keener both on marriage and remarriage. While she's luckier at settling with a lifelove, he's the more probable virgin on their wedding night. Although, despite her histrionics, he's the more emotional of the pair, if she strayed he'd be keener than most to try to work problems out. Other way round, she'd probably take a lover herself.

VIRGO MAN—SCORPIO WOMAN

Her rich, secret sensuality will act as a scorching catalyst to his warm sexuality, although neither finds the other earth-shatteringly attractive to start with. There is, despite this, a fair chance they could be partners. His ideal's got curves and a small waist, her voice purrs and she has the gentle manner of a geisha. Scorpio can play whatever role she chooses and enjoys masking her passionate nature! She's attracted to musclemen and rates a good provider—which he probably is. However, he's not keen on a homemaker, so may prefer her to be a joint breadwinner. Long-term, each wants a mate they can share a few jokes with.

Sexual attraction matters to both (she gives it the top female vote). But while she comes down heavily on the side of male loyalty, he'd rather have understanding.

Marriage risk levels? He's low on the register, she's second from top! But she's more likely to stay happily hitched for 10-plus years, and she is keener to wed. She is, however, more easily put off remarriage (though obviously not terminally). Both are likelier than average to be virgins and both have an even chance of marrying the loves of their lives. She finds marriage more of a sexlife-enhancer though. In fact, he's second lowest on our list and is also the male sign most likely to find this side of his marriage gets worse in time! He doesn't get much of a buzz from second or subsequent marriages, either. If an affair cropped up, both are more eager than most to calmly discuss the problems and try to talk them through. However, he could simply say nothing and cross his fingers, hoping against hope that her fling didn't last.

VIRGO MAN—SAGITTARIUS WOMAN

He looks too straight-faced for her to be attracted—at first. But she appeals to him very strongly, though, and he makes her one of his most popular partner choices. He thinks she's averagely sexy, too. She's likely to have the slim, yet extremely feminine form he goes for and a clear, attractive voice. She may have to work on the gentle manner he likes, though. She's more on the lookout than most signs for knock-you-out eyes and likes slim, tall, talkative—and kind—men.

Both want kindness and understanding from their life partner. But she rates a hard-working homelover more than most (which is a trifle hypocritical, given the amount of time she goes out herself!) He opts more for loyalty, generosity of spirit—and bags of sexiness! He's at low-risk of remarriage, she's an average rewedder. But he has slightly more chance of forming a bond that endures more than 10 years.

She's one of the most fancy-free females, but even she's not quite as keen as he is to stay single! He gets hitched to the love of his life in more instances. Both have a nearly average chance of being wedding day newcomers to sex. On the topic of sex, she's more likely than him to find that marriage gives it added zest. He's the man who most often says it's got worse! Her twinkling eyes and cheeky laugh may suggest otherwise, but statistically she's the zodiac's most faithful woman. He has an average chance of having affairs. If either's morals lapsed, both would want to know why— and put their relationship right.

VIRGO MAN—CAPRICORN WOMAN

There's a strong likelihood that this successful pair-up began with a work connection. But though it's a strong contender for a golden wedding celebration to come, this couple will have to beaver away to bring out the magic. He puts her name down as a favourite partner, and gives her a rather fanciable vote, too. She finds his a very sexy sign and there's an average chance she'll stand by him, once the first flush of attraction's worn off. She dreams of finding a tall, muscular man with a sit-up-and-notice voice and smile. She wants her mate to be faithful and kind and confident.

More than most males, he goes for curves (no podginess, though— he's too health-conscious for that). He appreciates Capricorn all the more if she's well-spoken and has a soothing manner. He's not that keen on a good homemaker, though, so if she's a would-be powerful career woman, so much the better. She gives top marks to a good provider, so he'll have to level-peg with her, workwise. Both want a loyal partner who shares their sense of humour. But sexual attraction is more of an issue for him than for her.

They're both less likely than average to remarry and have an even chance of staying married for 10 years or more. But he'd make the happier bachelor, and is less keen to remarry, too. Both may well end up with a Great Love, but he'll be the likelier virgin when they do. Marriage isn't guaranteed to help either's sexlife, though. She says it often stays the same. He's the man most likely to find it getting worse. She'd be much faster than most women to want a divorce if he admitted being unfaithful. If she was untrue, he'd want to smooth things over and start their love lives afresh.

VIRGO MAN—AQUARIUS WOMAN

He's nervous of her unusual way of thinking—and she doesn't always appreciate his pragmatic approach to life, either. But it can work. So what, if they're each other's least popular partners and neither finds the other especially sexy? How many unlikely long-term couples do you know? Feminine curves, soft voice and easy, unobtrusive manner will score a hit with him. And although she's quirkily hard to please, deepset, intelligent eyes, smart clothing and an attractive male voice will win her over. Long-term, she's the female starsign who most values a partner who really understands how she thinks. He gives this quality low marks, though, and votes instead for sexual attraction! But both like humour, appreciate good looks generally and—unlike most of their compatriot signs—go for a hard worker!

Lasting matches aren't a strongpoint for either, though he's less likely than her to go in for wiping the slate clean and starting anew with another partner. She is even less likely than him to nudge a relationship through the 10-year hoop. If she's a typical Aquarius woman, she'll be in more of a hurry than him both to get hitched, and to wed again.

He's luckier at getting the love of his life to marry him, though.

He's the more likely virgin—she's the zodiac's least sexually patient woman! But these signs are more likely than the others to report a worsening in their love relationship within marriage. There's an average chance of either of them having extramarital affairs. But both share a mission to find out why it happened and to solve problems so that their partner isn't tempted to stray again.

VIRGO MAN—PISCES WOMAN

Full marks for the physical side of their relationship—a feast that never stales. But they'll flummox each other emotionally, unless they're prepared to learn from one another. It's on the cards they'll end up together—the chances are average—but they wouldn't vote each other's sign as sexy. He'll get his womanly dream-come-true with her, though, for he loves neat curves, a musical voice with a nice tone and timbre, and a manner that's gentle as silk in the breeze. That's Pisces woman—until her next emotional crisis, anyway! And if she lets her figure bulge, he may go off her in a big way. She's smitten by a trim physique (like most Virgo men have) and a super smilability. They'll both be on the lookout for kindness, plus a sense of humour. He gives sexual attraction a bumper crop of votes, though, while she will want him to be an impossibly good mindreader!

There's a high chance she'll marry more than once in her life, but he's at low risk of having to start again. Neither get high marks for making bonds that last over 10 years, though. He couldn't fail to be happier than her to stay single—after all, she's the zodiac woman who hates this state the most! Despite her keenness on the idea of marriage, she's less prone than him to hook the love of a lifetime. She's a more likely wedding night virgin, however, and once she gets into the swing of it, she'll find marriage can do wonders for her sexlife! He's the husband, alas, who least often reports any improvement. In fact, he's likelier than most to say sex has got worse. He's the man who says nothing and hopes the problem goes away if his wife's unfaithful! Or he'd ask why and try to sort things out. If she were wronged, she'd take a revenge lover.

VIRGO MAN—ARIES WOMAN

One hot blast of her fiery temper could blow this relationship out! He'll never understand her seeming inability to handle life's stresses without short-circuiting—she'll wonder if he hails from planet Earth, he's always so controlled and cool. But even though it doesn't look that promising on paper—what with her lukewarm physical response to him and the fact he either finds her quite sexy or doesn't fancy her at all—there's still an average chance they'll get together. And stay together, despite their chalk-and-cheese clashes. Partly because he's more susceptible to sporty, yet curvy, female bodies like hers than he dares admit. He'll like her even more if she has an attractive voice (provided she turns the volume down a bit) but she might as well forget trying to ape the gentle manner he usually admires in a woman.

She'd like to put a bit more iron in his soul—but if she tries to push this subtly strongwilled man around, she'll find out how tough-minded he can be. She'll fall instantly for him, though, if he's muscly, tall, has vivid eyes—and is kind and faithful.

She's the sign who's keenest on kindness—he gives it only near-average marks. And she values homelovers more than most while he's not very keen on good homemakers. He rates loyalty, humour and sexual attraction highly instead.

This is the zodiac woman most likely to marry more than once—he's only at low risk. Although he's keener than her to stay single, he stands more chance of making his love last when he does commit himself and he's luckier at picking the love of his life, too. There's more chance she'll be a virgin when she weds and she finds marriage a sexlife highlighter. Yet both say loving can get worse (especially him!). She's quick to ask for divorce if cheated on. He'd say nothing or try to work problems out.

VIRGO MAN—TAURUS WOMAN

She gives the importance of sexual attraction in a relationship the lowest possible female vote in our survey. Which is just as well, for she may not be offended by his failure to pick her out as a potentially sexy starmatch—though she says she finds him moderately stimulating! There's only an average chance of them ending up together. And, with her expecting kindness, understanding and fun, while he's wanting humour and loyalty, they look pretty compatible. He goes notoriously weak at the knees at the sight of slender, yet shapely female flesh—and appreciates the gentle manner and strikingly attractive voice so many Taurus women possess. She'll be looking out for his ready smile and will be even more smitten if he turns out to be a good provider, who's confident and faithful.

He hasn't listed among his key desirabilities being a good homemaker, so may not fully appreciate her Taurus skills. He'd prefer a hard grafter to share the workload with. She quite likes her man to be a homelover. Sexual attraction matters more to him.

They're both low remarriage risks and have an even chance of staying wed more than 10 years. He's more than content to stay single than she is, but also keener to remarry (she's one of the least willing to try again). Taurus women are the ones who can most confidently expect to land their lifelove. He saves himself for marriage more often than she does, yet more frequently reports a downturn in sexual interest once the knot's tied. She gets a bigger sex boost from marriage than other signs. Usually, they'll want to work out infidelity problems—though he might stay quiet.

VIRGO MAN—GEMINI WOMAN

Mere mention of this mercurial female can set his heart racing with desire—or, on a bad day, it can leave him stone-cold. It rather depends if she's turning her nuclear reactor flirtation process onto him or a roomful of others! She only admits to finding him Mr Average, sexiness-wise. Yet, when the gloves are off, and probably the light as well, they name each other best partners. A girlish, yet well filled-out body, clear-as-a-bell voice and ungrating manner get top male vote from Virgo. She finds him totally irresistible when he puts his poshest clothes on—and she loves his sophisticated banter.

In the longer term, she'll need her man to grasp the butterfly logic of her speeding brain—and he gives this quality lowest male votes. Kindness gets higher ratings from her, too, while he appreciates sense of humour and sexual attraction far more.

Neither are high remarriage risks, though he's less likely than her to wed more than once. Yet both score low on the ten-years-plus scale and she does worse than him. She's the woman who most wants to hang onto her freedom! He's keener still! Once he does take the plunge, however, he's more likely to wed the love of his life and to be a virgin. She finds marriage does more for her sexlife—though both score highly for thinking it worsens it, too! If one strayed, the other would probably stay—asking why and attempting a make-up and makeover job on their relationship. He's the type who may just decide to keep his trap shut, and wait the storm out.

VIRGO MAN—CANCER WOMAN

He won't find a much milder-mannered, or more gently caring woman than her and women born under this starsign usually have siren voices (another bonus for him), too. They're both rather shy—and name each other as unlikely partners—with only average lustful stirrings on both sides! To make him notice her, she'll do best if she has a luscious, but never overweight, body.

She'll try to overcome her inhibitions if she spots that he has gorgeous eyes and dresses smartly. For long-term love, she wants to be shown plenty of kindness (of the kind she lavishes on others habitually) as well as understanding. He says shared humour and sexual attraction are the most important ingredients. But while she would rather have fun in the privacy of her own abode with another homeloving type, Virgo prefers the perks of a nice-looking partner who is good in bed!

He's a lower remarriage risk than her, but she's got more chance of passing the 10-year boundary. He actually scores second lowest among all male signs on this. She's keener on marriage (and luckier at getting the love of a lifetime). He's happy to stay single. She's the more probable wedding day virgin of the two. But neither report the earth moving more often once they're wed. He can even find sex gets worse. She's one of the least likely female signs to go in for an affair, while he's at average risk. If she turned her great moony eyes on another man, he'd either stay quiet and hope for the best, or try and work things out. She may well be first off the starting blocks and ask for divorce if he played the same trick on her.

VIRGO MAN—LEO WOMAN

Loyalty is the cement that bonds this duo—they both value this quality very highly in a partner. But their signblend relationship isn't common. He finds her very sexually alluring, but she doesn't really fancy him. And the chances of it going on from there aren't that high. Her sexy, stripper's body turns him on in a big way, though, and he also goes for an attractive voice and gentle manner— well, she can be quietly sophisticated if somewhat more tigerish than he's used to! She's the sign who most appreciates a trim male physique—and she likes a few glistening muscles, too! Both say sexual attraction is the be-all-and-end-all of any liaison. But he's keener than her on a long-term fun-lover with a sense of humour— and he also rates sex skills and good looks more than Leo does.

  She's less likely than most other women to marry more than once and he's another low risk. She's keener to wed and has more chance of taking her relationship beyond 10 years. But he's luckier at settling with his big all-time romance. She's likelier to be a virgin when they both walk down the aisle and generally goes on to find that sex improves once the ring's on her finger. He reports less of a perk-up than most! And while she's the female sign who's least likely to reckon that sex has worsened, he's the man who most often admits to a wilting of interest. Proud Leo might take a revenge lover prontissimo if she caught her man with his pants down. He'd want to know how he'd failed if she was untrue and logically try to tackle problems one by one.

VIRGO MAN—VIRGO WOMAN

She can set impossible high standards for sexual partners. Which is probably why she doesn't especially fancy her male zodiac matching number and reckons there's only an average chance she'd give him the winning partnership ticket. Conversely, he votes her quite a popular choice of partner and one of the sexiest signs. He's more upfront about his longings and more easily pleased—especially by her feminine lumps and bumps and slender waistline. He adores her melodious speaking voice and markedly gentle manner (nagging's 100% out). These qualities get top male vote from him. She looks deep into his psyche for faithfulness, then checks him out for reasonable height, slimness and muscular build!

Both ask Santa for loyal partners. But, while he appreciates a sense of humour and needs primal sexual attraction to fuel his relationship, she wants sheer fun.

She's the woman most likely of all signs to marry over again. He's at low risk. Both have an even chance of making a lasting match, but he may be twice as enthusiastic a bachelor. He's far happier to hear those wedding bells ring second time around, while she is the female sign most easily deterred form second marriage. She's slightly luckier than him at hand-picking the love of a lifetime, a likelier virgin and likely to think sex gets better after marriage. He's the man who most often moans that his physical relationship has got worse. Both tend to be faithful—her especially—but she's be faster than most to seek divorce if he erred. He'd want to know why, if she deceived him, and want to work things out.

THE VIRGO WOMAN'S LOVEMATCHES

VIRGO WOMAN—LIBRA MAN

There are no guarantees with Mr Libra. She may say he's her favourite partner (and he charms most women sooner or later) but he is one of the most likely men to stray! She doesn't find him sexy to start with, but this doesn't mean she won't succumb eventually.

Normally, she likes her men tall, muscular and slim—and above all, faithful. Reforming him could be a lifetime's mission. He's not that keen on her, initially, and doesn't fancy her much. But he could do—especially if she has a slightly topheavy body, a nice voice and a kind manner. He, too, wants a faithful partner (regardless of his own weaknesses) but Virgo's gentle manner won't win any prizes from him. He wants an understanding homeloving type, while she rates a hardworker (preferably loaded with cash) who's fun. Both expect loyalty.

Surprisingly, he's the male sign most likely to pass marriage's 10-year test, while she's the woman with the highest chance of marrying more than once. Being so fastidious, she's more wary than him of giving wedlock a second go. He wouldn't mind being single. She's the more probable bridal virgin and is luckier than him at getting hitched to her true love. Neither find marriage improves sex (he's more likely to find it stays much the same as before). She'll keep an eagle eye on him, but if he does step out of line and has an affair, she's faster than most women to ask for a divorce. He'd give her a spoonful of her own medicine if she wandered, and might take a lover himself.

VIRGO WOMAN—SCORPIO MAN

Physically, this can be a wonderful match and he needs no convincing of its physical potential. He picks her instantly as one of his most popular partners and isn't ambiguous about how much he fancies her. She's slightly more cautious—making him one of her middling choices both as a life partner and a sexmate. She generally likes her men to be taller and slimmer perhaps than Mr Scorpio (and she's not sure about his hairiness!). But she'll appreciate his muscularity. Another factor she's desperately seeking in a partner is faithfulness, so she'll need strong promises from him because he's likelier than many signs to falter. He gives her gentle manner top marks and wants her to make the best of her lovely legs—he loves split-side skirts. He appreciates her kind, faithful nature because he can't handle his own jealousy. Long-term, she looks for loyalty—he rates this less than other men. Both like a fun partner.

But while he reckons sex appeal's vital, humour and money matter to her. Each has a totally different marital profile. He's more likely than other male signs to mate for life, while she runs the highest risk of several marriages. But despite his approach, he's only slightly likelier than her to celebrate 10 years of wedded bliss with the same person! He's very passionate and is one of the keenest men to marry. She's more prone to ending up with the love of her life, and the more likely virgin of this couple. But even if she does have something to compare it with, she's none too sure that marriage improves her sexlife. He's the man who most often reports an improvement. Remarriage does more for her. He's keener than most to work out infidelity problems—she's quick to seek divorce if he wanders from her side.

VIRGO WOMAN—SAGITTARIUS MAN

He might wish she'd loosen up a bit and she might pray for him to grow more thoughtful. But they'll certainly both be relieved to learn that both these signs are the least likely to stray from a long-term relationship. He names her as one of his best partners (though he only gives her average sex appeal grades). She doesn't (theoretically) fancy him particularly and notes him down as one of her least likely matches. But he is more enthusiastic than most about her shyly encouraging smile.

Long-term, he craves lots of kindness and masses of understanding and wouldn't say no to a generous serving of humour. She rates having fun with a partner, too, and also rates loyalty more than most. But even more than the sound of shared laughter, she'd like to hear the sound of moneybags jangling!

He's an above-average remarriage risk and she's the female most likely to marry more than once in her endless quest for partnership perfection. She does have a better record than him at staying together for 10-plus years—he's the sign who manages this least often! She's keener to wed first time, but both signs are soundly put off remarriage. She more often picks the love of her life and is much likelier to keep herself for that special partner. There's a 50-50 chance they'll both report an upturn in their marital sex satisfaction graph—but nothing to go crazy about! If she did stray, he'd want to take the Lets Be Grown-up and Reasonable line and try to sit down and work things out. She, however, would rush to phone her solicitor to set a divorce in motion, if he ever wandered.

VIRGO WOMAN—CAPRICORN MAN

She'll have to get this walking success story with the guaranteed sex appeal to sign on the dotted line before setting up home with him because he's the male sign most likely to stray—and she needs her man to be faithful! She doesn't, in fact, particularly fancy him when faced with the entire zodiac to choose from and isn't quick off the mark to pick him out as lifepartner potential. He names her as a popular partner, though, and says she's averagely sexy.

She awards ticks to men who are of above-average height with slim, yet strong, well-muscled torsos. She also gives high ratings to men who are loyal and loads of fun. He goes for a melting smile, an attractive voice, wonderful legs and a gently supportive manner. Virgo's faithfulness appeals to him—he likes his life free of clutter and niggling worry—and he'd love it if they shared interests. He also values humour, sexual attraction and good looks in his spouse.

She is an average risk for marrying more than once—a less likely scenario for him—and he has more chance of notching up 10 years or more of wedded bliss. He's keener than her—and other men—to marry, but both are the signs who are wary of doing it a second time.

He's rather unlucky and rarely gets the love of his life (being too sensible to wed on rash impulse) while she does better here. She is more than three times likelier than him to be a wedding night virgin. Marriage gives more of a zip to her sexlife, though both score below average on this. But when it comes to remarriage, he gets more boost than she does. And if affairs ever divided them, neither would wait long before demanding a divorce!

VIRGO WOMAN—AQUARIUS MAN

He names her as quite a popular lifepartner, yet also votes her unsexy. Why? Because she asks him too many times if he loves her or not. All part of Virgo's need for constant reassurance. He's not exactly a Don Juan, but he does have a huge number of cronies and can't understand why she can't get more emotional nourishment outside her Big Relationship.

She files him as the male sign she's least likely to fancy. Yet there's an average chance she'll stay with him (constantly trying to reorganise him). Plus points in her eyes are height, trimness and supreme physical fitness, the kind that goes with rippling, glistening muscle power.

Her man must cross his heart to be faithful, too. He's attracted to her slim, shapely body and feels at ease with her gentle manner. But while independent Virgo least rates a good provider (though she likes money) she might want to be more of an equal, breadwinning partner than the great homemaker he needs.

Both demand loyalty and don't particularly value kindness. But where he gives understanding top ratings, she gives it the lowest female vote. Remarriage looms large in her future—but he's the man most likely to chalk up three wives! Somehow, he combines this with a good chance of managing 10 years of happy marriage with the same woman! So he can't waste much time in between. She's the woman most prone to call time on matrimony after one failure. He's one of the keenest to try again. She is luckier at settling with the love of her life—and more than six times likelier than experimental Aquarius to be a wedding virgin. She also finds marriage more of a libido massager—but neither of them score highly. He's likelier than most to find lovemaking stays the same.

VIRGO WOMAN—PISCES MAN

She's shot through with puritan work ethic, he's a man who likes to wait for the moment of inspiration! Yet he's more popular a partner with her than she is with him (she loves a cause to get her teeth into and few men look so much as if they need looking after as Pisces). He does think she's quite sexy, though. She names him as least sexy sign (he may not be tall enough for her tastes). He's often the faithful type, though, which does appeal to her—even though it's not a quality he rates himself in a partner.

Instead, he wants a slim and shapely body to hug, a sexy laugh and a gentle, unthreatening manner. He'd like to find himself a good homemaker to plump the cushions under his feet, but she gives a good provider one of the lowest votes. She may want shared roles. Both rate loyalty very highly and think fun's important, too, But while he hopes for skill in bed, she has her mind on how hard he works and the chink of plentiful loose change! At least she's partial to chipping in with the earnings.

This is the starwoman most likely to wed more than once. But he runs an even higher risk of remarriage than her! Despite this, he does have a better stay-together record for 10 years-plus, though. Both are highly likely virgins when they marry. She's in more of a dash to get to the altar than he is, though warier of remarriage. He gets luckier than her when it comes to monitoring the improvement of post-marital sexlives and more often reports an enhancement. They are both, as a rule, faithful to their partner. But they are also far speedier than most signs to ask for a divorce if they catch their other half straying.

VIRGO WOMAN—ARIES MAN

He'd really like her to stay home and look after him—he's the sign who most markedly rates a good homemaker—but she usually has other ideas. Anyway, she's the woman who values getting a man to do all the earning least! Chances are she'll want her own bank account, even though she's on the lookout for a hard worker with hard cash in his pocket. Still, housewife or career woman, he names her among his most popular partners and finds her sexy, too. She doesn't often fancy his sign, though, and nominates him The Man Most Unlikely to share her life. She likes tall, slim, muscular males. Long-term, she rates loyalty highly (instead, he gives top marks to sexual attraction). And she also demands faithfulness—and he's not as true as some—while he wants a good-looking home-loving lover.

This is the woman who's most likely to wed more than once. He's more hope of staying with the same partner for ten years or more. He's also keener on getting hitched (first time)—both are wary of marrying again. She is the zodiac's most patient woman and certainly more often makes it to her wedding day, still a virgin. He, though, is likelier to get the love of his life over the threshold. Once married, she finds more improvement in her sexlife than he does— he reports a bigger bonanza after a remarriage. He's the sort who'd take a lover himself if Virgo cast her net adulterously wide. If he strayed, she'd either play dumb and hope for the best, or ask for a divorce.

VIRGO WOMAN—TAURUS MAN

She'll find him mentally relaxing—and knows he'll always be there for her. Both put a strong emphasis on faithfulness. Physically, he finds her one of the sexiest signs around and it's pretty probable he'll pick her out as his partner. He really goes for her kind nature and slowburn smile and likes her other chief attributes; the model's body, attractive voice and mild, subtle manner. She's far more initially reserved with him, though, saying he's an unlikely choice for her and that she doesn't find him very fanciable. Generally, the slimmer he is, the more chance he'll stand with her.

They do have differing ideas about setting up home together. For while she's the sign who gives getting a good provider the lowest marks, he's very keen on finding a woman who is a good home-maker. She gives a big thumbs up to long-term fun with a partner, while he's the man who values this quality least. For the long haul, he wants kindness and understanding. She'd opt for loyalty and humour.

She's top of the list of multiple marriers while he runs the second lowest risk of all men. He's also far more prone than her sign to staying together with someone for 10-plus years. He's also keener to give the marital merryground a second go. He's luckier at wedding a lifetime's love, she's the more likely virgin and they both have an even chance of finding more sexual thrills within marriage than outside. She gets a bigger love boost than he does, though, from remarriage. Well, he's weaker than her when it comes to the temptation of an affair. And if he succumbs, she'll be fast to seek divorce. But if she strayed, he'd want to talk and try to solve problems logically and amicably.

VIRGO WOMAN—GEMINI MAN

She'll toss and turn and fret about this man's sexual loyalty and find it hard to see his flirting as the front it is—yet she often picks him as her favourite partner. And he returns the compliment. They both find each other sexy, too. As it turns out, they are also the signs who most appreciate a faithful partner! Good job both are among those signs least likely to stray, too. He's keener than most on her great legs, her softly provocative laugh, quietly capable manner and her slim, fit body.

He also appreciates her kindness, once it's allowed to peek past her critical veneer. Shared interests also get a top vote from him. For her part, she'll want an long-term lover to be loyal and to have a ready laugh. Being practical, too, she'd also like him to work hard (and play hard) and to have stacks of cash. Both this pair rate fun more than average, but he also values understanding and sexual attraction. He is the sign who most wants a partner who's a home lover.

She has the highest chance of all women of marrying more than once, while he does better at forming a long-lasting relationship. But while she always wants to find a husband, he's very keen to hang onto his freedom for as long as possible. Yet she is also likelier to say never again to marriage—he's less wary of getting his fingers burnt by matrimony. His luck's better when it comes to marrying the love of his life. Both may well be wedding virgins—they're the innocents of the zodiac. He's rather more prone to getting a sex boost from marriage. Both are less likely than most to stray, but quick to demand divorce if their partner does have an affair.

VIRGO WOMAN—CANCER MAN

Deep partner loyalty is what each member of this team wants, which is a good start. She says he is her favourite partner for life and she finds him far and away the sexiest sign, too. But he's not so keen on her sign and doesn't especially fancy her. She wants her men tall, strongly muscled and not an ounce overweight—like a men's singles tennis champ. He'll also need to be the faithful type—so Virgo will be pleased to note that this man is less likely than most to wander out of his marriage. He is usually smitten by nice eyes, a sexy laugh, mellow manner and a kind, thoughtful nature.

But while he gives a good homemaker top male vote (he wouldn't want her to do it all, merely to keep him company with the DIY), she is the female who least rates a sound provider. She may well prefer a cooperative, equal, working marriage. And whereas she wants fun, humour and a hard worker with money in his account, he just wants to be understood!

Both are likelier than others to marry more than once. He's better at making a lasting match and is also the man most willing to try wedlock again. She's the woman who's wariest of remarriage. Each has an average Great Love marriage chance and both are likely virgins. Marriage may be more of a sex tonic for her, while he reckons loving can actually go off the boil. Like him, she tends to be faithful but if she ever did wander, he may go all quiet and hope it didn't last. If he were untrue, she'd pitch in right away and demand a divorce.

VIRGO WOMAN—LEO MAN

She wants her partner to be perfect. He often thinks he is! Perhaps he manages to convince her, because not only do they name each other as among their partnership favourites, but she fancies him rotten! He does not, it must be added, put her in the immediately fanciable category but he does appreciate nice eyes more than other signs do. He also adores a body that curves and sways, shapely legs—the longer the better—and a sexy laugh like hers.

She'll fall extra heavily for him if this Leo is tall, slim and muscular. He'll need to be faithful, too, and despite his legendary vanity, there's an average chance he will be. In her partner, she wants loyalty—while he needs understanding.

Humour rates highly on both their desirable qualities lists. But he's twice as keen as her on getting someone for whom he feels deep, undying sexual attraction. He also nominates sex skills and good looks. So-practical Virgo isn't such a slave to her hormones. She wants a cash-heavy hard worker.

These two signs stand a high chance of marrying more than once (her especially). He's slightly likelier to notch up 10 happy years together, but both are only in the middle success range. Yet, he's three times keener to stay single—making him the man who most wants to keep his freedom! But both can be wary of remarriage, particularly Virgo. They're moderately lucky at getting together with the big love of their lives. She's more than twice as likely as him to wed as a virgin. He gets more of a sexual buzz from marriage—and the biggest boost of all from remarriage. But if either is unfaithful, the other will zip along to divorce lawyers immediately.

VIRGO WOMAN—VIRGO MAN

There's an average chance that these two will end up together in life, although he fancies bedding a same-sign lover more than she does. She doesn't find him that fanciable, whereas he names her as one of the sexiest starsigns. That's because of her legs, her nice eyes and her wicked laugh. He actually gives the highest male vote of all to her body—both shapely and slim—her pleasant vocal tones and her unfailingly gentle manner.

He is in the middle range for male straying—and she wants a partner who's faithful. Her other targets in an ideal man are commanding height, slimness and some good muscles. They both expect loyalty. But he rates sexual attraction more than she does. She gives top female marks to having fun together. She's also set on meeting a man with money, who doesn't mind hard work.

Virgo is the woman most prone to ordering more than one wedding cake—he's at low risk of remarriage. Yet both have an even chance of staying married for 10 years or more. When it comes to leaving the single life behind, he's twice as chary as her! And she's twice as likely as him to avoid remarriage altogether. Her luck's slightly stronger in marrying the love of her life and she's more chance of being a wedding night virgin. Both fail to find much sexlife boost from wedlock and he's the male sign who most often reports a worsening! If she ever wandered, he'd either want to mend their relationship or he'd stay silent and hope her affair ended. She is likelier than most to demand a divorce if her husband was untrue.

THE LIBRA MAN'S LOVEMATCHES

LIBRA MAN—SCORPIO WOMAN

He names her as a favourite partner and finds her fairly tasty, too. She says he's very sexy, but just a so-so choice. He's smitten by her curvy body, kind nature and attractive voice. Her strong-minded personality suits him well, too— he's the man who least rates a meek manner. She loves his gorgeous eyes and if he's tall and muscular, with a good voice, she's very taken. But while she gives a good provider the top female marks, he's not so interested in finding a good homemaker, so may prefer shared roles. Long-term, he asks for loyalty—she needs kindness. Both value fun and sexual attraction and adore each other's adventurous, intuitive approach to loving. But she wants a mate with a sense of humour, while he prefers a good-looking homelover.

She is at higher risk of marrying more than once—he's the man who most often makes a long-lasting match. She's keener to get hitched, but more easily put off giving matrimony a second try. She does better at marrying the love of her life and is more than twice as likely to wed as a virgin. And she's got a lot more chance of finding marriage a sex improver—he reports that loving often stays the same. Both are more at risk than most of having affairs. He's the sign likeliest to take a lover of his own if she strays, while she'll want to repair the damage if he gives her the runaround.

LIBRA MAN—SAGITTARIUS WOMAN

She's his first choice—but he's one of her least likelys. And neither nominate each other as especially sexy. Her curvy body, attractive voice and kind and faithful nature are attention grabbers here. She's more influenced than most by gorgeous eyes, a tall, muscular body and a good voice. Shared roles suit them both - neither especially rates a good provider or a good homemaker. He's looking for loyalty, while she's the sign keenest on a mate with a sense of humour. He likes a homelover who is sexy and good-looking, too.

But with jokey Sagittarius he may start wishing for a little less playfulness at bedtime—and a little more passion.

She is at higher risk than most of marrying more than once, while he's in the middle range. He's the man who most often makes a long-lasting match and she does well here, too. But she is in more of a hurry to marry, though she is warier than he is of wedding bells second-time around. She is luckier at marrying the love of her life—and is more than twice as likely to be a virgin when she does. Marriage gives her a bigger sex boost—he says loving often stays the same. And while she is the zodiac's most faithful woman, he's at high risk of an affair. She'll want to work things out if he does stray. He may dial up an old flame if she is untrue.

LIBRA MAN—CAPRICORN WOMAN

It's quite likely he'll pick her—but he's among her least popular partners and neither find the other especially sexy. He's drawn by a shapely body, kind nature and attractive voice and he values faithfulness, too. Her ideal man is tall, slim and kind with a good voice, a great smile and smart clothes. Confidence, a muscular build and being a good provider are other essential ingredients. But he may well prefer a partnership where roles are shared and that includes equal cash-earning, too. And while she enjoys his inventiveness in bed, (as long as he takes it slow), she may not give him all the flattery he craves. Long-term, both expect total loyalty. And he asks for a good looking, sexy and understanding homelover, while she wants a fun-loving, humorous mate.

He's a little likelier to marry more than once, but also has a higher chance of making a long-lasting match. Both are keen to marry and she's the sign happiest to hear wedding bells second time around. She is luckier than most, (certainly more than him), at marrying the love of her life and is more likely to be a virgin when she weds. Neither gets a big boost to their sexlife from marriage—mostly it stays the same. But she finds remarriage more fun in bed than he does. He may take his own lover if she ever wanders. She'd be calling the divorce lawyer if he two-times her.

LIBRA MAN—AQUARIUS WOMAN

She names him one of her best marriage bets and votes him quite sexy, too. But he says she's a least likely choice and he doesn't find her especially sexy. She's hard to please, but may fall for his smart clothes and good voice. Though what she's really looking for is a soulmate to share ideas and a busy social life. A curvy body gets his attention and he rates a kind and faithful nature and an attractive voice, too. But he may be puzzled if Aquarius seems more interested in talking about sex than doing it—he's far more physical. Long-term, both say loyalty and understanding are vital. And while he likes a sexy, good-looking homelover, she wants a mate with a sense of humour.

They both have an even chance of marrying more than once. But he's tops for sticking power, while she's less likely to pass marriage's 10-year mark. He's keener to stay single than she is—and he's in less of a hurry to give marriage a second go, too. They are not as lucky as some at marrying the love of their life and neither are likely to wed as virgins, especially her. She finds marriage a much bigger sex-booster than he does—but she's also likelier than most to say loving gets worse, while he often reports no change. If she ever strays, he may well take a lover of his own, while she's keener than most women to iron out any marital problems.

LIBRA MAN—PISCES WOMAN

He says she's a middle-range choice as a partner, but goes on to vote her most unsexy starsign! She nominates him as her least likely mate and she doesn't find him very sexy. His dream woman has a curvy body, a kind and faithful nature and an attractive voice. A gentle manner doesn't win many marks with him, though. She is attracted to slim men with great smiles, who promise faithfulness. He's looking for a good-looking partner who's both sexy and a loyal homelover. She's keener on kindness and humour. But both of them want understanding from a mate. They make romantic lovers, but he prefers sensual physical experiments, while her best turn-ons are all fantasy-based.

She is likelier than him to wed more than once—and he has more chance of notching up 10 years of marriage. He's far happier to stay single—she's the woman who least likes to be unattached. But he's more willing to give marriage a second go. She has better luck at marrying the love of her life —and is far likelier to wed as a virgin, too. Marriage gives her more of a sex boost—he often reports that loving stays the same. And she finds remarriage far sexier than he does. Both are at above average risk of having affairs. But if either ever does wander, the other may well take a lover of their own—or simply stay quiet and hope for the best, rather than sign divorce papers.

LIBRA MAN—ARIES WOMAN

Halfway down her list of sexy men, that's where she puts him! He either finds her very sexy, or not sexy at all. And they name each other as lukewarm popular partners. What she likes is his sociable self-confidence—and if he's tall and muscular, with a good voice and gorgeous eyes, she's interested. A well-stacked body, kind nature and attractive voice make him take notice. He is glad that she's more faithful than many and he likes her fiery personality, too—a gentle manner gets the lowest vote from him. Yet both need sweet romance and sexy compliments to keep passion red-hot. Partnerwise, he wants a loyal, understanding, good-looking homelover, while she's keener than most on a mate who is kind and full of humour.

She runs a high risk of getting hitched more than once, while he gets the top score for making a long-lasting match. But she does better at marrying a true love—he's less lucky than most here. And she's much more likely to be a wedding-day virgin. Marriage gives her a better sex boost—but she also says loving can get worse, while for him it often stays the same. She's a lot more likely to find sex sizzles second time around—he gets the joint lowest score. Aries is faster than other women to want a divorce if he's unfaithful. He may try to tip the scales by taking a lover of his own.

LIBRA MAN—TAURUS WOMAN

My favourite partner—they both say, and she often votes him sexy, too. Yet he says she's one of the least sexy starsigns! A curvy body, an attractive voice and a kind and faithful nature set his senses buzzing. She is drawn by kindness—and she likes a man who is confident, faithful and a good provider, too. If he is tall, muscular and slim, with a good line in chat, a great smile and smart clothes, even better! For the long haul, he demands loyalty and understanding and rates a good-looking, sexy, homelover. Ms Taurus likes a homelover too, especially the kind and witty variety.

He's likelier than her to marry more than once, yet he also has more chance of staying married for 10 years or more. She's far keener to marry—but he's more willing to give marriage a second go. She's much likelier to wed the love of her life and more often saves herself for that special person, while he rarely waits. Marriage is a lovelife improver for her—he's likelier to say loving stays the same. And remarriage is more of a sex-sizzler for her, too. But if he's unfaithful, she will want to know why and put things right, while he wastes little time in finding an extra lover, if it goes the other way.

LIBRA MAN—GEMINI WOMAN

Both find each other very sexy, but while she says he's a favourite partner, he names her among his least likely choices. Her curvy body and silvery voice make him first take notice, and if she's got a kind and faithful nature, he's a fan. He loves her outgoing personality, too—gentle-mannered women are not for him. She likes his sunny, sociable smile, his confidence, his smart clothes and his way with words. He values loyalty in a partnership and sexy good looks. She rates his kindness and understanding, but she needs to be certain of his love to fully relax and explore in bed.

She's less likely than him to marry more than once—but, while he's the man most likely to notch up 10 years of wedded bliss, she's the woman who does so least often . He's in more of a hurry to get attached and is much less easily put off remarriage. And he does better at marrying the love of his life, too. She's more likely than him to wed as a virgin and she finds marriage more of a sex-enhancer. He's likelier to report that sex stays the same. There's an above-average risk they will both have affairs. But she's keener than other signs to talk problems through if he does wander, while he may well say nothing or organise an extra lover for himself.

LIBRA MAN—CANCER WOMAN

Sexually, she's a mid-range choice for him and there's an average chance he'll choose her as a partner. But he's her least popular mate and she doesn't find him especially sexy. A curvy body, kind and faithful nature and attractive voice make him first sit up. But he he won't beg for more of her gentle manner—he prefers tough-minded types. She's keener than other women on the smart way sociable Libra dresses and loves his gorgeous eyes. He's glad she's more loyal than most, but he'll have to be patient with her in bed—she's less adventurous than him. She values kindness, understanding and fun. Both like a homelover more than most.

He's a little likelier than her to wed twice or more, but both often make a lasting bond. She's keener than him to marry and is luckier at marrying a true love and is more than twice as likely to wed as a virgin. But neither report a great sex-boost from matrimony—both often find that loving stays the same. Remarriage is more of a sex sizzler for her than for him, though. She's less likely than most to have an affair—he's not always so true. She may want a divorce if he does wander, while he may take a lover of his own, or simply say nothing, if she strays. He won't want to rock the boat.

LIBRA MAN—LEO WOMAN

She puts him near the top of her list of partnership picks and he says there's a fair chance he'll choose her, too. But they give each other just average marks for sexual sizzle. She likes her men to be slim and muscular, while he is attracted by her curvy body, sexy voice and kind nature. Both rate faithfulness and loyalty—she's the female sign keenest on this quality. Yet both are likelier than most to have affairs! To keep passion piping hot, mutual admiration is a must—she wants to star in bed, while he needs sexy compliments to stay steamy. Sexual attraction is vital to both for long-term success. But understanding, humour, fun, sex skills and good looks come higher on his list than on hers.

She's less likely than other women to marry more than once, while he's in the middle range. Yet she's not so sure to celebrate her 10th wedding anniversary. He is the man with the most marriage sticking-power. She is slightly keener to wed and is happier than most to try it for a second time, too. But he's a little luckier at marrying the love of his life. She's much more likely than him to marry as a virgin—and, if not, still finds marriage improves her sexlife. He is likelier than most to say that lovemaking stays the same. But if affairs ever cut into the relationship, both may decide to even the score by taking a lover of their own.

LIBRA MAN—VIRGO WOMAN

He's one of her favourite partners, though she doesn't rate him as a sex-object! He says she's his least likely love and he finds her unsexy. She likes her men tall, slim, muscular and faithful to only her—but she'll need promises in stone from wandering Libra. A curvy body and an attractive voice make him take notice and he likes faithful, kind-hearted women, too. But Virgo's gentle manner doesn't win many points from him. Both expect loyalty in a partner. But while he wants an understanding homelover who is sexy and good-looking, she values a mate with a sense of humour and gives fun the top female vote. In bed, he'll have to make the first move—

but she'll surprise him by being willing to try almost anything he sexily dreams up.

He's tops for notching up 10 years of wedded bliss. And he's far less wary about remarriage, while she's the woman most likely to say never again! She is luckier at marrying the love of her life— and is far likelier to be a virgin on the big day. And while she doesn't get a great sex-boost from marriage, she reports more improvement than him. He's at high risk of straying, she's at low risk. If he does wander, she is faster than most to call time, while he's the sign fastest to take a lover of his own (though he may do this with charming stealth).

LIBRA MAN—LIBRA WOMAN

She is physically pulled to him at first glance—and he says she's easily the sexiest starsign. There's a reasonable chance they will stay together, too, especially if she has a womanly body, attractive voice and kind nature. She loves his sociable line in chat and his stylish way of dressing—his great smile, muscular build and good voice appeal to her, too. Each want their partner to be faithful. Both are romantics who like a slow build-up to lovemaking. But while he needs spoiling, she has to have security before she'll truly let go. Long-term, she wants kindness and lots of laughs, but he gives humour the lowest vote. His Miss-to-Mrs Right is a sexy, understanding,good-looker who doesn't mind staying at home.

She's at low risk of marrying more than once, while he's in the middle range. These are the male and female starsigns who most often stay married for 10 years or more, with him doing better than her. She's keener to marry, and is a lot luckier at marrying the love of her life—he gets low marks for that. She finds marriage more of a sex-booster, while he's likelier than her to say lovemaking stays the same. But if either is ever untrue, the other will often reach out and draw another lover to his, or her, side.

THE LIBRA WOMAN'S LOVEMATCHES

LIBRA WOMAN— SCORPIO MAN

While he gets her vote as raunchiest sign, she doesn't often settle down domestically with him. She's keener than most on his mesmerising chat and if he has a great smile and is muscular, faithful and well-dressed, she may just stay around. He's the man who most appreciates a gentle manner. He also loves great legs and a kind and faithful nature. Long-term, so-physical Scorpio says he wants to have fun with a sexy partner who is good in bed and who appreciates his mastery of special sensual skills. Romantic Libra values sexual attraction least. She's looking for a loyal, kind and humorous mate. Overall, he puts her high on his wannabe partners list.

He is the man most likely to marry once, for life—and she is at lower risk of remarriage than most, too. She does a lot better when it comes to notching up 10 years of married life, though. Both can be keen to wed, but he's more easily put off matrimony second-time-around. She is luckier at marrying her lifelove, but he's more likely to be a wedding-day virgin. He finds the security of marriage improves his sex life. She doesn't report this so often. She may well take a lover of her own if he ever strays, while if she wanders, he'll do his best to work the love problems out.

LIBRA WOMAN—SAGITTARIUS MAN

She's his favourite partner of all, he votes her one of the sexiest signs. Yet he's among her least popular choices and she doesn't find him especially sexy. She's the woman who most appreciates a good communicator and she likes her men strong, smartly dressed and faithful, too. A warm smile, a slim body and shared interests win his heart—and he gives faithfulness top male ratings. Long-term, he needs kindness, understanding—and a sense of humour. She wants kindness, too, along with loyalty, which she often gets from him. But both give low marks to sexual attraction and while he takes a sporty all-action approach to loving, she dreams of slow, romantic build-ups between sensuous satin sheets.

She is the woman who most often makes a long-lasting match, while he's the man least likely to. He's also the sign most easily put off marriage second-time-around, while she's a lot less wary. She has much better luck at marrying the love of her life. But while both have an even chance of finding marriage increases their levels of sexual satisfaction, he finds remarriage more of a bodywarmer than she does. He is the zodiac's most faithful man, while she's one of the female signs most likely to wander! He's keen to solve marital problems if she does stray, while she'll simply shop for a lover of her own if her partner tangles with another woman.

LIBRA WOMAN—CAPRICORN MAN

She slots him in close to the top of her popular pairings list, while he says she's a middle-range choice—and neither finds the other especially sexy. She loves a communicative man she can really open up to—and if he is kind, with a muscular build, a great smile and a smart style of dressing, even better! Both appreciate a good voice—and need to know that their partner will be faithful, too. A winning smile and great legs grab his attention, and a gentle manner appeals to him, too. She needs kindness and loyalty if love is to last, while he wants a sexy, good-looking partner with a sense of humour—and money! She'll enjoy being swept off her feet by him—and straight into bed. But she could tire of his need to take control and he must learn not to rush romance.

He's likelier than her to wed more than once. But while she's the woman who most often notches up 10 years of marriage, he does better still. He is keener than her, and than other male signs, to wed, but he is in far less hurry than her to get married a second time. She's much likelier to land the love of her life—he gets one of the lowest results. Marriage improves her sexlife, too, but he reports a lot more improvement in remarriage. If she's unfaithful, he'll want to work things out—or ask for a divorce. She's likelier than most to take a lover of her own if he lets her down.

LIBRA WOMAN —AQUARIUS MAN

They name each other among their least favourite partners and neither votes the other very fanciable. She'll need to get her body in shape to appeal to him—he likes women to be curvy and slim. She'll need to be gentle and good at making a cosy home. But she's the sign who least rates a good provider, so she'll expect him to share the housework. Her dream man is a muscular hunk with a good voice, a great line in chat and an open smile. She says he has to be smartly dressed. And faithful. If it is to last, he must be kind to her—and hardworking. Aquarius wants to be understood and to have fun with a mate (who is good in bed). She needs security to set free her love skills—and he does, too, deep down. It's sexual variety and the silky compliments she's so good at giving that will keep this pairing aglow.

He's high on the remarriage risk register—she's low. She's more likely than others to make a long-lasting match and is keener to wed—but he enjoys the challenge of making a second marriage work more than she does. She's luckier at settling with the love of her life, while he's the sign who's least likely to. And he's also the man least likely to be a virgin when he weds, while she has an average chance. She finds being married makes for better sex—he often reports that it stays the same. If affairs divide them, he may ask for a divorce or, like her, he may take a lover of his own.

LIBRA WOMAN —PISCES MAN

They are among each other's least preferred partners and neither gives the other a high vote for sex-attraction power. He'll have to develop a good smatter of patter to pull her. And if he's kind and faithful, with a great smile, a good voice, muscular build and a wears smart clothes, he could yet grab her heart, too. Great legs appeal to him. So do a slim body and a sexy laugh do, too. But, while he rates a good homemaker, she's the sign that least rates a good provider, so she may not go for a stay-at-home role. Both want a partner who is loyal and it's only when there is total trust that each will unleash a passionate lovestyle. He also asks for humour, fun and sex-skills, while she likes a kind-hearted hardworker.

He's likelier to marry more than once—she's at low risk and is better than most at making a long-lasting bond. She's in much more of a hurry to marry, yet he's keener than other men, and than her, to wed a second time. He's the sign most likely to marry the love of his life, while she is often lucky, too. But he's likelier to save himself for that special person. He finds marriage more of a sex-booster than she does—and remarriage, too. If affairs hinder their love, she may even up the score by taking her own lover, while he'd try hard to mend the relationship, and only after that ask for a divorce.

LIBRA WOMAN—ARIES MAN

From opposite sides of the zodiac wheel, they do often end up as partners —yet they name each other among the least sexy signs. She loves a man who talks fluently, but won't like it if forceful Aries hogs the conversation— or takes over in bed too often. She fancies kind, muscular men in smart clothes who pledge faithfulness—and she likes a great smile and a good voice, too. He's attracted to a warm smile, nice eyes and curvy body. And he wants a good homemaker to look after him. But she doesn't rate a good provider and prefers shared roles. Long-term, she values loyalty, kindness and humour. He says that good looks and money are important, too. And while he gives sexual attraction top ratings, she gives it the lowest marks, putting emotional fulfilment before lust.

She often weds once, for life, while he is at average risk of remarriage. She is luckier than other signs at making a long-lasting match, while he does less well. Both are in a hurry to get hitched, but when it comes to marriage second-time-around, he's less keen to try than her. They often wed the love of their lives, but he's likelier to do so as a virgin. She finds marriage revs up her sex life, but he gets a bigger boost from remarriage. If either strays, the other may even the score by putting a lover of their own on the field.

LIBRA WOMAN—TAURUS MAN

They are not especially popular with each other—and don't usually rate each other as sexual superstars. She loves a man with a great smile and a good conversational line—and if he's muscular, smartly dressed, kind and faithful, she's smitten! He gives top marks to a warm smile and a kind nature—plus a curvy body, a sexy voice and a raunchy laugh. He's keen on a good homemaker, but she rates a good provider less than other women. He's the man who most values kindness in a partner—and understanding and sex skills also impress. She appreciates a kind and loyal hardworker. In bed she rewards him with praise worthy of a hero—but she may yearn for a more romantic, less sex-greedy style of loving.

Both are at less risk than most of marrying more than once. And while she is the woman most likely to stay wed more than 10 years, he does even better. Both are keen to marry, but remarriage appeals more to her than to him. They are often lucky at wedding the love of their lives, but he's likelier to be a virgin when he does. They have an average chance of finding sex improves within marriage. But both get less of a lovelife boost than most second-time-arounders. If she ever strays, he'd want to try to put marital problems right. If he wanders, she'll lasso a lover of her own.

LIBRA WOMAN—GEMINI MAN

They name each other among their favourite partners—and rate each other high on the sex-scale, too. She loves a good talker and smart clothing. A great smile, toned body and good voice win her over, too, and if he's kind and faithful, even better! He's the man most attracted to her superb legs, sexy laugh and slim body—and he loves their shared interest (socialising). If she's kind, faithful, gentle and a good homemaker, she's his dream woman! Both easily chat and charm each other into bed—but once there, she'll want commitment, which he can, at first, find hard to give. If this is to last, both say loyalty is vital. She also rates kindness and humour, while unlike her, he especially needs understanding, sexual attraction and fun.

Both are at lower risk than most of marrying more than once—and often successfully make long-lasting bonds, especially her. But she is much keener to wed and to remarry, too. She's a lot luckier at settling with the love of her life—but he's nearly twice as likely to go down the aisle as a virgin and is the sign who most often does. He finds matrimony more of a lovelife improver and is the man least likely to say sex has got worse. And he finds remarriage more of a love-booster, too. If she ever strays, he may well want a divorce, while she will match every betrayal of his with a sex adventure of her own!

LIBRA WOMAN—CANCER MAN

Quite sexy, she says and votes him a popular partner—but she's his least likely choice and he doesn't find her especially sexy. Smart clothes and muscular body make her first look up—and if he's got a great smile and winning way with words, she's hooked. A good voice and a kind and faithful nature appeal to her, too. His ideal woman is kind-hearted and gentle, with a sexy laugh—and he also rates a good homemaker. But she gives a good provider the lowest vote, preferring shared roles. Both ask for kindness and loyalty from a partner. She wants a hardworker, while he asks for a mate who understands him. If Libra learns to do so, she'll be rewarded with great sex and tender loving.

She usually marries once, for life, while he's the man most likely to wed twice or more. She is the sign best at making a bond last 10 years, while he has average success. He's happier than her to stay single—and he's a lot more likely to be a virgin when he weds, too. But she is luckier at marrying the love of her life and more often reports that marriage is a sex improver. When it comes to remarriage, though, she gets the bigger boost. If she wanders, he may well say nothing and hope it doesn't last, while she may cast her net for a lover of her own, if she discovers a partner's infidelity.

LIBRA WOMAN —LEO MAN

He's among her best-choice partners and she votes him one of the sexiest signs, too. But he says she's an unlikely partner and he doesn't find her very fanciable. He likes to look deep into his partner's eyes and he rates a warm smile, a curvy body, great legs and a sexy laugh. She's drawn by his radiant smile, smart clothes and good voice and she loves his sociable line in chat. If he's faithful, that's a big plus, too. Neither rate traditional roles, but she does expect kindness and loyalty from a partner, while he looks for a sexy and understanding mate who is nice-looking, witty and good in bed. And smooth charmer Libra knows just how to make proud performer Leo feel like he's the best lover ever.

She's one of the signs most likely to marry once, for life, while he's among those who most often remarry. She does a lot better at making a bond last 10 years or more, while he's over three times happier to stay single and is in a lot less of a hurry to remarry, too. Both do well at marrying the love of their lives, but she's more likely to go down the aisle as a virgin. He more often reports a lovemaking boost from marriage and gets far more improvement than her from second marriage. If she cheats, he may opt for divorce, while she is more likely to add a new lover to her list, if a partner proves to have a cheating heart.

LIBRA WOMAN—VIRGO MAN

They both give each other a guarded "yes" as suitable partners. Even though she votes him the least sexy sign, while he doesn't always see her sex-potential. His eyes will widen if she has a curvy and slim body, an attractive voice and a gentle manner. She'll fall for him only if he's a good speaker—but smart clothes, muscular build, great smile and good voice all help, too. Loyalty, laughter and kind hearts are key ingredients for both. But he's the more physical lover, asking for sexual attraction, lovemaking skills and good looks. And he likes a hardworker, too.

Both are at low risk of marrying more than once, but she more often makes a long-lasting match. He's over twice as keen as her on the single life—she's in more of a hurry to marry and to remarry, too. She is luckier at marrying the love of her life, but he's more likely to be the virgin. Marriage gives her a bigger sex boost—he's the male sign who most often reports a drop in interest. But neither get top marks for finding remarriage sexier. If he is ever unfaithful she may react by taking a lover of her own, while if she starts to wander, he'll write down all their problems and be sincere about wanting to solve them.

LIBRA WOMAN —LIBRA MAN

They top each other's "must-have" sex attraction lists. And there's a fair chance they will be partners. He's attracted to her curvy body, sexy voice and kind nature. She loves his verbal skills and appreciates his kindness, his great smile, and his smart style of dressing. If he has a muscular build and a good voice, even better! Both hope the other will be faithful and loyal. She especially needs to feel secure before she can open up to his highly adventurous lovestyle. She asks for kindness—and humour, which he awards lowest marks. Instead, he wants a good-looking, understanding and sexy homelover.

He's a little likelier than her to marry more than once, she's at low risk. But both are the signs who are best at making long-lasting bonds, with him ahead of her. He's much happier to stay single than she is, while she's luckier at settling with the love of her life. She says marriage is more of a sex-booster, while he reports loving often stays the same. But neither get high marks for finding remarriage a sex-sizzler. And if either ever strays, the other may take a lover of their own to make it fairer.

THE SCORPIO MAN'S LOVE MATCHES

SCORPIO MAN—SAGITTARIUS WOMAN

She rates him as red hot sexually, especially if he's tall and slim, but she'll have to flash a pretty leg to catch his eye, and be kind and gentle if she's going to win his heart, because she's not his instinctive first choice, either for a steamy affair, or for a lasting love match. She values closeness and communication. If he can't talk with her, or laugh with her at life's absurdities, if he's a slacker, or spends nights with the lads in the pub when there's grouting to be done and shelves to be hung, bitter resentment will set in. Home is where her heart is, (though she becomes too homey at her peril, and she dare not let herself go). He wants his partner to be a playmate. Physical attraction counts beyond all things for this lusty male in a lasting relationship, and marriage itself will not dampen his ardour, but he'll turn stone cold if love-making becomes too routine.

Strange that she, who is initially so compelled by his sexuality, and who is capable of deep, sustained passion, can be as quickly turned off by his boastfulness and exuberance in bed. Even stranger, he is more likely than she to save himself for his wedding night.

They both do well on their own, but flourish in a happy partnership. There is no woman more faithful than she; a pity he's not so dependable. Yet, though they will both want to work at their differences, if the going should get really tough, she will probably be first through the door. Because, in general, the Scorpio groom is more likely than the Sagittarius bride, to be dancing the anniversary waltz in 10 years' time.

SCORPIO MAN—CAPRICORN WOMAN

This is one of the more rare of zodiac pairings. He thinks she's not for him, but a well-turned ankle, natural warmth and a gentle manner may make him think again. She'll say she can take him or leave him, then be dazzled by his smile. And if he's tall and muscular she will be irresistibly physically drawn to him.

It is important that they sort out, at the start, the conduct of their relationship, because while she wants him to be supportive and self-confident, to keep her in comfort and lavish treats upon her, he believes she should make a decent contribution to the household kitty. He will not always share her sense of humour, but at least he has a sense of fun.

She may bring more sexual experience than him to the marriage, but he is very into love-making, and can enjoy sex with the same partner for ever if she is suitably responsive and admiring of his efforts, and if she participates with a whole heart. She, however, likes to be seduced, and may feel that his love marathons are lacking somewhat in old-fashioned romance. If he fails to cherish her she may show reluctance, and he, misunderstanding, will simply cool off. If they can only talk this out, however, her passion for him will be undiminished with the years.

Both make stable partnerships, and he's a real stayer. He is keener than her to say "I do", but should their relationship founder, she will be the more likely to marry again. She is adamant that he must be faithful; he takes a rather more indulgent view of infidelity, hers as well as his own! If she strays, he will want to work their problems out; if he does, it could be straight to the divorce courts.

SCORPIO MAN—AQUARIUS WOMAN

She votes him one of the sexiest of starsigns, but he is not particularly tuned in to her. This means they are not the likeliest of couples, but when the two do get together, we should all stand well clear, for fear of getting scorched in the white heat of their passion.

A lean thigh and a shapely calf will catch his eye, and a sweet, conciliatory manner will bring out the Romeo in him. She sets far more store by the higher values—loyalty, industry, understanding, good humour—than by the purely superficial, but she takes pride in a handsome partner, wants him to dress smartly and to have a pleasing voice.

He looks for a home-lover, but this social butterfly may not be pinned down. Never mind. If this leads to arguments, they can always make it up in bed. Both are sexually adventurous and curious, and will love to explore new techniques. She may teach him a trick or two on their honeymoon, for she is more likely than him— and all her sister starsigns—to have put in some serious research.

With so much shared enthusiasm for sex, it is surprising that their lovelife may now and then be in the doldrums. Should this happen, he will be the more likely to find solace in the arms of another, but if either is unfaithful, they will both try to work it out. He is better than she is at being single, but makes a very serious commitment to marriage and wants it to be for life. So does she, of course, but if one marriage fails, she will be less discouraged than him from trying it a second time.

SCORPIO MAN—PISCES WOMAN

What's a nice girl like her doing with a guy like him? Seriously, this is an improbable pairing since, while she rates him the hunk of hunks, he is inclined to overlook her, and doesn't generally regard her as his type. If she has won him round, it will have been with her gracious, unaggressive nature. And, since he's such a leg man, great pins may have helped. She, meanwhile, goes for a lithe body and a devastating smile

Unusual couple though they may be, they can be very pleasing to each other. Sexual attraction is paramount for him, it is the key for him to a successful love match, and she quite simply delights him in bed. She will weave a web of seductive fantasy to ensnare him, and she makes him feel like a sex-god when she thrills to his erotic skills. But she emphasises kindness and humour above the physical side of a relationship, and money comes high on her list of must haves, so he must attend to material considerations.

She is more anxious to have that ring on her third finger, because she dreads being left on the shelf. She may well be a virgin when she makes her vows, but he has more hope than her of enjoying lasting sexual satisfaction with a single partner, and she may find greater passion in a second marriage. He likes to think, when he plights his troth, that it will be for life. Well, so does Ms Pisces—every time.

SCORPIO MAN—ARIES WOMAN

Scorpio man's particular brand of sex appeal proves fatally attractive to a number of star signs that actually hold scant appeal for him. Aries is a case in point, and an odd one when you bear in mind that she adores to feel desired. She thinks he's top of the sexual pops, and she'd love to set up home with him. She goes for nice eyes, a high-voltage smile and Scorpio self-confidence. Yet he puts this Ms Bossy Boots at the very bottom of his shopping list. Somewhere below the soft soap and the salve for his ego. Is she selfish? He says so. And she can give him her most come-hither look, wear her shortest skirts, her most figure-hugging tops, but if she's too loud or brash he just won't want to know. Should they get together, it will be because he discerns in her the softer and more feminine qualities that he prizes. So if she is bent on having him, she should try a little tenderness.

Both bring a lot of energy and invention to their love-making, and everything is hunky-dory while she interprets his five-times-a-night antics as an act of worship. But if he wants to keep her really happy, he must constantly tell her how gorgeous she is.

Lusty individuals they may be, but both are quite likely to marry as virgins. They are both quite good at the partnership game, and often make lasting matches, but if it comes to a split, she is more likely than he is to have a second shot at matrimony. The Scorpio male can be just as turned on by his woman 10 years into the relationship, as he was by their first kiss. If the love-making palls, as it sometimes does, between these two signs, she should try being a bit less dictatorial, and he should pay her compliments.

In this challenging, not always comfortable partnership, tit-for-tat infidelity is a common feature. And, while he may well say "Let's talk it over" when she takes a lover, she will be a great deal less forgiving when he does.

SCORPIO MAN—TAURUS WOMAN

He votes her a loveable—but not necessarily a lust-afterable partner. She finds him more instantly attractive and more eminently go-offable. An appealing manner, kindness and constancy melt his heart, and he's mad for her if she's leggy, but her occasional bouts of boot-faced obduracy drives him to distraction. For her part, she is impressed by his self-belief, his eloquence, and the consideration of which he is capable.

If he wants her to pay her share there could be trouble, because she feels it's for him to be the breadwinner. Still, he will very much appreciate the energy she puts into home-making and having fun. He can laugh her into bed, but he'll need to keep the humour going if her enthusiasm is not to flag. For him, there are three things, above all, that make for a good partnership; sex, sex, and more sex. He fancies himself as an incredible love machine, but should remember that Taurus woman prefers to have a man to sleep with, and a machine to do washing-up.

Neither goes in for serial marriages, and both are quite keen to get hitched and stay hitched. Scorpio man in general scores slightly higher than Taurus woman at forging a relationship for life, but the fact that a marriage is long-lasting, does not necessarily mean that it is perfect, and she is luckier in love, with a keener instinct for choosing an ideal mate. Perhaps, then, he should draw encouragement from the fact that she's picked him!

She is the more likely to have had previous sexual partners, but both say that the security of marriage is a positive force in their intimate relations. Infidelity may not deal their partnership a death blow, since they both believe in discussing mutual problems and in dealing with them in an adult way.

SCORPIO MAN—GEMINI WOMAN

When she first sets eyes on him she thinks that he is sex personified, but he rates her as just so-so in the fanciability stakes, and neither sees the other as the obvious choice for a long-term partnership. He goes for the traditional female; caring, responsive, devoted, with home-making skills. She is impressed by self-possession, an infectious grin, a way with words, and she gives him high marks for his dress sense and his intuitive understanding. She looks for kindness in a partner, and would, on the whole, prefer it if he wasn't completely penniless.

Although sex is vital to him in a relationship, he should not lose sight of the fact that she is a mentally active person; he will need to stimulate her mind quite as much as her body.

She values her freedom, but is more keen than him to marry. Too keen, perhaps? Is she prone to marry in haste? Certainly she is less likely than other signs to marry Mr Right, and to be with him a decade from her wedding day. Still, since the Scorpio male so often marries the love of his life, and remains devoted to her, a stable and lasting partnership must be a strong possibility in this case.

She is more likely than he is to have had sexual partners before settling down, but he gets a continuing buzz from sex within marriage, and any loss of interest on his part may be a reaction to a cooling on hers. If either of them takes a lover, they will usually co-operate to try to save the marriage—though maybe not before he has a fling to get his own back on her for any infidelity.

He's not a great one for remarriage. She will often chance it, and find, with her new husband, the sexual magic that got lost somehow along the way in marriage number one.

SCORPIO MAN—CANCER WOMAN

These two, like opposite magnetic poles, are irresistibly mutually attracted. They not only fancy each other like nobody's business, but have a fair chance of making a permanent match. Ms Cancer is his kind of woman; sympathetic and sincere. And if she has beautiful legs, that's a tremendous bonus. She will admire his style of dress, and will lose herself in his lovely eyes.

She had better not be too passive, however, if she is going to keep him happy for ever. She will have to be fun-loving and great in bed.

He, meanwhile, must be at pains to reassure her sexually, for she will only relax, take powerful pleasure, and join in adventurous love-making, when he has earned her complete trust. "Gently does it" must be his maxim if he wants to unleash her true passions. They may well both be novices on their wedding night, and, provided they are sensitive to one another's needs, could embark together on a sexual exploration without end. They do well to heed the foregoing advice, since, while sex within marriage is often, for him, exciting and diverting, he can also find monogamy a turn-off.

They stand a better chance than many couples of making a match last, since Scorpio man so often marries for life, and Cancer woman reports a high success rate. They are both keen to tie the knot, though she may push it upon him before he is absolutely ready. And if the partnership should be dissolved, she will be the more likely to urge marriage upon another man.

She, to whom trust is everything, will be far less willing than him to overlook sexual indiscretion, and rather than try to work at their differences, he may well be hearing from her solicitors.

SCORPIO MAN—LEO WOMAN

These two get on so easily, they make a great team, and yet they simply don't fancy one another. above all it is shared interests that draw them together. That, at any rate, is what they'll tell you. But if Ms Leo has all his favourite womanly attributes—the sexy curves, the legs, the inviting smile and a mirthful laugh—he will be smitten. And, if he has a well-made, muscular physique, so will she.

Domestic arrangements require thorough discussion; she wants her man to be a provider. But, while he values his home life highly, and will hope that she does too, he most of all men, will want her to be in paid employment.

There are a few things to be squared on the sexual front, too. They can enjoy each other hugely in bed, but each wants to be the star performer. Self-conceited Scorpio, last of the red-hot lovers, has to be willing to share the limelight with Leo. He has to learn to receive pleasure as well as to give it. And if she's to relax, he must remember to show her plenty of affection, especially on their first night together, when she is more likely than him to be inexperienced.

The great news is that, for both of them, not only does sex enhance a marriage, but marriage enhances sex. This is doubly true of Scorpio man in a second or subsequent pairing. And, yes, there is a risk with these two that they won't celebrate their silver wedding. Or, at least, not with each other!

What will break them up? Infidelity, possibly, since they both tend to stray at some time. But, while she was more keen to marry in the first place, he may well be more anxious to sort out their problems if she takes a lover. And if it's him who has strayed? Then her attitude may well be that sauce for the goose is sauce for the gander.

SCORPIO MAN—VIRGO WOMAN

For a change, it is Mr Scorpio who must do the chasing. He not only likes her, but he fancies her like crazy, conforming as she does to his ideal of womanhood (gentle, affectionate, devoted and—in a perfect world—with legs to die for). For her part, she's suspicious of him, though she may be attracted to him if he is blessed with a lean, masculine physique. To begin with, can she trust him? Because fidelity is everything to her in a partnership, and he does have a roving eye.

If he should succeed in wooing her, they may prove surprisingly compatible. They agree that traditional male-female roles are not for them, and prefer to share responsibilities. Second only to loyalty, she values humour. But for him it is sexual attraction that counts all down the line, and he truly believes it is sustainable through years of marriage, though it can also die on him. They make good sexual partners, since he likes to lead and she is content to follow. She surprises and delights him with her willingness to experiment and, with his tendency to dominate, he will readily make the first move.

She is in less of a rush than he is to get hitched—not just to a sexy Scorpio, but to anyone. She believes in saving herself for that special person, and has a fair chance of making a good match. She is more likely than he is to find a true soul mate, but not necessarily in her first partnership.

Virgo women, though wary of marriage, are nevertheless the most prone of all the star signs to have a number of husbands, gaining in sexual confidence in the process.

In the unlikely event that she takes a lover, he will be anxious that they try to resolve their differences. But then, he holds light-hearted views on sexual infidelity, which Virgo will not condone.

SCORPIO MAN—LIBRA WOMAN

She's his number one choice as a partner, and he fancies her only slightly less than she fancies him. But while she rates his the sexiest sign, it is rare for her to settle down with him. If she does, it will be thanks to his articulacy, for she loves a finely-turned phrase. It will influence her if he dresses with style, has a disarming smile and a willingness to commit himself. He'll look first at her legs, and then at her face, to see if he can read in it the gentleness and generosity of spirit that he seeks.

Of all the signs, hers is the least enamoured of overt, swaggering sexuality. She is romantic, susceptible, beguiled by ideas, and by their expression in words. She yearns for adoration, craves reassurance, and may find rumbustious Scorpio, whose sensitivity is often subordinated to an obsession with bedmanship, simply too overwhelming.

Both of them make stable marriages, but she has better instincts than him for finding the love of her life. Sex is, for him, central to a relationship: if the sex isn't great, then nor, to his mind, is the partnership. With this make-or-break attitude, he will perform with ardour over the years—or he will turn away.

It is one of the paradoxes of Scorpio man's profile, that, while he is so motivated by the sexual urge, he is in many pairings the more likely to be a virgin on the wedding night. This holds true in this instance. But if love-struck Libra has fallen in the past for a silver-tongued seducer, she will not usually play around within marriage. If her Scorpio man should do so, she will get mad, and then she might just get even.

SCORPIO MAN—SCORPIO WOMAN

"We're great!" they agree. They rate each other as by far the sexiest sign—but then they would, wouldn't they? They don't necessarily reckon each other as possible life partners. They should keep a cool head here, and be guided by reason. Never mind how fantastic she looks in sheer stockings; never mind that she may have that softness that so appeals; if she's not a good home-maker, it will cause ructions. And though he may be of that fine, strong build that she admires, though she may go weak at the knees when she looks into his eyes, and tremble at the sound of his rich baritone voice, if he won't provide handsomely for her, there could be hell to pay in years to come.

Since they both enjoy that particular Scorpio brand of no-holds-barred sex, they will have exhilarating times in bed. But they each have to learn to take turns at giving and receiving pleasure.

Scorpio man often marries just the once. Scorpio woman has a more unerring instinct for finding her ideal partner—but it may take her a couple of tries. He is just as keen as she is to make his wedding vows, and there is an even chance that they'll both be virgins when they consummate their marriage. Because they are so sexually orientated, they can remain fervent lovers through a lifetime together. But if they are simply too similar in their approach to love-making, and cannot find some sort of compromise, their sex-life may fizzle out, and with it their relationship. They will not be indifferent to, or indulgent of, each other's affairs, but they will both have a brave try at setting marital matters to rights.

THE SCORPIO WOMAN'S LOVEMATCHES

SCORPIO WOMAN—SAGITTARIUS MAN

These two can agree on one thing at least; they wouldn't normally cross the street to get to know one another. She names him as the sign she least frequently fancies; and she leaves him quite unmoved, too. But there are exceptions to every rule in the zodiac. For Scorpio woman, a Sagittarian male with expressive eyes, a fine, strong, well-sculpted physique, and a distinctively sexy voice could be one of them. For Sagittarian man, a beautifully slim Scorpio woman with a 250-watt smile could be another. Then, if the pair of them have a strong interest in common, it can make for a powerful affinity.

They could have their differences on the home front, however; she favours the traditional male and female roles, while he may want her to go out to work. And if she likes to play mistress of the house, she should be warned; he may want to pitch in with the cooking and cleaning and show off his own skills.

She insists that sexual attraction is vital in a partnership, and she wants her mate to be witty as well as a great lover. He is game for a laugh, too, but rates kindness and understanding, not sexual dynamism, as the magic ingredients for long-term romance. She is a born seductress and sexually powerful, but she will anger and alienate him if she tries to use that power to manipulate him.

She will be keener than him to be Mr and Mrs, perhaps because she finds the marriage bed—with all the leisure and licence it affords—such a very sexy place. She is the more likely to be a virgin on their wedding night, and scores somewhat higher than he does for making a good and lasting marriage. Neither will make light of it if the other strays, but both say they would want to know why it happened, and would hope to put the problems right. Failing that, they might marry again, since both are more likely than most signs to do so.

SCORPIO WOMAN—CAPRICORN MAN

These two vote each other no more than passable—but she won't

437

pass him up if he is built like a gladiator, has a good, rich voice and eyes she could get lost in. Nor will he give her the go-by if she has the kind of legs that turn male heads, a sensuous smile and a sexy voice.

She likes her partner to earn plenty, to keep her in the manner to which she'd love to be accustomed. Well, money is certainly important to him; he's very into status and appearances. But that may mean he'll want her to go out to work, to boost their bank balance. At the same time, he will look to her to be gentle and loyal, and to share in his many interests.

They agree that sparky sex is the secret of long-term happiness in a partnership, and familiarity, in this case, seems to breed content, for neither finds that marriage dampens their ardour. She is more likely than him to be a virgin till she says "I do", but she is a fast learner, and there could be a battle for control, as they both like to dominate in bed.

Scorpio woman generally shows better judgement in her choice of partner. Capricorn man is keener to marry, perhaps too impatient to wait for Ms Right, though if he pledges himself tomorrow, there is a fair chance that he will stay married. He is rather less hasty when it comes to remarriage. She is usually game to give wedlock a second try. Both are capable of infidelity in some circumstances, and both would be keen to patch up the marriage. If they failed to do so, he would be quicker to ask for a divorce; she would be more inclined to wait and see.

SCORPIO WOMAN—AQUARIUS MAN

Sparks don't often fly at their first meeting, nor do they reckon each other as life partners, and yet, and yet... If he lives up to the Scorpio ideal, if he stands tall, has a wonderful physique, if his voice is pleasing and his gaze compels her, she may well fall for him. She'll catch his eye if she's slender, womanly, and not at all strident.

Here, at least, is a man who will play happy families with her, for both enjoy the traditional roles, whereby she makes a home and he earns the money. He will have to work hard, however, as she hopes to be well provided for.

He is more likely than she to have notched up a few lovers when he slips the wedding ring on her finger, but she has great enthusiasm for sex (or, rather, she has enthusiasm for great sex). He recognises the importance of skill and sensitivity in bed, and both thrive on experimentation, but he has a less rumbustious attitude, he wants a mate who loves him madly, and who truly, deeply understands him.

Scorpio woman is keener than him to marry in the first place, and is better at making a lasting match. Here's why. Sex within marriage can be endlessly fulfilling to her; so long as his love-making is erotic and unpredictable, she won't tire of the same partner. But marriage gives no such fillip to his libido. And, while she would be keen to effect a reconciliation were he to be unfaithful, if it were she who strayed he'd probably divorce her—or take a lover of his own!

She goes in for remarriage, too, though to a lesser extent, and if she finds yet more erotic pleasure with her second partner, Mr Aquarius will just be water under the bridge.

SCORPIO WOMAN—PISCES MAN

He is instinctively more drawn to her than she is to him, and sex is not usually on their minds when they meet. Unless, that is, he is powerfully built, with gorgeous eyes, and his voice is music to her ears. He'll go for her if she has model-girl proportions and a laugh to make his heart lift.

They could be a well-matched couple, since she looks for someone with a good income, who will provide well for her while she runs the home, and he likes his partner to care for his creature comforts.

She needs a mate with a high sex drive, who won't turn into a couch potato the minute he marries (a beer gut is a definite no-no). She wants him to make her laugh, and to be better than merely competent in bed. He wants a woman whom he can trust, and with whom he will have lots of fun, so regular sex with a loyal partner is particularly pleasing to him. Both are terrific instinctive lovers, they just know how to satisfy one another, but if wily Scorpio ever tries to manipulate sensitive Pisces, they could be in deep trouble.

Both sex and marriage mean commitment to him; he is not one to rush to the altar, and may well be a novice when he brushes the confetti out of his hair. Perhaps for this reason, he is luckier at settling with the love of his life, although both he and Ms Scorpio are game to make second and subsequent matches.

Neither is entirely immune to the temptations of illicit love, but if he is unfaithful she will probable want to talk it out, while if she is, his first impulse will be to call the whole thing off.

SCORPIO WOMAN—ARIES MAN

She doesn't go a bundle on Mr Aries—unless he's more Rambo than Ram. She votes his the least sexy of signs, though rippling pectorals and a smouldering gaze could cause her to have second thoughts. He says he can take her or leave her, and will probably leave her, unless the sway of slim hips, an encouraging smile and come-hither eyes turn his head.

In the rare event that these two do get together, theirs could be a truly viable marriage, since she looks to a man to support her in style and he, of all star signs, is most adamant that a woman's place is in the home. Mind you, if she has private income, some healthy investments, that will be to the good since he rates money—along with good looks and a love of home—as essential to lasting love.

Sex is paramount for her in a relationship; she wants a mate who will laugh with her, and will be past-master of love techniques. With the right partner she simply blossoms, and nothing of passion and responsiveness is lost with the years. He is more likely than she to be inexperienced on their honeymoon, and he must beware of treating love-making as mere contact sport, to scrum down between the sheets, without regard for her finer feelings.

He's not great on his own, so may rush into marriage, yet when he does so it is very often with the love of his life. She is better at making a lasting match, and will take a more adult view of his infidelity than

440

he of hers; while she opts for mature and reasonable discussion, he goes all out for revenge. Perhaps this is why she makes more stable alliances, though both may marry more than once, frequently finding deeper fulfilment with a second partner.

SCORPIO WOMAN—TAURUS MAN

Oh, the pain of unrequited love! There is she, smitten by Mr Taurus, especially if he's truly beefy and impales her with his gaze. But the hard fact is that only rarely does she turn him on. If she does, it is with her womanliness, the curl of her lips, the wiggle of her hips, her slender, curvy silhouette.

Where they score so well when they do get together is in her home-making skills (which he prizes), and his earning abilities, plus his bullish attitude to money (which is very important to her). His dream woman is not just kind and understanding, however, but also hardworking, so she had better get busy in the kitchen, and not just sit there painting her nails.

The physical side of a partnership figures large for both of them. She finds that sex puts the life into marriage, and marriage puts life into sex. He is slightly more likely than her to be a virgin when the banns are called, yet a little less likely to find that sex with one partner satisfies him. He is aroused by the overtly sexual, she by deeper, more subtle ideas and emotions. Silk stockings for him, then; delicious intrigue for her.

He is keen to tie the knot, and in spite of his roving eye and a tendency to boredom in the bedroom, he will often make a stable marriage, as he has good instincts for choosing the perfect partner. Much to his credit, he will make an effort to sort out marital differences, if infidelity on either side threatens the relationship. She is keen to find a solution, too.

SCORPIO WOMAN—GEMINI MAN

She is not very likely to play Juliet to his Romeo, or he Antony to her Cleopatra. Nothing personal, but they simply don't regard each other as suitable partner material... as a rule. She's a sucker, though, for a honed body, for bulging biceps and nice eyes, with which Mr Gemini is as likely as the next man to be endowed. And he won't say no to a trim waist, sensational legs and a mirthful, throaty laugh.

They may have problems from the start with the terms of their relationship, since old-fashioned Ms Scorpio wants to be a kept woman and a homemaker, while modern Mr Gemini thinks she should go out to work. At the same time, she should be a paragon of feminine virtue; faithful and gentle, with a lively interest in whatever interests him.

They agree that sex is important in a life partnership, are anxious to preserve the mystique, strive to please one another, and find that marriage has a positively aphrodisiac effect. If there is a problem, it is that he treats love-making too much as a game, while she looks for deeper emotional commitment. Still, they'll have lots of fun if she can lighten up, encouraged by his terrific sense of humour.

The bachelor Gemini doesn't readily give up his freedom, but he is more likely than she is to be a virgin on his wedding night, and to forge a lasting bond with one person. She can scarcely wait to whiz down the aisle, a couple of times if need be, is rather more successful than he in finding a true soul mate, and may discover that only in her second marriage are her true passions unleashed.

In his mind, her fidelity will have been a precondition of marriage, and he may very well call time on the partnership if she strays. He is less likely than she to have a bit on the side, but if he does she will either say "Let's have this out", or she'll pretend that she sees nothing in the hope that it will all come right in the end.

SCORPIO WOMAN—CANCER MAN

Yes, they quite fancy one another, and he sees her as a potential life partner, but as partner material she rates him very low. A he-man physique could give her pause, though, and if he has the kind of sexy, soulful eyes in which she feels she could drown, she'll be his. Still, she'll need a soft heart, an appealing persona and an infectious laugh if she is going to catch him.

In many ways, these two are meant for each other. They both fall happily into clear-cut, male-female roles, with him out there earning a crust (rather more than a crust, if she has her way), while she stays at home preparing candlelit dinners for two.

The bad news is that they are often less compatible in bed than out of it. She emphasises sex as the very key to a good relationship; she thinks that passion not only can but must be sustained in marriage, while it ranks low amongst his priorities, and he is less likely than her to have tried it before they got together. She needs to keep him simmering with a slow build-up to love, before bringing him to a rolling boil. A sense of security, and of deeper understanding, unlocks his sensibilities, while his humorous approach can dissuade her from being too heavy about love.

She is in more haste than he is to marry a first time, and both are quite likely to remarry (he, of all men, most commonly takes a second partner). If he shows increasing indifference to her physically, she may be driven to look for sex elsewhere, while he will tend to turn a blind eye. He is among the more faithful of men, but if he should take a lover, she will agonise about it, and try to find a way out of their deadlock.

SCORPIO WOMAN—LEO MAN

He is rather more inclined to seek her company than she his, and neither rates the other as an obvious sexual partner. She will lionise him, though, if he has all the items on the Scorpio shopping-list; if he's in really fine shape, with a well-pitched voice and that special light in his eyes. He wants her to share his interests, and finds a sexy laugh and supermodel statistics the biggest turn-on.

Will they make a go of it long-term? There could be trouble on the domestic front. She excels in creating a beautiful home, but she likes him to earn the money while she spends it, and he somehow can't see it her way.

Both want a sexy, funny, life partner, or laugh partner, who knows how to please them in bed. He is likely to be more sexually experienced than her when they embark on the sea of married love. They make adventurous lovers, and are agreed that sex improves in marriage. But proud Leo demands constant expressions of awe and admiration, which she is not disposed to supply, with the effect that he sometimes feels unappreciated.

In general, she makes a more solid marriage than he manages. And he is less eager to give up his precious freedom in the first instance, though he may remarry like a shot, and will often find greater sexual satisfaction with a second partner.

She is rather more likely than he is to cheat in marriage, and he is less forgiving, often refusing to discuss what is happening, (as she would do in his situation), instead demanding a divorce.

SCORPIO WOMAN—VIRGO MAN

This is quite a common partnership—surprisingly, since neither tops the other's Most Wanted list. His ideal woman is slim and feminine with a husky voice. Her perfect man is physically strong and well-made, with a twinkle in his eye.

They will have to work at their relationship if it is not to founder, since there is a big question mark over their compatibility. She would like him to pay all the bills, while she chooses the soft furnishings and cooks delicious meals, but he may insist that she hold down a job.

Because they are both very into sex, and value a sense of humour, they should have years of fun in bed. He surprises her with his erotic artistry and his appetite for love, but he can become tense and resistant to her ardent, intuitive love-making, while she clams up if she suspects that he doesn't understand her. She is far more likely than he is to say that marriage frees her to enjoy sex and enhances her pleasure; he is second-most-likely of all signs to say that sex in marriage is not so satisfying. Perhaps unexpectedly, she is more likely than him to be a virgin when she plights her troth.

He is slower to marry in the first instance—but quick to say "I do" for the second time. They stand about an even chance of finding true love in this world.

If affairs pose a threat, they will be keener than most to thrash the thing out in an adult manner, though there is a slight risk that, if she finds love outside marriage, he will withdraw into himself and be unprepared to acknowledge that they are in trouble.

SCORPIO WOMAN—LIBRA MAN

He is very drawn to her, more emotionally than sexually. She is very lured by him, more sexually than emotionally. Especially if he's a fine figure of a man, with a deep, mellow voice, she will feel a powerful physical attraction to him. And, who knows? If she embodies those attributes he most desires, a giving nature and a gorgeous figure, it might just tip the scales in her favour.

He likes her clear, rational way of thinking; the fact that she speaks her mind and knows what she wants (he has no time for doormats). He's not so keen on her game plan, however, which has her swanning around at home, in the lap of luxury if possible, while he provides the wherewithal. He is glad she's a home-lover, of course, but he may insist that she makes some kind of contribution to keep them solvent.

Both are keen to keep the sexual flame burning brightly, and they make adventurous love. She is far more likely than him to be a virgin till her wedding day, and says kindness and humour keep love alive, while he puts the stress on loyalty and good looks. Being half of a regular couple can actually increase her sex drive; his is unchanged by marriage.

Of all men, Mr Libra makes the most stable partnerships, but she is more likely to find the kind of deep, fulfilling romance that she dreams of. She's quicker off the mark when it comes to matrimony, but rather more likely than he is to be discouraged from trying it a second time.

They must both beware the distractions and temptations that

present themselves, this sexy, susceptible pair. If she takes a lover, he may shore up his ego by having a bit on the side himself. If he is the one who wanders, she will usually give him a second chance, so long as he is prepared to work with her at restoring the balance in their marriage.

SCORPIO WOMAN—SCORPIO MAN

What would you expect? Ms Scorpio, so enamoured of sex, says that by far the sexiest man for her is...Mr Scorpio. And, since he feels the same way, the atmosphere between them can simply crackle with electricity. Yet they do not necessarily see one another as partners.

Such is the magnetism between them, that it really wouldn't matter how he looked. But a powerful build will do very nicely, thank you, as will a great voice. He can't resist good legs, but he prizes a sweet nature, too, a certain feminine softness and a loyal heart.

Her ambitions to be a kept woman, while creating a splendid home, may cut little ice with him; of all men, he is least into home birds.

If this causes discord between them, things should look up at bedtime, since both argue that sexual attraction is fundamental to lasting marital happiness, and find profound satisfaction in sex within marriage. They are great at pleasing one another, though they both need to learn to take as well as give. They share a sense of fun, too, and will heighten their pleasure by dreaming up all kinds of naughty diversions. The downside is that he who so rates sex in marriage, can turn cold if it fails to live up to his high expectations.

She is less likely than him to make a sound marriage, and he will often mate for life, once he has passed the 10-year mark. Yet she is more likely than he is to find that one soulmate to love truly, madly, deeply. Both want and like to be married, though he is more reluctant a second time.

Because of their enthusiasm for sex, they are both at above average risk of being seduced by the charms of an outsider. But should either of them get up to hanky-panky, they will both have enough commitment to the marriage, to want to find a way out of their fix.

THE SAGITTARIUS MAN'S LOVEMATCHES

SAGITTARIUS MAN—CAPRICORN WOMAN

Neither score high with each other in the partner popularity stakes and it could take time before they find they fancy each other. A warm smile and a slim body grab his attention—and the promise of faithfulness makes him want to stick around. She's the type to turn to jelly at a sexy smile and likes a man who is tall, muscular and confident, with a good voice. She'll want him to be kind, faithful and able to provide for her and the children. Sagittarius may be happy to be breadwinner—but will expect her to chip in when she can. Humour is high on their list of essentials. And while she wants a loyal fun-lover, he especially asks for kindness. But his totally open, sporty, talk-dirty approach to sex might shock Capricorn, who likes to be gently wooed.

He's at higher risk of making remarriage a habit, while she has a better record for making the first one her last. She is keener to wed first time—and again. And she's likelier than most to marry her true love, while he's less often lucky. She's more often a virgin on her wedding night, but she's the sign least likely to vote marriage a lovelife booster, while he's more enthusiastic. Yet she finds remarriage brings her more of a sparkle that it does him. Both tend to be faithful, but if she does stray he'll hope to work problems out—she would be quick off the mark to divorce if he faltered.

SAGITTARIUS MAN—AQUARIUS WOMAN

Yummy, she says of him, but otherwise both give each other average marks as life partners and sexmates. They may well meet through a mutual interest—and her warm smile, slim body and faithful nature are her trump cards. She is looking for something special in a man beyond surface attraction—but gorgeous eyes, smart clothes and a good voice could help. Long-term, both say a mate with a sense of humour is vital. He also asks to be shown kindness and likes money, too, while she wants to be well understood by a loyal hardworker who is handsome and skilled in bed! Both are open and curious about sex, so there could be some sensational scenes between the sheets.

He is at higher risk of marrying more than once, but neither are particularly flighty. She's got more chance of making a long-lasting match—he's the man least likely to celebrate his 10th anniversary still hitched. She's keener to marry and to remarry, while he's more easily disillusioned than most by the whole business. Yet he's slightly luckier when it comes to marrying the love of his life. But both are less likely than most to wed as virgins. She finds marriage more sexually satisfying—or quite the opposite. He's pretty trustworthy, being the man least likely to have an affair. But both are keener than most to ask why and work things out if their partner ever looked for fun outside marriage.

SAGITTARIUS MAN—PISCES WOMAN

They love to lust after each other—yet he also names her as the sign he finds most unfanciable! And partnerwise, they give each other average ratings. Her warm smile and slim body move him to action—and if she is faithful and likes doing the same things as him, romance has a good chance. She thinks he's got the sexiest smile ever and she can't keep her hands off his well-honed body. His kind and faithful nature wins her over, too. Long-term, both say humour keeps them happy. Kindness also helps—and so does having enough money. Steamy fantasies and sex talk keeps mutual passions simmering here, but while he's all go between the sheets, she yearns for just a touch more romance.

Both may well get hitched more than once, especially him. She has a better record for making a bond last a decade or more—he's the man who least often does. She's far keener to wed and hates to feel left on the shelf. Meanwhile, he's the man most reluctant to give wedlock a second go. She is a little luckier at marrying a true love and is twice as likely to be a virgin when she does. Marriage, first time or second, is steamier for her, too. He's the man least likely to be unfaithful, while she's at above average risk. She would probably want to bin her marriage if he strayed. He'd ask what went wrong and try to work things out if she is ever untrue.

SAGITTARIUS MAN—ARIES WOMAN

He gives her the go-ahead as a partner, and finds her the sexiest sign of all. Yet she says she's unlikely to stick with him. She either fancies him—or says he's not her type. Her warm smile and sexy eyes are what makes his pulse race, and he's relieved that, like him, she tends to be faithful. His eyes and smile grab her attention, too, and she loves his chatty confidence and charitable personality. Both say their perfect partner must share their sense of humour and offer loyalty and understanding. And neither believe that sex is the be all and end all of a relationship. Yet both are adventurous under the covers, but he must remember to cheer her on with sexy compliments—and bite back on usual blunt talk.

Both may well tie the knot more than once—she's the sign most likely to. He's the man who least often makes a long-lasting match and she doesn't do much better. She's keener to marry, though. If his marriage fails, he's the man most likely to say never again. They are quite likely to marry the love of their life but, for all her brashness, she's far likelier than him to be a virgin. Unlike him, once wed, she finds sex either soars—or takes a dip, though second time around she gets surefire steamy results. If she ever strays, he'll want to know why and put things right. But if he wanders, she'll rush straight to a divorce lawyer.

SAGITTARIUS MAN—TAURUS WOMAN

He'd love to settle down with her, but she doesn't make him think of sex. She'd rather keep things casual because he's not often her type, bodywise. She'll have to stay slim if she does want to win his heart—and must work on her warm smile, too. If she is the faithful kind and shares the same outdoorsy hobbies, that's another plus. She wants a man who is kind, true, tall and muscular, confident, smart and slim. A great smile and a winning way with words work, too. And if he can provide well for her, they're on! But he worries about money, so he'll want her to chip in to the family budget, too. Long-term, both think kindness is essential—and a sense of humour keeps him hot, while she's the sign who most needs to have fun. Both are at their best sexually once fully committed—and his laugh-a-minute style of loving will stop her ever taking passion too seriously.

He's likelier to marry more than once and she does better at making a long-lasting bond. She's a lot keener to get a ring on her finger and is likelier than most to wed Mr Perfect. And she more often hangs onto her virginity until she does. Her sexlife really takes off within marriage—and she's a lot more fulfilled than him by sex in a second marriage, too. He's the man least likely to be unfaithful, while she runs an above average risk. But both would want to work mutual problems out if affairs threaten to split them.

SAGITTARIUS MAN—GEMINI WOMAN

Not a vast chance of a lifetime together—both are on the fickle side. But he gives her average marks as a sexual partner and companion. Her neat body and warm smile make him want to find out more— and he'll be pleased with what he finds if she can be faithful and shares his interests. A warm smile breaks the ice with Gemini—who says her Mr Right must be kind, confident, smartly dressed and easy to talk to. When it comes to lifelong commitment, both say kindness is vital—and having enough money helps. Humour keeps him keen, while she's the sign that most needs a man who understands her. This duo love spicy sex talk.

He's likelier than her to marry more than once. But both are the signs that least often make a long-lasting match. She's in less of a rush than any other woman to win marital status—he's even less hurried. But he's happier than her to give wedlock a second go and is luckier when it comes to settling with a true love. Sadly, she's the woman least likely to. She's more often a love newcomer. But neither are especially patient. Marriage gives her sexlife more of a perk up and so does a second bond. But both will want to look for solutions if their marriage is under fire from infidelity. Their main aim will be to stick together.

SAGITTARIUS MAN—CANCER WOMAN

She hums and haws over his fanciability, but might settle with him. He's not so keen on her and gives her the thumbs down. Her ideal man is well-dressed, with gorgeous eyes. But while he gives a great smile top marks, she's the woman least smitten by facial expressions. Shared interests strike a chord with him—and he can't resist a slim body. Surprisingly for the restless wanderer of the zodiac, he rates faithfulness highly and is the man least likely to stray. Long-term both long to be understood and to be treated with TLC. He says humour keeps happiness loves high. But he'll find her possessiveness goes beyond a joke and puts the dampers on his free and easy lovestyle.

He's likelier than her to remarry and is the man who least often makes a bond last 10 years or more, while she does better. Both want to wed, her especially. But she more often marries a true love and is nearly twice as likely to save herself for the wedding day. And while she's the sign most likely to find sex soars within a long-term bond, he gets revived, too. But having children could see passion take a nose-dive for him. Both are less likely than most to have affairs. But he'd want to sit down and sort things out if she went astray, while she may well want to see him squirm in the divorce court if he is caught playing away.

SAGITTARIUS MAN—LEO WOMAN

For two dynamic Fire signs, they're surprisingly dissatisfied with each other, both as partners and sexually. Firstly, there'll be diets all round here—both demand that their partner stays in trim. She wants him to develop his muscles, too, while he'll want her to join him in the gym and share his latest fad. Her warm smile cheers him on—but he'll expect her to stay faithful and gives this quality the top male vote. Loyalty matters most to her—and she'll be glad to know he is the man least likely to stray. He wants her to be kind, understanding and able to have a laugh. Leo may well want to dominate him in bed, though—bear hugs and rowdy fun will stop her treating him like a toy-boy.

He more often notches up at least two wives, while she does better at making love last a decade or more. Both want to marry, (she's almost too keen). But he may not have the heart to try a second time, unlike her. He is luckier at finding and keeping the love of his life, but Leo is more than twice as likely to hang onto her virginity until her wedding night. Marriage has a firecracker effect on her lovelife It may spark him off, too. He's Mr Faithful of the zodiac, while she's more likely than some to stray. Typically, he'll want to try to solve their problems if she does have an affair, while she may well take her own lover if he proves a let-down.

SAGITTARIUS MAN—VIRGO WOMAN

He names her as a favourite partner—and passion can burn brightly too here. But picky Virgo is not so stuck on him sexually and says he's her least likely partner. A warm smile melts his heart and promises of faithfulness wins it. She wants him to be trustworthy and true, too—and if he's tall, slim and muscular that's an added bonus. But independent Virgo doesn't expect him to keep her, which will please her cash-conscious mate. He'll want her to be kind, not critical, while she'll insist on—and probably get—loyalty. He needs to be understood and to share laughs, while she says love freeze-dries if it's not fun. Both rate being pals as much as lovers, but athletic Sagittarius will be surprised at just what sexy fun and games supposedly prim Virgo will go along with.

She's the sign likeliest to marry more than once and he's pretty high risk. But she does better at making a love bond last at least 10 years—his chances are lousy. She is keener to marry, but both can lose heart over the effort of getting hitched a second time. She's luckier at settling with a dream lover and is much likelier to save herself for them. And they have a fair, but not especially high chance, of a sizzling sexlife once wed. If she ever strays, he'll want to know why and try to put things right. She'll head for the divorce courts if she is deceived.

SAGITTARIUS MAN—LIBRA WOMAN

She's a favourite sexbomb and his first choice as a partner, too. Yet she doesn't go weak over him and he's not likely to be her life partner choice either. She needs a man who can keep her smiling with his lively chat, impress her with his muscles and surprise her with his good taste in clothes. Faithfulness wins her vote, too. A warm smile and a slim body is the way to his heart. He also wants his partner to be true—and if she shares his favourite pastime passions, even better. Long-term, he thrives on kindness and understanding—not forgetting humour, which keeps his heart skipping. She wants her mate to be kind and loyal—and she could have found the right man here. Security sets her loveskills free, but she'll be hard pressed to slow her fast-moving mate down so that they can take love the way she likes it, sexy and slow.

She's much likelier to marry only once and is the woman who most often makes a long-lasting match, while he's the man who least often does. She's keen to marry, while he's the man most easily disillusioned with wedlock. She is luckier at marrying the love of her life and is more likely to go down the aisle as a virgin. And both say that sex soars once married, but he finds remarriage steamier. She may well take her own lover if she ever catches him out, while he'd want to know why and put problems right if she had a fling.

SAGITTARIUS MAN—SCORPIO WOMAN

Their marriage might not take them to pensionable age and there's no special chemistry here. But her warm smile could yet win his heart—and if they have interests in common and she seems the faithful type, there's hope of success. Gorgeous eyes grab her and she likes a man to be tall and muscular, with a good voice. But while she wants him to be able to provide for her and any children that come along, he worries about money and will want her to have a stake in family finances. Long-term, he wants to be treated kindly and truly understood—and both rate a sense of humour. She also thinks lasting sexual attraction and being good in bed is vital. But this sporty, fun approach to loving could leave her unsatisfied—she wants to scale emotional peaks.

Both are at high risk of marrying more than once, especially her. But she's likelier to make a lasting match—he's the man who least often does. She's keener to marry, while he's the man most likely to want to give it a miss second time around. She's luckier at marrying the love of her life and is likelier to be a virgin when she weds. He's the impatient type! Getting hitched sets her sexlife alight and might warm his up, too. He's more faithful than most, she's less. But both would want to know what had gone wrong if the other strayed, and at least hope to mend bridges.

SAGITTARIUS MAN—SAGITTARIUS WOMAN

She thinks he makes a great partner, but he's not so sure about her. They quite fancy one another, though. Her slim body and warm smile go down well. If she is interested in the same things as him and seems the faithful sort, he'll ask her out. She likes men with Heathcliff-style flashing eyes, they'd best be tall, slim, kind-hearted and easy to talk to. Both want their life partner to share their sense of humour and understand how they think. He appreciates kindness, too, but says it's important they both have enough money. She wants a mate who works hard, but enjoys being at home. At bedtime there'll be rows, laughter—and delicious pleasure. But there will be no risk of boredom in a relationship built on the bedrock of friendship.

He's likelier than her to marry more than once. She rarely makes a bond last 10 years or more—and he's the man least likely to! She's in far more of a hurry to get hitched—and he can be warier than most of getting married a second time. But he's luckier at finding and keeping his dream love, while she is more likely to save herself for her own special person. Marriage sees her sexlife take off—and remarriage sees it skyrocket! He can report some favorable results, too. They are the signs least likely to have affairs. But if either ever does wander, both will want to sit down and try to work out what went wrong, then put it right.

THE SAGITTARIUS WOMAN'S LOVEMATCHES

SAGITTARIUS WOMAN—CAPRICORN MAN

She can't wait to settle down with him—but he gives her the cold shoulder at first and neither vote each other as super-sexy. She likes great eyes and a good line in chat and she'll fancy him if he's tall, slim and kind-hearted. Warm smiles, sexy tones and great legs make him want to pursue her. And if she is faithful, gentle and interested in the same things as him, romance could soon get on the road. For love to last, she needs to feel understood by a mate who shares her sense of humour, a worker bee who enjoys his homelife, too. He likes a laugh, too, but expects his partner to have money of her own and to stay mouth-wateringly attractive after marriage. She loves his tough-one-minute, tender-the-next lovemaking style—but she'll want a turn at being boss in bed sometimes!

They run an average risk of notching up spouses, but he does better at making a long-running bond. Both enjoy the single life, but she's keener to leave it. And he tends to be shyer of tying the knot a second time, too. She's luckier at marrying a dream lover and is far likelier to do so as a virgin. She finds marriage a steamier affair, and remarriage, too—though he doesn't do badly sexwise, either. He's the man likeliest to have affairs, while she doesn't. If she does stray though, he's not going to stick around. She's likelier to stay cool and try to sort things out between them if he wandered.

SAGITTARIUS WOMAN—AQUARIUS MAN

She's keener to settle with him than he is with her and neither find each other sexbombs. Kindness and a great way with words win her heart—and a tall slim physique makes her go weak, too. A curvy, trim body turns him on—and if it belongs to a good homemaker with a gentle manner, all the better! To let him stick around, she'll want him to share her sense of humour, understand her, work hard and tackle those jobs at home, too. He especially wants fun and understanding and values a loyal mate who is good in bed. Lovemaking between these two can be tender and imaginative—but spontaneous Sagittarius may find her lover's style too coolly premeditated, too rehearsed.

He's a lot likelier to marry more than once, yet he does better at making love last 10 years or more. Both enjoy the single life more than most, but she's happier than him to let it go. Yet marriage must suit him, as once he's tried it, he's hungry to wed again. She has better luck at settling with a true love—he's the male starsign least likely to. And he's the zodiac's least patient man when it comes to his own virginity. She finds matrimony a sexier state and remarriage is even spicier for her, while he reports less enhancement than most. She's less likely than him to stray, but if she does he may well want a divorce. She'd keep calm and ask why, then try to sort things out, if he admitted to seeing someone else.

SAGITTARIUS WOMAN—PISCES MAN

He says she's very sexy indeed and she'll probably fancy him, too. But he gives her only average marks partnerwise—and she hardly puts him in the picture! His sexy eyes could make her change her mind though—and if he is tall, slim, kind and easy to talk to, love could find a way. Her great legs, slim body and sexy laugh are his weakness. But while he wants her to stay at home and look after him, independent Sagittarius has broader horizons. Her perfect partner must share her sense of humour, understand her, enjoy being at home with her—and work hard. Long-term, he wants his mate to be loyal, amusing and full of fun—and good in bed, too. But while fantasy-filled sex will bond these two close at first, she'll soon want more commitment, more quickly, than Pisces usually gives.

He more often tots up a string of spouses. Yet he's also likelier to make a match last 10 years or more. Both enjoy single status. Yet she can be keen to wed and he's the man happiest to marry a second time (and the sign luckiest at wedding the love of his life). He's likelier than her to save himself for marriage, which he finds more sexually enhancing, too. But both are the signs least likely to report a drop in lovemaking. Her sexlife often hits the stratosphere when she remarries and he gets a good boost, too. Both are the faithful type. But if he wasn't, she'd hope they could stay together on a new basis. He may race for divorce if she were untrue.

SAGITTARIUS WOMAN—ARIES MAN

A love or hate pairing where they either fancy each other—or can't stand the sight of each other. And it's not very likely they'll settle together. Her warm smile makes him look twice—and her nice eyes and curvy body send him all the right signals, too. But while he's unashamedly after a homely type who'll devote herself to him, she's very independent. Her Mr Right has sexy eyes and is tall and slim, kind and easy to talk to. He shares her humour, understands her freestyle thinking, works hard and enjoys being at home. Aries wants her to be good-looking and to have some cash of her own. And she must be a sexbomb, too, to please him fully. Sagittarius will expect him to treat her as the individual she is, in bed or out. But he's so detached about lovemaking, he may even forget her name!

There's an average risk both will have more than one marriage. But he's a lot better at making wedlock stay blissful long-term. Both are keen to wed, especially him, but his attitude to remarriage is often once bitten, twice shy. He is luckier than most at settling with a true love and is likelier to be a virgin when he weds, too. Her sexlife gets a bigger boost from marriage though—and it turns technicolour second time around! She's the zodiac's most faithful woman, while he's at above average risk of affairs. If he does stray, she'll hope they can settle their differences and stick together. If she wanders, he may even the score by taking a lover of his own.

SAGITTARIUS WOMAN—TAURUS MAN

Natural partners for life, they aren't—and it's not often that they fancy each other. Her ideal man is easy to talk to, kind with sexy eyes, slim and tall. Taurus can't resist a warm smile and likes his woman to be curvy and kind-natured with a sexy voice and laugh. Faithfulness, gentleness and at least one shared interest keep him. He'll want his lady to be good about the house as well, but freedom-loving Sagittarius may have other goals in mind! She wants some-one she can have a laugh with, who understands the way she thinks. He must be hardworking—but able to enjoy simply being at home, too. Taurus wants to be treated kindly and also likes a hardworker who understands him. He wants his mate to be love-skilled—and his tender-tough sensuality will leave Ms Sagittarius primed to follow where he leads.

She is at higher risk of running up several spouses, while he's got a lot more chance of making marriage last over a decade. She's the woman most keen to get a ring on her finger and he's in some hurry, too. But he's better at finding and keeping a true love and is likelier to be a virgin when he weds. She says marriage is more of a sexlife improver and, unlike him, reports that remarriage is stunningly sexier that the single life. She's likelier to stay faithful. But if either ever looks elsewhere, these two may well want to sit down and talk their troubles through, hoping they can stay together.

SAGITTARIUS WOMAN—GEMINI MAN

Super-sexy hunk, she votes him. He finds her rather tasty, too. Yet he ends up keener than she is! They'll probably meet at evening classes or on a weekend walk. Her great legs and sexy laugh make him look twice. Deeper values like her kindness, faithfulness and gentleness mean a lot to him. She won't be able to resist gazing into his gorgeous eyes and will love his quicksilver way with words. If he is tall, slim and kind, too, she's won over. At first neither will want to seem too keen—but watch out for misunderstandings over too much game-playing! A shared sense of humour will save the situation. She's hoping for understanding and likes a man who'll work hard, but still enjoy his time at home with her. He says fun, good looks, sexual attraction and sex skills spell happiness for him.

She's at slightly higher risk of running up ex-husbands, while he more often makes a bond last 10 years. Yet he's far keener to stay single, while she's in a rush to wed. She's happier to marry a second time, too. But neither can bank on settling with the love of their life, though he's the luckier of the pair. And he's more patient when it comes to hanging onto his virginity, too. She gets better marital sex than he does, but reassuringly, they are the signs least likely to say loving gets worse. And she says her sexlife really takes off with husband number two. Both are faithful. But while she'll look for solutions if he wanders, he'll hire a divorce lawyer if she does.

SAGITTARIUS WOMAN—CANCER MAN

She wants to be out and about—he's a homebird. He says his mate must he kind, gentle and good about the house—and a sexy laugh keeps him tuned to her wavelength. She loves her man to be tall, slim and easy to talk to, with deeply tender eyes. Kindness and faithfulness count with her, too. But while he likes a stay-at-home partner, independent Sagittarius hates her horizons to shrink, so she may detest domesticity. Long-term, he wants to settle with someone who understands him and who he knows will be totally loyal. She says humour keeps romance on the boil—love freeze-dries for her without laughter. His sensuous after-dark manoeuvres keep her happy, but his moods cast a shadow she won't like—ever light and bright is her style.

He's the man who most often accumulates ex-wives, while she's at average risk. Yet he's better at making his marriage a long-term affair. Marriage holds more appeal for her, yet he's luckier at marrying the love of his life and is likelier to be a virgin. She finds wedlock really perks up her sexlife—while it can all go off for him. And second marriages can be stunningly better for her, if not quite so steamy for him. Both tend to be faithful, but if he is ever untrue, she'll want to air their problems—while he may quietly hope for the best if he finds she's having a wicked fling.

SAGITTARIUS WOMAN—LEO MAN

She says he oozes sex appeal and he certainly likes the look of her! But she's the one who is likelier to want to put their affair on a long-term basis. Right from the start, they can't keep their eyes off each other. She falls for him if he is tall and slim with a kind face and an easy way of talking, while her sexy laugh and warm smile make him want to know her life history. That curvy body and those great legs spur his interest, too. If they have an interest in common, so much the better. Both want a long-term mate who understands them well and laughs at the same jokes. But he's the sexier of the two, giving higher marks to sexual attraction, good looks and sex-skills. Jokey Sagittarius must watch a tendency to tease proud Leo between the sheets. He hates that. He needs applause for being her best lover ever—mockery makes his love ebb away!

He's likely to have more weddings than her, yet he also stands a better chance of making his marriage(s) last 10-years-plus. Both enjoy being single. She's likelier to stroll down the aisle as a virgin. Marriage is even more sexually fulfilling for him than it is for her, though. If he does ever wander, she'll hope to put their relationship problems right. He may well want a quickie divorce if she is untrue.

SAGITTARIUS WOMAN—VIRGO MAN

He sees her future spouse material—and there's a fair chance she'll choose him. But he fancies her more than the other way round. A curvy, slim body and an attractive voice appeal, and a gentle manner are what it takes to win his heart. Sexy eyes make her go weak—

and if he's tall, slim, kind-hearted and easy to talk to, he fits her bill! To put love on a long-term footing, he must show understanding and humour, work hard and make the most of his homelife. He shares her need for understanding and humour—and loyalty, kindness and sexual attraction come high up his list, too. But while she yearns for spontaneous passion and surprises, he insists on timetabling love. This could easily get her down.

Neither are particularly likely to marry more than once—certainly not him. Yet they don't do especially well at making long-lasting matches either, though his record's better than hers. Both enjoy the single life, but she's in more of a hurry to get to the altar and to remarry, too. She finds the state of matrimony a lot sexier than he does—he gets low marks here. And while he's the man most likely to find loving gets worse, she's the sign least likely to report this. Despite her flirty, boisterous style, she's the zodiac's most faithful woman, he's at average risk. But both would want to talk troubles through if affairs ever cropped up. He's also likely to bury his head in the sand if she were unfaithful.

SAGITTARIUS WOMAN—LIBRA MAN

He's so impatient to carry her over that threshold. But he may never get the chance,, as he's one of her least likely choices. And neither votes the other super-sexy. Her curvy body and attractive voice appeal to him first, but it's her kind and faithful nature that always makes him want to stick around. She might like his gorgeous eyes, and if he is tall, slim and kind-hearted, with a pleasing voice, he could yet be her type. Shared roles suit them both—neither wants to do all the paid work, or all the dusting! Long-term he needs a mate who will be loyal, which this lady often is. And she'll want him to have a good sense of humour. Both like a homelover, but he says that good looks and sexual attraction keep marriage afloat, while she simply wants friendship with an equal. And it could grate with no-nonsense Sagittarius that Libra expects to be treated like a hero and titillated in bed.

She's far more sexually spontaneous than him. But both are good at notching up a full 10 happy years. She is keener to wed—but he is in more of a hurry, second time around. She has better luck at settling with a true love and is more than twice as likely to be the virgin. Marriage stokes up her sexlife—he says loving often stays the same. She's at low risk of affairs—he's high . But she'll want to talk their troubles through if he does let her down, while he may take a lover himself if she is ever untrue.

SAGITTARIUS WOMAN—SCORPIO MAN

He's a sex-idol in her eyes, but he's not so bowled over by her and there's only a middling chance they'll choose to spend their whole lives together. Great legs are his weakness—and a gentle, kind and faithful nature tells him he's struck lucky. A flash from his eyes gets her going—and if he's tall, slim, great to talk to and kind-hearted as well, she's won over. Long-term, she wants a mate who understands her, shares her sense of humour, works hard and enjoys doing jobs around the house. He wants a fun-loving homebird who is good in bed and keeps him alive sexually. But his emotional intensity and serious love expertise could prove too much for pillow-fighting Sagittarius, who likes a giggle anytime, anywhere.

He is the man least likely to make a string of marriages, while she's average. He's better too at making marital bliss last 10 years, while she scores rather low here. Both enjoy being single—yet they are still happier than most to head for the altar. But he can be wary of going through those vows a second time. He is luckier at marrying a true love and is likelier to do so as a virgin. And he either finds matrimony a more arousing state than she does or reports back with a noticeable drop in interest. Her sexlife takes off with remarriage though, while he scores less highly. He's at high risk of affairs—she's the most faithful sign. Wait for the fireworks. But both would hope to stick together if affairs ever occurred

SAGITTARIUS WOMAN—SAGITTARIUS MAN

So alike, yet not when it comes to singling out partners! He's her ideal, she says. He rarely makes a beeline for her—would you believe, he actually fancies her more than she fancies him. They'll probably meet through mutual pals—and it will be her dazzling smile and slim body that first register. As she's also the faithful type, there could be a future with him after all... His gorgeous eyes make her want to know more. If he is kind-hearted, easy to talk to and tall and slim, he could turn out to be her Mr. Perfect after all. Humour could ease out any bumps in their romance. She hopes he'll also understand her, work hard and enjoy his homelife, while he wants to be treated kindly. She dreads being trapped and bored, his biggest fear is being short of money. Both appreciate openness and honesty between the sheets, but she'll have to get this sporty, speedy male to slow down if she wants to maximise pleasure. And be prepared to spell this out.

He's likelier to marry more than once, and both score very low for making a bond last 10 years or more. She's far keener to marry and is much less easily put off remarriage, too. But he has better luck when it comes to settling with a true love. She's the more likely virgin. Marriage, and especially remarriage, sees her sexlife really perk up, while doing far less for his. These two are the most faithful pair in the zodiac. But if affairs ever do threaten to divide them, both will hope they can work their problems through and may end up staying together.

THE CAPRICORN MAN'S LOVEMATCHES

CAPRICORN MAN—AQUARIUS WOMAN

A lifelong match between these two is the exception rather than the rule and it's not often they turn each other on. Great legs spell lust at first sight for him and a warm smile and an attractive voice usually make him ask for her phone number. If she turns out to be faithful, gentle and interested in the same things as him, even better. It's hard to pin down her fanciability factors—but a subtle smile, melifluous voice and smart clothes are included. For love to last, she demands loyalty and wants her man to understand her offbeat way of thinking. Love goes cold without laughs, she says—but hard work is also required and he must keep his looks and stay sensational in bed. He says humour and looks count, too, and he wants his mate to be able to pay her way. But there could be a power tussle in bed. He likes to be big boss—she wants to stay on top!

Both may marry more than once, but he's likelier to keep a ring on his finger for 10 years. The single life suits him better, yet he's keener to wed than she is. But she's in more of a hurry to remarry—he's reluctant to risk it. She is luckier at settling with a true love. But though she's the woman least likely to wed as a virgin, she stands more chance than him! Marriage can send her sex life sky-high or make it fizzle. His love life is less of a rollercoaster, but he finds remarriage more satisfactory. Both will look for answers if the other is untrue. But if a solution can't be found, he'll want divorce.

CAPRICORN MAN—PISCES WOMAN

She scores a hit with him, sexually and as a partner. But he's not one of her favourites and she doesn't find him very sexy. Faithfulness means a lot to him in a woman, despite being the man most likely to stray! He's also looking for gentleness and shared interests—and a warm smile, great legs and an attractive voice don't go amiss either. The man she marries must be kind and true—and if he's slim, with a ready smile he'll win points with her, too. Both say that being able to share a laugh and having enough money help to keep marriage well afloat. He wants his mate to keep her looks and stay sexy, too. He'll be thrilled at the world of fantasy love this daring lady opens up to him—and she'll feel well protected by her own he-man.

Both may marry more than once, especially her. But he's likelier to tot up 10 years of married bliss. The single life suits him better— she can't bear to be unattached. Yet he's keener to actually get married. But second-time-around, both are easily put off, especially him. She is luckier at marrying a dream lover and is a lot likelier to do so as a virgin—he's too inquisitive to save himself. She finds marriage more physically satisfying than he does—but both say sex soars in a second marriage. There is a risk of affairs, especially for him. But he'll try to find ways to stay together if she strays, before resorting to divorce. If he lets her down, she may well take a lover of her own.

CAPRICORN MAN—ARIES WOMAN

He would love to set up home with her and fancies her a lot—except when she turns bossy and won't let him be in charge. She's not so sure she wants to spend years with him and she's in no rush to share his bed, either. Her warm smile, great legs and attractive voice slow workaholic Capricorn down. And if she's the gentle, faithful type and they have an interest in common, he may well want to stick around. Her Mr Right brims with confidence and is kind-hearted and faithful, tall and well-spoken. Best of all, she loves looking deep into his gorgeous eyes. Long-term, she'll settle for a kind and loyal homelover, while he wants his mate to be amusing, good-looking, sexy and rich! But if he chooses her, he'll have to compromise on his love of early morning sex—Aries is night owl.

She's the female sign likeliest to run up a string of ex-husbands, while he's better at making a bond last 10 years or more. But though he's keener to get to the altar, he's wary of making a second mistake. She's luckier at marrying a true love, while he scores low here. And she's far likelier to wed as a virgin—he rarely waits for his wedding night. Marriage either makes her sex life sizzle or go stone cold, while he finds sex within a second marriage is far better. He's the man most at risk of having affairs, while she's truer than most. But she'll sprint to court if she catches him straying, while he'd attempt to talk things through before going for divorce, if he felt let down.

CAPRICORN MAN—TAURUS WOMAN

She loves being swept off her feet and into bed by him—and sees this as a lasting love affair. But surprisingly, he's not keen on this fellow Earth sign and he votes her unsexiest woman of all! Well-turned legs spell instant lust to him and he's smitten by a warm smile, an attractive voice and a soothing manner. She can't resist his quiet confidence, his tall, muscular build and his great taste in clothes. She feels she can confide in him and hopes he will be kind, fun and faithful. But there are no guarantees here—he has one of the worst reputation for wandering in the zodiac! While she wants her man to provide for her, he says her nestbuilding ways don't appeal, so he'll probably want her to go out to work. His perfect mate has sexy good looks, wit—and money of her own in the bank.

Neither are at high risk of multiple marriages, but he scores better for making a bond last a decade or more. He enjoys his single status much more than she does. Yet he's also the man keenest to be a husband—and she's keener still to wed than he is. She strikes lucky more often than most at marrying a true love. And she's likelier to be a virgin when she does—he rarely is. She flourishes within wedlock, getting the best boost of all to her sexlife. But both find that loving is even better second time around. If either admits to an affair, these two will hope to find a way of solving their problems and staying together. If solutions can't be found, however, he'll go for divorce.

CAPRICORN MAN—GEMINI WOMAN

He says she's the sign he most often lusts after—but she says no thanks, he's not her type sexually. Yet there's a fair chance they'll spend a lifetime together. They may well meet through a shared interest and it'll be her lithe legs and inviting voice that first set his passion pulses racing. If her smile is warm and gentle, he's hers! But although he's the zodiac's least faithful man, he may find Gemini's flirting too jealousy-inducing. She can't resist a man in smart clothes, especially if he has a neat chat-up line and oozes confidence. A kind smile clinches it for her! Both say cash worries can undermine love. Instead, she wants kindness and understanding, while he asks for laughs and sexy good looks. And it will be wildfire lovemaking that superglues this unpredictable pair together.

He's likelier to marry twice, but he's also got a high chance of making a bond last 10 years, while she doesn't. Both like being single, but he's secretly keener to get down the aisle, while she often holds tight to her freedom. And neither rush to remarry—he's the man wariest of trying again. She's twice as likely to be a virgin when she weds. She gets a surprise sex boost from marriage, while he may wait until remarriage to find what he's been missing. She's the woman keenest to find a stay-together solution to love triangle problems. He wants answers, too, before resorting to divorce.

CAPRICORN MAN—CANCER WOMAN

They see themselves spending a lifetime together and both find each other reassuring to snuggle up to. Her warm smile, soothing voice and sexy legs first take his fancy. And if she seems the faithful sort and likes the same things he does, he'll want to find out more. A lingering glance from his sexy eyes makes her heart start to thump—and she loves his power-dressed style. To put this on a long-term footing, he'll have to show that he's kind and understanding—and that he finds it fun to create a cosy home with her. But he wants a good-looking, sexy partner with money.

There's a one-in-three chance both will marry more than once. But he's a better bet for making a long-lasting bond. He is in more of a hurry to wed. But while she's the woman keenest to marry a second time, he's the man who is least eager, held back by his pride. She is luckier at marrying her dream lover—he scores low here. And she's likelier to wed as a virgin—he rarely waits. Neither report a big boost to lovemaking from marriage, but he finds remarriage far sexier. She's more faithful than most, while he has the zodiac's worst reputation. Divorce is often the chosen option if affairs come between them. But he'll have a good go at working things out before doing anything drastic because he's realistic.

CAPRICORN MAN—LEO WOMAN

He thinks radiant Leo would make a wonderful partner, but she's not so sure she wants to settle with strong, silent him and neither vote each other ideal bedmates. She says her Mr Right is a slim and muscular hunk—while he describes his ideal woman as having a warm smile, great legs and a lovely voice. She must be faithful, too, that gets his top vote—and interested in the same things as him. Proud Leo demands loyalty from any man she makes her mate. But Capricorn may have a poor record here, the survey shows. He is far keener that his partner has a sense of humour, though both say it's vital that the sexual buzz stays good and strong.

He's higher on the marriage risk register—she's the sign least likely to rewed. Yet he does better at making a bond last 10 years or more and is the man who most dreams of being a husband. But second time around, she's in more of a hurry. Neither can bank on ending up with the love of their life. But while she's one of the signs likeliest to wed as a virgin, he's among the men who least often do. Her sexlife often soars with marriage, while he may have to wait until he's taken the plunge a second time to see a big improvement. Both are at risk of affairs, especially him. She may take a lover herself or stay quiet, hoping for the best if she finds he has let her down. He'd hope for answers if the situation was reversed—or would press for a divorce.

CAPRICORN MAN—VIRGO WOMAN

He's keen to settle with helpful Virgo and can fancy her, too. But she says he's not often her type. Her kind of man is tall, muscular, slim—and faithful. But there are no guarantees here as Capricorn is the man most likely to stray. He may well fall for her warm smile, soothing voice and neat, shapely legs. And if she's gentle and faithful and takes an interest in what he likes doing in his spare time, he'll hope they can put things on a long-term footing. But she'll expect pledges of loyalty first—plus the promise of fun. He appreciates her humour and he'll want her to keep her sweetly sexy looks. Their lovemaking may not move mountains in its early days, but it's rich in potential—a slow burn.

Virgo is the sign who most often switches marriage partners and she's likelier than him to bale out before the 10-year mark. He's the man most set on being a husband—she's in less of a hurry to wed. But both are the signs least keen to marry a second time. She is likelier to settle with her true love—he's less fortunate here. And she's more than three times more likely to be a virgin when she gets in the marital bed. Sex soars more for her than for him after the wedding, but neither score highly. He may well see sex enhanced after a second marriage, though. Any love triangle troubles would make both race to a divorce lawyer. But he might want to discuss things rationally first, unlike her. She's unforgiving.

CAPRICORN MAN—LIBRA WOMAN

He's a favourite of hers for long-term loving and there's a fair chance he'll choose her, too. Both find each other more cuddly than sexy—but their slow-to-get-off-the-ground romance can work its way up to a crescendo of mutual pleasure. She loves a smooth-talking, chunky hunk with a great smile, a muscular build, smart clothes and a kind heart. But, ironically, for two of the signs most likely to stray, this pair both demand that their partner stays faithful. He can't resist a pair of great legs and loves a warm smile and a silky voice. Let's hope they're all hers. He says he wants to settle with a gentle soul, who likes doing the same things he does. Libra's recipe for lasting love is kindness and loyalty—while he says he needs a sexy, funny, good-looker with cash of her own.

He's at higher risk of remarriage, yet he does even better than her at notching up 10 years of marital bliss—and she's the zodiac woman most likely to succeed here. Both are keen to get down the aisle, particularly him. But he's in far less of a hurry than her, second time around. She may well get hitched to the love of her life, while he tends to be less lucky. And she's also likelier to marry as a virgin. Sex simmers more hotly for her within marriage, but his love life really takes off second time around. If affairs do occur, both partners will want a heart-to-heart to work things out. If that doesn't work, she'll take a lover—and he'll want a divorce.

CAPRICORN MAN—SCORPIO WOMAN

This match gets middle-of-the-road marks, for sex and life-companionship. But his gorgeous eyes could make her blink as he goes past—and if he's tall and muscular, with a good voice, she'll do a double-take. It'll be her voice, too, that first attracts him and her warm smile and wickedly good legs will clinch the deal. He hopes she'll be faithful and gentle, and interested in the same things as him. But she'll want him to provide for her and any children that arrive—and he tends to think women should work, to avoid money worries. Both say sexual attraction is vital to a long-term bond—and her exotic blend of forbidden excitement and sensual abandon could get him well and truly addicted—if he can stand the pace! Humour is another essential. She says a mate must also be skilled in bed, while retaining her good looks keeps him happy.

She's likelier to remarry, while he does slightly better at making love a lasting pleasure. He's even keener than her to get a ring on his finger—but both can feel twice as shy second time around. She's likelier to marry her true love—he's not extra lucky here. And she's a lot more often a virgin when she weds—he hardly ever waits. Marriage doesn't give either an especially big sex boost, but on remarriage these two get a real perk-up. Both are at risk of affairs, but are likelier than most to look for solutions if the other wanders, though he might just give up and seek a divorce.

CAPRICORN MAN—SAGITTARIUS WOMAN

She thinks she's struck lucky here—he's everything she ever wanted, partnerwise at least. Yet he may give her few points as a mate and goes so far as to say they could well be a sexual mismatch. She can't resist a pair of gorgeous eyes, especially if they belong to someone tall, slim and kind-hearted, with a witty line in chat. Great legs and a warm smile are the way to his heart—and he goes weak at the sound of a sexy voice. If they share interests and she's the faithful sort, he could yet be hers! Her long-term dream is to settle with an understanding homelover who works hard and shares her ever-ready sense of humour. This chap wants plenty of laughter too—but he says that sexy good-looks and practical earning power also matter to him.

There's an average chance both will marry more than once, but he's much likelier to stay married 10 years or more. He's the man in the most rush to wed—she's among the women keenest to stay unshackled. Yet she's luckier at marrying a true love. But neither do especially well here. And she's over twice as likely to take her vows as a virgin. Marriage is sexier for her—but both find second marriages steamier than expected. He's the zodiac's least faithful man, while she's its most faithful woman. If they give way to affairs, they'd hope to talk their troubles through and stick together. But he might as easily file for divorce.

CAPRICORN MAN—CAPRICORN WOMAN

He finds her irresistibly sexy and she wants to touch him, too. Yet they're not especially popular with each other as marriage partners. But their lovemaking stamina can make for some memorable marathons and their squabbles are often the preamble to their best sex! She fancies him if he's a tall, slim, muscular love contender who radiates confidence and dresses sensationally. He must have a kind heart, a great smile and a good voice. And if he's faithful, fun and able to provide for her, even better! But this man will want her to work—he doesn't rate a stay-at-home and hates money worries. Both say a sense of humour is vital. His Ms Right is also faithful and gentle with a warm smile, a soothing voice and sexy, good looks. She does like doing the same things he does, so it's hopeful.

He may be slightly likelier to remarry, but he has a better track record for staying wed 10 years or more. He likes being single more than she does—but once he's made up his mind to marry, he's a faster mover. Second time around, she's the woman keenest to wed, while he's the most reluctant male. She's likelier to land a dream lover—he's not often so lucky. And she's likelier to save herself for someone. Neither finds sex an all-consuming passion within marriage, but both say remarriage can get really steamy. Divorce looms large if either strays. But he may have a try at working things out first before saying goodbye.

THE CAPRICORN WOMAN'S LOVEMATCHES

CAPRICORN WOMAN—AQUARIUS MAN

She's keener on him than he is on her, but neither find the other sexiest sign. She's an enthusiastic man-watcher, giving top marks to tall, muscular men who are confident, kind and faithful. A good voice, a great smile behind which lies a good earner, get her top vote. He appreciates a good homemaker, so he may well be happy to take on the bread-winning role for both of them, as long as she stays curvy, slim and gentle, the way he likes. For love to last, both say loyalty is vital—and so is fun! She likes her love feast spiced with humour, while he asks for understanding of his quirky way of thinking. Sex skills keep him happy—and bookish Capricorn surprises him once her inhibitions are stripped away.

She tends to be a one-marriage woman, while he's the man likeliest to amass three wives! Yet both score average marks for making a long-lasting match. He likes the single life—she prefers to be married. But wedlock can suit them both, as they are among the signs keenest to get hitched again. He's the man who least often settles with the love of his life, though, while she's far luckier. And he's least likely to be a virgin on his wedding night, too. Neither say lovemaking changes after marrying—but she finds remarriage more of a sex booster. And both are likely to want a divorce if their partner strays, though he may take a lover himself in revenge.

CAPRICORN WOMAN—PISCES MAN

There's more chance she'll find him a desirable, suitable mate than vice versa. He votes organised Capricorn his least favourite partner and the sign he's least likely to find sexy, too! She likes her men to be men—tall, muscular and confidently spoken. A good earner gets her top vote, too, but he must be faithful and kind to keep her. Pisces can't resist long legs on a slim body, and a sexy laugh turns him on, too. And he may well be happy to be the breadwinner—though she's often much better with money than he is. For love to last long-term, both say loyalty, humour and fun are essential. He values sex skills—and his tender, intuitive loving could release passionate abilities in her she never knew she had!

 Though he's likelier than her to take his marriage vows more than once, he does better at making a bond last 10 years or more. But she's in more of a hurry to marry—he's the male sign least set on getting wed. Once married they both thrive as proved by the fact they're the signs who are keenest to remarry. Both score highly at wedding the love of their lives—he's the man most likely to. There's also a high chance he'll marry as a virgin—and he often gets more of a boost to his sexlife once hitched. She can find it stays the same, though remarriage may work wonders. This pair are more faithful than most but are fast to demand a divorce if the other wanders. But he may decide to quietly hope for the best instead.

CAPRICORN WOMAN—ARIES MAN

She rather fancies him and hopes they'll have a happy future together. But he's not always so struck on her. Her Mr Right is tall and muscular, with a great smile and a confident voice—sounds just like macho Mr Aries! She wants him to be kind, faithful and a good earner. He's the sign who most appreciates a good homemaker, so he may well be happy to bring home the bacon for both of them—for a time—if Capricorn doesn't feel like being her usual ambitious self. Nice eyes, a curvy body and a warm smile are other ways she can win his heart. Her recipe for long-term success is loyalty, humour and fun. He likes the idea of a good-looking home lover who has money of her own and is sensationally sexy!

Neither are at high risk of remarrying, but he does slightly better at making a match last 10 years or more. He's keener to marry—being single doesn't suit him, as he loves being looked after. But she is the woman in the biggest hurry to remarry, while he's more often wary. Both can be lucky at settling with the love of their lives, but he's likelier to remain a virgin until his wedding night. His sexlife either gets a big lift, or comes down to earth with a bump after the wedding—hers more often stays on course. If affairs come between them, she'll turf him out, then shout through the letterbox that she'll see him in court. He may take a lover of his own if she has a fling.

CAPRICORN WOMAN—TAURUS MAN

There's a high chance of marital happiness here—he says she's his favourite partner and she finds him the sexiest sign, too. She can't keep her hands off his tall, muscular frame and she goes all gooey when he smiles. His confident voice captures her imagination—and if he's kind and faithful and earns enough to keep them, she's his. He first notes her warm smile, curvy body and sexy laugh. He wants her to cosset him kindly and gently—and to be faithful and good at creating a cosy home. In return for this domestic bliss, she says he must offer loyalty, humour and fun. He asks her to show understanding, work hard, which she usually does, and be a sexpot in bed. An earthy duo, their passion can stay volcanically hot—as long as they are prepared to try new techniques that keep the risk of bedtime boredom at bay.

He's at low risk of multiple marriages and she often sticks to one match, too. But he has more chance of staying married a decade. He's likelier to do the proposing—but she's the woman keenest to get a ring on her finger second time around. She's a little luckier at marrying a true love, but he more often saves himself until he's hitched. Her sexlife often carries on the same after marriage—while his either soars or sinks without trace. And she finds remarriage a lot sexier. He'll hope to work things out between them, if she ever admits to an affair—she may well want a divorce if he does.

CAPRICORN WOMAN—GEMINI MAN

She'd like to spend a lifetime with sparky Gemini and finds him fairly sexy, too. But he says she's not often his type and her earthbound lovestyle can bring him down. She loves his confident, sociable smile, his tall, muscular build, his sexy voice and smart clothes. But she wants him to be kind, faithful and able to provide for her—and he may well expect her to share the breadwinning. His top rated heart-stoppers are great legs, a slim body and a sexy laugh. Kindness, faithfulness and a gentle manner win his love and he likes a woman he has a lot in common with. She says her magic ingredients for a happy bond are loyalty, humour and lots of fun, which he also rates. He dreams, too, of an understanding, sexy, good-looking homelover who is superb in bed.

Neither runs a high risk of multiple marriages, but he does better at making a bond last 10 years or more. Yet he's the man who most enjoys the single life—and he could take some pushing down the aisle, first and second time around! His reluctance means he can miss out on marrying the love of his life, while Capricorn is lucky here. But he's the man who most often hangs onto his virginity. That's probably why he finds marriage a bigger sexlife booster than her. She says loving usually carries on the same, though remarriage can improve it for her. Usually the faithful type, these two are faster than most to ask for a divorce if the other strays.

CAPRICORN WOMAN—CANCER MAN

She'd love to settle down with him and there's a fair chance he'd choose her, too—but this match is more often cuddly than clinchy. She can't resist his warm smile, his kind face and his soothing voice, just what she needs after a hard day. If he's confident, faithful, tall and muscular, she's coming over right now. Surprisingly for an ambitious, businesslike sign, she wants a man who can provide for her, while he needs a mate who'll make a cosy home for him. He hopes she'll be kind and gentle, too, and he can't resist her sexy laugh. Long-term, he's the man who most expects loyalty from a mate—and he asks for plenty of understanding, too. She says humour is vital for happiness—and his warm hugs will make her feel softer and more sensually alive than she ever knew possible.

He's the man most at risk of remarriage, while she more often enters wedlock only once. But both signs score near even for making a match last 10 years or more. He enjoys his single status, while she's the woman in the most rush to remarry. She's likelier to wed a true love, but he's more often a virgin until his wedding night. These two are the signs most likely to see their sexlife take a nose-dive as time goes by, but he's equally likely to report improvements, so no real worries! Both tend to be faithful, but she's faster than other women to file for divorce if her partner strays, while he's the man likeliest to say nothing if she moved behind his back.

CAPRICORN WOMAN—LEO MAN

He'd love to spend a lifetime with reliable her, but she's not so sure she wants to hitch up with attention-grabbing him. And neither find each other extra-fanciable. He's the man most entranced by sexy eyes—and a warm smile, a curvy body, great legs and a raunchy laugh. If these assets belong to a woman with whom he has interests in common, great! She's rather taken by a sexy smile and a good voice and likes her man to be tall, muscular, faithful, confident and able to keep her in style. But Leo may well expect a joint effort on the earning front. And they don't see eye-to-eye on the importance of loyalty and kindness, which she feels are vital, either. But both say humour keeps a marriage afloat. He adds that he wants an understanding, sexy, good-looking partner who has the hots for him in bed. But he could find this lady takes some nudging to be imaginatively spontaneous, the way he likes.

He's far likelier to remarry, yet he scores slightly better for making a long-lasting bond. He enjoys the single life more than she does—she's in more of a hurry to marry and to wed again, for the company, security and sex. Both signs may well tie the knot with a true love, but she's likelier to do so as a virgin. He gets a bigger sexlife boost from wedlock—she's the woman who least often gets refuelled. These two are more faithful than most. But both will feel badly let down and in need of a divorce lawyer if the other proves untrue.

CAPRICORN WOMAN—VIRGO MAN

He'd love to rely on her—she's so sensible and he can find her quite a tasty number, too. She secretly dreams of getting him into bed and says she could do worse than choose him as a partner. He can't resist her curvy, slim body, her attractive voice and gentle manner. She goes for him if he's kind, faithful and confident—and if he's tall and muscular, with a good voice, it's a cert. But while she might want him to be the main breadwinner, he'll expect her to chip in with the pennies, too. Both say loyalty and humour are the keys to lasting happiness. But he says sexual attraction must stay strong—so they must watch that long working hours and petty problems don't make both too drained to replenish that valuable lovemaking stock!

He's less likely than most to have a string of spouses and she's at below average risk, too. There's an even chance they will stay married a decade or more, but he's keener to remain single than her and is warier of remarriage, too. Both have a good chance of marrying the love of their life, but he more often stays a virgin until his wedding night. They are less likely than most to find marriage a lovelife booster—and while she usually finds sex stays the same, he's the man most likely to say it's got worse. She's more faithful than most—but fast to demand a divorce if he wanders, while he'll look for ways of resolving any marital hiccups brought on by her.

CAPRICORN WOMAN—LIBRA MAN

He may dream of marching down the aisle with her—but she says the chances of her going willingly are slim. And neither finds the other ultra-sexy. A curvy body, kind nature and attractive voice are his priorities—and he says faithfulness is vital, although his own record can be dodgy. Her ideal man is tall and muscular, with a good voice, a great smile and smart clothes. He must be kind and confident—and able to earn enough to support them. But Libra may prefer a more up-to-date arrangement, where she uses her earning power, too. Both say that loyalty is vital. But "serious" Capricorn surprises by saying she looks forward to lots of laughs with a fun-loving mate. Libra yearns for an understanding homelover who is good-looking and packed with sex appeal. And he'll find this lady's powerful go-for-it nature and her sheer physical stamina make for a lovestyle that could easily grow on him.

He's a little likelier to marry more than once, but also does better at making a match last 10 years or more. Both are keen to wed and she's the sign happiest to get a ring on her finger second time around. She is luckier than most, and than him, at marrying the love of her life and is more likely to save herself for that special person. Neither say that marriage makes their sexlife better. But she finds remarriage more of a toe-toaster than he does. Extra-marital affairs could kibosh their relationship. He'd find his own lover—she'd demand divorce.

CAPRICORN WOMAN—SCORPIO MAN

They are not very likely to want to spend a lifetime together—but she fancies him more than he fancies her. His Ms Right has to have a gentle manner, so he may find thrusting Capricorn too businesslike by half. Great legs grab his attention—and he likes his women kind and faithful, even if he isn't always so himself. But while she's looking for a man who can provide for her, he's the man who least rates a good homemaker, so it's likely he'll want to send her out to work! His great smile makes her do a double take—and he'll match her ideal if he is tall and muscular, confident, kind and faithful, with a sexy voice. But they disagree over loyalty, which she says is essential and he gives the lowest marks. Both want fun, but she says it must be spiced with humour, while he likes the sound of a sexy homelover who is sensational in bed.

Both are at low risk of marrying more than once—and he especially tends to be a one-marriage man. He's slightly likelier to notch up 10 years of marriage and is in more of a hurry to go down the aisle, first time around. Second time, she's the keenest sign of all, being at her best when wed. She is luckier at marrying a true love, but he's likelier to save himself until his wedding night. Sex can soar or plummet for him after saying, I Do—she is likelier to find it stays the same. Remarriage does the trick for her. She'll want a divorce if he strays—he'll want to know why, if she's untrue.

CAPRICORN WOMAN—SAGITTARIUS MAN

He's a carefree optimist. She wants life to run to a plan. With different outlooks, it's hardly surprising they don't often gel and neither finds the other sizzlingly sexy. Yet they may well meet through a shared interest and it will be her warm smile and slim body that first catch his attention. Her faithful nature makes him want to stick around and she's bowled over by his great smile. She hates wimps and likes her men to be tall, muscular and confident, with good voices and good incomes, too. Kindness and faithfulness also get him in her good books—and he's got a good record here. To win his heart long-term, he says he must be treated kindly and spared serious money worries. She says loyalty and fun are vital and both feel it's great to have someone they can laugh with.

He's at higher risk of remarriage—and she more often makes a match that lasts a decade at least. She's in more of a hurry to get that ring on her finger and is the lady keenest to marry second time around, while he's easily put off. She's luckier at getting hitched to the love of her life and is likelier to stay a virgin until her wedding night—he rarely does. But she's the sign least likely to vote marriage a lovelife booster, while he's more enthusiastic. Remarriage often shows her what she was missing, though. Both tend to be true to each other. He'd want to work problems out if she ever strayed—she'd hire a divorce lawyer if he strayed.

CAPRICORN WOMAN—CAPRICORN MAN

Two hard heads—and a pair of soft hearts! They can find each other very sexy, but their habit of driving a hard bargain with each other may put them off staying together long-term. If he is tall and muscular with a confident voice and smile, he'll be her best man. But he must be kind, faithful and able to provide well for her, too. He demands that she stays true, too—and she has a far better record for loyalty than him! But he's less keen than her on traditional roles and may expect her to work. He'll be glad if they share interests—and even happier if she is warm and gentle, with great legs and a lovely voice. Both say humour keeps marriage off the rocks. But she wants loyalty and fun, too, while he says his ideal partner is sexy, good-looking and rich!

He's slightly likelier than her to marry more than once, yet has far more chance of making a long-lasting bond. He likes the single life more—but once he's made up his mind to marry he's in more of a hurry to tie the knot. Second time around she's far keener to get hitched, though. She does a lot better at marrying the love of her life—he's less likely than most to. And he's also less often a virgin when he weds. Neither find marriage a great sex improver, but both get a big boost from remarriage. They are faster than most to shout "Divorce!" if their mate admits to affairs—but he may be more prepared to give the marriage a second chance.

THE AQUARIUS MAN'S LOVEMATCHES

AQUARIUS MAN—PISCES WOMAN

They are not big hits with each other—naming each other among their least likely choices as partners. And sex ratings aren't high here, either. His Ms Right is curvy and slim, with a gentle manner and a knack for making a comfortable home, where he feels well looked after. Pisces doesn't often rate traditional roles though, preferring to share chores and breadwinning. She wants a man who is slim, faithful and kind, with a smile that knocks her for six. Long-term he must keep her amused—and free of money worries. He wants to be well understood by her and expects her to be loyal, fun to be with and good in bed. Patience helps if he wants to tease out the sexual daredevil in her—she's full of secret, wild fantasies just waiting to be acted out!

He's likelier to remarry—three or even four times. But she runs a risk here, too. He does a little better at making a bond last 10 years or more. Yet he's keener than her on the single life—she's the woman who least likes to be unattached. Though second time around, he's in more of a hurry to wed. She's luckier at marrying the love of her life and is likelier to be a virgin when she does. He's too impatient to wait! And she finds marriage more of a sexlife improver—he says loving usually stays the same. Divorce is his answer if he finds that she has a secret lover. She'd stay quiet and hope for the best if the situation was reversed.

AQUARIUS MAN—ARIES WOMAN

These two say they'd love to settle down together—and both can find each other electrifyingly attractive. Her curvy, slim body takes his eyes. He hopes she'll treat him gently, too, and be able to take care of the home front, leaving him time for his own adventurous interests. But compromises could be needed, as dynamic Aries often has strong ambitions of her own. Gorgeous eyes make her look twice at him, and if he is tall and muscular, confident, kind and faithful, she'll want to delve deeper. She says a kind-hearted homelover will suit her fine as a husband. He wants a mate on the same wavelength who is loyal, fun and good in bed. But when it comes to getting into that bed, she'll want to tell him to stop his wild fantasising, come back to earth and get on with it!

Both are at high risk of remarriage, especially her, and he is the man most likely to tie the knot three times. He does a little better at making a bond last 10 years or more. But while he's keener to stay single, he's in more of a hurry to wed second time around. She is luckier at marrying a true love—he's the man least likely to. And he is almost six times less likely than her to be a virgin when he kneels at the altar. Sex either skyrockets or nosedives for her after the wedding, while he says it stays the same. Both are the signs keenest to get divorced if their partner ever strays. But they'd give a passing thought to taking a lover of their own, too.

AQUARIUS MAN—TAURUS WOMAN

She's his favourite candidate for a trip down the aisle and he finds her sensationally sexy, too. But he's not so popular with her. Her ideal man is a slim, muscular he-man, a smart dresser with a confident smile and a great line in chat. Kind and faithful, too, he needs to earn enough money to provide for them both. Aquarius wants his mate to be a good homemaker, so he may be happy enough to take on the breadwinning role himself. He also asks her to treat him tenderly and to stay curvy and slim. For love to last, both say being able to have fun is vital. She likes the idea of a kind-hearted homelover, while he wants a mate who is loyal, understanding—and great in bed. It's here she'll softly bring out the sensualist in him, while he stops her getting fixed ideas.

He's likelier to sign up for marriage more than once—yet he reports more chance of making a long-lasting match, too. He likes the single life better than her, but marriage must suit him, as second time around he's much keener than her to get rehitched. She's the woman likeliest to marry a true love—he's the man who least often

483

does. And he's also least likely to wed as a virgin, while she stands more chance. She finds marriage opens up a new world of sex—he usually finds loving stays the same. And remarriage is far more gratifying for her, too. He'd race for a divorce if she was ever untrue. She'd want to know why he wandered and put things right.

AQUARIUS MAN—GEMINI WOMAN

He either finds her erotically supercharged—or not worth the effort of persuading her to lay her head on his pillow. She doesn't vote him sexual dynamite—yet there's a fair chance this extra-sociable pair will want to get together. He may not be able to resist her curvy, slim body and will fall for her if she treats him gently and creates a happy home for him to come back to. She's bowled over by his great smile and his headful of brilliant ideas and she loves the way he explains things. She wants him to be kind, confident and to dress smartly. And long-term, he must understand her well and try to keep her free of money worries. He wants someone on his quirky wavelength, loyal, fun and a megastar in bed.

  He's likelier than her to get re-hitched and is the man who's wifetally most often totals three! Yet he does have a far better record for making a bond last 10 years or more. Neither are in a big rush to wed, but he's in more hurry the second time. Both score low when it comes to marrying the love of their lives. And he is the man least likely to wed as a virgin, while she's the impatient sort, too! She finds sex takes an upturn after marriage—he says it usually carries on the same. And she finds remarriage sexier, too. He's the man likeliest to want a divorce if he catches her straying. She scores top marks for wanting to work things out if he's untrue.

AQUARIUS MAN—CANCER WOMAN

She's one of his favourite partners and he finds her distractingly sexy. There's a fair chance she'll pick him, too, and she votes him quite a dish himself. Lightning first strikes when she looks into his gorgeous eyes—and she can't resist the smart way he dresses, either. It's her curvy and slim body and the gentle way she talks that make him want to know more about her. If caring Cancer is good at looking after him, leaving him more time for his adventurous interests, he's putty in her paws! For love to last, both say that mutual understanding is vital, (especially for him)—and so is the ability to have fun. She wants to settle with a kind-hearted homelover; he wants a loyal mate. But both agree that there's more to happy partnership than sexual attraction.

He's a lot likelier than her to marry several times and is the man who most often ends up with three wives! She does better at making a lasting match and is keener to wed. But matrimony suits them both as they are in more of a hurry than most to remarry. She's luckier at marrying the love of her life—he's the sign who least often does. And he's five times less likely than her to wed as a virgin,(and is the man least likely to). Their sexlives usually carry on business as normal after the wedding and neither are at high risk of affairs. But if she did stray, he'd want to talk things through, while she would be faster than most to file for divorce.

AQUARIUS MAN—LEO WOMAN

He's keener to spend a lifetime with her than she is with him, but both find each other fairly fanciable, as long as they stay slim! She likes her man to be muscular, too, while a curvaceous body is just his ticket. He asks her to treat him gently and look after him well— which big-hearted Leo will do as long as he doesn't eclipse her need to reach her own potential by selfishly concentrating on his own needs. She'll let him know—and loudly—if he does! He can make her happy by proving how loyal he is—and by being great in bed. Worryingly for her, he's the sign that least rates sexual attraction long-term, but he thinks sex skills matter, so she'll have to puzzle that out! He says it's vital she's on his wavelength—and that being fun-seeking keeps love hot.

She's the woman least likely to marry more than once, while he's at high risk, with a one-in-10 chance of having three wives! She's slightly more successful at staying married a decade or more, while he likes the single life better. But once he's tried marriage, it suits him, and he's the man keenest to give wedlock a second go. Neither are especially lucky at marrying the love of their lives—he's the man least likely to. He also scores lowest for wedding as a virgin, while she's second most likely to. Marriage more often makes her sexlife soar, while his usually stay the same. If she ever proved untrue, he may want a divorce, while she'd take a lover of her own or say nothing if he strayed.

AQUARIUS MAN—VIRGO WOMAN

She gets the thumbs down, dubbed the unsexiest sign because she keeps asking him if he loves her! Yet she's among his most popular partner choices. She may well choose him, too, but gives him poor marks for sex. Her Mr Right must, above all, be faithful—and if he is tall, slim and muscular, so much the better. His ideal woman is curvy and slim and treats him gently. She's great at looking after him and the home—but independent Virgo doesn't expect her man to provide for her and may well work very hard at a career instead. Long-term, both want loyalty from a partner. But while he gives understanding top marks, she gives it the lowest score. She wants a sexy, funny, hardworker—and asks to be spared money worries, too. He hopes she'll be good in bed—and finds she is indeed powerfully sexy under her cool, girl guide exterior.

She's the woman most at risk of multiple marriages and he's even more likely to remarry, with one in 10 notching up three wives! Yet he does slightly better at staying married a decade. And second time around he's the man keenest to wed, while she's the woman likeliest to say never again! She does better at marrying the love of her life and is more than six times likelier to save herself for that special person. Neither get a big boost to their sexlife from marriage, though remarriage smoulders more for her. But if either ever strays, both are faster than most to ask for a divorce.

AQUARIUS MAN—LIBRA WOMAN

They aren't especially keen to settle down together and find each other no more than averagely sexy. Her Mr Right is a great talker, and that, Aquarius is. But she may think he voices some strange ideas! If he's kind and faithful, with a great smile, a muscular build and a smart style of dressing, he could yet win her heart. He's lured by a slim, curvaceous body and wants his mate to be gentle and good about the house. But Libra gives a good provider the lowest score, so may well have ambitions, socially and at work, that divert her attention from his domestic needs. Her partner must be a kind, loyal, hardworker—while what he wants more than other men is true understanding and endless fun. Sex skills get his vote, too—but his analytical sex-in-the-head approach to loving could clash with her strong need for romance.

He's at high risk of marrying more than once, she's at low risk and is the woman who is best at making a long-lasting match. She's keener to wed—but he enjoys the challenge of making a second marriage work even more than she does. She's luckier at marrying the love of her life—he's the man least likely to. And he's also the sign least likely to wed as a virgin. She often finds that marriage perks up her sexlife—he's more likely to find it stays the same. If either ever wanders, these two may well take their own lovers in revenge. But he may also decide divorce is the only answer.

AQUARIUS MAN—SCORPIO WOMAN

They're in no big hurry to settle down together, or even to share the same bed for the night. Her right-on romancer has gorgeous eyes and is tall, muscular, with a sexy voice and a sense of humour. He should earn enough to provide for them both—and Aquarius may oblige here, as he likes his woman to be a caring homemaker who concentrates on looking after him. She must also be curvy, slim and gentle and, in the long-term, fun, loyal and able to understand his sometimes outrageous thoughts and ideas. Sensual Scorpio thinks sexual attraction is far more vital than he does, though both rate sex skills. But while she likes her passion strong, hot and abandoned, he could spend too much time thinking and talking about sex—and not enough getting on with it!

He's the man likeliest to get hitched three times, while she more often makes a long-lasting bond. The single life appeals more to him, she's more easily put off than he is, marrying a second time. She's luckier at settling with the love of her life—he's the man least likely to. And she's a lot more likely to marry as a virgin—he scores lowest here. She gets more of a boost to her sexlife from marriage— he's likelier than most to find it stays the same. And she finds remarriage a lot more physically stimulating than he does. Both are at risk of affairs, especially her. If she does stray, he'll want a divorce, or may take his own lover. She will try to find ways to stay together if he did the dirty on her.

AQUARIUS MAN—SAGITTARIUS WOMAN

He's more popular with her than she is with him—but neither vote each other hot property, sexwise. She loves a man with a good line in chat—and finds this one has enough outrageous ideas to keep her talking for a lifetime. If he's tall, slim and kind-hearted, so much the better. He likes his women curvy and slim, gentle and good at making a cosy home for him. But she doesn't especially ask for a good provider, so may prefer shared roles. For this to work long-term, both say mutual understanding is vital. She wants a humorous, hardworker who will help around the house. He asks for a loyal fun-lover who is good in bed. These two are great companions, but sex could fizzle instead of sizzle if they forget those romantic touches of their early days.

He's at higher risk than her of marrying more than once, yet he does better at making a lasting bond. Both love the freedom of being single. But she secretly yearns to marry—and he's the man in the most hurry to wed second time around. She is luckier at settling with a true love—he's the male starsign least likely to. And he's far less likely to be a virgin until his wedding night. Marriage really ups the

488

sexual temperature for her, while loving often stays the same for him. She tends to be faithful—but if affairs do come between them, he'll want a divorce or will take his own lover. She'll do all she can to put their marriage right.

AQUARIUS MAN—CAPRICORN WOMAN

She'd like to settle with him, but he's not so sure—and neither finds the other highly sexually attractive. She likes her men to be tall and muscular, confident and able to provide for her. If he has a good voice, a great smile and promises to be kind and faithful, she'll accept his offer. He wants his mate to be curvy, slim, gentle and keen to look after him and their cosy home. So he may well be happy to play the sole breadwinner role, which she , unexpectedly, seems to ask of him. Both say loyalty is vital to any lasting match, which must be fun-packed as well to keep them interested. She needs humour, too, while he asks her to understand his quirky way of thinking. He'll also want her to be good in bed—and she can surprise with passion once her conventional inhibitions fall away.

She usually marries just once, while he is the man most likely to have three spouses! Yet both are near-average for making a bond last a decade or more. He's happier than her to be single, while she longs to be married. But matrimony clearly suits them both, as they are keener than most to wed second time around. He's least lucky at wedding the love of his life, while she does well here, and he's also least likely to hang onto his virginity until after he's hitched. Sex usually carries on the same for these two, once wed, but she finds a second marriage extra-sexy. If affairs ever come between them though, both will probably want to part.

AQUARIUS MAN—AQUARIUS WOMAN

She votes him her favourite partner, while he says she's a real sexbomb and makes quite a good lifemate, too. And though she's not equally bowled over by him, she still rather fancies him. Her curvy, slim body first grabs his attention. If she treats him gently and knows how to look after him, leaving him time for his own interests, he's on line! She thinks he might be the soulmate she's looking for, as she takes in his gorgeous eyes, good voice and smart clothes. Both are the signs keenest to find a partner who understands them and that they know will be loyal. She asks for a humorous, good-looking hardworker, while he rates a sexy fun-lover. She wants him to be good in bed, too—and because she knows his needs, gets a hotter response from him than others would.

He's likelier to remarry—even to have three spouses. But he scores higher than her for making a long-lasting match. She's keener to wed, but second time around, he's in the most hurry, enjoying the challenge. Neither are very lucky at marrying the love of their life, but she does better than him. And both are the pair least likely to wed as virgins. She finds matrimony a sexier state, but says loving can get worse, too, while he reports it usually stays the same. She's the sign keenest to unravel a love tangle and stay together. He'd take his own lover, or demand divorce if she strayed.

THE AQUARIUS WOMAN'S LOVEMATCHES

AQUARIUS WOMAN—PISCES MAN

She's more popular with him than he is with her, both sexually and for marriage. He's smitten by great legs, a slim body and a sexy laugh and he appreciates a woman who can create a cosy home. She's simply after a soulmate—but she may well take notice of smart clothes and a good voice. Long-term, she's more specific— he must be loyal and understanding, amusing and good-looking. Hard work is required, too—and he has to be great in bed. She will indeed find Pisces a very sensitive lover—the only danger is that non-stop snuggles could prove suffocating for her at times. Partnerwise, he appreciates a sexpert, too, but says loyalty, humour and fun are also vital to create his brand of marital happiness.

He's likelier to remarry than she is, yet has a better record for staying wed for 10 years or more. She's in more of a hurry to get into wedding white—he's wary of the changes it would bring. But wed once, he is the sign that most wants to marry again. He's also the lucky man most likely to wed the love of his life. And while she's the woman likeliest to lose her virginity before marriage, he's keener than most to save himself. Both say sex soars after marriage, especially him. But she can report that loving takes a break, while he's the man least likely to find its splendour dims. If he ever wanders, she'll look for ways that they can get close again. He's keener than most on divorce if his mate proves untrue.

AQUARIUS WOMAN—ARIES MAN

She can rather fancy him—but they basically give each other nil points for sex appeal. Despite this initial response, there's an average chance they'll still want to stick together long-term. She's hard to please when it comes to attraction factors—and prizes mental qualities more highly than physical ones. But smart clothes and a good voice could catch her fancy. He can't resist a warm smile, sexy glance and curvy body. He's also keener than other men to grab a good homemaker to look after him. But she's in no hurry to find someone to support her and may well have ambitions and schemes of her own to keep her busy. Both say good looks help towards long-term happiness. He wants his mate to be a sexy homelover, with money of her own. She asks for a loyal, understanding and humorous hardworker who is great in bed. And she'll love experimenting with daredevil Aries—he seems tireless!

They are at middle-range risk of remarriage, but he does better at staying wed a decade plus. Neither really value their single status. But second time around, she's keener to remarry. He has better luck at marrying the love of his life and he is twice as likely as her to wed as a virgin. She finds marriage either puts a smile into her sexlife, or adds a damper. But remarriage is a more hotted-up affair for him. If a love tangle ever threatens to bust them up, both would look for solutions, rather than divorce, though he might take a lover.

AQUARIUS WOMAN—TAURUS MAN

He dreams of matrimony with her—she's his favourite partner and he finds her quite sexy, too. There's a fair chance she'll choose him, too, though she doesn't vote him a sex-sensation. What attracts her to a man is hard to pin down, though smart clothes and a good voice may appeal. What she's really after is a soulmate who understands her totally. A warm smile, a sexy laugh and a curvy body is enough to turn on sensual Taurus. He dreams of settling with a kind, gentle and faithful woman—one who can create a cosy, welcoming home for him. But Aquarius is not desperate to find a good provider and may make Taurus uneasy by putting outside interests before homelife. For marriage to work, both say that being on the same wavelength helps—and so does hardwork and bedroom skills. He's the man who most rates kindness, while she wants loyalty, looks and a sense of humour.

 He's a better bet for long-lasting marriage and is less likely than her to remarry. Both are keen to wed, but she is more easily put off doing it a second time. He is luckier at marrying the love of his life and is likelier to wed as a virgin—she's the woman least likely to. She finds sex either lifts off after marriage, or falls flat, while his lovelife stays more level. He's at more risk than she is of having affairs. But both are the signs keenest to work marital problems out, so that they can end up still together.

AQUARIUS WOMAN—GEMINI MAN

She says she'd love to spend a lifetime with him and she finds him so-sexy, too. Yet he says she's one of his least likely choices and he doesn't give her high sex-ratings either. She wants to find a mate who truly understands her and is not much interested in surface attractions, though smart clothes and a good voice can work. He's very taken with great legs and a slim body—and can't resist a sexy laugh. He wants his mate to be kind, faithful and gentle and hopes she'll share his busy social life, which Aquarius probably will.

Long-term, he says she'll need to stay on his wavelength and be sexy, good-looking, fun and homeloving. She wants him to be loyal, humorous, hardworking, good looking and great in bed. And he probably will be, though hot loving will be mixed with giggles and friendship.

He's less likely than her to marry more than once, but neither are at high risk. He more often notches up years of marriage—yet is the man who is happiest to stay single. She's far keener than him to wed, but neither are especially lucky at marrying a true love. He's the man likeliest to get hitched as a virgin—she's the woman who least often does. And though she often finds marriage sexier, she is twice as likely as him to say loving gets worse. If he ever wanders, she'll be keener than most to find a way they can stay together. But he'll be fast to ask for a divorce if she strays.

AQUARIUS WOMAN—CANCER MAN

This needs work if it's to be more than a one-way ticket. He's keener to settle with her than she is to stick with him and neither vote each other fanciable. To appeal to him, she'll need a sexy laugh and gentle manner. Deeper values attract her, though his smart clothes and sexy voice are OK for starters. But while he wants a nest-builder, Aquarius says her horizons must stay wide, so she may not take to domestic life. They also differ about kindness. He says it's essential, she gives it lowest vote of all. She says she needs a man who understands her (sometimes unusual) way of thinking. He wants a loyal mate who'll stick by him whatever. Sexy nights and fun-packed days don't seem to be what either wants, though.

He's likelier to notch up a string of ex-spouses, while she is more often a one-marriage woman. Yet he has more hope of reaching his 10th wedding anniversary. At first more reluctant to wed, second time around he's raring to go compared with her. He's luckier at wedding a true love and likelier to be a wedding-day virgin, while she often lacks patience. She gets a bigger kick out of sex within marriage than he does, though both signs say that loving can take a downturn. She'll question him until she finds out what went wrong if he ever proves untrue. He's likelier than most to clam up and hope that any fling she has soon comes to an end.

AQUARIUS WOMAN—LEO MAN

He gets higher popularity ratings from her than she gets from him, but both quite fancy each other. Hard to please Ms Aquarius is looking for something deeper than surface attraction—yet a sexy voice and smart clothes could make her want to know more. Nice eyes and a warm smile send all the right messages to him—and great legs, a curvy body and a sexy laugh get him really interested. If they share interests, so much the better! Both say love only grows if there is humour and understanding—and being great-looking and good in bed are bonuses! But while she likes a man who'll work hard, he wants a mate who has time to spend on him—and staying sexy is important from his point of view, too. There's a danger that radiant Leo's ego could suffer under her microscope of analysis—less thinking, more loving would help!

He's likelier than most to take marriage vows more than once, while she's nearer average. But he also has a better record for making a lasting match. She's keener on marriage all round though— he often likes to hang onto his single status. Yet he does a lot better at finding and keeping the love of his life. Neither are very patient about saving their virginity, but sex often peaks for both after formally tying the knot. If he ever admits to an affair, she'll want to do what she can to put their relationship right and stay together. He'll head off to hire a good divorce lawyer without a backward glance if he catches her being untrue.

AQUARIUS WOMAN—VIRGO MAN

They may well leave each other rather cold, both as marriage and sex partners. A curvy and slim body knocks him sideways at first sight and he loves a gentle, soothing voice, too. She's in search of a soulmate—but there's a chance that sexy eyes, smart clothes and a good voice could add up to initial attraction. To put things on a long-term footing, she'll want to feel truly understood, while he thinks that keeping mutual sexual attraction buzzing is the way to happiness. Both want their mate to work hard—and reckon that good looks and a great sense of humour help love stay microwave hot. These two may well be so curious to find out everything they can about each other that they will often stay up half the night talking, forgetting that they're missing out on sex.

He's likelier than her to marry for life—she's at average risk of getting hitched more than once. Yet neither score highly when it comes to making a match last a decade or more. He's far keener than her on the single life, while she's in more of a hurry than most to wed. But he is luckier at settling with a true love and is likelier to wed as a virgin—she's the female sign least likely to. Her sexlife can turn turbo-charged once wed—his often carries on the same. But both may report a drop in interest, too. There's an average risk they'll have affairs—but if they do, both will want to find out just what went wrong and have a go at rebuilding the relationship.

AQUARIUS WOMAN—LIBRA MAN

She can't wait to get his ring round her third finger and she says he's sexier than most, too. But he reports she's rarely his type and it's not often he fancies her either. His attention could, however, be grabbed by a curvy body and an attractive voice—and a kind and faithful nature makes him want to stick around. She wants a life partner she can share ideas and an active social life with—and thinks that outgoing Libra could be just the man. His smart clothes and sexy voice make him all the more enticing. For long-term loving, both say that loyalty and understanding are vital. Sexual attraction and good looks are other essentials in his book, and he likes a homelover, too. She says humour is the secret of happy loving. But passionate kisses will be needed to halt her tendency to pillow-talk too much—he wants her full concentration on his great performance.

There's an even chance they'll both wed more than once. But he's the man who does best at making a lasting bond, while she's less often so lucky. She's more the marrying type—he tends to enjoy his freedom for longer. Neither are especially lucky at wedding the love of their life and are less patient than most about hanging on to their virginity. Wedlock often gives her the sexual satisfaction she's been looking for. But she can report a turn for the worse, while his sexlife usually carries on the same. If he ever strays, she'll want to know why—in detail—then try to put things right between them. He may well take a lover of his own, if she is ever untrue.

AQUARIUS WOMAN—SCORPIO MAN

She finds him breathtakingly sexy, but he's not so taken with her and it's not very often they go down the aisle together. Gentle, kind and faithful women make him feel warm inside—and great legs really turn him on. She's out to find a man who understands her, heart and quirky soul, and isn't too bothered by surface attraction. But a good voice and smart clothes may catch her interest. Long-term, she wants a mate who is loyal, great looking, humorous and hardworking. He likes a homelover—which socially-minded Aquarius may not be. But both agree their partner must be dynamite in bed, with Scorpio saying sexual attraction is at the heart of married life. He won't be disappointed in Aquarius, whose love of experimentation means he's served an ever-changing menu of sensual treats.

He's usually a one-marriage man, while she runs a near-average risk of entering wedlock more than once. He does better at making a bond last a good ten years of more. But he can be happier than her to hang onto his single status, first or second time around. He is luckier at marrying the love of his life and is likelier to do so as a virgin—she's the woman with the least patience in the entire zodiac! He's likelier than other men to find that sex takes an upturn after getting hitched—and she often gets a boost, too. But, sadly, both also report high chances of an interest downturn. Both would hope to talk marital problems through if affairs ever occurred. But he may also choose to take his own lover, if she strays.

AQUARIUS WOMAN—SAGITTARIUS MAN

As a sexpot he may well get her vote—but both generally see each other as a middle-range life-partner choice. An interest in common may well bring them together—but he'll have to be something special to take her fancy. She's after a soulmate, though gorgeous eyes, a good voice and a smart style of dressing may catch her fancy. Her warm smile, slim body and faithful nature first draw him to her. But if he's intending to stick around, he'll have to learn to understand her eccentric ways and be loyal, hardworking and hot stuff in bed! Both say humour is vital to keep a relationship running smoothly. He wants kindness, too, and says that having enough money makes all the difference. She'll introduce a streak of wild fantasy into their lovemaking that he will adore—and they'll share an Aladdin's cave of private jokes that will keep both smiling.

Both have a fair chance of marrying for life, especially her. And she's ahead when it comes to reaching the 10-year mark still hitched—he's the man least likely to. She finds marriage more appealing all round, while he can be easily put off ever giving wedlock a second chance. Yet he can be luckier at settling with a true love, though neither often go down the aisle still a virgin. Marriage more often sends her sexlife soaring—but she's also likelier than him to find it takes a dip. She's at average risk of affairs—he's the man least likely to play away. If either does, the other will do their best to put the relationship right, to stop it happening again

AQUARIUS WOMAN—CAPRICORN MAN

These two are rarely favourites with each other—and they don't often fancy each other either! Her Mr Right understands her heart and soul—but she'll still look twice at a man with gorgeous eyes, a great smile and a snappy style of dressing. He can't resist a warm smile, great legs and a sexy voice. If their owner is faithful and gentle, she'll score even more points with him. And if they share interests watch out! For love to last, she demands loyalty, humour—and hard work. Being good looking and sensational in bed helps. He wants to have a lot of laughs with a sexy good-looker—and says money helps smooth the path of true romance. But her behaviour in bed could baffle—she won't play by his rules, let him be in charge. His rock-steady loving could grow on her, though.

Both are at average risk of running up a plurality of spouses, but he scores far higher for making marriage last a good 10 years or more. He's a little keener than her to get hitched—but second time around she's in more of a hurry, while he can be too proud to risk failing again. She more often marries a true love, but neither are very lucky. And there is not much chance either will wed as a virgin. Marriage gives her more of a sex-boost, but she can report that loving gets worse, while he says remarriage works well for him. He's the man most at risk of affairs—she's at average risk. But he may holler for divorce if she wanders, while she's the woman keenest to know what went wrong, then put it right, if he is ever untrue.

AQUARIUS WOMAN—AQUARIUS MAN

She says she'd simply love to be his mate—while he says she's one of the sexiest starsigns going. She doesn't vote him quite such a sex-machine though—and he says she only makes an averagely good partner. Her curvy and slim body first sets his temperature rising—and if she is gentle by nature and good about the house, he's halfway hers. It's hard to nail down what she actually fancies in a man—apart from his soul! But gorgeous eyes, a good voice and smart wardrobe of clothes may well get her vote. For loving that lasts, she says she must have a mate who understands her rather odd little ways. He must be loyal, too, good-looking, hardworking, funny and great in bed! He gives understanding a top rating, too, and says he wants a loyal mate who is fun to be with and X-rated material behind closed bedroom doors

He's at more risk of remarrying and is the man most likely to have three wives. But he does better than her at making a long-lasting match. She's keener to wed, yet second time around, he's in more of a hurry, enjoying the challenge. Neither can bank on wedding a true love, but she does better than him. They are the male and female signs least likely to be virgins on their wedding day. And while wedlock often boosts her sexlife, she can report a downturn, while he says it stays the same. She'll be keen to find a way to stay together if he ever wanders—but he'll want a divorce if she strays.

THE PISCES MAN'S LOVEMATCHES

PISCES MAN—ARIES WOMAN
He wants her around, all right, but she gives him just average marks, as a partner—and sex mark-ups are not high on either side. Her dream man is tall, muscular and confident with sexy eyes and a strong voice. In an ideal world he must be kind and faithful, too. Slim, leggy women make Pisces go weak and a sexy laugh really turns him on. But he'll want his mate to concentrate on looking after him—while dynamic Aries says she'd rather be out forging ahead in the big, wide world. She wants a long-term mate who helps at home and always treats her kindly, while his perfect partner makes him laugh and is loyal, fun and ace at bedtime. But though Aries loves being drawn into this marvellous web of sexual and romantic fantasies, he says she can spoil it all by being over-controlling.

She's the woman most likely to have a string of ex-husbands—and he's at high risk too, (though he does better at making a long-lasting match). He enjoys the single life, but second time around, he's the man in the most hurry to marry, while she gets cold feet. He's likelier than her to be a virgin on his wedding day, though she scores high here, too. And he is the lucky man who most often weds a true love. Once hitched, he says sex improves no end, while she reports it can take a turn for the worse. But both get a fair helping within remarriage. If either were unfaithful, the other may well demand a divorce, especially Aries who can't stand being let down.

PISCES MAN—TAURUS WOMAN
It's not often that they choose to stick together for life—and neither rate each other highly, as lovers. Her chap should be tall, slim and smartly dressed, with a great smile. He ought to be fun to talk to, kind, confident and always faithful. She says he must provide for her, too, which suits Pisces as he wants to settle with a warm-hearted homemaker, like traditional Taurus. He'll be even happier if she has great legs, a slim body and a sexy laugh. Long-term, she says her

man must be a kind homelover, while he asks for a loyal mate who has a sense of humour and well-honed sexpertise. Both want to have endless fun together. But though he loves the way she pampers him, they can descend into hypersensual greed at times—for food, for drink, for sex, for everything.

He's at higher risk than most of marrying more than once, yet does better than her at making love linger at least a decade. He likes being single, fearing the changes marriage brings, while she's in more of a hurry than most to get a ring on her finger. Yet matrimony obviously suits him, as he is the sign keenest to wed again, well ahead of her. He's also the man who is luckiest at wedding a true love and he's likelier than most, a lot likelier than her, to do so as a virgin. Both get a good boost to their sexlife from marriage, especially her. If affairs ever came between them, though, he'd either say nothing or ask for a divorce. But she'd do her best to save the relationship before letting go.

PISCES MAN—GEMINI WOMAN

They well end up Mr and Mrs—but neither are in a rush to share the same bed! A great pair of legs, a slim body and a sexy laugh turn his resolve to jelly. But he wants a woman who'll concentrate on making him feel cosily looked after at home—and Gemini spends far too much time socialising for his liking! She loves a man who has a confident smile, a snappy way of dressing and a powerful way with words. But he must be kind-hearted too, to truly win her round. And for long-term loving, she says it's vital he understands her—and has enough money to keep their finances off the rocks. He wants a loyal fun-lover with a sense of humour who knows exactly what she's doing in bed. To take their loving to new heights, though, he should keep her guessing more often and hide his over-possessive nature.

He's at far more risk of marrying more than once than she is. Yet he does a lot better at making a bond last 10 years—she scores low here. These two are in less of a hurry than other signs to wed. But once hitched, marriage suits him better than most. He is luckier than

501

other signs at wedding the love of his life—and is the man in the most hurry to remarry, while she may say never again! He's likelier to wed as a virgin. And he finds sex more of a treat within marriage, while she is twice as likely to say loving has got worse. If he ever wanders, she'll want to know why, in detail—and try to put things right. Pisces would either say nothing, or demand a divorce.

PISCES MAN—CANCER WOMAN

She finds him sensuously sexy and says she'd love to set up home with him. But he's not so keen to settle down with her and doesn't vote her especially fanciable. She can't resist the smart way he dresses—and a sexy glance from him makes her feel weak. He'll take a shine to her great legs, slim body and sexy laugh. Her homemaking skills will impress him, too—she looks after him just the way he's always wanted. If love is to last, both say they must be able to have fun together, too—though neither say their mate must have money. She simply wants a kind-hearted, understanding homelover, while he says a partner who is loyal, humorous and great in bed will suit him fine. But both can be slow to unfold strong secret passions that lie hidden within. Patience, trust and lingering sessions in their very own love-cave help the process.

He is at more risk of remarriage, yet does better at making a bond last a decade at least. He enjoys being single more than she does, but once he's tried marriage, he likes it and is in more of a hurry than her to repeat it. He's the luckiest man in the zodiac when it comes to marrying the love of his life, while she's not always so fortunate. And he's likelier than her to wed as a virgin, too. He finds marriage improves his sexlife more and, unlike her, he hardly ever reports that loving goes off the boil. But if a love betrayal ever does loom on the horizon, divorce may be first choice option for both.

PISCES MAN—LEO WOMAN

They'd love to spend a lifetime together—yet neither feel any great urgency to get their hands on each other. However, if he's slim and

502

muscular, she can grow to fancy him, while he won't be able to resist her if she has great legs, a slim body and a sexy laugh. But she must be able to create the soothing home environment he needs—and she may well have other projects in mind, than looking after him! Both rate a loyal mate more than others do—but while he's at lower than average risk of affairs, she's more of a liability than most. She expects her partner to stay sexy, while he's not so bothered, (though he does say she must be a fun lover who is great between the sheets). At bedtime, he's tender, she's torrid. So they complement—and often compliment—each other nicely.

She's likelier than other women to marry just once, for life, while he runs more risk of remarrying. But they score neck-and-neck for staying wed a decade or more. He'll need some coaxing down the aisle, though, while she's keen to marry. Yet matrimony suits him more than most—he's the man who is luckiest at wedding a true love, well ahead of her, and he is also the starsign in the most hurry to wed again. Both are likelier than most to stay virgins until their wedding night, especially him. But he finds marriage—and remarriage—a more-rewarding experience. These are the signs least likely to say loving has got worse. But if affairs ever come between them, he'll want a divorce, while she may take her own lover.

PISCES MAN—VIRGO WOMAN

She's quite keen to settle down with him—he's not so sure. Yet he finds her fairly fanciable, while she votes him the least sexy sign! A tall, slim, muscular man may well appeal to Virgo. But he must swear to be faithful—and Pisces scores quite well here. Yet, oddly, he's the sign who least appreciates faithfulness in a partner. Instead, he can't resist a woman who is curvy, slim and gentle with a sexy laugh. He wants his mate to create a cosy home for him—but though independent Virgo is the tidy type, she likes the idea of working for a living, so she'll expect him to help with the dusting! Both say their long-term partner must fun to be with. Practical Virgo admires a man who works hard and earns plenty, while Pisces wants a partner

503

with a sense of humour, who is great in bed. And this lady is perfect for his strict-nurse fantasy, if she'll put on her apron and stockings and play along!

She is the woman most at risk of remarriage—and he's even likelier to wed again. Yet he does better at making a match last a decade or more. She's keener to marry, but second time around, he is in more of a hurry—she's easily put off trying again. He's the man who does best at marrying the love of his life—and both are likelier than most to be virgins when they take their vows. Marriage turns out to be a sexier experience for him. But neither are the type who tends to stray. If they ever got tangled in a love triangle, though, both would be mighty fast to find a way out through divorce.

PISCES MAN—LIBRA WOMAN

They are not especially keen to walz down the aisle together—and sex-ratings are fairly low here, too. Her Mr Right has a way with words and is kind and faithful, too—which caring Pisces often is. But he'll also need to have a great smile, smart clothes, a good voice and a muscular build to truly please her. His ideal woman is leggy and slim, with a sexy laugh. She is good about the house and makes him feel so welcome when he comes home. But sociable Libra is the sign least keen to find a man who'll provide for her—so she'll probably see her main role as being out in the workplace, not home in his kitchen. Long-term, both ask for a mate who'll be loyal. She says she'd stick with a kind-hearted hardworker, while he'd be happiest with a fun-lover who has a good sense of humour, and is great in bed. And, in Libra, he may well find a treasury of sensual delights to keep him truly occupied!

He's more likely to accumulate spouses—she's at low risk of remarrying and is better at making a bond last at least 10 years. First time around, she's in more of a rush to marry—he's worried about what the big change might bring. But marriage must suit him after all, as he's keener than other signs to marry again. Both often marry the love of their lives—he is the luckiest man of all here. He more

504

often weds as a virgin. Marriage is more of a sex-improver for him—so is remarriage. If she wanders, he'll want a divorce, but she may get even by taking her own lover, if he's untrue.

PISCES MAN—SCORPIO WOMAN

He's in more of a hurry to set up home with her than she is to settle with him—and neither rates the other as super-sexy. She's looking for a man who is tall and muscular with a good voice and gorgeous eyes. He's got to be prepared to provide for her, too—which may suit Pisces, as he rather likes his mate to be at home, ever-tending to his needs. He'll also be happy if she has great legs, a slim body and a sexy laugh. For long-term loving, both say their mate must share their sense of humour—and know the erotic alphabet. She wants him to be good-looking, too, while he says she must be great fun. These two can learn to satisfy each other deeply, mind and body. But while she can calm his worst fears, she can also provoke them by—naughtily using sex to manipulate his feelings.

Both stand a fair chance of marrying more than once, especially her—yet she's likelier to make a long-lasting match. She is in more of a hurry to get hitched. But while he is the man in the least rush to commit himself, second time around he's the sign that most wants to wed. He is luckier at marrying the love of his life, and is likelier to do so as a virgin. Matrimony gives him more of a sex-boost, too—and he's the man least likely to say that lovemaking has got worse. Affairs trigger a different reaction from each of this pair. He may well ask for a divorce, but she's likelier to do all she can to solve their problems, in a brave bid to stay together.

PISCES MAN—SAGITTARIUS WOMAN

He finds her highly fanciable—and she may well have the hots for him, too. But he votes her only an averagely popular partner—and she says he's usually a no-no long-term. His sexy eyes and his tall, slim body could make her think twice though, especially if he is kind and fun to talk to. He'll find he can't resist her great legs, slim body and sexy laugh. But he'd like to find a mate who can make cosy home for him—and free-ranging Sagittarius prefers being out and about, with housework low on her list. Her Mr Right must understand her well, share her sense of humour, be hardworking and good about the house. He wants his life-mate to be loyal, humorous and fun-loving and to know what she's doing at bedtime. Their bodies are drawn together like powerful magnets, but both tend to play it cool emotionally. Secretly, she'll want more commitment than he may he ready to give.

He's likelier to sign up for marriage more than once, yet he does better at making a lasting bond. Both like the single life. But she's keener than him to wed, though he's the man in the most hurry second time around. He's luckier than most at marrying a true love—and he's likelier to do so as a virgin. Marriage sends his sexlife soaring higher—but both are the signs least likely to find that loving loses its pace. And she gets a massive boost from a second bond. They tend to be faithful, but he'll want a divorce if she does stray, while she'll hope to work things out, if he is untrue.

PISCES MAN—CAPRICORN WOMAN

She's keener on him—both as a life partner and sexmate. He says she's the sign that least appeals to him as a life partner and as a bedmate, too! She likes the he-man type—tall, muscular and confident with a good voice and a deep pocket. He must be kind and faithful, too, to win her heart. Pisces could yet fall for her if she is slim, with great legs and a sexy laugh. And he says that if she'll do the homemaking, he'll do the breadwinning, as she seems to ask—which is surprising, as she's often thought of as the businesswoman of the zodiac. For long-term success, both say loyalty, humour and fun are vital ingredients. He wants a partner who knows how to turn him on—and Capricorn will surprise even herself, as his tender loving unleashes deep passions within.

He's likelier than her to go down on bended knee more than once—yet he does better at making a marriage last past the 10-year mark.

But she's keener to get a ring on her finger—he's the man in the least hurry to get hitched. Once married, they both find it better than they thought, and second time around they are the signs who are keenest to wed again. Both do well at wedding a true love, with him getting topmost score here. He's likelier to wed as a virgin, though—and finds marital sex a more exciting experience, too. She reports that loving often stays the same, and doesn't really take off unless she marries. They tend to be faithful—but if either strays, the other could well see divorce as the only option.

PISCES MAN—AQUARIUS WOMAN

He'll wonder if she'll ever feel exactly the way he does about her. She has so many friends—while he wants her full concentration on him! He can't resist her great legs, slim body and sexy laugh. But he'll want her to make their comfy home the centre of their lives— and she's often so busy elsewhere! Her ideal man understands her, heart and soul—but she'll want him to dress smartly and have a good voice, too. Long-term, he must be understanding and loyal, with rugged good looks and a great sense of humour. He must work hard by day, and be great between the sheets by night, to live up to her dreams! Pisces' bedroom technique is bound to satisfy—as long as constant cuddles don't keep her from her busy social life! He appreciates an expert lover, too—but says that loyalty, humour and fun and also vital to married life.

He's likelier than her to remarry, yet he does better at making a lasting bond. She's in more of a hurry to be a spouse, while he worries his life would change if wed. But once hitched, he's happy—and is the man keenest to marry again. He's also likelier than most to wed a true love. And while she's the woman who least often marries as a virgin, he's quite keen to save himself. Both report a boom in lovemaking after tying the knot. But she says love sessions can also plummet, while he's the man least likely to experience a drop. If he proves untrue, she'll do all she can to mend their marriage. But he may bale out with a divorce if she strays.

PISCES MAN—PISCES WOMAN

She's his number one favourite in the pairing-off stakes—and he votes her by far the sexiest sign, too. She says he'd make a fairly suitable life-partner, too—but has no strong opinions about his sex power. He can't resist her if she is slim, with great legs and a sexy laugh—while she says she'll fall for him, if he is kind and faithful with a firm body and a great smile. But while she might be great at creating the cosy home he longs to come back to, she'll have other things on her mind, apart from looking after him. For lasting happiness, both say their mate must have a sense of humour. She also asks to be kept free of money worries, while he wants a loyal funster who is a great lover. And this same-sign soulmate knows the secrets of his innermost fantasies—so there'll be few complaints here!

He's likelier to take his marriage vows more than once, though both are at risk. Yet he does better at making love last a decade or more. She wants to wed as soon as possible, while he's more wary. But once he's tried wedlock, he loves it—and is the man in the most hurry to marry again. He's also luckier than other signs at wedding a true love, and is likelier than her to save himself for that special person. He finds marriage more sexually satisfying, too, being the man least likely to report a drop in interest. But remarriage hots things up for her. If she strays, he may want a divorce, while she'll say nothing, or take her own lover if he wanders.

THE PISCES WOMAN'S LOVEMATCHES

PISCES WOMAN—ARIES MAN

They'd love to settle down together and both find each other fairly fanciable—though he can vote her the least sexy sign of all, if she turns on the waterworks too often! His great smile and slim body make her first take notice—but she says he must be kind and faithful to win her heart. He's very attracted to her warm smile, sexy eyes and curvaceous body—and hopes she'll create a cosy home where he feels warmly cared for. In gentle Pisces, he may believe he's found his dream woman! And she may well see powerful Aries as the strong protector she needs. For lasting love, he says she must be homeloving, but able to earn money of her own. He wants her to be good-looking, too, and will love how Pisces combines sexiness and romance in one package. She wants a man who is kind, shares her sense of humour and keeps her free of cash crises.

She's a little likelier to marry more than once—he does better at staying wed a decade or more. But she's the woman least keen to stay single, and he'd rather be wed as well. Second time around, though, she's in slightly more of a hurry than him. He does well at marrying a true love and both stand a fair chance of being virgins at their wedding. She's likelier to find being a Mrs soups up her sexdrive and says second marriages are especially sexy. But both would be tempted to take a lover themselves if they ever caught their partner straying—though she might just say nothing and hope the mistress would move away.

PISCES WOMAN—TAURUS MAN

She'd love to go down the aisle with him. She does, however, give him both the sexy—and unsexy—vote. He finds her fairly fanciable, yet names her among the women he's least keen to settle with. She likes his sexy smile and hopes he'll be kind and faithful. But she may have to put food-loving Taurus on a diet—she likes her man to stay slim. A warm smile and a curvy body grab him and he loves a sexy voice and laugh. He especially wants his mate to be kind—and to be faithful, gentle and good at creating a home he'll want to come back to, as well. For long-term loving, she says there are two essentials— a sense of humour and cash! He wants someone on his wavelength, who works hard and who's hot stuff in bed. So he'll like Pisces' wicked fantasising and willingness to try almost anything. She seems to mind-read his every desire!

She's at higher risk of marrying more than once—he's at low risk and does a lot better at staying wed a decade or more. He's twice as happy to stay single, though, while she's one of the women most desperate to hook a man. But he does better at finding and keeping the love of his life. And he's likelier to be a virgin when he weds, though both score high here. These two get a fair boost to their lovelife once wed, but he can find it gets worse—while she says remarriage is even sexier. If she ever strays, he's the man who most wants to know why and put things right. She'll pretend she doesn't know, or quietly take a lover of her own, if he proves untrue.

PISCES WOMAN—GEMINI MAN

She's keen to get him to the altar and says he's quite sexy because he shares her love of fantasy. There's a fair chance he'll choose her, too, but he doesn't give her high sex ratings. She can't resist his great smile and his slim body—and his kindness and faithfulness win him high marks, too. He's the leg man of the zodiac—but his Ms Right must also be slim with a sexy laugh. She should treat him gently, be kind and faithful—and take an interest in the things he does. For long-term happiness, she says it's essential they share the same sense of humour, treat each other kindly and have enough cash to get by. He says he wants an understanding homelover, who is fun to be with, sexy, good-looking and great in bed. Her feminine, romantic lovestyle grows on him—and while he isn't the shining knight on a white charger she's usually looking for, he's a tingling electric charge instead!

She's likelier to remarry—while "flirty" Gemini turns the tables by being better at making a lasting bond. But he's more than four times keener to stay single than she is. She does slightly better at wedding a true love. But he's likelier to marry as a virgin and is the sign that most often does. Both get average marks for finding marriage a sex improver, with him least likely to say loving has got worse. But she finds remarriage sexier than he does. He'd consider divorce if he ever caught her playing away, while she'd say nothing, or take her own lover if he turned out to be unfaithful.

PISCES WOMAN—CANCER MAN

There's a reasonably strong chance they'll want to stroll down the aisle together. But while she finds him quite sexy, he either votes her a real sizzler—or a sex fizzler! Her sexy laugh and her kind and gentle ways warm his tender heart—and if she can create a cosy, welcoming home, he'll stick around. She loves his sexy smile and slim body and appreciates his kind and faithful nature, too. For this to work long-term, she says humour is essential—and that having enough money keeps strife at bay, too. He gives top votes to a woman who is loyal—and he wants to be well understood and treated kindly as well. But neither especially expect their partner to be hardworking—both want someone who will lavish time on them. And they don't really care if their mate is good in bed or not. These two are capable of wild, imaginative lovemaking, but may hide it. Sharing fantasies is a beginning.

Both are at risk of signing up for marriage more than once, especially him. But he does better at making a bond last 10 years or more and is likelier to marry the love of his life, too. She's keener to wed though and hates being without a man. He goes to the altar as a virgin more often. But wedlock proves more sexually satisfying for her and she finds remarriage really steamy! He's the faithful type, while she's at above average risk of affairs. If a partner does stray, they are likelier than most to say nothing, hoping it soon ends.

PISCES WOMAN—LEO MAN

Radiant Leo feels all at sea with tearfully emotional Pisces—and she says he's one of her least favourite mates, too. Sex ratings aren't much better on either side. Yet a warm smile at the right moment could melt both their hearts. She goes weak at the sight of a slim body, but says her man must be faithful if she's going to let him stay around. He likes great legs, a curvy body and a sexy laugh—and loves looking deep into his partner's eyes. Both say being on the same wavelength helps long-term—and so does a sense of humour! And she says having enough money avoids rows. But while she feels kindness is vital, he thinks other things matter more, like being sexy, good-looking and great in bed! But he must watch he doesn't overwhelm romantic Pisces with his need to be star of the bedtime show. She'd like some praise, too!

They both stand a high chance of taking marriage vows twice or more, especially him. He's better than her at lasting out until at least his 10th wedding anniversary though. But while he's the man who most enjoys his single status, she's the woman in the biggest hurry to find a husband. He has better luck at finding, and keeping, the love of his life—but she is likelier to remain a virgin until after her wedding. Marriage is a sexier affair for him, though both say that second marriages are usually warmer. He's faster than most to demand a divorce if she strays. She may take a lover of her own, or simply stay quiet and hope for the best, if he ever wanders.

PISCES WOMAN—VIRGO MAN

They are not often bowled over by each other's sex appeal, yet there's a fair chance they'll choose each other as partners. Her curvy, slim body first catches his eye and he gives top ratings to her sexy laugh and soothing voice. If she is kind and gentle, that will appeal, too. He must be slim, with a smile that knocks her out, to be her sort of man—but he must be faithful, too, which there's an average chance he will be. But Pisces won't appreciate his impeccable dress sense—she's the sign that least rates smart clothes. Both want their long-term mate to treat them kindly and to share their sense of humour. But he's more interested than her in sexual attraction—though her fantasy lovestyle could be just what he needs, to take his mind off worries that can sidetrack his sexdrive.

He's at low risk of taking more than one trip down the aisle, while she's a high risk. But neither do especially well at making a bond last a decade or more. She's in a scramble to find a husband—but he's in no hurry to marry. And his patience often pays off—he's likelier to wed the love of his life. She is happier to stay a virgin until hitched and finds marriage a more sexually enhancing experience. He's the man who least often gets a boost and who is most likely to say love-making tails off! He'll be torn between saying nothing and trying to talk problems through, if she is ever caught straying. She may well take her own lover, if he is untrue.

PISCES WOMAN—LIBRA MAN

There's a fair chance he'll want her to wear his ring—but she says he's the man she's least likely to settle with. And while he votes her the sign he's in the least hurry to bed, she says she doesn't fancy him much herself, thank you. He wants his woman to be kind and faithful. But he doesn't like the gentle type, which she may be—he prefers strong-minded, dynamic females. She likes a man to have a trim body and a dazzling smile. And he must pledge to be true—but Pisces is likelier than most to wander. Though given a little Libran romance, she'll unlock the secrets of her love fantasy store—and that should keep him far too busy to look elsewhere! For love to last, he says his partner must be sexy, great-looking, loyal and home-loving. She says kindness and humour matter more, but both want a mate who is on their wavelength.

She's higher on the marriage risk register than him—he has more chance of making a love-match last 10 years or more. He likes the single life, while she hates being unattached—though he's in more of a hurry to wed second time around. She is luckier at marrying the love of her life and is likelier to do so as a virgin. And she finds marriage really perks up her sexlife, while he says it usually carries on the same. Both run a higher than average risk of affairs, but are likelier than most to say nothing and hope for the best, if their partner proves untrue. Or they may just take lovers of their own.

PISCES WOMAN—SCORPIO MAN

She says he's the sexiest man she's ever met and can't wait to get him all to herself. Pisces is fairly popular with him, too, and he finds her quite sexy. She's likely to be kind, gentle and faithful—just the qualities that most appeal to Mr Scorpio, who likes his partner to be all woman. If she has great legs, that seals it! She can't resist his sexy smile and his slim body. But she hopes he will treat her kindly and never wander—and he doesn't have the best of records here. Long-term, she asks for someone kind and funny, who earns enough to keep them clear of cash worries. He's looking for a sexy homelover who enjoys fun and is great between the sheets. So he should love Pisces' blend of fantasy love, daring and romance and she'll appreciate his firm guidance and expertise.

He tends to marry for life, while she is likelier than most to have more than one spouse. He is slightly better at making marriage last 10 years or more. But she's keener to wed, hating to be left on the shelf. She is a little luckier at settling with a true love and is more likely to wed as a virgin. But he thrives within wedlock and is the man who most often finds it a sex booster. She says remarriage is more sexually satisfying, though. If he proves untrue, she may well take her own lover in revenge. But he'll do all he can to work things out between them if she ever wanders.

PISCES WOMAN—SAGITTARIUS MAN

They vote each other a super-sexy duo—yet he says he finds her the most unfanciable sign of all, when she turns soppily emotional. And as partners, they give each other just an average score. He won't resist her warm smile and slim body though—and if she turns out to be the faithful type and interested in the same things as him, love can really take hold. His slim, well-kept body tempts her and his sexy smile and kind, faithful nature win her heart. For long-term success, both agree they must show each other kindness, share the same sense of humour and have enough money for their needs. Neither see sexual attraction as the most vital ingredient in a happy marriage, but steamy sex talk and fantasy fun will keep lust temperature high. He shouldn't forget the romantic touches of their early days, though—Pisces needs to feel loved.

Both may well marry more than once, especially him. She does better at making a love bond last 10 years—he's the man least likely to. And while she's in more of a rush to get to the altar, he's the man in the least hurry second time around. She does better at marrying the love of her life and is twice as likely to do so as a virgin. And she finds matrimony more of a sex booster, too. But she's at above average risk of having affairs, while he is the man most likely to stay faithful. He'd want to know why and work things out if she did ever wander. She'd want a fast divorce if he strayed.

PISCES WOMAN—CAPRICORN MAN

He thinks she'd make a great partner and a sexy bedmate, too. But she says he's not a favourite of hers and she doesn't really fancy him. He'll fall for her if she has great legs, a warm smile and a sexy voice. He says she should treat him gently, take an interest in the things he likes—and be faithful, despite the fact that he's the man who least often is. Her Mr Right is kind and faithful, too. She'll want him to stay slim, as well—and to keep smiling, to cheer her up. A shared sense of humour is vital to both to make this work long-term—and they say that being free of money worries helps a lot, too. He also wants his mate to be good-looking—and to stay hot stuff. And sexwise she can learn to let go under the protective wing of he-man Capricorn, giving full rein to secret fantasies that make their love sessions so deliciously daring.

Both are at risk of remarrying, especially her. But he does better at sticking 10 years of marriage. He enjoys being single, while she dreads being left on the shelf. But once he's made up his mind, he's even keener than her to wed. When it comes to remarriage though, it's a case of once bitten, twice shy for both. She has better luck at marrying the love of her life and is a lot likelier to wed as a virgin, while he's usually too impatient. She finds wedlock sexier than he does—but both say sex soars second time around. If he ever strays, she may take a lover of her own. He'd look for ways they could stay together before considering a divorce.

PISCES WOMAN—AQUARIUS MAN

They don't often hit it off, both voting the other among their least likelys. And sex ratings are low here, too. He's looking for a slim and curvaceous partner who treats him gently and makes a comfy, cosy, tidy home for him. But Pisces is rarely that organised and she may well prefer sharing roles, allowing her more freedom. Her Mr Right has a trim physique and a knockout smile—and he is faithful and kind-hearted, too. For long-lasting happiness, she says a sense of humour is essential—and so is enough money to keep strife at bay. He wants a life partner who understands him well and is loyal, fun and great in bed. With warm and patient handling Pisces can be— she has a secret store of outrageous fantasies just waiting for the right person to unlock them.

He stands slightly more chance of marrying twice—and is the man who most often ends up having three spouses! He's a little better at making a bond last 10 years, though. But while she's in a hurry to wed, dreading that she's leaving it too late, he's quite happy to hang onto the single life. Second time around, though, he's in more of a rush. She is luckier at wedding the love of her life and is likelier to save herself for that special person—he rarely waits! And she finds marriage more of a sexlife booster, too—he says lovemaking carries on the same. He'd want a divorce if he found she was carrying on behind his back. She'd stay quiet and hope any fling he had soon came to an end.

PISCES WOMAN—PISCES MAN

She's his favourite choice as life partner—and he votes her by far the sexiest sign, too. She says he's a fairly good match for her as well, but has no strong feelings about him sexwise. A firm body and a great smile first grab her attention—and kindness and faithfulness make it bond like superglue. He likes his woman to be slim, with great legs and a sexy laugh. And she must be good at creating a cosy home—which arty Pisces may well be. But she also has other ambitions on her mind apart from playing house. For love to last, both say a sense of humour is essential. She says being free of money worries helps, too, while his dream partner is a loyal funlover who is great in bed. He won't be disappointed—it takes one Pisces to unlock the other's full range of romantic and x-rated fantasies simmering away unseen!

He takes more trips down the aisle than her, on average, but both are at risk of remarrying. He does better at making a lasting bond. But he's happier to stay single—she hates being unattached. Yet marriage suits him as he is the sign keenest to remarry and the man who most often weds the love of his life. He's also likelier to marry as a virgin and finds wedlock sexier, being least likely to report that loving gets worse. If illicit affairs do come to light, both may well say nothing, hoping the other's fling soon ends. Or she may take a lover herself, while he could have divorce in mind.

APPENDIX I

ZODIAC SIGN TABLES

with British Summer Time and World Time Zones

YOUR TRUE ZODIAC SIGN

Our year has 365 days but the sun takes an extra five hours and 50 minutes each year to move through all the signs of the zodiac. So the time of day, and the date, it enters each sign varies from year to year. When dates like July 23 to August 23 are given for Leo, for example, this can only mean that most years the sun was in Leo for most of July 23. But some years it was already in Leo by the evening of July 22, sometimes it spends quite a lot of July 23 still in Cancer.

If you were born near the beginning or end of your zodiac sign, please turn to that sign in these tables and check your year, day and time of birth to get your true zodiac sign.

Times used in the tables are GMT.

SUN INTO ARIES

DAY	YEAR	TIME OF DAY	DAY	YEAR	TIME OF DAY
21 March	1900	01:38	21 March	1933	01:43
21 March	1901	07:23	21 March	1934	07:28
21 March	1902	13:16	21 March	1935	13:18
21 March	1903	19:14	20 March	1936	18:57
21 March	1904	00:58	21 March	1937	00:45
21 March	1905	06:57	21 March	1938	06:43
21 March	1906	12:52	21 March	1939	12:28
21 March	1907	18:32	20 March	1940	18:24
21 March	1908	00:27	21 March	1941	00:20
21 March	1909	06:13	21 March	1942	06:10
21 March	1910	12:02	21 March	1943	12:03
21 March	1911	17:54	20 March	1944	17:48
20 March	1912	23:28	20 March	1945	23:37
21 March	1913	05:18	21 March	1946	05:32
21 March	1914	11:10	20 March	1947	11:12
21 March	1915	16:51	20 March	1948	16:57
20 March	1916	22:47	20 March	1949	22:48
21 March	1917	04:37	21 March	1950	04:35
21 March	1918	10:25	21 March	1951	10:26
21 March	1919	16:19	20 March	1952	16:14
20 March	1920	21:59	20 March	1953	22:00
21 March	1921	03:51	21 March	1954	03:53
21 March	1922	09:48	21 March	1955	09:35
21 March	1923	15:28	20 March	1956	15:21
20 March	1924	21:21	20 March	1957	21:16
21 March	1925	03:12	21 March	1958	03:06
21 March	1926	09:01	21 March	1959	08:55
21 March	1927	14:59	20 March	1960	14:43
20 March	1928	20:44	20 March	1961	20:32
21 March	1929	02:35	21 March	1962	02:30
21 March	1930	08:30	21 March	1963	08:20
21 March	1931	14:06	20 March	1964	14:10
20 March	1932	19:54	20 March	1965	20:05

21 March	1966	01:53	20 March	1984	10:25
21 March	1967	07:37	20 March	1985	16:14
20 March	1968	13:22	20 March	1986	22:03
20 March	1969	19:09	21 March	1987	03:52
21 March	1970	00:57	20 March	1988	09:40
21 March	1971	06:38	20 March	1989	15:29
20 March	1972	12:21	20 March	1990	21:20
20 March	1973	18:13	21 March	1991	03:02
21 March	1974	00:07	20 March	1992	08:49
21 March	1975	05:57	20 March	1993	14:41
20 March	1976	11:50	20 March	1994	20:29
20 March	1977	17:43	21 March	1995	02:15
20 March	1978	23:34	20 March	1996	08:04
21 March	1979	05:22	20 March	1997	13:56
20 March	1980	11:10	20 March	1998	19:55
20 March	1981	17:03	21 March	1999	01:47
20 March	1982	22:56	20 March	2000	07:36
21 March	1983	04:39	20 March	2001	13:32

SUN INTO TAURUS

DAY	YEAR	TIME OF DAY	DAY	YEAR	TIME OF DAY
20 April	1900	13:27	20 April	1914	22:53
20 April	1901	19:13	21 April	1915	04:28
21 April	1902	01:04	20 April	1916	10:24
21 April	1903	06:58	20 April	1917	16:17
20 April	1904	12:41	20 April	1918	22:05
20 April	1905	18:43	21 April	1919	03:59
21 April	1906	00:39	20 April	1920	09:39
21 April	1907	06:17	20 April	1921	15:32
20 April	1908	12:11	20 April	1922	21:28
20 April	1909	17:58	21 April	1923	03:05
20 April	1910	23:45	20 April	1924	08:59
21 April	1911	05:36	20 April	1925	14:51
20 April	1912	11:11	20 April	1926	20:36
20 April	1913	17:02	21 April	1927	02:32

20 April	1928	08:16	20 April	1965	07:26
20 April	1929	14:10	20 April	1966	13:12
20 April	1930	20:06	20 April	1967	18:56
21 April	1931	01:39	20 April	1968	00:42
20 April	1932	07:28	20 April	1969	06:27
20 April	1933	13:19	20 April	1970	12:16
20 April	1934	19:00	20 April	1971	17:54
21 April	1935	00:50	19 April	1972	23:38
20 April	1936	06:31	20 April	1973	05:31
20 April	1937	12:19	20 April	1974	11:19
20 April	1938	18:15	20 April	1975	17:08
20 April	1939	23:55	19 April	1976	23:03
20 April	1940	05:51	20 April	1977	04:58
20 April	1941	11:51	20 April	1978	10:50
20 April	1942	17:39	20 April	1979	16:36
20 April	1943	23:32	19 April	1980	22:23
20 April	1944	05:17	20 April	1981	04:19
20 April	1945	11:07	20 April	1982	10:08
20 April	1946	17:02	20 April	1983	15:50
20 April	1947	22:39	19 April	1984	21:38
20 April	1948	04:25	20 April	1985	03:26
20 April	1949	10:17	20 April	1986	09:13
20 April	1950	15:59	20 April	1987	14:58
20 April	1951	21:48	19 April	1988	20:46
20 April	1952	03:36	20 April	1989	02:39
20 April	1953	09:25	20 April	1990	08:27
20 April	1954	15:19	20 April	1991	14:09
20 April	1955	20:57	19 April	1992	19:57
20 April	1956	02:44	20 April	1993	01:49
20 April	1957	08:41	20 April	1994	07:37
20 April	1958	14:27	20 April	1995	13:22
20 April	1959	20:17	19 April	1996	19:11
20 April	1960	02:06	20 April	1997	01:04
20 April	1961	07:55	20 April	1998	06:58
20 April	1962	13:51	20 April	2099	12:47
20 April	1963	19:36	19 April	2000	18:40
20 April	1964	01:27	20 April	2001	00:37

SUN INTO GEMINI

DAY	YEAR	TIME OF DAY	DAY	YEAR	TIME OF DAY
21 May	1900	13:17	21 May	1934	18:35
21 May	1901	19:04	22 May	1935	00:25
22 May	1902	00:53	21 May	1936	06:07
22 May	1903	06:45	21 May	1937	11:57
21 May	1904	12:28	21 May	1938	17:50
21 May	1905	18:31	21 May	1939	23:26
22 May	1906	00:24	21 May	1940	05:23
22 May	1907	06:03	21 May	1941	11:23
21 May	1908	11:58	21 May	1942	17:09
21 May	1909	17:45	21 May	1943	23:03
21 May	1910	23:30	21 May	1944	04:50
22 May	1911	05:18	21 May	1945	10:41
21 May	1912	10:56	21 May	1946	16:34
21 May	1913	16:49	21 May	1947	22:09
21 May	1914	22:37	21 May	1948	03:57
22 May	1915	04:10	21 May	1949	09:51
21 May	1916	10:05	21 May	1950	15:27
21 May	1917	15:58	21 May	1951	21:15
21 May	1918	21:45	21 May	1952	03:04
22 May	1919	03:39	21 May	1953	08:53
21 May	1920	09:21	21 May	1954	14:48
21 May	1921	15:16	21 May	1955	20:24
21 May	1922	21:10	21 May	1956	02:13
22 May	1923	02:45	21 May	1957	08:10
21 May	1924	08:40	21 May	1958	13:51
21 May	1925	14:33	21 May	1959	19:42
21 May	1926	20:15	21 May	1960	01:34
22 May	1927	02:08	21 May	1961	07:22
21 May	1928	07:52	21 May	1962	13:17
21 May	1929	13:47	21 May	1963	18:58
21 May	1930	19:42	21 May	1964	00:50
22 May	1931	01:15	21 May	1965	06:51
21 May	1932	07:07	21 May	1966	12:32
21 May	1933	12:57	21 May	1967	18:18

Zodiac Sign Tables

21 May	1968	00:06	21 May	1985	02:43
21 May	1969	05:50	21 May	1986	08:28
21 May	1970	11:38	21 May	1987	14:11
21 May	1971	17:15	20 May	1988	19:57
20 May	1972	23:00	21 May	1989	01:54
21 May	1973	04:55	21 May	1990	07:38
21 May	1974	10:36	21 May	1991	13:20
21 May	1975	16:24	20 May	1992	19:13
20 May	1976	22:21	21 May	1993	01:02
21 May	1977	04:15	21 May	1994	06:49
21 May	1978	10:10	21 May	1995	12:35
21 May	1979	15:55	20 May	1996	18:24
20 May	1980	21:43	21 May	1997	00:19
21 May	1981	03:40	21 May	1998	06:06
21 May	1982	19:23	21 May	1999	11:53
21 May	1983	15:07	20 May	2000	17:50
20 May	1984	20:58	20 May	2001	23:45

SUN INTO CANCER

DAY	YEAR	TIME OF DAY	DAY	YEAR	TIME OF DAY
21 June	1900	21:40	22 June	1917	00:14
22 June	1901	03:27	22 June	1918	05:59
22 June	1902	09:15	22 June	1919	11:53
22 June	1903	15:04	21 June	1920	17:40
21 June	1904	20:51	21 June	1921	23:35
22 June	1905	02:51	22 June	1922	05:26
22 June	1906	08:41	22 June	1923	11:02
22 June	1907	14:23	21 June	1924	16:59
21 June	1908	20:19	21 June	1925	22:50
22 June	1909	02:06	22 June	1926	04:30
22 June	1910	07:49	22 June	1927	10:22
22 June	1911	13:35	21 June	1928	16:06
21 June	1912	19:16	21 June	1929	22:00
22 June	1913	01:09	22 June	1930	03:53
22 June	1914	06:51	22 June	1931	09:28
22 June	1915	12:29	21 June	1932	15:23
21 June	1916	18:24	21 June	1933	21:12

22 June	1934	02:48	21 June	1968	08:13
22 June	1935	08:38	21 June	1969	13:56
21 June	1936	14:22	21 June	1970	19:43
21 June	1937	20:12	22 June	1971	01:20
22 June	1938	02:04	21 June	1972	07:06
22 June	1939	07:39	21 June	1973	13:01
21 June	1940	13:36	21 June	1974	18:38
21 June	1941	19:33	22 June	1975	00:27
22 June	1942	01:16	21 June	1976	06:24
22 June	1943	07:13	21 June	1977	12:15
21 June	1944	13:02	21 June	1978	18:11
21 June	1945	18:52	21 June	1979	23:57
22 June	1946	00:45	21 June	1980	05:47
22 June	1947	06:19	21 June	1981	11:46
21 June	1948	12:10	21 June	1982	17:24
21 June	1949	18:02	21 June	1983	23:09
21 June	1950	23:36	21 June	1984	05:03
22 June	1951	05:25	21 June	1985	10:45
21 June	1952	11:12	21 June	1986	16:30
21 June	1953	17:00	21 June	1987	22:11
21 June	1954	22:54	21 June	1988	03:57
22 June	1955	04:32	21 June	1989	09:54
21 June	1956	10:42	21 June	1990	15:33
21 June	1957	16:20	21 June	1991	21:19
21 June	1958	21:57	21 June	1992	03:15
22 June	1959	03:49	21 June	1993	09:00
21 June	1960	09:42	21 June	1994	14:48
21 June	1961	15:30	21 June	1995	20:35
21 June	1962	21:25	21 June	1996	02:24
22 June	1963	03:04	21 June	1997	08:21
21 June	1964	08:57	21 June	1998	14:03
21 June	1965	14:56	21 June	1999	19:50
21 June	1966	20:34	21 June	2000	01:48
22 June	1967	02:23	21 June	2001	07:38

SUN INTO LEO

DAY	YEAR	TIME OF DAY	DAY	YEAR	TIME OF DAY
23 July	1900	08:36	23 July	1934	13:42
23 July	1901	14:23	23 July	1935	19:33
23 July	1902	20:10	23 July	1936	01:18
24 July	1903	01:58	23 July	1937	07:07
23 July	1904	07:49	23 July	1938	12:57
23 July	1905	13:45	23 July	1939	18:36
23 July	1906	19:32	23 July	1940	00:34
24 July	1907	01:17	23 July	1941	06:26
23 July	1908	07:14	23 July	1942	12:07
23 July	1909	13:00	23 July	1943	18:04
23 July	1910	18:43	22 July	1944	23:56
24 July	1911	00:28	23 July	1945	05:46
23 July	1912	06:13	23 July	1946	11:37
23 July	1913	12:04	23 July	1947	17:14
23 July	1914	17:46	22 July	1948	23:07
23 July	1915	23:26	23 July	1949	04:57
23 July	1916	05:21	23 July	1950	10:26
23 July	1917	11:07	23 July	1951	16:21
23 July	1918	16:51	22 July	1952	22:08
23 July	1919	22:44	23 July	1953	03:52
23 July	1920	04:35	23 July	1954	09:45
23 July	1921	10:30	23 July	1955	15:25
23 July	1922	16:19	22 July	1956	21:20
23 July	1923	22:00	23 July	1957	03:15
23 July	1924	03:57	23 July	1958	08:50
23 July	1925	09:44	23 July	1959	14:45
23 July	1926	15:24	22 July	1960	20:37
23 July	1927	21:16	23 July	1961	02:23
23 July	1928	03:02	23 July	1962	08:18
23 July	1929	08:53	23 July	1963	13:59
23 July	1930	14:42	22 July	1964	19:53
23 July	1931	20:21	23 July	1965	01:48
23 July	1932	02:18	23 July	1966	07:23
23 July	1933	08:05	23 July	1967	13:16

22 July	1968	19:08	22 July	1985	21:37
23 July	1969	00:48	23 July	1986	03:25
23 July	1970	06:37	23 July	1987	09:07
23 July	1971	12:15	22 July	1988	14:51
22 July	1972	18:03	22 July	1989	20:46
22 July	1973	23:56	23 July	1990	02:22
23 July	1974	05:31	23 July	1991	08:11
23 July	1975	11:22	22 July	1992	14:09
22 July	1976	17:19	22 July	1993	19:51
22 July	1977	23:04	23 July	1994	01:42
23 July	1978	05:01	23 July	1995	07:30
23 July	1979	10:49	22 July	1996	13:19
22 July	1980	16:42	22 July	1997	19:16
22 July	1981	22:40	23 July	1998	00:56
23 July	1982	04:16	23 July	1999	06:45
23 July	1983	10:05	22 July	2000	12:43
22 July	1984	10:59	22 July	2001	18:27

SUN INTO VIRGO

DAY	YEAR	TIME OF DAY	DAY	YEAR	TIME OF DAY
23 Aug	1900	15:20	23 Aug	1916	12:08
23 Aug	1901	21:07	23 Aug	1917	17:53
24 Aug	1902	02:53	23 Aug	1918	23:36
24 Aug	1903	08:41	24 Aug	1919	05:28
23 Aug	1904	14:36	23 Aug	1920	11:21
23 Aug	1905	20:28	23 Aug	1921	17:15
24 Aug	1906	02:13	23 Aug	1922	23:04
24 Aug	1907	08:03	24 Aug	1923	04:51
23 Aug	1908	13:57	23 Aug	1924	10:47
23 Aug	1909	19:43	23 Aug	1925	16:33
24 Aug	1910	01:27	23 Aug	1926	22:14
24 Aug	1911	07:13	24 Aug	1927	04:05
23 Aug	1912	13:01	23 Aug	1928	09:53
23 Aug	1913	18:48	23 Aug	1929	15:41
24 Aug	1914	00:29	23 Aug	1930	21:26
24 Aug	1915	06:15	24 Aug	1931	03:10

23 Aug	1932	09:06	23 Aug	1967	20:12
23 Aug	1933	14:51	23 Aug	1968	02:03
23 Aug	1934	20:32	23 Aug	1969	07:43
24 Aug	1935	02:24	23 Aug	1970	13:34
23 Aug	1936	08:10	23 Aug	1971	19:15
23 Aug	1937	13:58	23 Aug	1972	01:03
23 Aug	1938	19:46	23 Aug	1973	06:54
24 Aug	1939	01:31	23 Aug	1974	12:29
23 Aug	1940	07:28	23 Aug	1975	18:24
23 Aug	1941	13:17	23 Aug	1976	00:19
23 Aug	1942	18:58	23 Aug	1977	06:01
24 Aug	1943	00:55	23 Aug	1978	11:57
23 Aug	1944	06:46	23 Aug	1979	17:47
23 Aug	1945	12:35	22 Aug	1980	23:41
23 Aug	1946	18:27	23 Aug	1981	05:39
24 Aug	1947	00:09	23 Aug	1982	11:16
23 Aug	1948	06:02	23 Aug	1983	17:08
23 Aug	1949	11:48	22 Aug	1984	23:01
23 Aug	1950	17:23	23 Aug	1985	04:36
23 Aug	1951	23:16	23 Aug	1986	10:26
23 Aug	1952	05:03	23 Aug	1987	16:10
23 Aug	1953	10:45	22 Aug	1988	21:55
23 Aug	1954	16:36	23 Aug	1989	03:47
23 Aug	1955	22:19	23 Aug	1990	09:21
23 Aug	1956	04:15	23 Aug	1991	15:13
23 Aug	1957	10:08	22 Aug	1992	21:11
23 Aug	1958	15:46	23 Aug	1993	02:51
23 Aug	1959	21:43	23 Aug	1994	08:44
23 Aug	1960	03:34	23 Aug	1995	14:35
23 Aug	1961	09:18	22 Aug	1996	20:23
23 Aug	1962	15:13	23 Aug	1997	02:19
23 Aug	1963	20:57	23 Aug	1998	08:00
23 Aug	1964	02:51	23 Aug	1999	13:52
23 Aug	1965	08:42	22 Aug	2000	19:49
23 Aug	1966	14:18	23 Aug	2001	01:28

SUN INTO LIBRA

DAY	YEAR	TIME OF DAY	DAY	YEAR	TIME OF DAY
23 Sept	1900	12:20	23 Sept	1934	17:44
23 Sept	1901	18:08	23 Sept	1935	23:38
23 Sept	1902	23:55	23 Sept	1936	05:26
24 Sept	1903	05:43	23 Sept	1937	11:13
23 Sept	1904	11:40	23 Sept	1938	17:00
23 Sept	1905	17:29	23 Sept	1939	22:49
23 Sept	1906	23:14	23 Sept	1940	04:45
24 Sept	1907	05:08	23 Sept	1941	10:32
23 Sept	1908	10:58	23 Sept	1942	16:16
23 Sept	1909	16:44	23 Sept	1943	22:11
23 Sept	1910	22:30	23 Sept	1944	04:01
24 Sept	1911	04:17	23 Sept	1945	09:49
23 Sept	1912	10:08	23 Sept	1946	15:41
23 Sept	1913	15:52	23 Sept	1947	21:29
23 Sept	1914	21:33	23 Sept	1948	03:21
24 Sept	1915	03:23	23 Sept	1949	09:06
23 Sept	1916	09:14	23 Sept	1950	14:43
23 Sept	1917	15:00	23 Sept	1951	20:37
23 Sept	1918	20:45	23 Sept	1952	02:23
24 Sept	1919	02:35	23 Sept	1953	08:06
23 Sept	1920	08:28	23 Sept	1954	13:55
23 Sept	1921	14:19	23 Sept	1955	19:41
23 Sept	1922	20:09	23 Sept	1956	01:35
24 Sept	1923	02:03	23 Sept	1957	07:26
23 Sept	1924	07:58	23 Sept	1958	13:09
23 Sept	1925	13:43	23 Sept	1959	19:08
23 Sept	1926	19:26	23 Sept	1960	00:58
24 Sept	1927	01:17	23 Sept	1961	06:42
23 Sept	1928	07:05	23 Sept	1962	12:36
23 Sept	1929	12:52	23 Sept	1963	18:23
23 Sept	1930	18:36	23 Sept	1964	00:17
24 Sept	1931	00:23	23 Sept	1965	06:06
23 Sept	1932	06:15	23 Sept	1966	11:43
23 Sept	1933	12:00	23 Sept	1967	17:38

22 Sept	1968	23:26	23 Sept	1985	02:08
23 Sept	1969	05:06	23 Sept	1986	07:59
23 Sept	1970	10:59	23 Sept	1987	13:45
23 Sept	1971	16:45	22 Sept	1988	19:29
22 Sept	1972	22:33	23 Sept	1989	01:20
23 Sept	1973	04:21	23 Sept	1990	06:56
23 Sept	1974	09:59	23 Sept	1991	12:49
23 Sept	1975	15:55	22 Sept	1992	18:43
22 Sept	1976	21:48	23 Sept	1993	00:23
23 Sept	1977	03:30	23 Sept	1994	06:20
23 Sept	1978	09:26	23 Sept	1995	12:13
23 Sept	1979	15:17	22 Sept	1996	18:00
22 Sept	1980	21:09	22 Sept	1997	23:56
23 Sept	1981	03:06	23 Sept	1998	05:38
23 Sept	1982	08:47	23 Sept	1999	11:32
23 Sept	1983	14:42	22 Sept	2000	17:28
22 Sept	1984	20:33	22 Sept	2001	23:05

SUN INTO SCORPIO

DAY	YEAR	TIME OF DAY	DAY	YEAR	TIME OF DAY
23 Oct	1900	20:54	23 Oct	1916	17:56
24 Oct	1901	02:45	23 Oct	1917	23:43
24 Oct	1902	08:35	24 Oct	1918	05:32
24 Oct	1903	14:22	24 Oct	1919	11:21
23 Oct	1904	20:18	23 Oct	1920	17:12
24 Oct	1905	02:07	23 Oct	1921	23:02
24 Oct	1906	07:54	24 Oct	1922	04:52
24 Oct	1907	13:50	24 Oct	1923	10:50
23 Oct	1908	19:36	23 Oct	1924	16:44
24 Oct	1909	01:22	23 Oct	1925	22:30
24 Oct	1910	07:11	24 Oct	1926	04:18
24 Oct	1911	12:58	24 Oct	1927	10:07
23 Oct	1912	18:50	23 Oct	1928	15:54
24 Oct	1913	00:34	23 Oct	1929	21:41
24 Oct	1914	06:17	24 Oct	1930	03:26
24 Oct	1915	12:09	24 Oct	1931	09:15

23 Oct	1932	15:03		24 Oct	1967	02:44
23 Oct	1933	20:47		23 Oct	1968	08:29
24 Oct	1934	02:35		23 Oct	1969	14:10
24 Oct	1935	08:28		23 Oct	1970	20:04
23 Oct	1936	14:18		24 Oct	1971	01:53
23 Oct	1937	20:06		23 Oct	1972	07:41
24 Oct	1938	01:54		23 Oct	1973	13:30
24 Oct	1939	07:46		23 Oct	1974	19:11
23 Oct	1940	13:39		24 Oct	1975	01:06
23 Oct	1941	19:27		23 Oct	1976	06:58
24 Oct	1942	01:15		23 Oct	1977	12:41
24 Oct	1943	07:08		23 Oct	1978	18:37
23 Oct	1944	12:55		24 Oct	1979	00:28
23 Oct	1945	18:43		23 Oct	1980	06:17
24 Oct	1946	00:35		23 Oct	1981	12:13
24 Oct	1947	06:26		23 Oct	1982	17:58
23 Oct	1948	12:18		23 Oct	1983	23:55
23 Oct	1949	18:13		23 Oct	1984	05:46
23 Oct	1950	23:44		23 Oct	1985	11;22
24 Oct	1951	05:36		23 Oct	1986	17:14
23 Oct	1952	11:22		23 Oct	1987	23:01
23 Oct	1953	17:06		23 Oct	1988	04:44
23 Oct	1954	22;56		23 Oct	1989	10:36
24 Oct	1955	04:43		23 Oct	1990	16:15
23 Oct	1956	10:34		23 Oct	1991	22:06
23 Oct	1957	16:24		23 Oct	1992	03:58
23 Oct	1958	22:11		23 Oct	1993	09:38
24 Oct	1959	04:11		23 Oct	1994	15:37
23 Oct	1960	10:01		23 Oct	1995	21:32
23 Oct	1961	15:47		23 Oct	1996	03:19
23 Oct	1962	21:40		23 Oct	1997	09:15
24 Oct	1963	03:29		23 Oct	1998	14:59
23 Oct	1964	09:20		23 Oct	1999	20:53
23 Oct	1965	15:10		23 Oct	2000	02:48
23 Oct	1966	20:51		23 Oct	2001	08:26

SUN INTO SAGITTARIUS

DAY	YEAR	TIME OF DAY	DAY	YEAR	TIME OF DAY
22 Nov	1900	17:47	23 Nov	1902	05:34
22 Nov	1901	23:40	23 Nov	1903	11:20
22 Nov	1904	17:15	22 Nov	1941	16:37
22 Nov	1905	23:04	22 Nov	1942	22:30
23 Nov	1906	04:53	23 Nov	1943	04:21
23 Nov	1907	10:51	22 Nov	1944	10:07
22 Nov	1908	16:34	22 Nov	1945	15:55
22 Nov	1909	22:20	22 Nov	1946	21:46
23 Nov	1910	04:11	23 Nov	1947	03:37
23 Nov	1911	09:55	22 Nov	1948	09:29
22 Nov	1912	15:48	22 Nov	1949	15:16
22 Nov	1913	21:35	22 Nov	1950	21:02
23 Nov	1914	03:20	23 Nov	1951	02:51
23 Nov	1915	09:13	22 Nov	1952	08:35
22 Nov	1916	14:57	22 Nov	1953	14:22
22 Nov	1917	20:44	22 Nov	1954	20:14
23 Nov	1918	02:37	23 Nov	1955	02:01
23 Nov	1919	08:25	22 Nov	1956	07:50
22 Nov	1920	14:15	22 Nov	1957	13:39
22 Nov	1921	20:05	22 Nov	1958	19:29
23 Nov	1922	01:55	23 Nov	1959	01:27
23 Nov	1923	07:53	22 Nov	1960	07:18
22 Nov	1924	13:46	22 Nov	1961	13:07
22 Nov	1925	19:35	22 Nov	1962	19:01
23 Nov	1926	01:27	23 Nov	1963	00:49
23 Nov	1927	07:14	22 Nov	1964	06:39
22 Nov	1928	13:00	22 Nov	1965	12:29
22 Nov	1929	18:48	22 Nov	1966	18:14
23 Nov	1930	00:34	23 Nov	1967	00:05
23 Nov	1931	06:24	22 Nov	1968	05:49
22 Nov	1932	12:10	22 Nov	1969	11:31
22 Nov	1933	17:53	22 Nov	1970	17:24

22 Nov	1934	23:43	22 Nov	1971	23:13
23 Nov	1935	05:34	22 Nov	1972	05:02
22 Nov	1936	11:25	22 Nov	1973	10:54
22 Nov	1937	17:16	22 Nov	1974	16:39
22 Nov	1938	23:06	22 Nov	1975	22:31
23 Nov	1939	05:58	22 Nov	1976	04:21
22 Nov	1940	10:49	22 Nov	1977	10:07
22 Nov	1978	16:04	22 Nov	1990	13:47
22 Nov	1979	21:54	22 Nov	1991	19:36
22 Nov	1980	03:41	22 Nov	1992	01:26
22 Nov	1981	09:36	22 Nov	1993	07:07
22 Nov	1982	15:24	22 Nov	1994	13:06
22 Nov	1983	21:19	22 Nov	1995	19:02
22 Nov	1984	03:11	22 Nov	1996	00:55
22 Nov	1985	08:51	22 Nov	1997	06:48
22 Nov	1986	14:44	22 Nov	1998	12:35
22 Nov	1987	20:30	22 Nov	1999	18:25
22 Nov	1988	02:12	22 Nov	2000	00:20
22 Nov	1989	08:05	22 Nov	2001	06:01

SUN INTO CAPRICORN

DAY	YEAR	TIME OF DAY	DAY	YEAR	TIME OF DAY
22 Dec	1900	06:40	22 Dec	1922	14:57
22 Dec	1901	12:36	22 Dec	1923	20:53
22 Dec	1902	18:34	22 Dec	1924	02:45
23 Dec	1903	00:19	22 Dec	1925	08:37
22 Dec	1904	06:13	22 Dec	1926	14:33
22 Dec	1905	12:03	22 Dec	1927	20:18
22 Dec	1906	17:52	22 Dec	1928	02:03
22 Dec	1907	23:50	22 Dec	1929	07:52
22 Dec	1908	05:33	22 Dec	1930	13:39
22 Dec	1909	11:19	22 Dec	1931	19:29
22 Dec	1910	17:11	22 Dec	1932	01:14
22 Dec	1911	22:53	22 Dec	1933	06:57
22 Dec	1912	04:44	22 Dec	1934	12:49
22 Dec	1913	10:34	22 Dec	1935	18:36

22 Dec	1914	16:22	22 Dec	1936	00:26
22 Dec	1915	22:15	22 Dec	1937	06:21
22 Dec	1916	03:58	22 Dec	1938	12:13
22 Dec	1917	09:45	22 Dec	1939	18:05
22 Dec	1918	15:41	21 Dec	1940	23:54
22 Dec	1919	21:27	22 Dec	1941	05:44
22 Dec	1920	03:17	22 Dec	1942	11:39
22 Dec	1921	09:08	22 Dec	1943	17:28
21 Dec	1944	23:14	22 Dec	1973	00:08
22 Dec	1945	05:03	22 Dec	1974	05:56
22 Dec	1946	10:53	22 Dec	1975	11:46
22 Dec	1947	16:42	21 Dec	1976	17:35
21 Dec	1948	22:33	21 Dec	1977	23:23
22 Dec	1949	04:23	22 Dec	1978	05:21
22 Dec	1950	10:13	22 Dec	1979	11:10
22 Dec	1951	16:00	21 Dec	1980	16:56
21 Dec	1952	21:43	21 Dec	1981	22:51
22 Dec	1953	03:31	22 Dec	1982	04:38
22 Dec	1954	09:24	22 Dec	1983	10:31
22 Dec	1955	15:11	21 Dec	1984	16:23
21 Dec	1956	21:00	21 Dec	1985	22:08
22 Dec	1957	02:49	22 Dec	1986	04:02
22 Dec	1958	08:40	22 Dec	1987	09:46
22 Dec	1959	14:34	21 Dec	1988	15:28
21 Dec	1960	20:26	21 Dec	1989	21:22
22 Dec	1961	02:19	22 Dec	1990	03:07
22 Dec	1962	08:15	22 Dec	1991	08:54
22 Dec	1963	14:02	21 Dec	1992	14:44
21 Dec	1964	19:50	21 Dec	1993	20:27
22 Dec	1965	01:41	22 Dec	1994	02:23
22 Dec	1966	07:28	22 Dec	1995	08:18
22 Dec	1967	13:16	21 Dec	1996	14:07
21 Dec	1968	19:00	21 Dec	1997	20:08
22 Dec	1969	00:44	22 Dec	1998	01:57
22 Dec	1970	06:35	22 Dec	1999	07:44
22 Dec	1971	12:23	21 Dec	2000	13:38
21 Dec	1972	18:13	21 Dec	2001	19:22

SUN INTO AQUARIUS

DAY	YEAR	TIME OF DAY	DAY	YEAR	TIME OF DAY
22 Jan	1900	11:03	21 Jan	1904	10:57
20 Jan	1901	17:16	20 Jan	1905	16:51
20 Jan	1902	23:11	20 Jan	1906	22:42
21 Jan	1903	05:13	21 Jan	1907	04:30
21 Jan	1908	10:27	20 Jan	1946	15:44
20 Jan	1909	16:10	20 Jan	1947	21:31
20 Jan	1910	21:58	21 Jan	1948	03:18
21 Jan	1911	03:51	20 Jan	1949	09:09
21 Jan	1912	09:29	20 Jan	1950	15:00
20 Jan	1913	15:19	20 Jan	1951	20:52
20 Jan	1914	21:11	21 Jan	1952	02:38
21 Jan	1915	02:59	20 Jan	1953	08:21
21 Jan	1916	08:53	20 Jan	1954	14:11
20 Jan	1917	14:37	20 Jan	1955	20:01
20 Jan	1918	20:24	21 Jan	1956	01:49
21 Jan	1919	02:20	20 Jan	1957	07:39
21 Jan	1920	08:04	20 Jan	1958	13:29
20 Jan	1921	13:54	20 Jan	1959	19:19
20 Jan	1922	19:48	21 Jan	1960	01:10
21 Jan	1923	01:35	20 Jan	1961	07:01
21 Jan	1924	07:29	20 Jan	1962	12:58
20 Jan	1925	13:20	20 Jan	1963	18:54
20 Jan	1926	19:13	21 Jan	1964	00:41
21 Jan	1927	01:12	20 Jan	1965	06:29
21 Jan	1928	06:56	20 Jan	1966	12:20
20 Jan	1929	12:42	20 Jan	1967	18:08
20 Jan	1930	18:33	20 Jan	1968	23:54
21 Jan	1931	00:17	20 Jan	1969	05:39
21 Jan	1932	06:07	20 Jan	1970	11:24
20 Jan	1933	11:52	20 Jan	1971	17:13

DAY	YEAR	TIME	DAY	YEAR	TIME
20 Jan	1934	17:37	20 Jan	1972	22:59
20 Jan	1935	23:28	20 Jan	1973	04:49
21 Jan	1936	05:11	20 Jan	1974	10:46
20 Jan	1937	11:01	20 Jan	1975	16:36
20 Jan	1938	16:58	20 Jan	1976	22:25
20 Jan	1939	22:50	20 Jan	1977	04:15
21 Jan	1940	04:43	20 Jan	1978	10:04
20 Jan	1941	10:33	20 Jan	1979	16:00
20 Jan	1942	16:23	20 Jan	1980	21:49
20 Jan	1943	22:19	20 Jan	1981	03:36
21 Jan	1944	04:06	20 Jan	1982	09:31
20 Jan	1945	09:53	20 Jan	1983	15:17
20 Jan	1984	21:06	20 Jan	1993	01:24
20 Jan	1985	02:58	20 Jan	1994	07:08
20 Jan	1986	08:47	20 Jan	1995	13:01
20 Jan	1987	14:40	20 Jan	1996	18:54
20 Jan	1988	20:25	20 Jan	1997	00:44
20 Jan	1989	02:07	20 Jan	1998	06:47
20 Jan	1990	08:02	20 Jan	1999	12:38
20 Jan	1991	13:47	20 Jan	2000	18:24
20 Jan	1992	19:33	20 Jan	2001	00:14

SUN INTO PISCES

DAY	YEAR	TIME OF DAY	DAY	YEAR	TIME OF DAY
19 Feb	1900	02:01	19 Feb	1924	21:52
19 Feb	1901	07:44	19 Feb	1925	03:43
19 Feb	1902	13:39	19 Feb	1926	09:35
19 Feb	1903	19:40	19 Feb	1927	15:34
20 Feb	1904	01:24	19 Feb	1928	21:19
19 Feb	1905	07:20	19 Feb	1929	03:07
19 Feb	1906	13:14	19 Feb	1930	09:00
19 Feb	1907	18:57	19 Feb	1931	14:40
20 Feb	1908	00:53	19 Feb	1932	20:29
19 Feb	1909	06:38	19 Feb	1933	02:16
19 Feb	1910	12:27	19 Feb	1934	08:01
19 Feb	1911	18:20	19 Feb	1935	13:52
19 Feb	1912	23:55	19 Feb	1936	19:32
19 Feb	1913	05:44	19 Feb	1937	01:20

19 Feb	1914	11:37	19 Feb	1938	07:19
19 Feb	1915	17:23	19 Feb	1939	13:09
19 Feb	1916	23:18	19 Feb	1940	19:03
19 Feb	1917	05:04	19 Feb	1941	00:56
19 Feb	1918	10:52	19 Feb	1942	06:46
19 Feb	1919	16:47	19 Feb	1943	42:40
19 Feb	1920	22:29	19 Feb	1944	18:27
19 Feb	1921	04:20	19 Feb	1945	00:14
19 Feb	1922	10:16	19 Feb	1946	06:08
19 Feb	1923	15:59	19 Feb	1947	11:52
19 Feb	1948	17:37	19 Feb	1975	06:50
18 Feb	1949	23:27	19 Feb	1976	12:40
19 Feb	1950	05:18	18 Feb	1977	18:31
19 Feb	1951	11:10	19 Feb	1978	00:21
19 Feb	1952	16:56	19 Feb	1979	06:13
18 Feb	1953	22:41	19 Feb	1980	12:02
19 Feb	1954	04:32	18 Feb	1981	17:52
19 Feb	1955	10:18	18 Feb	1982	23:46
19 Feb	1956	16:05	19 Feb	1983	05:31
18 Feb	1957	21:58	19 Feb	1984	11:17
19 Feb	1958	03:49	18 Feb	1985	17:08
19 Feb	1959	09:38	18 Feb	1986	22:58
19 Feb	1960	15:27	19 Feb	1987	04:50
18 Feb	1961	21:17	19 Feb	1988	10:36
19 Feb	1962	03:15	18 Feb	1989	16:21
19 Feb	1963	09:09	18 Feb	1990	22:14
19 Feb	1964	14:57	19 Feb	1991	03:58
18 Feb	1965	20:48	19 Feb	1992	09:44
19 Feb	1966	02:38	18 Feb	1993	15:36
19 Feb	1967	08:24	18 Feb	1994	21:22
19 Feb	1968	14:09	19 Feb	1995	03:12
18 Feb	1969	19:55	19 Feb	1996	09:02
19 Feb	1970	01:42	18 Feb	1997	14:53
19 Feb	1971	07:27	18 Feb	1998	20:56
19 Feb	1972	13:11	19 Feb	1999	02:47
18 Feb	1973	19:02	19 Feb	2000	08:34
19 Feb	1974	00:59	18 Feb	2001	14:28

BRITISH SUMMER TIME
(DAYLIGHT SAVING TIME)

If you were born during the times when the clocks were put forward, you need to deduct one hour (or two where double summer time is marked) to get back to Greenwich Mean Time. The changes happen at 02.00 (but double summer time at 03.00).

1900-1915	No time changes	1942	all year (deduct two hours from 05 April to 09 Aug)
1916	21 April to 01 October	1943	all year (deduct two hours from 04 April to 15 Aug)
1917	08 April to 17 September		
1918	24 March to 30 September	1944	all year (deduct two hours from 02 April to 17 Sep)
1919	30 March to 29 September		
1920	28 March to 25 October	1945	all year (deduct two hours from 02 April to 15 July)
1921	03 April to 03 October		
1922	26 March to 08 October	1946	14 April to 06 October (no doubles this year)
1923	22 April to 08 October		
1924	13 April to 21 September	1947	16 March to 2 November (deduct two hours from 13 April to 10 August.)
1925	19 April to 04 October		
1926	18 April to 03 October		
1927	10 April to 02 October	1948	18 April to 31 October
1928	22 April to 07 October	1949	03 April to 30 October
1929	21 April to 06 October	1950	16 April to 22 October
1930	04 April to 05 October	1951	15 April to 21 October
1931	19 April to 04 October	1952	20 April to 26 October
1932	17 April to 02 October	1953	19 April to 04 October
1933	09 April to 08 October	1954	11 April to 03 October
1934	22 April to 07 October	1955	17 April to 02 October
1935	14 April to 06 October	1956	22 April to 07 October
1936	19 April to 04 October	1957	14 April to 06 October
1937	18 April to 03 October	1958	02 April to 05 October
1938	10 April to 02 October	1959	19 April to 04 October
1939	16 April to 19 November	1960	10 April to 02 October
1940	25 February to 31 Dec	1961	26 March to 29 October
1941	all year (deduct two hours from 04 May to 10 Aug)	1962	24 March to 28 October
		1963	31 March to 27 October

537

1964	22 March to 25 October
1965	21 March to 24 October
1966	20 March to 23 October
1967	19 March to 23 October
1968	18 February, then all year
1969	all year
1970	all year
1971	all year, up to 31 October
1972	19 March to 29 October
1973	18 March to 28 October
1974	17 March to 27 October
1975	16 March to 26 October
1976	21 March to 24 October
1977	20 March to 23 October
1978	19 March to 22 October
1979	18 March to 28 October
1980	16 March to 26 October
1981	28 March to 25 October
1982	28 March to 24 October
1983	27 March to 23 October
1984	25 March to 28 October

1985	31 March to 27 October
1986	30 March to 26 October
1987	29 March to 25 October
1988	27 March to 23 October
1989	26 March to 29 October
1990	25 March to 28 October
1991	31 March to 27 October
1992	29 March to 25 October
1993	28 March to 24 October
1994	27 March to 23 October
1995	26 March to 29 October
1996*	31 March to 27 October
1997	30 March to 26 October
1998	29 March to 25 October
1999	28 March to 24 October
2000	26 March to 29 October

*From 1996 dates are estimates and could be changed by the government.

WORLD TIME ZONES

Astrological timings are traditionally based on Greenwich Mean Time (GMT) which is the time used in the United Kingdom and Eire. If you were born outside this time zone you need to adjust your time of birth to use the tables. Where there is a minus sign next to your country, you are behind GMT so you need to add the number of hours shown. If there is a plus sign next to your country, you are ahead of GMT so you need to deduct the number of hours shown. You should also allow for that country's own summer or winter daylight saving time.

Adelaide	+09.30	Madrid	+01.00
Alexandria	+02.00	Malta	+01.00
Amsterdam	+01.00	Melbourne	+10.00
Athens	+02.00	Montreal	-05.00
Bombay	+05.30	Moscow	+03.00
Brussels	+01.00	Nairobi	+03.00
Buenos Aires	-03.00	New York	-05.00
Cairo	+02.00	Oslo	+01.00
Calcutta	+05.30	Paris	+01.00
Calgary	-07.00	Peking	+08.00
Cape Town	+02.00	Perth WA	+08.00
Chicago	-06.00	Rangoon	+06.30
Christchurch NZ	+12.00	Rio de Janeiro	-03.00
Colombo	+05.30	Rome	+01.00
Copenhagen	+01.00	St Petersburg	+02.00
Durban	+02.00	San Francisco	-08.00
Gibraltar	+01.00	Singapore	+08.00
Helsinki	+02.00	Stockholm	+01.00
Hong Kong	+08.00	Sydney NSW	+10.00
Karachi	+05.00	Tokyo	+09.00
Lagos	+01.00	Toronto	-05.00
Lima	-05.00	Vancouver	-08.00
Lisbon	00.00	Wellington NZ	+12.00
London	00.00	Winnipeg	-06.00
Los Angeles	-08.00	Yokohama	+09.00

THE ASTROSEX SURVEY

5 million copies of this questionnaire were distributed. The answers form the basis of this book.

SURVEY QUESTIONNAIRE

Please indicate your answers to all the questions below by circling the number that applies to you. In some cases you may wish to give more than one reply.

1 Please circle number to show if you are
Male 1 Female 2

2 What is your own starsign?

Aries (March 21 to April 20)	1
Taurus (April 21 to May 21)	2
Gemini (May 22 to June 21)	3
Cancer (June 22 to July 22)	4
Leo (July 23 to August 23)	5
Virgo (August 24 to September 22)	6
Libra (September 23 to October 23)	7
Scorpio (October 24 to November 22)	8
Sagittarius (November 23 to December 21)	9
Capricorn (December 22 to January 20)	10
Aquarius (January 21 to February 18).	11
Pisces (February 19 to March 20)	12

3 What is your age group?

16 to 21	1
22 to 30.	2
31 to 40	3
41 to 50	4
Over 50	5

4 What is your partner's starsign?

Aries (March 21 to April 20)   1
Taurus (April 21 to May 21)   2
Gemini (May 22 to June 21)   3
Cancer (June 22 to July 22)   4
Leo (July 23 to August 23)   5
Virgo (August 24 to September 22)   6
Libra (September 23 to October 23).   7
Scorpio (October 24 to November 22).   8
Sagittarius (November 23 to December 21)   9
Capricorn (December 22 to January 20)   10
Aquarius (January 21 to February 18)   11
Pisces (February 19 to March 20)   12

5 Which starsign have you found to be the most sexy?

Aries (March 21 to April 20)   1
Taurus (April 21 to May 21)   2
Gemini (May 22 to June 21)   3
Cancer (June 22 to July 22)   4
Leo (July 23 to August 23)   5
Virgo (August 24 to September 22)   6
Libra (September 23 to October 23)   7
Scorpio (October 24 to November 22).   8
Sagittarius (November 23 to December 21)   9
Capricorn (December 22 to January 20)   10
Aquarius (January 21 to February 18)   11
Pisces (February 19 to March 20).   12

6 Which starsign have you found to be the least sexy?

Aries (March 21 to April 20)   1
Taurus (April 21 to May 21)   2
Gemini (May 22 to June 21)   3
Cancer (June 22 to July 22)   4
Leo (July 23 to August 23)   5
Virgo (August 24 to September 22)   6
Libra (September 23 to October 23)   7
Scorpio (October 24 to November 22)   8

Sagittarius (November 23 to December 21)   9
Capricorn (December 22 to January 20)   10
Aquarius (January 21 to February 18)   11
Pisces (February 19 to March 20)   12

7 If you are married, how many times?

Once   1
Twice   2
Three times   3
Four   4
Five   5
Six or more   6

8 How long have you been married (if more than one marriage, choose the one that lasted longest)?

One year   1
Two to five   2
Six to 10   3
Over 10 (please give years)   4

9 If you are not married, are you

Single and plan to stay that way   1
Single but hope to marry   2
Have been married, but never again   3
Have been married and hope to marry again   4

10 How does your sex drive compare with your partner's?

Higher   1
Lower   2
Same   3

11 How often do you make love?

Every day   1
More than four times a week   2
One to three times a week.   3
Once to three times a month   4
Rarely   5
I am celibate at this time   6
I plan to stay celibate   7

12 Would you like to make love

Less often	1
More often	2

13 In which of these places have you made love? Circle as many as apply to you.

Bed	1
Sofa	2
Floor	3
Shower	4
Bath	5
Kitchen	6
Table	7
Chair	8
Cinema	9
Car	10
Bus	11
Train	12
Plane	13
Swimming pool	14
Beach	15
Park	16
Office	17
Changing cubicle	18

14 Do you prefer to have sex with:

Men	1
Women	2
Either	3

15 Did you marry the love of your life?

Yes	1
No	2

16 Were you still a virgin when you got married?

Yes	1
No	2

17 Are you doing all the sexual things you want to do with your partner?

Yes	1
No	2

18 Has a long-term relationship/marriage made you:

More interested in sex	1
Less interested in sex	2
Your interest has stayed the same	3

19 While making love, do you ever imagine your partner is someone else?

Yes	1
No	2

20 Do you like your partner to talk and make sounds of pleasure during sex?

Yes	1
No	2

21 Which of these would put you in the mood for love? Circle as many as apply.

Shared romantic meal	1
Hot dancing	2
Slow dancing	3
Watching sexy movie	4
Listening to music in softly-lit room	5
A gift of flowers	6
A sexy phone call at work	7
Playing sport together	8
Shared bath	9
Shared shower	10
Massage	11
Compliments	12
The words "I love you"	13
Holiday in the sun	14
Being caressed on hair	15

Face	16
Throat	17
Breast/Chest	18
Stomach	19
Thighs	20
Feet	21

22 How many sexual partners have you had?

One	1
Two to Five	2
Six to 10	3
11 to 20	4
Over 20	5

23 Which of these best describes your view of sex?

Pure magic	1
Over-rated	2
Normal part of life	3
Pleasurable	4
Expression of love that keeps us together	5

24 Has being married improved your sex life?

Yes	1
Made it worse	2
It's the same.	3

25 Does having children together make your partner seem:

More sexy	1
Less sexy	2
The same	3

26 Which of these have you tried? Circle as many as apply to you.

Wearing special sexy undies	1
Eating food off each other's bodies	2
Bondage	3
Spanking	4
Sensual massage	5

Paid-for sex	6
Watching erotic videos	7
Telephone sex	8
Using sex toys	9
Wearing rubber	10
Oral sex	11
Threesomes	12
Swapping partners	13

27 Which of these would you like to try?

Wearing special sexy undies	1
Eating food off each other's bodies	2
Bondage	3
Spanking	4
Sensual massage	5
Paid-for sex.	6
Watching erotic videos	7
Telephone sex	8
Using sex toys	9
Wearing rubber	10
Oral sex	11
Threesomes	12
Swapping partners	13

28 Which of these sexual positions or techniques excites you most?

Man on top	1
Woman on top	2
Both on your side	3
Woman face down	4
Sitting on each other's lap	5
Both standing	6
Woman on hands and knees	7
Oral sex	8
Manual sex	9

29 How much time would you most like to spend on foreplay?

None, I like instant sex	1

Five minutes	2
15 minutes	3
30 minutes	4
Hours	5

30 How long do you spend on the penetration stage of lovemaking?

Five minutes or less	
Six to 10 minutes	1
11 to 15 minutes	2
16 to 30 minutes	3
30 to 60 minutes	4
Over an hour	5

31 Circle as many of these as you agree with. Sexlife would be more exciting if:

I was the right weight	1
My partner was right weight	2
I had bigger breasts/muscles	3
My partner had bigger breasts/muscles	4
I/my partner had a bigger penis	5
I/my partner had better job	6
I/my partner had more money	7

32 If married, have you had an affair?

No	1
Yes, once	2
Yes, between 2 and 5 times	3
Yes, more than 5 times	4

33 If you found out your partner had an affair, would you:

Ask for divorce	1
Take a lover of your own	2
Say nothing and hope it wouldn't last	3
Ask why and adjust your relationship to stop it happening again	4

34 If you had an affair, why?

Not enough sex at home	1
Bored with partner	2
Pure physical attraction.	3
Thrill of the chase	4
Made me feel more attractive	5
Younger lover revitalised me	6
Older lover taught me so much	7
A way out of my marriage	8
I fell in love	9

35 How many orgasms would you expect to have in one session?

None	1
One	2
Two	3
Three	4
Four	5
More	6

36 Do you ever fake orgasms?

Yes	1
No	2

37 Are your friends mostly:

Same sex	1
Opposite sex	2

38 If you have remarried, was sex better in your second or subsequent marriages?

Yes	1
No	2
The same	3

39 Circle the one quality that matters most of all to you in a partner.

Kindness.	1
Sexual attraction	2
Money	3

Sense of humour	4
Fun	5
Understanding how I think	6
Loyalty	7
Hard worker	8
Home lover	9
Good looks	10
Sex skills	11

40 If you found your sex life with marriage partner unbearable, would you:

Move on	1
Avoid sex but stay together	2
Go for counselling	3
Take a lover and have sex with partner occasionally	4

41 Do you enjoy a kiss and cuddle when it isn't going to lead to sex?

Yes	1
No	2

42 When your partner is in the mood, and you are not, will you:

Enjoy giving pleasure	1
Say no	2

43 How do you like to be caressed?

Slow, gently, lovingly	1
Fast, firmly, and passionately	2

44 Which of these settings do you find the sexiest?

A luxury hotel with a round bed, satin sheets, champagne	1
A private apartment with scented candles, black walls and sheets	2
A warm, deserted beach at sunset, half lying in the sea	3
A secluded piece of wild moor land, rough grasses and cool breeze on your skin	4

45 What first attracts you to someone (men go to second part of this)?
Part 1

Gorgeous eyes	1
Great smile	2
Good voice	3
Tall	4
Muscular	5
Slim	6
Smart clothes	7
Confidence	8
Good line in chat	9
Good provider	10
Kindness	11
Faithfulness	12

Part 2 (for men)

Nice eyes	1
Warm smile	2
Curvy body	3
Slim body	4
Great legs	5
Attractive voice	6
Sexy laugh	7
Shared interests	8
Good homemaker	9
Kind nature	10
Gentle manner	11
Faithfulness	12

46 Do you expect to make love:

Until age 50	1
Until age 60	2
Until 70	3
As long as I live	4